HISTORY

OF THE

STATE OF OHIO.

BY

JAMES W. TAYLOR.

FIRST PERIOD.

1650—1787.

CINCINNATI:
H. W. DERBY & CO., PUBLISHERS.
SANDUSKY:
C. L. DERBY & CO.
1854.

FRANKLIN PRINTING CO.
Columbus, Ohio.

PREFACE.

The History of that region of North America, which constitutes the State of Ohio, may properly be divided into four epochs.

The First Period, or the ante-territorial epoch, engrosses the present volume. Commencing with the obscure memorials and traditions of the early Indian tribes, which are preserved in the faithful relations of Jesuit adventure upon the inland lakes and rivers of the continent—tracing the rise and progress of the fearful struggle for the Ohio and St. Lawrence valleys, between those European powers, that the lapse of a century finds in zealous alliance and with apprehensive gaze turned in an opposite direction—dwelling, once more, upon fragmentary relics of that Indian occupation in Ohio, which the first European settlers found in the Wyandot, Delaware, Ottawa and Shawanese successors of the almost mythical Eries of the seventeenth century—repeating the simple chronicles of Moravian zeal and courage, which, not unfruitful of beneficent influence upon the children of the forest, are also recognized by an intelligent reader to have been an agency extremely salutary and effective, in the protection of an exposed frontier during the disastrous hours of the American Revolution—narrating the incidental effect of that great struggle upon the rude communities of savage life, which, at remote intervals, were familiar to the trader and missionary between Lake Erie and the Ohio; and, finally, preserving, with the fullness of detail which authenticity demands, those early monuments of continental legislation, that have proved, in their fuller development, the deep and broad foundations of the Commonwealth of Ohio, the following pages, as the author needs not to be reminded by others, hardly emerge from those mists of time, which distinguish an antiquarian era from the more sharply defined annals of our subsequent history. The dates of the title-page—1650–1787—are made conspicuous, as an epitome of the author's design, which perhaps may be deemed more curious than useful. Its execution was certainly undertaken—at first without any view of permanent publication—mainly upon that sort of impulse, so admirably illustrated by Walter Scott, in his delineation of the Antiquary. The subsequent periods of Ohio history, according to the classification above referred to, are as follows: The Second Period, 1787–1802, may be denominated the Territorial; the Third, 1802–1815, that of State Organization; and the Fourth, 1815–1851, that of State Development, until, with the adoption of the Constitution of the latter year, our Ohio has reached a career of Progress—a period when the heterogeneous elements of her population may be expected to maturo into a type of character, and the refinements of society and culture will become prevalent.

The first is unlike the subsequent periods in several particulars, that have not been without their influence upon the style and arrangement of the present volume. Of course, prior to 1787, the materials existed only in libraries—in books or manuscripts—while, since that date, much which would arrest the attention and investigation of a historical student, rests in the *memory of the living*. Besides, the authorities for whatever relates to Ohio from 1650 to 1787, are not numerous, and consist of rare volumes long since out of print. The details contained in this work, have been wrested, therefore, from the dead hand—*mort gage*—of old books, and because these were inaccessible to most readers, and unlikely to transpire in new editions, I have not restrained myself from ample quotations. In doing so, it has been an unavoidable result, that every variety of style breaks the currents of the following chapters; but I have resisted the disposition to paraphrase, whenever it seemed that the *language of the witness* was in any respect desirable, either for the statement or elucidation of a doubt, or as an illustration of men or times. If the freedom and fullness of citation from such unique publications as the Journal of Rogers, James Smith's story of Indian captivity, or the truthful and quaint narratives of the Moravians, Heckewelder and Loskiel, is irksome to the reader, the only apology here offered, or which the nature of the case admits, is, that the practice in question was adopted from a sentiment entirely opposite to the vanity of authorship. It was deliberately adopted for the sake of authenticity, although sacrificing, in a considerable degree, the unity of the volume.

In respect to Indian orthography, also, the indulgence of the reader is entreated. The names of places and personages are written with infinite variety, and I have preferred, especially when a quotation was in hand, to forbear any effort to conform the orthography in these instances to any other than the writers' own standard. The names of "Coshocton," still applied to the Forks of the Muskingum, and of "Bockengehelas," the noted war-chief of the Delawares, may be particularly mentioned, as illustrations of the confusion of tongues which pervade aboriginal nomenclature.

Indeed, these pages aim at little more than a compilation of memorials and traditions, hitherto dispersed and often inaccessible. The writer, perhaps from force of habit, has been indisposed to assume a relation to their contents much different from that of an Editor. Hereafter, it may be, he may sustain with more confidence, the independent bearing of authorship. Meanwhile, the Press of Ohio are urged to verify or expand the suggestions of this volume, so far as connected with their respective localities. The book may thus constitute a nucleus of historical inquiry, and if so, notwithstanding in many particulars it may be convicted of mistake or omission, yet the aggregate of historical knowledge will probably be increased.

The Indian, during the period which bounds the present publication, is of course the central, almost the exclusive, figure in the scenes described. There has been no attempt to urge any hypothesis upon his antecedents—no disposition to dogmatize upon his character or destiny. So far as his personality has been inseparable from the progress of events, he has moved into view, but also been suffered to pass from view without special challenge. In Ohio, the Indian was a temporary sojourner,—not linked so inseparably to the soil as the Six Nations to their "Long House," between Niagara and the Hudson. But while the tribes who were found in occupation of Ohio, were comparatively strangers to that region —having moved thither between 1720 and 1750— yet they are so far identified with its plains, forests and waters, that any inquiry, however cursory or incidental, into their habits and history, is likely to become an enthusiasm. The geography of the State is likewise suggestive of the aboriginal dwellers. The streams, more than the political subdivisions, illustrate their vanished dialects, as has been beautifully expressed in some lines by William J. Sperry, formerly of the Cincinnati *Globe*, entitled "A Lament for the Ancient People," and which, although a digression and not historically exact, are here inserted, as well for their intrinsic merit as from a personal regard to the writer:

"Sad are fair Muskingum's waters,
  Sadly, blue Mahoning raves;
Tuscarawas' plains are lonely,
  Lonely are Hockhocking's waves.

From where headlong Cuyahoga
  Thunders down its rocky way,
And the billows of blue Erie
  Whiten in Sandusky's bay,

Unto where Potomac rushes,
  Arrowy from the mountain side,
And Kanawha's gloomy waters
  Mingle with Ohio's tide;

From the valley of Scioto,
  And the Huron sisters three,
To the foaming Susquehanna,
  And the leaping Genesee;

Over hill and plain and valley—
  Over river, lake and bay—

On the water—in the forest,
  Ruled and reigned the Seneca.

But sad are fair Muskingum's waters,
  Sadly, blue Mahoning raves;
Tuscarawas' plains are lonely,
  Lonely are Hockhocking's waves.

By Kanawha dwells the stranger,
  Cuyahoga feels the chain,
Stranger ships vex Erie's billows,
  Strangers plow Scioto's plain.

And the Iroquois have wasted,
  From the hill and plain away;
On the waters—in the valley,
  Reigns no more the Seneca.

Only by the Cattaraugus,
  Or by Lake Chautauque's side,
Or among the scanty woodlands,
  By the Alleghany's tide—

There, in spots, like sad oases,
  Lone amid the sandy plains,
There the Seneca, still wasting,
  Amid desolation reigns."

Even more total than the disappearance of the Senecas, is the migration of the remnants of the Ohio Tribes, who succeeded the New York confederates upon the Muskingum, the Scioto and the Sandusky, and of whom not even a "sad oasis" is visible, except upon the distant waters of the Kanzas or Nebraska. This volume leaves the indomitable

Wyandot, the sagacious Delaware, the fierce Shawnee, and the cunning Ottawa as yet unconquered, although slowly and sternly retreating before the insolent column of white emigration. Another epoch witnessed the downfall of their savage pride, before the battalions of Wayne: while thenceforth, wholly unchecked by Indian resistance, swelled within our borders the rising tide of population, civil structure and material development. Upon these scenes the curtain is here unlifted. The task, delicate and responsible in manifold aspects, extends immediately over the threshold laid by these pages. He will be fortunate to whom its proper execution shall be allotted in the contingencies of the future.

To the writings of the late JAMES H. PERKINS, and for valuable suggestions personally communicated to the author by Hon. EBENEZER LANE, Hon. ELIJAH HAYWARD, Col. JOHN JOHNSTON, THOMAS MEANS, Esq., and other citizens of the State, an expression of acknowledgment is due, and is gratefully tendered.

J. W. T.

CONTENTS.

CHAPTER I. Page

The Fate of the Ancient Eries, - - - - - - 13

CHAPTER II.

The Nature and Extent of Iroquois Conquest in the Mississippi Valley, - - - - - - - - - 22

CHAPTER III.

Indian Occupation of Ohio in 1750, - - - - - 29

CHAPTER IV.

Lake Erie in the Seventeenth Century, - - - - 41

CHAPTER V.

The French Establish Fort Sandusky—The English Explore the Ohio Valley, - - - - - - - - 55

CHAPTER VI.

The Ascendancy of France upon the Ohio, - - - 69

CHAPTER VII.

A Picture of Ohio One Hundred Years since, - - - 81

CHAPTER VIII.

The Surrender of the Western Posts to England, - - 115

CHAPTER IX.

Conspiracy of Pontiac, - - - - - - - 127

CHAPTER X.

The Expeditions against the Western Tribes under Bradstreet and Bouquet, - - - - - - - 140

CHAPTER XI.

Old Maps and Indian Trails, - - - - - - 156

CHAPTER XII.

Submission and Fate of Pontiac, - - - - - 166

CHAPTER XIII.

English Negotiations with the Western Tribes—The Claim to Kentucky, - - - - - - - - - 178

CHAPTER XIV.

The Moravian Missions on the Muskingum, - - - 186

CHAPTER XV.

The Society of United Brethren, - - - - - 202

CHAPTER XVI.

Dunmore's Expedition in 1774—The Story of Logan, - - 238

CHAPTER XVII. Page

The Relation of the Western Tribes to the Revolutionary Contest, - - - - - - - - - - 261

CHAPTER XVIII.

Border War of the Revolution, - - - - - - 275

CHAPTER XIX.

The Conquest of Illinois by George Rogers Clark—Indian Sieges of Fort Laurens, - - - - - - - - 280

CHAPTER XX.

The Kentucky Campaigns against the Shawanese, - - 309

CHAPTER XXI.

The Moravian Missions on the Muskingum, from 1772 to 1782, 328

CHAPTER XXII.

Pennsylvania Campaigns against the Ohio Indians, - - 374

CHAPTER XXIII.

Subsequent Movements of the Moravian Congregation, - 380

CHAPTER XXIV.

Embassies and Negotiations between the United States and the Ohio Tribes, - - - - - - - - 412

Treaty of Fort Stanwix in 1784, 425; Treaty of Fort McIntosh in 1785, 438; Treaty of Fort Finney in 1786, 442.

CHAPTER XXV.

Colonial Claims to Western Lands, and their Cession to the United States, - - - - - - - - - 465

CHAPTER XXVI.

The Settlement of the North-Western Territory—Ordinance of 1787, - - - - - - - - 493

APPENDIX.

I. Further Particulars of the Eries, Neutrals, and Andastes, - 517
II. French Occupation by a Process Verbal, - - - 520
III. The Delaware Villages on the Scioto, - - - - 521
IV. The Locality of the Canesadooharie, - - - - 521
V. Contemporary Accounts of the Indian Hostilities in 1774, - 522
VI. Further Particulars of Connolly's Scheme, - - - 525
VII. Incidents in the Life of James Dean, - - - - 527
VIII. Netawatwes, and other Delaware Chiefs, - - - 530
IX. Lewis Wetzell, the Borderer, - - - - - 532
X. Surrender of the Moravian Tract to the United States, - 539
XI. Bockengahelas, the War-Chief of the Delawares, - - 545
XII. Subsequent Indian Treaties, - - - - - 550
XIII. Ordinance of 1787, - - - - - - 55'

HISTORY OF OHIO.

CHAPTER I.

THE FATE OF THE ANCIENT ERIES.

A PERIOD of two centuries prior to 1850, comprises our knowledge of that region of the American Continent, which is bounded by Lake Erie on the north, and the Ohio River on the south; and even within that brief segment of time, many statements rest upon vague tradition.

An attempt to ascend beyond 1650, would involve a profitless discussion of the probable origin of the Indian race. We shall decline the inquiry, whether the lost tribes of Israel yet linger in the aborigines of the American woods; or whether the latter are an off-shoot from the Tartars of Asia; or, abandoning the unitary theory of the race, whether the Creator has not given to the continent of America its peculiar inhabitants. These are ethnological problems, which are aside from the purpose of the present volume.

The Ohio of 1650 we assume to have been a forest wilderness, principally occupied by a tribe of Indians, called the ERIES, whose villages skirted the shores of the lake so designated.

There is some conflict of opinion, whether the Eries were not confined to the eastern shore of the lake, but the preponderance of authority is in favor of their occupation of the southern shore. Dewitt Clinton, in his celebrated Historical Discourse upon the Indians of North America, speaks of "the nation of the Eries or Erigas *on the south side of Lake Erie*." Louis Hennepin, a Franciscan friar, whose travels in New France were published in 1698, mentions the return of the Iroquois to their villages, bringing Erie Indians as captives "*from beyond the lake*." Brant, the distinguished Mohawk chief, in a letter to Timothy Pickering, dated Nov. 20, 1794, alludes to the Eries as "a powerful nation formerly living *southward of Buffalo creek*." Charlevoix, the historian of New France, may be cited as an authority that the nation of Eries lived where the State of Ohio now is. The recent discovery of ancient earthworks, and two inscriptions in the pictographic character, on Cunningham's Island (now Kelley's Island, a township of Erie county, Ohio), are supposed by Schoolcraft to indicate that the archipelago of islands in the western part of Lake Erie, was one of the strongholds of the tribe.[1]

1) Kelley's Island has an area of about 3000 acres, and is situated ten miles north of the mouth of Sandusky Bay. It consists of a basis of horizontal limestone, of the species common to Lake Erie, rising about fifteen feet above the water level. The surface, where it is exposed, discloses the polish created by former diluvial or glacial action — a trait which is so remarkable on the rocks of the adjoining shores of Sandusky. This is covered with a fertile limestone soil, and at the earliest period, all, except the old fields, bore a heavy growth of hard wood timber.

On the south shore of the Island are two crescent-shaped embankments, apparently intended to inclose and defend villages; (a third circumvallation is situated inland.) One has a front of 400 feet, and the other of 614 feet, on the rocky and precipitous margin of the lake. Within these enclosures have been found stone axes, pipes, perforators, bone fish hooks, net sinkers, and fragments of human bones. In the vicinity is a rock, 32 by 21 feet on the surface, in which a great variety of figures and devices are deeply sunk. The summit of the rock is elevated eleven feet above the water. "It is by far the most extensive and well-sculptured, and well preserved inscription of the antiquarian period, ever found in America. Being on an islet sepa-

It is generally admitted that the Eries were a member of the Iroquois family, as distinguished from the Algonquin tribes. In 1650, the Iroquois, as the confederated Mohawks, Oneidas, Onondagas, Cayugas and Senecas were called by the French, occupied what is now New York and Northern Pennsylvania; the Hurons or Wyandots, and a kindred Neutral Nation, held the peninsula between Lakes Huron, Erie and Ontario; the Eries were seated on the southern shore of Lake Erie; while the Andastes possessed the valleys of the Alleghany or Upper Ohio River,—but all were generically Iroquois, speaking dialects of the same lingual stock. The Western tribes were singly more powerful than either of the New York tribes, except perhaps the Senecas; but the Five Nations (afterwards increased to Six by the accession of the Tuscaroras) had formed their celebrated alliance at least as early as 1605, and, by the strength of union, become the terror of their less sagacious neighbors.

Before proceeding with our immediate topic—the fortunes of the Eries, Hurons and Andastes—we will briefly classify the other Indian tribes, as they were found by the first discoverers of the continent.

rated from the shore, with precipitous sides, it has remained undiscovered till within late years. It is in the pictographic character of the natives. Its leading symbols are readily interpreted. The human figures, the pipes, smoking groups, the presents and other figures, denote tribes, negotiations, crimes, turmoils, which tell a story of thrilling interest, in which the white man or European plays a part. There are many subordinate figures which require study. There are some in which the effects of atmospheric and lake action have destroyed the connection, and others of an anomalous character. The whole inscription is manifestly connected with the occupation of the basin of the lake by the Eries—of the coming of the Wyandots—of the final triumph of the Iroquois, and the flight of the people who have left their name to the lake."—*History, Condition and Prospects of the Indian tribes of the United States: by H. R. Schoolcraft, LL.D. Illustrated by S. Eastman, U. S. A. Part second,* 86–7.

Except the Iroquois, antiquarians describe all other northern tribes as Algonquin, which term, though generic, was the special designation of a nation living on the St. Lawrence River, where also was the seat of the Utawawas or Ottowas. The leading tribe of the Algonquins, however, were the Lenno Lenapees or Delawares, who were found by the first colonists about the waters of the Delaware and its tributary streams, within the present limits of New Jersey and Eastern Pennsylvania. Their traditions declare them to be the parent stem whence other Algonquin tribes have sprung—a claim recognized by the latter, who accord to the ancient Lenapees the title of Grandfather. The Lenapees, on their part, call the other Algonquin tribes Children, Grandchildren, Nephews, or Younger Brothers; but they confess the superiority of the Wyandots and the Five Nations by yielding them the title of Uncles, while they, in return, call the Lenapees Nephews, or more frequently Cousins.[2]

"Except the detached nation of the Tuscaroras, and a few smaller tribes adhering to them," to quote from the accomplished historian of Pontiac's Conspiracy, "the Iroquois family were confined to the region south of the Lakes Erie and Ontario, and the peninsula east of Lake Huron. They formed, as it were, an island in the vast expanse of Algonquin population, extending from Hudson's Bay on the north to the Carolinas on the south; from the Atlantic on the east to the Mississippi and Lake Winnipeg on the west. They were Algonquins who greeted Jacques Cartier as his ships ascended the St. Lawrence. The first British colonists found savages of the same race hunting and fishing along the coasts and inlets of Virginia; and it was the daughter of an Algonquin chief who interceded with her father for the life of the

2) Parkman's Conspiracy of Pontiac, 26.

adventurous Englishman. They were Algonquins who, under Sassacus the Pequot and Phillip of Mount Hope, waged deadly war against the Puritans of New England; who dwelt at Penacook under the rule of the great magician Passaconaway, and trembled before the evil spirits of the Crystal Hills; and who sang *Aves* and told their beads in the forest chapel of Father Rasles by the banks of the Kennebec. They were Algonquins who, under the great tree at Kensington, made the covenant of peace with William Penn; and when the French Jesuits and fur traders explored the Wabash and the Ohio, they found their valleys tenanted by the same far-extended race. At the present day, the traveler, perchance, may find them pitching their bark lodges along the beach at Mackinaw, spearing fish among the boiling rapids of St. Marys, or skimming the waves of Lake Superior in their birch canoes."

Bancroft, in a map of aboriginal America, concurs with Parkman, but limits the Algonquins to the thirty-sixth degree of north latitude, and gives four-fifths of the country south of that parallel to the Mobilian race. The other southern races were the Cherokees, who were mountaineers, and occupied the upper valley of the Tennessee River, as far west as Muscle Shoals, and the highlands of Carolina, Georgia and Alabama, the Switzerland of the south; the Uchees and Catawbas, who occupied small areas adjacent to the Cherokee country on the south and east; and the Natchez, residing in scarcely more than four or five villages, of which the largest was near the site of the city thus called. Bancroft has a general classification of Dacotah for the numerous tribes west of the Mississippi, and within the valleys of the Arkansas and the Missouri. These distinctions have little other foundation than language, of which eight radically different varieties are said to have been spoken east of the Mississippi.[3]

To return to the kindred but hostile Iroquois tribes. About the middle of the seventeenth century, the Five Nations of New York, grown arrogant by fifty years of confederation, invaded the territory of the Hurons or Wyandots. The ancient seats of this nation were on the eastern shores of the lake which now bears their name, and thither the enemy penetrated, undisturbed by the Neutral Nation, who occupied the eastern portion of the peninsula adjacent to Lake Ontario, and probably extended beyond the Niagara River.[4] The Hurons were driven with great slaughter to the Manitouline islands of the lake. They next occupied the island of Michillimacinac, thinking its isolated position and precipitous cliffs would prove a shelter. But the enraged enemy drove them thence. They fled into the territories of the Odjibwas, in Lake Superior. But even there their enemies attempted to follow them, until they were defeated by the Chippewas, in a battle fought at the foot of the south cape of its outlet; at a prominent elevation, which, in allusion to this incident, is still called Point Iroquois.

The extinction of the Neutral Nation soon followed, and then the victorious Iroquois turned against their Erie brethren. In the year 1655, using their canoes as scaling ladders, they stormed the Erie strongholds, leaped down like tigers among the defenders, and butchered them without mercy. The greater part of the nation was involved in the massacre, and the remnant was incorporated with the conquerors, or with other tribes, to which they fled for refuge.[4]

3) History of the United States, vol. iii., p. 235.

4) We accede to what seems the weight of tradition, that the Neutral Nation were a distinct tribe, and so called from their neutrality in the contest between the Iroquois and the Hurons; but Schoolcraft, in speaking of

The Andastes shared the same fate, but their resistance postponed their dispersion until 1672, when their ruin was also accomplished. It seems likely that a tribe called by the Iroquois, Satanas, by the French, Chaouanons, and whom we suppose to have been the Shawanese, were, about this period, driven from the valley of the Ohio to the vicinity of the Mexican Gulf. Thus, at the commencement of the eighteenth century, the territory now Ohio was derelict, except as the indomitable confederates of the North made it a trail for further hostilities, or roamed its hunting grounds.

Attached to "Baron La Hontan's Voyages and Adventures in North America between 1683 and 1694," is a map, upon which, near the source and mouth of the Sandusky River, are indices of "savage villages destroyed by ye Iroquese." The latter would be the site of Sandusky, or the vicinity near the outlet of the Bay and River. Parallel with the southern shore of "Errie or Conti Lake," and apparently at an average distance of thirty miles, is a line drawn connecting the Mississippi with Western New York, which, according to the map, "represents ye way that ye Illinese march through a vast tract of ground to make War against ye Iroquese: The same being ye Passage of ye Iroquese in their incursions upon ye other Savages, as far as the river Missisipi." Upon the Maumee River a tribe of "Errieronons" are put down, and in the country south of the source of the Sandusky river, "Andastognerons" are mentioned, probably remnants of the Eries and Andastes.[5]

the Eries, remarks, that "there can be no question, from the early accounts of the French missionaries, that they were at the head of that singular confederation of tribes called the Neutral Nation, which extended from the extreme west to the extreme eastern shores of Lake Erie, including the Niagara."

5) The outline of Lake Erie on La Hontan's map is curious enough. It

This incidental reference to detachments of the Eries and Andastes, which we presume that La Hontan here makes, confirms the belief that they were not exterminated by the war of 1655. Like the conquered Hurons, they were fugitives from their villages on the borders of the lake, but it is quite likely that they became the allies of the formidable Miamis or Twahtwahs, whose residence was on the Miami of the Lakes and the Miami of the Ohio. According to the French missionary authors, cited by Schoolcraft, the Iroquois fell on the Miamis and Chictaghicks or Illinois (enraged, we may suppose, at their friendly reception of the vanquished Indians) who were encamped together on the banks of the Maumee River in the year 1680, being twenty-five years after the final defeat of the Eries. In this attack they killed thirty and took three hundred prisoners. But the Illinois and Miamis rallied, and by a dexterous movement, got ahead of the retreating Iroquois, waylaid their path, and recovered their prisoners, killing many of the enemy.

The future fate of the Eries is involved in obscurity. General Lewis Cass has expressed the opinion that the Kickapoos and Shawanese are remnants of the Eries, and adds that the Canadians, to this day, term the Shawanese the Nation of the Cat or Raccoon, which is well known to be the

is made broader at the eastern extremity than elsewhere, the shore running due south from the mouth of Niagara River to the southeast corner, where is the mouth of a "Conde River"—as if the line from Buffalo to Erie was due south. Thence at right angles, but slightly indented now and then, we have the southern shore, without any streams until the Sandusky and Maumee Rivers are noted with a fair degree of accuracy, except that Sandusky Bay is not put down otherwise than as the mouth of the river. There is a liberal allowance of islands opposite, and the river itself is represented as rising at a distance of 100 miles (according to the scale given) in a circular lake of at least 15 miles in diameter.

origin of the word Erie. On the other hand, some traditions of the Catawbas of the South, render it not improbable that they are the survivors of the vanquished Eries.[6]

6) For further details of these traditionary tribes, see Appendix No. I.

CHAPTER II.

THE NATURE AND EXTENT OF IROQUOIS CONQUEST IN THE MISSISSIPPI VALLEY.

THE extent of Iroquois conquest in the seventeenth century was the subject of much controversy between the French and English, while Canada was under the dominion of the former. The French title, by discovery of the Lakes and the Mississippi, was sought to be overcome by a grant of sovereignty from the Five Nations. This sovereignty was claimed to result from a conquest of the entire country east of the Mississippi. Colden in 1727, and Clinton in 1811, are the prominent champions of the Iroquois pretension—the former advancing it as a matter of vital importance to the English colonies, and the latter reiterating it with the interest of an antiquarian and the pride of a New Yorker. It is interesting to observe how closely recent writers have pursued the authority, almost the text, of Gov. Clinton. The following extract discloses the partisan tenor of his discourse:

"The conquests of the Iroquois, previous to the discovery of America, are only known to us through the imperfect channels of tradition; but it is well authenticated, that since that memorable era, they exterminated the nation of the Eries or Erigas, on the south side of Lake Erie, which has given a name to that Lake. They nearly extirpated the Andastes and the Chouanons; they conquered the Hurons, and drove them and their allies, the Ottawas, among the Sioux, on the head waters of the Mississippi. They also subdued the Illinois, the Miamis, the Algonkins, the Delawares, the Shawanese, and several tribes of the Abenagins. * * * The Illinois fled to the westward, after being attacked by the Confederates, and did not return until a general peace; and were permitted in 1760, by the Confederates, to settle in the country between the Wabash and the Scioto rivers. The banks of Lake Superior were lined with Algonkins, who sought an asylum from the Five Nations. They also harassed all the Northern Indians, as far as Hudson's Bay, and they even attacked the nations on the Missouri. When La Salle was among the Natchez, in 1683, he saw a party of that people who had been on an expedition against the Iroquois. Smith, the founder of Virginia, in an expedition up the Bay of Chesapeake, in 1608, met a war party of the Confederates then going to attack their enemies. They were at peace with the Cowetas or Creeks, but they warred against the Catawbas, the Cherokees, and almost all the Southern Indians. The two former sent deputies to Albany, where they effected a peace through the mediation of the English. In a word, the Confederates were, with a few exceptions, the conquerors and masters of all the Indian nations east of the Mississippi. * * * * * *

"In consequence of their sovereignty over the other nations, the Confederates exercised a proprietary right in their lands. In 1742 they granted to the province of Pennsylvania certain lands on the west side of the Susquehannah, having formerly done so on the east side. In 1744 they released to Maryland and Virginia certain lands claimed by them in those colonies; and they declared at this treaty, that they had conquered the several nations living on the Susquehannah and Potomac rivers, and on the back of the Great Mountains in Virginia. In 1754, a number of the inhabitants of Connecticut purchased of them a large tract of land west of the Delaware River, and from thence spreading over the east and west branches of the Susquehannah River. In 1768 they gave a deed to William Trent and others, for land between the Ohio and Monongahela. They claimed and sold the land on the north side of the Kentucky River."

This is a skillful statement of the grounds for the Iroquois claim, and was doubtless compiled by the learned writer from the archives of the colonies, and whatever of the diplomatic correspondence between the English and French governments had then transpired. The provincial authorities took early measures to obtain a transfer of whatever rights the New York confederates had obtained. As early as 1684, Lord Howard, governor of Virginia, held a treaty with the Six Nations, at Albany, when, at the request of Colonel Dungan, the Governor of New York, they placed themselves under the protection of the mother country. This was again done in 1701; and, upon the 14th of September, 1726, a formal deed was drawn up, and signed by the chiefs, by which their lands were conveyed to England, in trust, "to be protected and defended by his majesty to and for the use of the grantors and their heirs."[1]

Without repeating the French argument in the premises, it may be mentioned as an interesting coincidence, that Gen. William H. Harrison, as recently as 1837, responded with intelligent zeal to the exaggerated narrative of Clinton, and vindicated the warlike qualities of the Western Indians, by a denial that the Miami Confederacy of Illinois and Ohio could have been conquered by the Iroquois. He cites nu-

1) Writings of James H. Perkins, Vol. II, p. 186. Pownall's Administration of the Colonies, 4th Ed., London, 1768, p. 269.

merous evidences that in 1700 the Miami nation was very numerous; and, even within the memory of those living in 1837, that the Illinois tribes could bring into the field four thousand warriors. "In the year 1734," he adds, "M. de Vincennes, a captain in the French army, found them in possession of the whole of the Wabash, and their principal town occupying the place of Fort Wayne, which was actually the key of the country below. This officer was the first Frenchman who followed the route of the Miami of the Lake and the Wabash, in passing from Canada to their western settlements. Long before this period, the French must have known of the shorter and easier route, and no reason can be assigned for their never having used it, but from its being formerly the seat of war on some portion of it between the Wyandots and Iroquois. De Vincennes found the Miamis in the possession of the entire Wabash."

Briefly, Gen. Harrison admits the subjection of the Delawares, in Pennsylvania, the dispersion of the Hurons, Eries and Andastes, and that the Iroquois advanced as far west as Sandusky; but denies that there is any tradition among the Miamis of their ever having been conquered by the Iroquois. He remarks that, at the treaty of Greenville, there was no allusion to a claim, on the part of the Five Nations, to any right of property in the soil, or jurisdiction over the territory of the Miamis.[2]

Upon a careful review of all the evidence, we think the hypothesis of Gen. Harrison deserves to be adopted in preference to that of Colden and Clinton; and for the following reasons, in addition to those already adduced:

1. The distance from their homes to which war parties

2) Harrison's Discourse before the Ohio Historical Society. See Transactions, Vol. I, p. 257.

were accustomed to march, has little significance when we consider that, within the immense area eastward of the Mississippi, the entire Indian population, two hundred years ago, is estimated by Bancroft at only one hundred and eighty thousand; and that skill in eluding a foe, until the moment chosen for a blow, has always been a favorite portion of Indian tactics.

2. So far as the Lake region is concerned, the map of La Hontan, above described, indicates that the "Illinese" were as ready to make inroads upon the "Irroquese" as the latter were to make westward incursions.

3. We have already shown that the Iroquois were repulsed by the Chippewas from the pursuit of the Hurons (a circumstance unnoticed by Clinton); and Schoolcraft's narrative of the successful reprisal, in 1680, by the Illinois and Miamis, on the banks of the Maumee River, should not be forgotten.

4. In this connection, we should not overlook the relations of the New York Indians, and their Canadian neighbors, the French. Prior to 1663, their intercourse had been very precarious, but in that year a deputation from the Iroquois cantons, who proposed an errand of pacification to Montreal, were surprised, and most of them killed by a party of Algonquins, allies of the French. Of course, all prospects of peace vanished, and a furious war raged along the Canadian frontier. At the first outbreak, these hostilities were most disastrous to the French; but the Canadian Governors, at the head of disciplined troops, more than retaliated on their savage enemies during the thirty years' war which followed. Courcelles, Tracy, De la Barre, and De Nonville, invaded by turns, with various success, the country of the Confederates; and at length, in the year 1696, the veteran Count

Frontenac, who was then, for the second time, Governor of Canada, marched upon their cantons with all the force of the province.[3] He burned their deserted villages, and devastated their maize fields. Even the fierce courage of the Iroquois began to quail before these repeated attacks, while the gradual growth of the colony, and the arrival of troops from France, at length convinced them that they could not destroy Canada. In 1700 a pacification was effected, and the numerous prisoners on both sides were allowed to return. In the year 1726, the French succeeded in erecting a permanent military post at the important pass of Niagara, within the limits of the Confederacy. On the 14th of September, in the same year, the Six Nations made the well known cession of their lands to England, in "trust to be protected and defended by his Majesty, to and for the use of the grantors and their heirs." The fact that the haughty Iroquois submitted to such a measure, is a proof that their power was on the wane, and that they had ceased to occupy the arrogant position of conquering tribes.

It will be remembered that the conquest of the Eries was in 1655, only eight years before the commencement of the war between the French and the Iroquois; and the resistance of the Andastes was prolonged until 1672, seven years after the massacre of the Indian deputation to Montreal. Our inference is, that before the removal of the Eries and Andastes from the path to the Mississippi, Iroquois excursions against the Miamis and Illinois were of course impracticable; and afterwards, all the energies of the New York tribes were summoned to resist the French, by whom their country was frequently invaded and their villages destroyed. It is evident, therefore, that they could have no leisure or force

3) Parkman's Pontiac, 61, 63.

for western expeditions while these desperate hostilities were in progress at home; and after the peace of 1700, and especially after the French occupation of Niagara, in 1726, the denizens of Ohio had no ground to apprehend any disturbance in their possession.

Upon the whole, we are willing to compromise between the positions respectively assumed by Clinton and Harrison. We admit that the Indians of Pennsylvania and New England were tributary to the Five Nations, made so by conquest, and that the country on both sides of Lake Erie—the seats of the Hurons and Neutrals in Canada, and the Eries, Andastes and Shawanese in Ohio—were swept of their aboriginal occupants by their merciless enemies, but beyond the Potomac, the Ohio and the Miamis, it seems to us that there was a drawn battle, constantly renewing, and variable in results. It may be that the Miamis and their Illinois confederates were more frequently repulsed, but they cannot be said to have been subjugated, nor even conquered. Very likely, on the conclusion of peace with Western and Southern tribes, there may have been stipulations in the nature of quit claim, but these did not necessarily imply the previous relation of victor and vanquished, no more than a bill to quiet title recognizes that alleged by a claimant to be paramount.

After 1663, however, when the long war with the Canadian colonists broke out, and until the peace of 1700, the dominion of the Five Nations over the territory of Ohio was nominal, never enforced to the exclusion of other Indian tribes, who hastened to occupy the beautiful and vacant realm.

CHAPTER III.

INDIAN OCCUPATION OF OHIO IN 1750.

THIS chapter will be devoted to a brief sketch of the Indian tribes, who, during the interval between the inroads of the Iroquois (vacating forcibly the region between the Ohio and Lake Erie) and the earliest settlement by Europeans in 1750, gradually occupied the country. The reader may expect some unavoidable repetition, especially in a sketch of the Wyandots, for the materials of which we are greatly indebted to the ethnological and historical labors of Albert Gallatin.[1]

Four tribes were prominent within the limits of Ohio a century since—the Wyandots, Delawares, Shawanese and Ottawas.

1. THE WYANDOTS OR HURONS.—When Champlain arrived in Canada, the Wyandots were the head and principal support of the Algonquin tribes against the Five Nations. In our first chapter we have given their geographical position, and their relations with the Neutral Nation, or Attiouandarons, north, and the Eries and Andastes or Guandastogues (Guyandots,) south of Lake Erie. The extent of their influence and of the consideration in which they were held, may be found in the fact, that even the Delawares, who claimed to be the elder branch of the Lenape Nation, and

1) Gallatin's Synopsis of the Indian Tribes within the United States, east of the Rocky Mountains, and in the British and Russian Possessions of North America; in Transactions of the American Antiquarian Society, II, 68, 72.

called themselves the grandfathers of their kindred tribes, recognized the superiority of the Wyandots, whom to this day they call their uncles. And though reduced to a very small number, the right of the Wyandots, derived either from ancient sovereignty, or from the incorporation of the remnants of the three extinct tribes, to the country between Lake Erie and the Ohio, from the Alleghany to the Great Miami, has never been disputed by any other than the Five Nations.

Their real name *Yendots*, was well known to the French, who gave them the nickname of Hurons. They were called *Quatoghee* by the Five Nations, and one of their tribes *Dionondadies* or *Tuinontatek*. They were visited in 1615 by Champlain, and in 1624 by Father Sigard; and the Jesuits, who subsequently established missions among them, have given, in the "Relations of New France," some account of their language, and ample information of their means of subsistence, manners and religious superstitions. They had, probably on account of their wars with the Five Nations, concentrated their settlements in thirty-one villages, not extending more altogether than twenty leagues either way, and situated along or in the vicinity of Lake Huron, about one hundred miles southwardly of the mouth of the French River. They consisted of five confederated tribes, viz: the *Ataronch*-ronons, four villages; the *Attiquenongnahai*, three villages; the *Attignaouentan* or "Nation de l'Ours," twelve villages; the *Ahrendah*-ronons, the most northeastern tribe, and with which Champlain resided, three villages; and the *Tionontate*, or "Nation of the Petun," the most southwesterly, which formerly had been at war with the other tribes, and had entered the confederation recently, nine villages.[2]

2) Father Lallemand, 1640; Relations, &c.

The small-pox carried off about twelve hundred souls in the year 1639. The Missionaries, principally with a view of baptizing dying children, visited at that time every village, and, with few exceptions, every cabin; and embraced the opportunity of making a complete enumeration of the whole nation. They give the general result in round numbers, seven hundred cabins, and two thousand families, which they estimate at twelve, but which could not have exceeded ten thousand souls. They were not only more warlike, but, in every respect, more advanced in civilization than the Northern Algonquins, particularly in agriculture, to which they appear, probably from their concentrated situation, to have been obliged to attend more extensively than any other Northern Indian nation. The Missionaries had at first great hardships to encounter, and found them less tractable than the Algonquins. But, whether owing to the superior talents of Father Brebeuf and his associates, or to the national character, they made ultimately more progress in converting the Hurons, and have left a more permanent impression of their labors in the remnant of that tribe, than appears to have been done by them, in any other nation without the boundaries of the French settlements.

The only communication of the Hurons, with the infant colony of Canada, was by the river Ottawa, of a difficult navigation, interrupted by portages. The Five Nations directed their attacks to that quarter, cut off the several trading parties, which were in the habit of descending and ascending the river once a year, and intercepted the communication so effectually, that, about the year 1646, the Missionaries on Lake Huron were three years without receiving any supplies from Quebec. The Hurons, who had lost several hundred warriors in those engagements, became dispirited and careless. They indeed abandoned the smaller villages and fortified the larger. This only accelerated their ruin. In the year 1649, the Five Nations invaded the country with all their forces, attacked and carried the most considerable of those places of refuge, and massacred all the inhabitants. The destruction was completed in the course of the ensuing year. A part of the Hurons fled down the Ottawa River and sought an asylum in Canada, where they were pursued by their implacable enemies even under the walls of Quebec. The greater part of the Ahrendas and several detached bands surrendered, and were incorporated into the Five Nations. The remnant of the Tionontates took refuge among the Chippewas of Lake Superior. Others were dispersed towards Michillimacinac, or in some more remote quarters. This event was immediately followed by the dispersion of the Algonquin nations of the Ottawa River.

In 1671, the Tionontates, after an unsuccessful war with the Sioux, left Lake Superior for Michillimacinac, where they rallied around them the dispersed remnants of the other tribes of their nation, and probably of the Andastes and other kindred tribes, which had been likewise nearly exterminated by the Five Nations. Some years later they removed to Detroit, in the vicinity of their ancient seats. And, though reduced to two villages, they resumed their ascendancy over the Algonquin tribes, and acted a conspicuous part with great sagacity in the ensuing conflicts between the French and the Five Nations. Charlevoix, in 1721, writes, that they were still the soul of the councils of all the Western Indians. They claimed the sovereignty over the country between Lake Erie and the Ohio River, which was exercised by frequent grants and cessions hereafter to be mentioned. Col. John Johnston, of Piqua, the well known Indian agent, says that their actual settlements extended from Detroit along the south shore of Lake Erie, as far east as Sandusky Bay.

2. The Delawares.—This interesting tribe has been awarded a higher rank in the page of Cooper, the American novelist, and in the Memoirs of the Moravian Missionaries, than Indian tradition seems to warrant. John Heckewelder, as their annalist, and David Zeisberger, as their philologist, have contributed largely to this favorable impression. The former has preserved a Delaware tradition, that many hundred years ago, the Lenni Lenape resided in the western part of the American continent; thence by a slow emigration, they at length reached the Alleghany River, so called from a nation of giants, the *Allegewi*, against whom the Delawares and Iroquois (the latter also emigrants from the westward) carried on successful war; and, still proceeding eastward, settled on the Delaware, Hudson, Susquehannah and Potomac rivers, making the Delaware the center of their possessions. The Delawares, thus seated on the Atlantic, divided themselves into three tribes, distinguished by the names of the Turtle, the Turkey and the Wolf; or the Unamis, Unalachtgo and Minsi. The latter, also called Mon seys or Muncies, were considered the most warlike and active branch of the Lenape. We shall see hereafter that the latter designation was revived, with important consequences, in Ohio.

Heckewelder seeks unsuccessfully to explain the subjection of the Delawares to the Five Nations, whom they called Mengwe, as a stratagem by the latter; but there is no doubt that a tribe who, more readily than any other, accepted Christianity, found themselves unable to cope with their more warlike neighbors on the war path.[3]

3) Loskiel's History of the Moravian Missions in North America; Part 1, 130. Heckewelder's History Indian Nations.

About 1740–50, a party of Delawares, who had been disturbed in Pennsylvania by European emigration, determined to remove west of the Alleghany Mountains, and obtained from their ancient allies and uncles, the Wyandots, the grant of a derelict tract of land lying principally on the Muskingum. Here they flourished and became a very powerful tribe. From 1765 to 1795, they were at the height of their influence, but the treaty of Greenville, and the disasters sustained by the Delawares in Wayne's campaign, were a death blow to their ascendancy.

3. THE SHAWANESE.—The conflicting testimony, relative to these Bedouins of the American wilderness, is accurately stated by Gallatin.[4] He conjectures that the "Shawnoes," as he writes the word, separated at an early date from the other Lenape tribes, and established themselves south of the Ohio, in what is now the State of Kentucky; that having been driven away from that Territory, probably by the Chickasaws and Cherokees, some portion found their way, during the first half of the seventeenth century, as far east as the country of the Susquehannocks, a kindred Lenape tribe; that the main body of the nation, invited by the Miamis and the Andastes, crossed the Ohio, occupied the country on and adjacent to the Scioto, and joined in the war against the Five Nations; and that, after their final defeat, and that of their allies, in the year 1672, they were again dispersed in several directions. A considerable portion made about that time a forcible settlement on the head waters of the rivers of Carolina; and these, after having been driven away by the Catawbas, found, as others had already done, an asylum in different parts of the Creek country. Another portion joined their brethren in Pennsylvania; and some may

4) Gallatin's Synopsis, 65. Drake's Life of Tecumseh, 10.

have remained in the vicinity of the Scioto and Sandusky. Those in Pennsylvania, who seem to have been the most considerable part of the nation, were not entirely subjugated and reduced to the humiliating state of women by the Six Nations. But they held their lands on the Susquehannah only as tenants at will, and were always obliged to acknowledge a kind of sovereignty or superiority in their landlords. They appear to have been more early and unanimous than the Delawares in their determination to return to the country north of the Ohio. This they effected under the auspices of the Wyandots, and on the invitation of the French, during the years 1740–55. They occupied there the Scioto country, extending to Sandusky, and westwardly towards the Great Miami, and they have also left there the names of two of their tribes, to wit: Chillicothe and Piqua. Those who were settled among the Creeks joined them; and the nation was once more reunited. Mr. Johnston, the Indian agent, says that this southern party lived on the Sawanee River, which empties into the Gulf of Mexico, and is supposed to derive its name from them; and that they returned thence, about the year 1755, to the vicinity of Sandusky, under the conduct of a chief called Black Hoof. It has been reported that Tecumseh and his brother, the Prophet, were sons of a Creek woman married during that migration to a Shawnoe.

During the forty following years, the Shawanese were in an almost perpetual state of war with America, either as British colonies or as independent States. They were among the most active allies of the French during the seven years' war; and, after the conquest of Canada, continued, in concert with the Delawares, hostilities which were only terminated after the successful campaign of General Bouquet. The first permanent settlements of the Americans beyond the Alleghany mountains, in the vicinity of the Ohio, were commenced in the year 1769, and were soon followed by a war with the Shawanese, which ended in 1774, after they had been repulsed in a severe engagement at the mouth of the Kanhawa, and the Virginians had penetrated into their country. They took a most active part against America, both during the war of Independence, and in the Indian war which followed, and which was terminated in 1795 at Greenville. They lost, by that treaty, nearly the whole territory which they held from the Wyandots; and a part of them, under the guidance of Tecumseh, again joined the British standard during the war of 1812.

4. OTTAWAS.—The name of this tribe was either derived from, or communicated to the Canadian River, on whose banks they lived until driven westward by the Five Nations, where they took refuge among the Pottawatamies and Ojibwas. The western shore of Lake Huron, and the northern portion of the Michigan peninsula, was the asylum of the fugitive Ottawas. The tribe has been distinguished in the person of Pontiac, chief of the Ottawas, whose conspiracy against the British garrisons in 1763, was a master stroke of Indian sagacity, ranking its instigator with Phillip and Tecumseh. The honor of his birth has been claimed by other tribes, and his mother was said to be an Ojibwa woman, but he was doubtless born among the Ottawas. He obtained a controlling influence over the Ojibwas and Pottawatamies, and made their confederacy with the Ottawas the basis of his combination against the English. But we must not anticipate. We have mentioned him in these terms, because the practice of antiquarian writers is to depreciate the Ottawas, and the name of the great Ottawa chief is their best vindication.

It has been remarked that, among the Ottawas alone, the

heavenly bodies were an object of veneration—the Sun ranking as their Supreme Deity. This tribe, whose mythology was more complicated than usual with the Indians, were accustomed to keep a regular festival to celebrate the beneficence of the Sun; on which occasion the luminary was told that this service was in return for the good hunting he had procured for his people, and as an encouragement to persevere in his friendly cares. They were also observed to erect an idol in the middle of their town, and sacrifice to it; but such ceremonies were by no means general. On first witnessing Christian worship, the only idea suggested by it was that of asking some temporal good, which was either granted or refused.[5]

Bancroft states that the word "Ottowa," signifies "trader," and was probably applied by the Hurons from the fact that the tribe was principally settled on and in the vicinity of an island in the Ottawa River, where they exacted a tribute from all the Indians and canoes going to, or comimg from the country of the Hurons. It is observed by a Jesuit father, Le Jeune, that although the Hurons were ten times as numerous, they submitted to that imposition; which seems to prove that the right of sovereignty over the Ottawa River was generally recognized. After their expulsion from this aboriginal custom house, the memory of their island home seems to have been preserved; for during the last century they sought and were suffered to take possession of the islands of Lake Erie and the peninsula of Sandusky, where their fishing and trapping parties were found by the French traders as early as 1750.

Soon after the period now under consideration, straggling parties of New York Indians were occasionally found near

5) Missions en la Nouvelle France, 1635, p. 72.

Lake Erie; and at least one Mingo town (the term designating any of the Six Nations, but, in this instance, a party of Cayuga Indians,) was situated on the Ohio River, just below the present site of Steubenville. Logan, celebrated for the specimen of Indian eloquence attributed to him by Jefferson, was a Mingo or Cayuga, and resided in the village above mentioned. We shall have further occasion to mention the arrival of Caughnewagas and Senecas (the former, a tribe from Canada, supposed by Heckewelder to be the old Connecticut Mohicans, mingled with various Iroquois Indians,) in different sections of the southern coast of Lake Erie. Th four tribes above named, however, alone deserve the designa tion of Ohio Indians at the date before us.

Some idea of the Indian occupation of Ohio in 1750 is now attainable. It will be seen by what precedes, that the Delawares occupied the valley of the Muskingum, and thence to Lake Erie and the River Ohio, asserting a possession over about one-half of the State; the Shawanese were soon admitted to the valleys of the Scioto and Miami Rivers, adjoining the Twigtwees or Miami Indians; while the Wyandots, and a few bands of Ottawas, dwelt upon the waters of Sandusky and Maumee, but nearer the bays into which they fell than their sources. As for the Wyandots, it should be remembered that the principal seat of the tribe was opposite Detroit, and the Ohio settlements were in the nature of colonies from the peninsulas bordering Lake Huron. This was also the case with the Ottawas, whose villages were scattered along the shore; although, on a map drawn in 1763, the remains of an "Ottowa fort" are visible near the present site of Plymouth, Huron county, while an Ottawa town is put down on the Cuyahoga River, about thirty miles from its mouth. The Ohio Indians, it may be necessary to add, were superior specimens of the race. The Delawares were the ancestral tribe, and their biography contains an unusual number of remarkable personages, though none of so extraordinary career or character as to be known to the present generation. They will receive a large degree of our notice when the history of the Moravian mission comes before us; for it was principally among the Delawares that the missionaries were successful in making conversions. The Shawanese, whose rovings might vindicate their claim, at least, to be a lost tribe of Israel, have been frequently characterized as the "Spartans" of the race; and certainly their constancy in braving danger and enduring all the consequences of defeat, merits the appellation. But it is by the name of Tecumseh, a son of the nation, though by an alien mother, as we have before observed of his great Ottawa prototype, that the name "Shawnee," will be commemorated in the wild annals of our aboriginal history. The Ottawas, so far as they have ever been observed on the soil of Ohio, have hardly sustained the gravity and dignity of position, which we spontaneously assign to the Wyandot and the Delaware. Compared with his forest brethren, the Ottawa, or Tahwah, (as the early settlers called him,) whose life was nearly amphibious, by his joint avocations of trapper and fisher, seems to be rather a Pariah among his brethren, but to whom history will be more indulgent, in deference to the name of Pontiac. As for the Wyandots, ever recurring as the tribe will be in these chapters, we can do no better than to give a paragraph from Gen. Harrison's discourse, to which we have frequently referred. He gives the Wyandots the unquestioned preference among the Western Indians on the score of bravery. With the other tribes, flight in battle, when occasioned by unexpected resistance and obstacles, brought with it no disgrace, and was rather a part of their strategy: but otherwise with the Wyandots. In the battle of the Rapids of the Miami, in which the confederated tribes were broken by Gen. Wayne, of thirteen chiefs of the Wyandots one only survived, and he badly wounded. The following anecdote illustrates this trait in their character:

"When General Wayne assumed the position of Greenville, in 1793, he sent for Captain Wells, who commanded a company of scouts, and told him that 'he wished him to go to Sandusky and take a prisoner, for the purpose of obtaining information.' Wells (who, having been taken from Kentucky when a boy, and brought up among the Indians, was perfectly acquainted with their character,) answered, that 'he could take a prisoner, but not from Sandusky.' 'And why not from Sandusky?' said the General. 'Because,' answered the Captain, 'there are only Wyandots there.' 'Well, why will not Wyandots do?' 'For the best of reasons,' said Wells, 'because Wyandots will not be taken alive.'"

CHAPTER IV.

LAKE ERIE IN THE SEVENTEENTH CENTURY.

CLOSELY related as Ohio is to the mighty current of the St. Lawrence, a rapid outline of its early exploration will not be deemed too discursive, although our attention will thus be recalled to events which transpired during the seventeenth century.

The magnificent water-course which constitutes the northern border of the Atlantic and Mississippi States, aided materially in the colonization of its extended coast. As at Plymouth, it was religious sentiment which first opened the adventurous way to the borders of our inland lakes. As early as 1616, Le Caron, an unambitious Franciscan monk, the companion of the noted Champlain, had traversed New York, and threading the Canadian peninsula, reached the rivers of Lake Huron. As Quebec was founded only eight years before, the voyage of the missionary probably deserves the distinction of a first discovery. In 1625, we hear of the Franciscans laboring with the Neutral Hurons near the Niagara river.

Tempting as the theme may be, we must be content with a mere chronology of the French missions on the great lakes. They were repelled from the south shore of Lake Erie during the following fifty years, which was the period of their greatest activity, by the hostility of the Iroquois, who were often at war with the natives of the soil.[1]

1) Charles Whittlesey relates (Discourse before Ohio Historical Society in 1840, p. 8.) that trees have been found on the Western Reserve, bearing the marks of an axe, which, judging from the rings, were made in 1660.

The Jesuits succeeded all other religious orders in the labor of evangelization, and from 1634 to 1647, no less than forty-two missionaries of that society were devoted to the tribes in Upper Canada—assembling twice or thrice a year at St. Marys, a central spot upon the banks of the Matchedash, between Lakes Toronto or Simcoe and Huron. Perhaps no passage of colonial history is so full of romantic interest as the narrative of the Wyandot Mission, of which Bancroft has furnished a faithful and fascinating picture; but as early as 1649, the principal seat of the Jesuit Fathers, the village of St. Ignatius, was destroyed by the ruthless Mohawks, and the peaceful inmates involved in a general massacre. The names of Anthony Daniel, Jean de Brebeuf and Gabriel Lallemand, have been preserved to us, fragrant with their martyrdom in the wilderness.

Every dispassionate reader will readily respond to the tribute by the single-hearted annalist of New France. "It is certain," says Charlevoix, "as well from the annual relations of those happy times, as from the constant tradition of that country, that a peculiar unction attached to this savage mission, giving it a preference over many others far more brilliant and fruitful. The reason no doubt was, that nature, finding nothing there to gratify the senses or to flatter vanity—stumbling blocks too common even to the holiest—grace worked without obstacle. The Lord, who never allows himself to be outdone, communicates himself without measure to those who sacrifice themselves without reserve; who, dead to all, detached entirely from themselves and the world, possess their souls in unalterable peace, perfectly established in that child-like spirituality which Jesus Christ has recommended to his disciples as that which ought to be the most marked trait of their character." "Such is the portrait," adds Charlevoix, "drawn of the missionaries of New France by those who knew them best. I myself knew some of them in my youth, and I found them such as I have painted them, bending under the labor of a long apostleship, with bodies exhausted by fatigues and broken with age, but still preserving all the vigor of the apostolic spirit, and I have thought it but right to do them here the same justice universally done them in the country of their labors."

The Relations or Journals of the Jesuit Fathers contain incidental descriptions of the lake coast from "Unghiara," or Niagara, to Lake Superior, otherwise called "Tracy" and "Upper Lake." A map, published at Paris, in 1660, indicates a discovery of Lake Michigan, or "Lake of the Illinois."

In 1668, the mission of Sault St. Mary was established by Claude Dablon and James Marquette—the oldest settlement in Michigan.

In 1671, Marquette gathered some wandering Hurons round a chapel at point St. Ignace, on the main land north of the peninsula of Michigan.

In 1673, Marquette, accompanied by Joliet, a trader of Quebec, and five other Frenchmen, with a number of Indian guides, paddled up Green Bay in birch bark canoes, ascended Fox River to the head of navigation and crossed the Portage to the banks of the Wisconsin. Here their guides deserted the party, from fear of the Sioux, but the Frenchmen fearlessly followed the current of the Wisconsin, until, on the 17th of June, the Mississippi was discovered.

In 1678, La Salle, accompanied by Tonti, an Italian soldier, and Lewis Hennepin, a Flemish friar of the order of Recollects, commenced the construction of the "Griffin," a bark of sixty tons, near the present site of Buffalo. During the next summer, this bark was ready for the voyage, and on the 7th of August, 1679, the surface of Lake Erie was first parted by the keel of civilization. The crew was thirty-four in all—sailors, hunters and soldiers—while father Hennepin was accompanied by several friars of his order.

Our purpose is not to follow this exploring expedition after leaving Lake Erie. The present digression only relates to their adventures from Niagara to Detroit. The voyage to Mackinaw—the return of the Griffin loaded with furs, and the wreck of the bark in Lake Erie—La Salle's subsequent wanderings in Illinois among innumerable discouragements—his weary journey to Fort Frontenac on Lake Ontario, traversing the ridge which divides the basin of the Ohio from that of the lakes—his return to the Illinois in 1681, these and subsequent particulars of his heroic adventures and untimely end in the wilderness of Louisiana, belong to general history, and we must resist the temptation to pursue the romantic record.

His companion, Hennepin, has left to us a readable book, which, authentic for our purposes of reference, has been sharply criticised and also lustily defended,[2] in respect to its narrative of exploration and discovery in the valley of the Mississippi. With that controversy we have nothing to do. His sketch of Lake Erie, as it was in 1679, is our only concern with the gray-coated Franciscan. We even suppress the inclination to give a personal history of the doughty friar.

We repeat Hennepin's description of Niagara Falls in his own words, preserving also the typography of 1698, the date of the edition in our possession:

"Betwixt the Lake *Ontario*, and *Erie*, there is a vast and prodigious Cadence of Water which falls down after a sur-

2) Democratic Review, v. 190, 381.

prising and astonishing manner, insomuch that the Universe does not afford its Parallel. 'Tis true *Italy* and *Suedeland* boast of some such things; but we may well say they are but sorry Patterns, when compared to this of which we now speak. At the foot of this horrible Prescipice, we meet with the River *Niagara*, which is not above half a quarter of a League broad, but is wonderfully deep in some places. It is so rapid above this Descent, that it violently hurries down the wild Beasts while endeavoring to pass it to feed on the other side, they not being able to withstand the force of its Current, which inevitably casts them down above Six hundred feet.

"This wonderful Downfall is compounded of two great Cross-streams of Water, and two Falls, with an Isle sloping along the middle of it. The waters which fall from this vast height do foam and boil after the most hideous manner imaginable, making an outrageous noise, more terrible than that of Thunder, for when the Wind blows from off the South, their dismal roaring may be heard above fifteen Leagues off.

"The River *Niagara* having thrown itself down this incredible Precipice, continues its impetuous course for two Leagues together, to the great Rock above mentioned, with an inexpressible rapidity: But having passed that, its Impetuosity relents, gliding along more gently for two Leagues, till it arrives at the Lake *Ontario* or *Frontenac*.

"Any Barque or greater vessel may pass from the Fort to the foot of this huge rock above mentioned. This rock lies to the Westward, and is cut off from the Land by the River *Niagara*, about two Leagues farther down than the great Fall; for which two Leagues the people are oblig'd to carry their Goods over-land; but the way is very good and the Trees are but few and they chiefly Firr and Oaks. From the great Fall unto this Rock, which is to the West of the River, the two Brinks of it are so prodigious high, that it would make one tremble to look steadily upon the Water, rolling along with a Rapidity not to be imagined. Were it not for this vast Cataract, which interrupts Navigation, they might sail with Barks or greater Vessels, above Four hundred and fifty Leagues farther, cross the Lake of the *Hurons*, and up to the farther end of the Lake *Illinois;* which two Lakes we may well say are little Seas of fresh Water."

A chapter in Hennepin's Discoveries is devoted to Lake Erie, which is written with an accent on the last letter, and appears to have been pronounced in three syllables. He says the lake is called Erie Tejocharontiong, and "extends itself from east to west, a hundred and forty leagues in length. But (he boastfully adds) no European has ever surveyed it at all; only I, and those who accompanied me in this discovery, have viewed the greater part of it. This lake encloses on its southern bank a tract of land as large as the Kingdom of France. It divides itself at a certain place into two channels, because of a great island enclosed betwixt them." In the narrative of the Griffin's "Trial Trip," some further particulars are given of Lake Erie:

"On the 7th of August, 1679, we went on board,[3] and sailed from the mouth of Lake Erie, steering our course west-south-west with a favorable wind; and though the enemies of our Discovery had given out, on purpose to deter us from our enterprise, that the Lake Erie was full of rocks and sands, which rendered the navigation impracticable, we run above twenty leagues during the night, though we

3) The typography of 1698 is conformed to the present usage.

sounded all that while. The next day, the wind being more favorable, we made above five and forty leagues, keeping at an equal distance from the banks of the lake, and doubled a cape to the westward, which we called the Cape of St. Francis. The next day we doubled two other capes, and met with no manner of rocks or sands. We discovered a pretty large island towards the southwest, about seven or eight leagues from the northern coast; that island faces the strait that comes from the Lake Huron.

"The 10th, very early in the morning, we passed between that island and seven or eight lesser ones; and having sailed near another, which is nothing but sand, to the west of the lake, we came to an anchor at the mouth of the strait, which runs from the Lake Huron into that of Erie. The 11th, we went farther into the strait, and passed between two small islands, which make one of the finest prospects in the world. This strait is finer than that of Niagara, being thirty leagues long and everywhere one league broad, except in the middle, which is wider, forming the lake we have called St. Clair. The navigation is easy on both sides, the coast being low and even. It runs directly from north to south.

"The country between those two lakes is very well situated, and the soil very fertile. The banks of the strait are vast meadows, and the prospect is terminated by some hills covered with vineyards. Trees bearing good fruit, groves and forests so well disposed that one would think nature alone could not have made, without the help of art, so charming a prospect. That country is stocked with stags, wild goats and bears, which are good for food, and not fierce as in other countries: some think they are better than our pork. Turkey cocks and swans are there also very common; and our men brought several other beasts and birds, whose names are unknown to us, but they are extraordinary relishing. The forests are chiefly made up of walnut trees, chestnut trees, plum trees, and pear trees, loaded with their own fruit and vines. There is also abundance of timber fit for building; so that those who shall be so happy as to inhabit that noble country, cannot but remember with gratitude those who have discovered the way, by venturing to sail upon an unknown lake for above one hundred leagues. That charming strait lies between forty and forty-one degrees of northern latitude."

La Salle visited the Hurons, "who inhabited the Point of Missilimakinak," and the "Outtaouatz," or Ottawas, who were three or four leagues more northward, who are described as "in confederacy together against the Iroquese, their common enemy. They sow Indian corn, which is their ordinary food; for they have nothing else to live upon, except some fish they take in the lakes." Of the latter, the Indians "brought abundance of whitings and some trouts of 50 and 60 pound weight."

Late in 1680, Father Hennepin returned from his explorations of the valley of the Mississippi and the upper lakes, and passed the winter of 1681 at Michillimacinac, in company with Father Pierson, a Jesuit, whom he found with the Indians. We quote again:

"During the winter, we broke holes in the ice of Lake Huron, and by means of several large stones, sunk our nets sometimes twenty, sometimes twenty-five fathom under water, to catch fish, which we did in great abundance. We took salmon trouts which often weighed from forty to fifty pounds. These made our Indian wheat go down the better, which was our ordinary diet. Our beverage was nothing but broth made of whiteings, which we drank hot, because as it cools it turns to jelly, as if it had been made of veal.

"During our stay here, Father Pierson and I would often divert ourselves on the ice, where we skated on the lake, as they do in Holland. I had learned this slight when I was at Ghent." Hennepin here admitted forty-two Canadians to the order of Saint Francis.

In Easter week, 1681, the Franciscan and his companions left Michillimacinac, and after drawing their canoes for twelve or thirteen leagues over the ice, embarked on Lake Huron, "the sides of which still continued froze five or six leagues broad." After rowing a hundred leagues, they passed the straits, and arrived at "the Lake Erie, or of the Cat," where they spent some time "to kill sturgeon, which come here in great numbers to cast their spawn on the side of the Lake." They took nothing but "the belly of the fish, which is the most delicious part, and threw away the rest." Their further adventures in Lake Erie are narrated as follows:

"This place afforded also plenty of venison and fowl. As we were standing in the lake, upon a large point of land which runs itself very far into the water, we perceived a bear in it as far as we could see. We could not imagine how this creature got there; 'twas very improbable that he should swim from one side to t' other, that was thirty or forty leagues over. It happened to be very calm; and so two of our men, leaving us on the point, put off to attack the bear, that was near a quarter of a league out in the lake. They made two shots at him, one after another, otherwise the beast would certainly have sunk them. As soon as they had fired, they were forced to sheer off as fast as they could to charge again; which when they had done, they returned to the attack. The bear was forced to stand it, and it cost them no less than seven shot before they could compass him.

"As they endeavored to get him aboard, they were like

to have been overset; which, if they had, they must have been infallibly lost: All they could do was to fasten him to the bar that is in the middle of the canoe, and so drag him on shore; which they did at last with much ado and great hazard of their lives. We had all the leisure that was requisite for the dressing and ordering him, so as to make him keep; and in the meantime took out his entrails, and having cleansed and boiled them, eat heartily of them. These are as good a dish as those of our sucking pigs in Europe. His flesh served us the rest of our voyage, which we usually eat with lean goats' flesh, because it is too fat to eat by itself; so that we lived for an hundred leagues upon the game that we killed in this place.

"There was a certain captain of the Outtaonacts, (Ottawas,) to whom the Intendant Talon gave his own name, whilst he was at Quebec. He used to come often to that city with those of his nation who brought furs thither. We were strangely surprised at the sight of this man, whom we found almost famished, and more like a skeleton than a living man. He told us the name of Talon would be soon extinct in this country, since he resolved not to survive the loss of six of his family who had been starved to death. He added, that the Fishery and the Chase had both failed this year, which was the occasion of this sad disaster.

"He told us, moreover, that though the Iroquois were not in war with his nation, yet had they taken and carried into slavery an entire family of twelve souls. He begged very earnestly of me, that I would use my utmost endeavors to have them released, if they were yet alive, and gave me two necklaces of black and white porcelain that I might be sure not to neglect a business which he had so much to heart. 'I can rely upon thee, Barefoot, (for so they always called us,) and am confident that the Iroquese will hearken to thy reasons sooner than any one's. Thou didst often advise them at their Councils, which were held then at the Fort of Katarockoni,[4] where thou hast caused a great cabin to be built. Had I been at my village when thou cam'st through it, I would have done all that I could to have kept thee instead of the Black Coat, (so they call the Jesuits,) which was there.' When the poor Captain had done speaking, I solemnly promised him to use my utmost interest with the Iroquese for the releasement of his friends.

"After we had rowed above a hundred and forty leagues upon the Lake Erie, by reason of the many windings of the bays and creeks which we were forced to coast, we passed by the Great Fall of Niagara, and spent half a day in considering the wonders of that prodigious cascade."

"I could not conceive how it came to pass that four great lakes, the least of which is 400 leagues in compass, should empty themselves one into another, and then all centre and discharge themselves at this Great Fall, and yet not drown good part of America."

Whereupon Hennepin, after modestly wishing that somebody had been with him "who could have described the wonders of this prodigious frightful fall so as to give the reader a just and natural idea of it," proceeds to submit "the following Draught such as it is," but which we do not choose to transcribe. On his route to Fort Frontenac, he claims to have visited the Iroquois, and obtained the "releasement" of the twelve prisoners whom they had taken, and notices the flight of pigeons over their heads in clouds as "a thing worthy of admiration. The birds that were flying at the head of the others, keep often back to ease and

4) Fort Frontenac, now Kingston, at the foot of Lake Ontario.

help those among them that are tired; which may be a lesson to men to help one another in time of need."

There is a map attached to Hennepin's work which shows how little was known of the interior of this continent in 1698. "Lake Erie or of the Cat," is represented as three times as large as Lake Ontario, and equal to Superior. It is wider at the western extremity than elsewhere, extending four degrees of latitude from the straits on the northwest nearly south to the line of the 36th degree, or the latitude of Nashville. One degree below the southwest angle of the lake, the "Hohio," as it is called near the mouth, or the "Ouye," as elsewhere styled, is laid down as flowing between "Apalachin Hills," which range east and west from Virginia towards the Mississippi. A lake nearly as large as Ontario is placed on the south side of these hills, apparently the supposed source of the Savannah River. The Mischasipi, or Mississippi, is laid down in reasonable proportion, the foreshortening of the country east of it being the most ludicrous feature of the map. It is the same, as if the Ohio was sixty miles south of Sandusky Bay, a mountain chain intervening, and then the whole country as far south as Alabama ignored, sunk by a geographical earthquake. The direction of the north shore of Lake Erie is not inaccurate, for it was twice coasted by Hennepin, and the relation between the Niagara and St. Clair rivers is about as we now find it; but instead of narrowing the lake west of the mouth of Cuyahoga river, it sheers off to the south, making a broad angle with the north and south line of the western coast, which is represented as 240 miles long; and thus full one-third of what is now the State of Ohio is swallowed up by an imaginary sea, or an imaginary extension of an actual sea.

Sandusky Bay and River, as well as the Maumee River,

are drawn at an accurate angle to the southern shore, and rightly placed as to each other, yet their channels run from east to west, as indeed might be expected when an area as large as Lake Huron is dropped so unceremoniously at the entrance of the strait of St. Clair. Between these streams is found the only reference to an Indian tribe south of Lake Erie, and that is the "Erieckronois," probably a detachment of the unfortunate Eries, availing themselves of the protection of the adjoining Miami and Illinois tribes. As Hennepin's first publication was in 1683, it is probable that this map includes the observations and traditions made and collected by him in 1679–'81, and this record of the Eries twenty-five years after the disastrous campaign of 1655, is an additional proof, in the first instance, that they were not exterminated by their enemies; and secondly, that the power of the Iroquois had been previously checked on the Miami frontier.

Father Hennepin's description of the "pretty large island towards the southwest," is doubtless a modified form of his previous statement that the lake "divides itself at a certain place into two channels because of a great island enclosed betwixt them." In both cases, (the first is from his general description of Lake Erie, and the other from his narration of the Griffin's cruise,) he probably refers to Point Pelee Island, which, in connection with Kelley's Island, would naturally arrest the notice of the explorer. Cape St. Francis is now called Long Point, and the two other capes doubled in the westward and coastwise progress of La Salle's party, must have been Point aux Pines or Landguard Point, and Point Pelee. La Hontan, in his later map, while far more accurate than Hennepin in his outline of the southern coast of Lake Erie, interrupts his northern shore, about midway from Niagara to St. Clair, by a projection of a cape or peninsula two-thirds across the lake. Hennepin places and delineates Long Point with reasonable accuracy.

We have mentioned La Hontan, whom we have had occasion to cite elsewhere. His letters include the period of 1683–'93, and are racy productions. He also explored Lake Erie. Not to be outdone by his gray-coated predecessor, he describes Niagara as "seven or eight hundred foot high and half a league broad." After entering Lake Erie, his party coasted along the north coast, "being favored by the calms," for it was August, 1687. "Upon the brink of this lake (he says) we frequently saw flocks of fifty or sixty Turkeys, which run incredibly fast upon the sands, and the savages of our company kill'd great numbers of 'em, which they gave to us in exchange for the fish that we catched. The 25th we arrived at a long point of land which shoots out 14 or 15 leagues into the Lake, and the heat being excessive we chose to transport our boats and baggage two hundred paces over land, rather than coast about for thirty-five leagues." On the 6th of September, La Hontan entered the Straits of St. Clair, and pursued his western route, whither we will not follow him.

CHAPTER V.

THE FRENCH ESTABLISH FORT SANDUSKY—THE ENGLISH EXPLORE THE OHIO VALLEY.

WE have given a synopsis of French discovery in the west. These explorations were promptly followed by settlements. In 1701, soon after the peace between the Iroquois and the French in Canada, the latter effected a settlement at Detroit. The party that first took possession of that important position were De la Motte Cadillac, with a Jesuit missionary and one hundred Frenchmen. The fort, which, by its early establishment, made Michigan the oldest of the inland States, except perhaps Illinois, soon became the centre of a valuable trade with the Indians, and the Hurons returned to its vicinity from their fifty years' exile, while above, in Upper Canada, was a colony of Ottawas. Thence, as we have shown, these tribes, who became inseparable companions, soon extended to the Sandusky Basin, where they were firmly established long before any European exploration of the country south of Lake Erie.

At New Orleans and in Illinois were the principal seats of the French in the valley of the Mississippi. As early as 1729, the settlers in the vicinity of New Orleans amounted to nearly six thousand, although a third of that number were slaves; while on the Mississippi, near the Illinois, there were in 1750, five French villages, containing one hundred and forty families, and three villages of colonized natives, numbering not less than six hundred.

Prior to 1750, the communication between Canada and Louisiana was carried on by the distant routes of Green Bay and the Wisconsin, Lake Michigan and the Illinois, and more recently by the Maumee and the Wabash, which latter river was regarded by the French as the main stream to which the Ohio was but a tributary. At the straits of Michillimacinac and the mouth of the St. Josephs river, at the head of Green Bay, and on the site of Fort Wayne, were French settlements, convenient for Indian traffic and contributing to the armed occupation of the country. There is some doubt whether Fort Miamis on the Maumee, (now Fort Wayne,) was founded before 1750, but it is mentioned by Vaudrueil, then Governor of Louisiana and afterwards of Canada, as existing in 1751. Its real date is probably contemporaneous with Fort Sandusky, namely, 1750. Detroit, a post of great importance, had been occupied since 1701.

It was nearly fifty years after the settlement of Detroit by the French, that the attention of France or England was turned to the region between Lake Erie and the Ohio River. Perhaps its dense forests repelled the luxurious Gaul, while the savannahs nearer the Mississippi tempted his occupation. But at length a dispute arose, with the increasing strength of the colonies, about the respective limits of the Atlantic colonies and of Louisiana. Under the treaties of Utrecht and Aix la Chapelle, England claimed that the valley of the lakes and the country east of the Mississippi should be recognized as an Iroquois conquest, and by compact with those tribes, as under the protectorate or dominion (in our days the terms are yet synonyms) of Great Britain. In reply, France cited discovery and occupation—the history of a hundred years of missions, expeditions and colonization. The missions had declined, but the Indian trade continued, and their posts, planted at the most eligible positions from Detroit to New Orleans, were regular garrisons, relieved once in six years. The boats from the Illinois country, descending annually to New Orleans, carried flour, Indian corn, bacon, both of hog and bear, beef and pork, buffalo robes, hides and tallow. The downward voyage was made in December; in February the boat returned with European goods for consumption and Indian traffic.[1] The Northwestern Indians were almost universally in the French interest. As respected the country on the upper lakes, the Mississippi, the Illinois, and the Wabash, the French title, according to European usage, was complete. To forestall the English pretensions to the country immediately south of Lake Erie, the Count de la Galissonniere, shortly after assuming office as Governor General of Canada, sent Monsieur Celeron de Bienville, in 1749, with three hundred men, to traverse the country from Detroit east to the mountains, to bury at the most important points, leaden plates with the arms of France engraved, to take possession with a formal process verbal, and to warn the English traders out of the country.[2]

As will more fully appear in the sequel, the French, in the winter of 1750–'51, followed their formal claim to the territory between Lake Erie and the Ohio, which the exploring party of Celeron de Bienville had reasserted, by taking actual occupation of the northern frontier. This was done by founding a fort and trading station at Sandusky.

Meanwhile, the English colonies of Pennsylvania and Virginia, deeply interested in the trade and pacification of the Ohio Indians, no less than in the political questions at issue, were far from inactive. One George Croghan, an English

1) Hildreth's History United States, II, 434.

2) See Appendix, No. II.

trader, was also an envoy from the Government of Pennsylvania—distributing, on one occasion, goods to the value of a thousand pistoles among the Indians settled on the Ohio and Miami rivers. Licenses to trade with the Indian tribes even to the Mississippi, were also granted by the Governor of Pennsylvania.[3] As early as June, 1744, the colonies of Pennsylvania, Virginia and Maryland, went through another ceremonial of receiving from a deputation of Iroquois, at Lancaster, "a deed recognizing the King's right to all lands *beyond the mountains*." Still stimulated by a sense of danger from the French and their Indian allies, Pennsylvania, at the instigation of Benjamin Franklin, organized her militia.

We have now reached, in order of time, the organization of the Ohio Land Company of 1748, the exploration of Christopher Gist, and our first item of circumstantial evidence as to the period when Fort Sandusky was built and occupied by the French. In 1748, Thomas Lee, with twelve other Virginians, among whom were Lawrence and Augustine, brothers of George Washington, and also Mr. Hanbury, of London, formed an association which was called the "Ohio Company," and petitioned the King for a grant of lands beyond the mountains. This petition was approved by the monarch, and the government of Virginia was ordered to grant the petitioners half a million of acres within the bounds of that colony, beyond the Alleghanies, two hundred thousand of which were to be located at once. This portion was to be held for ten years free of quit-rent, provided the company would put there one hundred families within seven years, and build a

3) In 1749, La Jonquiere, the governor of Canada, learned to his great indignation, that several English traders had reached Sandusky, and were exerting a bad influence upon the Indians of that quarter; and two years later he caused four of the intruders to be seized near the Ohio and sent prisoners to Canada."—*Parkman's Pontiac*, 64.

fort sufficient to protect the settlement; all of which the company proposed, and prepared to do at once, and sent to London for a cargo suited to the Indian trade, which was to come out so as to arrive in November, 1749. This grant was to be taken *principally* on the *south* side of the Ohio river, between the Monongahela and Kanawha rivers.[4]

In the autumn of 1750, the agents of the Ohio Company employed Christopher Gist, a land surveyor and familiar with the woods, to explore their contemplated possessions on the Ohio River, as well as the adjacent country. He kept a journal of his proceedings, which was published, and is entitled: "A journal of Christopher Gist's journey, began from Colonel Cresap's, at the old town on the Potomac River, Maryland, October 31, 1750, continued down the Ohio within fifteen miles of the falls thereof; and from thence to Roanoke River in North Carolina, where he arrived in May, 1751."[5] Mr. Craig, in his notes on the early history of Pittsburgh, thinks, from what he can ascertain, that he ascended the Juniata, after crossing over from the Potomac, and descended the Kiskeminetas to the Alleghany, which stream he crossed about four miles above Pittsburgh, and passed on to the Ohio. From the mouth of Beaver creek he passed over to the Tuscarawas, or Muskingum River, called by him and by the Indians Elk Eye creek; striking it on the 5th of December, or thirty-five days after leaving the Potomac, at a point about fifty miles above the present town of Coshocton, probably within the county of Stark. On the 7th, he crossed over the Elk Eye to a small village of Ottawas, who were in the French interest. He speaks of the land as broken, and the

4) Perkins' Writings, ii, 191. Sparks' Washington, ii, 478.

5) S. P. Hildreth's Pioneer History, 26—a valuable publication of the Ohio Historical Society.

bottoms rather narrow on this stream. On the 14th December he reached an Indian town, a few miles above the mouth of Whitewoman creek, called Muskingum, inhabited by Wyandots, who, he says, are half of them attached to the French and half to the English, containing about one hundred families. "When we came in sight of it, we perceived English colors hoisted on the King's house and at George Croghan's. Upon inquiring the reason, I was informed that the French had lately taken several English traders, and that Mr. Croghan had ordered all the white men to come into this town, and had sent expresses to the traders of the lower towns, and among the Piquatiners, and that the Indians had sent to their people to come to council about it."

From this passage, it is evident that the Pennsylvania traders had traversed the Indian villages, and obtained the good will of their inhabitants in a considerable degree. George Croghan was apparently at the head of a trading party, and he and Andrew Montour accompanied Gist in his further exploration. The latter, who acted as interpreter, and was influential among the Delawares and Shawanese, was a son of the famous Canadian half breed, Catharine Montour, whose residence was at the head of Seneca Lake, in New York.[6] Catharine had two sons, Andrew and Henry,

6) Of this woman W. L. Stone (Life of Brant, i, 340) says: "She was a native of Canada, a half-breed, her father having been one of the early French governors—probably Count Frontenac, as he must have been in the government of that country at about the time of her birth. During the wars between the Six Nations and the French and Hurons, Catharine, when about ten years of age, was made a captive, taken into the Seneca country, adopted and reared as one of their own children. When arrived at a suitable age, she was married to one of the distinguished chiefs of her tribe, who signalized himself in the wars of the Six Nations against the Catawbas, then a great nation living southwestward of Virginia. She had several children by this chieftain, who fell in battle about the year 1750, after which she did not marry again. She is said to have been a handsome woman when

who were three-fourths of Indian blood. The late James H. Perkins supposed that the companion of Gist was Henry, who was a chief among the Six Nations, and says that Andrew had been taken by the French in 1749. But Gist gives the name of his interpreter and companion as "Andrew," and it is unreasonable to suppose him mistaken. It is more likely that Andrew Montour had escaped from his Canadian captors, and was ready to make reprisals on them. Besides Croghan and Montour, Gist was accompanied by Robert Kalender during the latter portion of his journey. We resume the diary of Gist:

"Monday, 17th December, 1750. Two traders belonging to Mr. Croghan came into town and informed us that two of his people had been taken by forty Frenchmen and twenty Indians, who had carried them with seven horse loads of skins *to a new fort the French were building on one of the branches of Lake Erie.*"

This we claim to have been Fort Sandusky. Bancroft recognizes no doubt on the point, but quotes Gist as stating that the captives were "*carried to the new fort at Sandusky.*"[7] There was certainly no other fort or station on any branch of Lake Erie at the close of 1750. Two years afterwards, or early in 1753, twelve hundred men from Montreal built a fort at Presque Isle, now Erie, and crossing thence to the

young, genteel, and of polite address, notwithstanding her Indian associations. It was frequently her lot to accompany the chiefs of the Six Nations to Philadelphia, and other places in Pennsylvania, where treaties were holden; and, from her character and manners, she was greatly caressed by the American ladies—particularly in Philadelphia, where she was invited by the ladies of the best circles, and entertained at their houses. Her residence was at the head of Seneca Lake." This account is mostly derived from Witham Marshe's Journal of a Treaty with the Six Nations, held at Lancaster in 1744, where Madame Montour (as Marshe calls her) was.

7) History of the United States, iv, 77.

waters flowing south, they established posts at La Boeuf and Venango, the one on French creek, the other on the main stream of the Alleghany. All accounts concur in fixing this date for the posts at Erie, Waterford and Venango. Du Quesne, afterwards Fort Pitt and now Pittsburgh, was occupied in 1754. It is true that Niagara and Detroit commanded the extremities of Lake Erie, but in 1750–1, the only French fort on a branch of the lake was Sandusky. This will appear more distinctly as we proceed with Gist's diary.

"Tuesday, 18th December. I acquainted Mr. Croghan and Mr. Montour with my business with the Indians, and talked much of a regulation of trade, with which they were pleased, and treated me well."

"Tuesday, 25th. This being Christmas day, I intended to read prayers, but after inviting some of the white men, they informed each other of my intentions, and being of several persuasions and few of them inclined to hear any good, they refused to come; but one Thomas Barney, a blacksmith, who is settled there, went about and talked to them, and then several of the well disposed Indians came freely, being invited by Andrew Montour." Mr. Gist delivered a discourse, which was interpreted to the Indians, and read the English church service. He then says: "The Indians seem to be well pleased, and came up to me and returned me their thanks and then invited me to live among them," &c.

"Friday, 4th January, 1751. One Taaf, an Indian trader, came to town from near Lake Erie, and informed us that the Wyandots had advised him to keep clear of the Ottawas, (a nation firmly attached to the French, living near the lakes,) and told him that the branches of the lakes were claimed by the French, but that all the branches of the Ohio belonged to them and their brothers, the English, and that the

French had no business there, and that it was expected that the other part of the Wyandots would desert the French and come over to the English interest, and join their brethren on the Elk Eye creek, and build a strong fort and town there."

"Wednesday, 9th. This day came into town two traders from among the Piquatiners (a tribe of the Tawightees) and brought news that another English trader was taken prisoner by the French, and that three French soldiers had deserted and come over to the English, and surrendered themselves to some of the traders of the Picktown, and that the Indians would have put them to death to revenge the taking of our traders; but as the French had surrendered themselves to the English, they would not let the Indians hurt them, but had ordered them to be sent under the care of three of our traders, and delivered at this town to George Croghan."

"Saturday, 12th. Proposed a council—postponed—Indians drunk.

"Monday, 14th. This day George Croghan, by the assistance of Andrew Montour, acquainted the King and council of this nation (presenting them with four strings of wampum) that their Roggony [father] had sent, under care of the Governor of Virginia, their brother, a large present of goods, which were now safe landed in Virginia, and that the governor had sent me to invite them to come and see him, and partake of their father's charity to all his children on the branches of the Ohio. In answer to which, one of the chiefs stood up and said that their King and all of them thanked their brother, the governor of Virginia, for his care, and me for bringing them the news; but that they could not give an answer until they had a full and general council of the several nations of Indians, which could not be until next spring; and so the king and council shaking hands with us, we took our leave."

"Tuesday, 15th. We left Muskingum and went west five miles to the White Woman's creek, on which is a small town. This white woman was taken away from New England, when she was not above ten years old by the French Indians. She is now upwards of fifty—has an Indian husband and several children. Her name is Mary Harris. She still remembers they used to be very religious in New England; and wonders how the white men can be so wicked as she has seen them in the woods."

Having crossed the Licking and Hockhocking, Gist descended the east bank of the Scioto, was favorably received at several Delaware villages, and estimated the strength of the tribe at about five hundred fighting men.[8] On the 28th, he reached Shawnee town, "situated on both sides of the Ohio, just below the mouth of Scioto creek, and containing about three hundred men. There were about forty houses on the south side of the river, and about a hundred on the north side, with a kind of state house, about ninety feet long, with a tight cover of bark in which councils were held."

Thence on the 12th of February, the party as before enumerated, crossed to the Great Miami, and were received at the Tawightwi town, which was on the northwest side of the river, and consisted of about four hundred families. The Tawightwi, or Miami Indians, are described as a numerous people, consisting of many different tribes, under the same form of government. A chief of the confederacy was chosen indifferently from the tribes, and at this time, was the king of the Piankeshaws. Gist was kindly received, and notwithstanding four Ottawas were present as envoys from the

8) See Appendix, No. III.

French, with tempting presents and offers of renewals of friendship, the latter were rejected, and the powerful Miamis gave the English envoy a promise to meet the Virginia commissioners at Logstown, seventeen miles below Pittsburg, for a general treaty. The scene of this interview was probably at the mouth of Loramies Creek, or just above Piqua.

The king of the Piankeshaws, setting up the English colors in the council, as well as the French, rose and replied to the overtures of the Ottawa messengers. "The path to the French is bloody, and was made so by them. We have cleared a road for our brothers, the English, and your fathers have made it foul, and have taken some of our brothers prisoners." "This," added the king, "we look upon as done to us," and turning suddenly from them, he strode out of the council. At this the representative of the French, an Ottawa, wept and howled, predicting sorrow for the Miamis.

To the English, the Weas and Piankeshaws, after deliberation, sent a speech by the great orator of the Weas. "You have taken us by the hand," were his words, "into the great chain of friendship. Therefore we present you with these two bundles of skins to make shoes for your people, and this pipe to smoke in, to assure you our hearts are good towards you, our brothers."

In the presence of the Ottawa ambassadors, the great war chief of the Picqua stood up, and summoning in imagination the French to be present, he spoke—

"Fathers! you have desired we should go home to you, but I tell you it is not our home; for we have made a path to the sun rising, and have been taken by the hand by our brothers, the English, the Six Nations, the Delawares, the Shawanese, and the Wyandots; and we assure you in that road we will go. And as you threaten us with war in the spring, we tell you, if you are angry, we are ready to receive you, and resolve to die here, before we will go to you. That you may know this to be our mind, we send you this string of black wampum.

"Brothers, the Ottawas, you hear what I say, tell that to your fathers, the French, for that is our mind, and we speak it from our hearts."

"The French colors are taken down," adds Bancroft, "and the Ottawas *are dismissed to the French fort of Sandusky.*"[9]

On the 1st of March, Gist left on his return by the falls of Ohio, and through the Cumberland mountains, to North Carolina; but in April, 1751, the Miami chiefs were revisited by Croghan, with similar results, as narrated in his published journal.

The Shawanese, found by Gist at the mouth of the Scioto, were lately returned from their southern wanderings, but as the scattered portions of the tribe came to Ohio, they established themselves higher up the stream and on the waters of the Miami, building several towns.

Having thus generally examined the land upon the Ohio, in November Gist commenced a thorough survey of the tract south of the Ohio, and east of the Kanawha, granted to the Ohio Company, and spent the winter in that labor.

Early in 1752, a settlement of English traders was attempted on the Great Miami, at the mouth of Loramie's Creek. A party of French soldiers having heard of it, came to the Twigtwees or Miamis, and demanded the traders as intruders. The Indians refused—the trading house was destroyed—fourteen natives killed, and the traders were carried into Canada, and some of them, according to one account, burned alive. This fort or trading house, was

9) History of the United States, iv, 81.

called by the English writers Pickawillany. These traders were probably Pennsylvanians, for that State made a gift of condolence to the Twigtwees for those slain in their defence.[10]

On the 9th June, 1752, Messrs. Fry, Lomax and Patton, Virginia Commissioners, met the Indians at Logstown, fourteen miles below Pittsburg, on the right bank of the Ohio, which had long been a trading point, but had been abandoned by the Indians in 1750. Gist appeared as agent for the Ohio Company. The Commissioners urged a confirmation of the treaty of Lancaster. The Indians claimed that the treaty at Lancaster did not cede any lands west of the warrior's road, which ran at the foot of the Alleghany ridge. Two old chiefs asked Mr. Gist where the Indians' land lay—for the French claimed all the land on one side of the Ohio river, and the English on the other? Mr. Gist found the question difficult to answer. "However," said the savages, "as the French have already struck the Twigtwees, we shall be pleased to have your assistance and protection, and wish you would build a fort at once at the Fork of the Ohio." The Virginians asked much more, and at length, by bribing one of the Montours to exert his influence, induced the Indians to sign a deed, confirming the Lancaster treaty in its full extent, consenting to a settlement southeast of the Ohio, and guarantying that it should not be disturbed by them.

Hildreth says in 1752, "a band of the Miamis, or Twigtwees, as the English called them, settled at Sandusky,

10) This was in May, 1753. The present to the Miamis was two hundred pounds, besides a grant of six hundred pounds for general distribution among the tribes; but so great was the apprehension of the French, that the money probably was not sent, though Conrad Weiser was dispatched as a messenger in August to learn how things stood. *Sparks' Franklin*, iii, 219; *N. A. Review*, xlix, 83.

having refused to remove to Detroit, and persisting in trade with the English, their village was burned, the English traders were seized, and their merchandize confiscated."[11] This is probably an inaccurate version of the affair at Loramies or Pickawillany.

Early in 1753, Gist had established a plantation near the Youghiogany, west of Laurel Hill, consisting of eleven families, but his purpose to lay off a town and fort near the mouth of Chartier's creek, about two miles below the Fork, on the southeast side of the river, was relinquished.

In the summer and fall of 1753, the French landed at Erie, and planted their garrisons at Presq' Isle, Le Boeuf and Venango.

In November of the same year, George Washington, as the envoy of Virginia, had his unsatisfactory interview of remonstrance with the French commandant.

11) History of the United States, by Richard Hildreth, II, 436.

CHAPTER VI.

THE ASCENDANCY OF FRANCE UPON THE OHIO.

THE year 1754 may be indicated as the period when the favorable sentiments which Croghan and Gist had ascertained and cultivated among the Ohio Indians, began to change to hostility. It was a year of French activity and English folly. The colonies were alarmed, but inefficient and parsimonious; while the French labored zealously to conciliate the Indians by gifts and flatteries. The envoys of the latter did not alarm the savages by any demands—their only object was to conciliate good will. "During the autumn of 1754," says Perkins, "the pleasant Frenchmen were securing the west step by step; settling Vincennes, gallanting with the Delawares, and coquetting with the Iroquois, who still balanced between them and the English. The forests along the Ohio shed their leaves, and the prairies filled the sky with the smoke of their burning; and along the great rivers, and on the lakes, and amid the pathless woods of the west, no European was seen whose tongue spoke other language than that of France."[1]

On the other hand, the infatuation of the colonists in seeking a grant of extensive tracts, occupied by Ohio Indians, from the Iroquois—the increasing numbers and influence of the Shawanese, who were the hereditary enemies of the English, and whose professions otherwise to Gist were probably hypocritical or mercenary—the failure of the colonies to

1) Perkins' Writings, ii, 280.

continue their donations to the western Indians, while French emissaries swarmed in every village, with gifts of trinkets and exchanges of ammunition and ardent spirits; and finally the evidences of French activity and strength afforded by the erection of forts at Sandusky, Vincennes, Miamis, Presque Isle, Du Quesne, &c.—all these circumstances conspired to alienate even the Delawares and Miamis from the English, and to make all the tribes either allies or acquiescent spectators of the French inroad. The main body of the Wyandots, and the Ottawas, without exception, became the active allies of the French.

Perhaps no one was more keenly sensitive to the approaching danger, and more sagacious in devising means to avert it, than Benjamin Franklin. He was the life and soul of the Albany Congress of 1754, which was summoned to promote the common defence and general welfare of the colonies, and his writings reflect vividly the weakness of the English counsels as contrasted with his clear perception of the exigencies of the crisis. No western annalist should omit a cordial recognition of Franklin's timely and valuable suggestions on the eve of that momentous struggle which terminated French dominion upon the St. Lawrence and the Ohio.

As is well known, the Albany Convention of 1754, resulted in a plan of union, drawn by the sagacious Franklin, which was deemed too loyal to the crown by the colonies, and too democratic by the Court of England, and therefore was universally rejected. There were present delegates from New Hampshire, Rhode Island, Connecticut, New York, Pennsylvania and Maryland. The Six Nations were also represented by Hendrick, the Mohawk Sachem, and certainly no one was more capable than an Iroquois chieftain to impress upon the delegates the necessity of union. The policy of a confederacy had been the secret of the strength of the Five Nations, and it was a remarkable incident at the council of Lancaster, in 1744, that a recommendation of *Union* came from Cannastego, one of their orators. At the session of the FOURTH OF JULY, of that year, the eloquent Onondaga warrior used this language:

"We have one thing further to say, and that is, we heartily recommend union and good agreement between you and your brethren. Never disagree, but preserve a strict friendship for each other, and thereby you, as well as we, will become the stronger.

"Our wise forefathers established union and amity between the Five Nations; this has made us formidable: this has given us great weight and authority with our neighboring nations. We are a powerful confederacy; and by your observing the same methods which our wise forefathers have taken, you will acquire fresh strength and power; therefore, whatsoever befalls you, never fall out with each other."

There are evidences that Franklin's thoughts had been for some time turned to a union of the colonies. He had thrown out hints to that effect in his newspaper. The *Pennsylvania Gazette* for May 9, 1754, contains an account of the capture by the French of Captain Trent's party, who were erecting a fort (afterwards Fort Du Quesne) at the fork of the Ohio. The article was undoubtedly written by the editor. After narrating the particulars and urging union to resist aggression, he adds: "The confidence of the French in this undertaking seems well grounded in the present disunited state of the British colonies, and the extreme difficulty of bringing so many different governments and assemblies to agree in any speedy and effectual measures for our common defence and security; while our enemies have the very great advantage of being under one direction, with one council and one purse." At the end of the article is a wood cut, in which is the figure of a snake, separated into parts, to each of which is affixed the initial of one of the colonies, and at the bottom, in larger capitals, the motto, "JOIN OR DIE." It is well known that this device was adopted with considerable effect at the beginning of the Revolution. In some of the newspapers of that day, the mutilated snake makes a conspicuous head-piece, running across the page, and accompanied by the same significant motto.[2]

Not discouraged by the Albany failure, Franklin persisted in devising other measures of relief for the colonial crisis. He brought forward his "Plan for settling two Western Colonies in North America, with reasons for the plan," dated 1754, and probably written shortly after the Albany Convention of that year. One of these barrier colonies was to guard the Niagara frontier, and the other to occupy the northern bank of the Ohio. This was to be done by organizing a joint stock, one share of which, calling for a blank number of acres, was to be transferred to every settler or subscriber of a given amount of money—by which he anticipated that sufficient men and means would be collected, "provided only," added the shrewd Franklin, "that the crown would be at the expense of removing the little forts the French have erected in their encroachments on his Majesty's territories, and supporting a strong one near the Falls of Niagara, with a few small armed vessels, or half-galleys to cruise on the lakes."

For the security of the Lake Colony in its infancy, he proposed a temporary fort on French Creek, the principal

2) Sparks' Franklin, iii, 25.

branch of the Alleghany River, but which Franklin calls "Buffalo creek of the Ohio," and "another at the mouth of the Tioga, on the south side of Lake Erie, where a port should be formed and a town erected for the trade of the lakes." I presume that "Tioga" was intended for Cuyahoga, for he immediately adds, that "the colonists for *this settlement* might march by land through Pennsylvania."

The next paragraph contains an allusion to Fort Sandusky, which demonstrates that it was founded before 1754 at least.

"The river Scioto, which runs into the Ohio about two hundred miles below Logstown, is supposed the fittest seat of the *other colony;* there being for forty miles on each side of it, and quite up to its head, a body of all rich land: the finest spot of its bigness in all North America, and has the particular advantage of sea-coal in plenty (even above ground in two places,) for fuel, when the wood shall be destroyed. This colony would have the trade of the Miamis or Twightwees; and should, at first, have a small fort near Hochockin, at the head of the river, and another near the mouth of the Wabash. *Sandusky*, (in the earliest edition of Franklin's Works written *Sanduski*,) *a French Fort near the Lake Erie, should also be taken;* and all the little French forts south and west of the lakes, quite to the Mississippi, be removed, or taken and garrisoned by the English."

These colonies were to be on the French plan of western colonization, every fort having a small settlement around it, one furnishing protection and the other provisions; and Franklin assumes that "there are already in all the old colonies many thousands of families that are ready to swarm, wanting more land," who would be attracted by "the richness and natural advantages of the Ohio country." He opens his essay, indeed, by observing that "the great country back of the Appalachian mountains, on both sides of the Ohio and between that river and the lakes, is now well known, both to the English and French, to be one of the finest in North America, for the extreme richness and fertility of the land, the healthy temperature of the air, and mildness of the climate ; the plenty of hunting, fishing and fowling ; the facility of trade with the Indians ; and the vast convenience of inland navigation or water carriage by the lakes and great rivers, many hundreds of leagues around." "From these natural advantages," he predicts "it must undoubtedly (perhaps in less than another century,) *become a populous and powerful dominion.*"

In favor of his project of charters and encouragement to two border colonies, as above sketched, Franklin gives so characteristic an outline of the evils to be prevented, and the benefits to be attained, that we cannot refrain from a quotation of some extent:

"The French are now making open encroachments on these territories, in defiance of our known rights ; and if we longer delay to settle that country, and suffer them to possess it, these *inconveniencies and mischiefs* will probably follow :

1. Our people being confined to the country between the sea and the mountains, cannot much more increase in number : people increasing in proportion to their room and means of subsistence.

2. The French will increase much more, by that acquired room and plenty of subsistence, and become a great people behind us.

3. Many of our debtors and loose English people, our German servants and slaves, will probably desert to them, and increase their numbers and strength, to the lessening and weakening of ours.

4. They will cut us off from all commerce and alliance with the western Indians, to the great prejudice of Britain, by preventing the sale and consumption of its manufactures.

5. They will, both in time of peace and war, (as they have always done against New England,) set the Indians on to harrass our frontiers, kill and scalp our people, and drive in the advanced settlers; and so, in preventing our obtaining more subsistence by cultivating of new lands, they discourage our marriages, and keep our people from increasing; thus (if the expression may be allowed,) killing thousands of our children before they are born.

"If two strong colonies of English were settled between the Ohio and Lake Erie, in the places hereafter to be mentioned, these advantages might be expected:

1. They would be a great security to the frontiers of our other colonies, by preventing the incursions of the French and French Indians of Canada, on the back parts of Pennsylvania, Maryland, Virginia and the Carolinas; and the frontiers of such new colonies would be much more easily defended than those of the colonies last mentioned now can be, as will appear hereafter.

2. The dreaded junction of the French settlements in Canada with those of Louisiana would be prevented.

3. In case of a war, it would be easy, from those new colonies, to annoy Louisiana, by going down the Ohio and the Mississippi; and the southern part of Canada, by sailing over the lakes, and thereby confine the French within narrow limits.

4. We could secure the friendship and trade of the Miamis or Twigtwees, (a numerous people, consisting of many tribes, inhabiting the country between the west end of Lake Erie and the south end of Lake Huron, [Michigan rather,] and

the Ohio,) who are at present dissatisfied with the French and fond of the English, and would gladly encourage and protect an infant English settlement in or near their country, as some of their chiefs have declared to the writer of this memoir. Further, by means of the Lakes, the Ohio and Mississippi, our trade might be extended through a vast country, among many numerous and distant nations, greatly to the benefit of Britain.

5. The settlement of all the intermediate lands, between the present frontiers of our colonies on one side, and the Lakes and Mississippi on the other, would be facilitated and speedily executed, to the great increase of Englishmen, English trade, and English power.

"The grants to most of the colonies, are of long narrow slips of land, extending west from the Atlantic to the South Sea. They are much too long for their breadth; the extremes are at too great distance: and therefore unfit to be continued under their present dimensions. Several of the old colonies may conveniently be limited westward by the Alleghany or Apalachian mountains, and new colonies formed west of those mountains."

Tempting as this relic is, we will not further pursue the extract. It is certainly the prophecy of history, and perhaps no passage in the useful life of Franklin, has been more productive of service to his country, than his early labors to unite the colonies. They were the germ of the confederacy of the Revolution, and the Constitution of 1789. The foregoing project was in the alternative—only in case the Albany scheme was not adopted. Both, however, were one generation too soon. These councils were unheeded, and after 1754, the reaction in favor of the French, so extensively prevailed among the Western tribes, for the reasons already indicated, that Braddock's defeat became the signal of a general rising against the colonies.

Our record of the subsequent occurrences of the French and English war, can only be chronological.

On the 17th of April, 1754, while a small party of Virginians were erecting a fort at the forks of the Ohio, Contrecoeur, a French officer, appeared on the Alleghany with sixty batteaux, three hundred canoes and eighteen cannon. Ensign Ward, who, in the absence of Capt. Trent and Lieut. Fraser, was in command of only forty-one men, surrendered to a force of one thousand French and Indians, and was permitted to lead his party, with their tools, to Virginia. The French erected Fort Du Quesne at once, and their communication from Lake Erie to the Ohio was complete.

The retreating company fell in with a force of one hundred and fifty men, under Col. Washington, who, instead of turning back, resolved to push boldly on, strike the Monongahela at the mouth of Redstone, (now Brownsville,) and establish a fort there. Informed by Tanacharison, a friendly Indian chief, otherwise called Half King, that a French party was seeking him, Washington advanced, a skirmish ensued, M. de Junonville, the French commandant, and ten of his men were killed, and twenty-two taken prisoners, one of whom was wounded. One of Col. Washington's men was killed, and two or three wounded. This event occurred on the 28th of May, 1754.

Washington was soon joined by the rest of his regiment (his rank was Lieut. Colonel, but he had succeeded to the command on the death of Col. Joseph Fry,) raising his force to six hundred men. He erected a stockade at Great Meadows, called Fort Necessity, and pushed on towards Fort Du Quesne. The approach of a much superior force under M. de Villiers, brother of Junonville, obliged him to fall back to Fort Necessity. His troops were fatigued, discouraged and short of provisions; and, after a day's fighting, he agreed to give up the fort, and to retire with his arms and baggage. Having retired to Wills creek, Washington's troops assisted in the erection of Fort Cumberland, which now became the frontier post of Virginia.

We need not repeat the tale of Braddock's defeat. It occurred on the 9th of July, 1755. An expedition against Niagara also failed.

Singular as it may seem in this paper age, war was not declared between England and France until May, 1756. This year was also barren of results.

Nothing decisive until 1758. Then, among other triumphs of English arms, Fort Du Quesne was abandoned on the approach of Gen. Forbes through Pennsylvania. With the fall of this fort ceased all direct contest in the West. From that time, Canada was the scene of operations, but in 1759, Ticonderoga, Crown Point, Niagara, and at length Quebec itself, yielded to the English; and, on the 8th of September, 1760, Montreal, Detroit, and all Canada were given up by Vaudreuil, the French Governor.

Our statement that Fort Sandusky was built and occupied by the French as early as 1750–1, is now seen to be fully sustained by the journal of Gist, and the essay of Franklin (both contemporary documents) as well as by the opinion of Bancroft. The exact locality of this stockade cannot be ascertained, but the probability is, on a comparison of all the references which have fallen under our notice, that the site was about three miles west of the city of Sandusky, near the village of Venice, on Sandusky Bay. The trail from Fort Du Quesne, afterwards Fort Pitt, and now Pittsburg, to

Detroit, evidently struck Sandusky Bay, near the locality above mentioned, and Fort Sandusky was not probably far from that trail.

All the Revolutionary treaties with the Ohio Indians, as well as the treaties of January 9, 1789, at Fort Harmar, and August 3, 1795, at Greenville, contain grants to the United States of "six miles square upon Sandusky Lake, *where the Fort formerly stood.*" On a map of Ohio, published in 1803, this tract is clearly delineated as extending from the south shore of Sandusky Bay, and including the locality which we have supposed to be the situation of Fort Sandusky. Parkman, in a chart of "Forts and Settlements in America, A. D. 1763," places nothing within the present limits of the State of Ohio, except Fort Sandusky, which is situated on the Bay or Lake of that name. The allusions to Fort Sandusky imply so distinctly that it was near Lake Erie, or easily accessible therefrom, that the opinion has been expressed, that the Fort was situated on the peninsula north of the Bay; and Evans' "Map of the British Colonies," published in 1755, represents Fort Sandusky on the *left side* of the outlet of the Bay, and marks a Fort Junandat (a probable corruption of Wyandot) near the mouth of the Sandusky River, on the south side. This location of Fort Sandusky, placing it in Danbury township, Ottawa county, is universally contradicted by subsequent charts and descriptions, and we have adopted an opinion in favor of the location on the great northwestern trail. That trail we suppose to have struck a point on the Tuscarawas River, near the junction of Sandy creek, on the southern border of Stark county; thence westward through the southern tier of townships in Wayne county, and the towns of Mohican and Vermillion, in Ashland county; thence turning northwest through

Mifflin, Franklin and Plymouth townships, of Richland county, crossing the Black Fork of the Walhonding or Whitewoman River twice ; still more northwardly through the townships of New Haven, Greenfield, Peru and Ridgefield, of Huron county, striking across a bend in the Huron River ; and so through Erie county northwestwardly in the direction of Detroit.

CHAPTER VII.

A PICTURE OF OHIO ONE HUNDRED YEARS SINCE.

It is in our power, by transcribing freely from a Narrative of the Captivity of Col. James Smith among the Ohio Indians, between May, 1755, and April, 1759, to present a picture of the wilderness and its savage occupants, which, bearing intrinsic evidence of faithful accuracy, is also corroborated by the public and private character of the writer.

Col. James Smith was a native of Pennsylvania, and after his return from Indian captivity, was entrusted, in 1763, with the command of a company of riflemen. He trained his men in the Indian tactics and discipline, and directed them to assume the dress of warriors, and to paint their faces red and black, so that in appearance they were hardly distinguishable from the enemy. Some of his exploits in the defence of the Pennsylvania border are less creditable to him than his services in the war of the Revolution. He lived until the year 1812, and is the author of a Treatise on the Indian mode of warfare. In Kentucky, where he spent the latter part of his life, he was much respected, and several times elected to the Legislature.

The first edition of Smith's Journal was published in Lexington, Kentucky, by John Bradford, in 1799.[1] Samuel G. Drake, the Indian antiquarian and author, accompanies

1) See a volume entitled "Indian Captivities, or Life in the Wigwam;" by S. G. Drake, author of the "Book of the Indians;" Derby & Miller, publishers, Auburn, N. Y

its republication in 1851 by a tribute to Smith as "an exemplary Christian and unwavering patriot."

In the spring of 1755, James Smith, then eighteen years of age, was captured by three Indians, (two Delawares and one Canasatauga,) about four or five miles above Bedford, in Western Pennsylvania. He was immediately led to the banks of the Alleghany River, opposite Fort Du Quesne, where he was compelled to run the gauntlet between two long ranks of Indians, each stationed about two or three rods apart. His treatment was not severe, until near the end of the lines, when he was felled by a blow from a stick or tomahawk handle, and, on attempting to rise, was blinded by sand thrown into his eyes. The blows continued until he became insensible, and when he recovered his consciousness, he found himself within the fort, much bruised, and under the charge of a French physician.

While yet unrecovered from his wounds, Smith was a witness of the French exultation and the Indian orgies over the disastrous defeat of Braddock. A few days afterwards, his Indian captors placed him in a canoe, and ascended the Alleghany River to an Indian town on the north side of the river, about forty miles above Fort Du Quesne. Here they remained three weeks, when the party proceeded to a village on the west branch of the Muskingum, about twenty miles above the forks. This village was called Tullihas, and was inhabited by Delawares, Caughnewagas and Mohicans.[2] The

2) Heckewelder, in his History of the Indian Nations (p. 77), says that the *Cochnewago* Indians were a remnant of the Mohicans of New England, who had fled to the shores of the St. Lawrence, where they incorporated themselves with the Iroquois, and became a mixed race, of course under French influence. A number of the Mohicans from Connecticut emigrated to Ohio in 1762, and their chief was "Mohican John," whose village was on the trail from Sandusky to Fort Pitt, near the township of Mohican, in Ashland county, according to our reckoning.

soil between the Alleghany and Muskingum rivers, on the route here designated, is described as "chiefly black oak and white oak land, which appeared generally to be good wheat land, chiefly second and third rate, intermixed with some rich bottoms."

While remaining at Tullihas, Smith describes the manner of his adoption by the Indians and other ceremonies, which we prefer to give in his own words:

"The day after my arrival at the aforesaid town, a number of Indians collected about me, and one of them began to pull the hair out of my head. He had some ashes on a piece of bark, in which he frequently dipped his fingers in order to take the firmer hold, and so he went on, as if he had been plucking a turkey, until he had all the hair clean out of my head, except a small spot about three or four inches square on my crown. This they cut off with a pair of scissors, excepting three locks, which they dressed up in their own mode. Two of these they wrapped round with a narrow beaded garter, made by themselves for that purpose, and the other they plaited at full length, and then stuck it full of silver brooches. After this they bored my nose and ears, and fixed me off with ear-rings and nose-jewels. Then they ordered me to strip off my clothes and put on a breech-clout, which I did. They then painted my head, face and body, in various colors. They put a large belt of wampum on my neck, and silver bands on my hands and right arm; and so an old Chief led me out on the street, and gave the alarm halloo, *coo-wigh*, several times, repeated quick; and on this, all that were in the town came running and stood round the old Chief, who held me by the hand in the midst. As I at that time knew nothing of their mode of adoption, and had seen them put to death all they had taken, and as I never could find that they saved a man alive at Braddock's defeat, I made no doubt but they were about putting me to death in some cruel manner. The old Chief holding me by the hand, made a long speech, very loud, and when he had done, he handed me to three young squaws, who led me by the hand down the bank, into the river, until the water was up to our middle. The squaws then made signs to me to plunge myself into the water, but I did not understand them. I thought the result of the council was that I should be drowned, and that these young ladies were to be the executioners. They all three laid violent hold of me, and I for some time opposed them with all my might, which occasioned loud laughter by the multitude that were on the bank of the river. At length one of the squaws made out to speak a little English (for I believe they began to be afraid of me) and said '*No hurt you.*' On this I gave myself up to their ladyships, who were as good as their word; for though they plunged me under water, and washed and rubbed me severely, yet I could not say they hurt me much.

"These young women then led me up to the council house, where some of the tribe were ready with new clothes for me. They gave me a new ruffled shirt, which I put on, also a pair of leggins done off with ribbons and beads, likewise a pair of moccasins, and garters dressed with beads, porcupine quills and red hair—also a tinsel-laced cappo. They again painted my head and face with various colors, and tied a bunch of red feathers to one of those locks they had left on the crown of my head, which stood up five or six inches. They seated me on a bear-skin and gave me a pipe, tomahawk and polecat-skin pouch, which had been skinned pocket-fashion, and contained tobacco, killegenico, or dry sumach leaves, which they mix with their tobacco; also spunk, flint and steel. When I was thus seated, the Indians came in, dressed and painted in their grandest manner. As they came in, they took their seats, and for a considerable time there was a profound silence—every one was smoking; but not a word was spoken among them. At length one of the Chiefs made a speech, which was delivered to me by an interpreter, and was as followeth: 'My son, you are now flesh of our flesh and bone of our bone. By the ceremony which was performed this day, every drop of white blood was washed out of your veins; you are taken into the Caughnewago nation and initiated into a war-like tribe; you are adopted into a great family, and now received with great seriousness and solemnity in the room and place of a great man. After what has passed this day, you are now one of us by an old strong law and custom. My son, you have now nothing to fear—we are now under the same obligations to love, support and defend you that we are to love and defend one another; therefore you are to consider yourself as one of our people.' At this time I did not believe this fine speech, especially that of the white blood being washed out of me; but since that time I have found that there was much sincerity in said speech; for, from that day, I never knew them to make any distinction between me and themselves, in any respect whatever, until I left them. If they had plenty of clothing, I had plenty; if we were scarce, we all shared one fate.

"After this ceremony was over, I was introduced to my new kin, and told that I was to attend a feast that evening, which I did. And as the custom was, they gave me also a bowl and wooden spoon, which I carried with me to the place, where there was a number of large brass kettles, full of boiled venison and green corn; every one advanced with his bowl and spoon, and had his share given him. After this, one of the chiefs made a short speech, and then we began to eat.

"The name of one of the chiefs in this town, was Tecanyaterighto, alias Pluggy, and the other Asallecoa, alias Mohawk Solomon. As Pluggy and his party were to start the next day to war, to the frontiers of Virginia, the next thing to be performed was the war dance, and their war songs. At their war dance, they had both vocal and instrumental music; they had a short hollow gum, closed at one end, with water in it, and parchment stretched over the open end thereof, which they beat with one stick, and made a sound nearly like a muffled drum. All those who were going on this expedition, collected together and formed. An old Indian then began to sing, and timed the music by beating on this drum, as the ancients formerly timed their music by beating the tabor. On this, the warriors began to advance, or move forward in concert, like well disciplined troops would march to the fife and drum. Each warrior had a tomahawk, spear, or war-mallet in his hand, and they all moved regularly toward the east, or the way they intended to go to war. At length they all stretched their tomahawks toward the Potomac, and giving a hideous shout or yell, they wheeled quick about, and danced in the same manner back. The next was the war song. In performing this, only one sung at a time, in a moving posture, with a tomahawk in his hand, while all the other warriors were engaged in calling aloud, *he uh, he uh*, which they constantly repeated while the war song was going on. When the warrior that was singing had ended his song, he struck a war-post with his tomahawk, and with a loud voice told what warlike exploits he had done, and what he now intended to do, which were answered by the other warriors with loud shouts of applause. Some who had not before intended to go to war at this time, were so animated by this performance, that they took up the tomahawk and sung the war song, which was answered with shouts of joy, as they were then initiated into the present marching company. The next morning this company all collected at one place, with their heads and faces painted with various colors, and packs upon their backs; they marched off, all silent, except the commander, who, in the front, sung the traveling song, which began in this manner: *hoo caughtainteheegana.* Just as the rear passed the end of the town, they began to fire in their slow manner, from the front to the rear, which was accompanied with shouts and yells from all quarters.

"This evening I was invited to another sort of dance, which was a kind of promiscuous dance. The young men stood in one rank, and the young women in another, about one rod apart, facing each other. The one that raised the tune, or started the song, held a small gourd or dry shell of a squash in his hand, which contained beads or small stones, which rattled. When he began to sing, he timed the tune with his rattle; both men and women danced and sung together, advancing towards each other, stooping until their heads would be touching together, and then ceased from dancing, with loud shouts, and retreated and formed again, and so repeated the same thing over and over, for three or four hours, without intermission. This exercise appeared to me at first irrational and insipid; but I found that in singing their tunes *ya ne no hoo wa ne*, &c., like our *fa sol la*, and though they have no such thing as jingling verse, yet they can intermix sentences with their notes, and say what they please to each other, and carry on the tune in concert.

I found that this was a kind of wooing or courting dance, and as they advanced stooping with their heads together, they could say what they pleased in each other's ear, without disconcerting their rough music, and the others, or those near, not hear what they said."

Smith describes an expedition, about thirty or forty miles southwardly, to a spot which he supposed to be between the Muskingum, Ohio and Scioto rivers—perhaps in Licking county. It was a buffalo lick, where the Indians killed several buffalo, and in their small brass kettles made about half a bushel of salt. Here were clear open woods, and thin white oak land, with several paths, like wagon roads, leading to the lick.

Returning to the Indian village on the Muskingum, Smith obtained an English Bible, which Pluggy and his party had brought back among other spoils of an expedition as far as the south branch of the Potomac. He remained at Tullihas until October, when he accompanied his adopted brother, whose name was Tontileaugo, and who had married a Wyandot woman, to Lake Erie. Their route was up the west branch of the Muskingum, through a country which for some distance was "hilly, but intermixed with large bodies of tolerable rich upland and excellent bottoms." They proceeded to the head waters of the west branch of Muskingum, and thence crossed to the waters of a stream, called by Smith the Canesadooharie. This was probably the Black River, which, rising in Ashland, and traversing Medina and Lorain counties, (at least by the course of its east branch,) falls into Lake Erie a few miles north of Elyria.[3] If we suppose that Tullihas, situated twenty miles above the principal forks of Muskingum, was near the junction of the Vernon and Mo-

3) See Appendix, No. V.

hican Rivers, on the border of Knox and Coshocton counties, Smith and his companion probably followed what is called on Thayers' Map of Ohio the " Lake fork of the Mohican," until they reached the northern portion of Ashland county, and there struck the headwaters of the Canesadooharie, where, as Smith testifies, they found " a large body of rich, well-lying land; the timber, ash, walnut, sugartree, buckeye, honey-locust and cherry, intermixed with some oak and hickory." Let us here resume the Narrative:

" On this route we had no horses with us, and when we started from the town, all the pack I carried was a pouch, containing my books, a little dried venison, and my blanket. I had then no gun, but Tontileaugo, who was a first rate hunter, carried a rifle gun, and every day killed deer, raccoons or bears. We left the meat, excepting a little for present use, and carried the skins with us until we encamped, and then stretched them with elm bark on a frame made with poles stuck in the ground, and tied together with lynn or elm bark; and when the skins were dried by the fire, we packed them up and carried them with us the next day.

" As Tontileaugo could not speak English, I had to make use of all the Caughnewaga I had learned, even to talk very imperfectly with him; but I found I learned to talk Indian faster this way than when I had those with me who could speak English.

" As we proceeded down the Canesadooharie waters, our packs increased by the skins that were daily killed, and became so very heavy that we could not march more than eight or ten miles per day. We came to Lake Erie about six miles west of the mouth of Canesadooharie. As the wind was very high the evening we came to the lake, I was surprised to hear the roaring of the water, and see the high waves that dashed against the shore like the ocean. We encamped on a run near the lake, and as the wind fell that night, the next morning the surface was only in a moderate motion, and we marched on the sand along the side of the water, frequently resting ourselves as we were heavy laden. I saw on the strand a number of large fish that had been left in flat or hollow places: as the wind fell and the waves abated, they were left without water, or only a small quantity, and numbers of bald and gray eagles, &c., were along the shore devouring them.

"Some time in the afternoon we came to a large camp of Wyandots, at the mouth of Canesadooharie, where Tontileaugo's wife was. Here we were kindly received: they gave us a kind of rough brown potatoes, which grew spontaneously, and were called by the Caughnewagas *ohnenata.* These potatoes peeled, and dipped in raccoon's fat, taste nearly like our sweet potatoes. They also gave us what they called *caneheanta,* which is a kind of hominy made of green corn, dried, and beans mixed together.

"From the headwaters of Canesadooharie to this place the land is generally good—chiefly first or second rate, and comparatively little or no third rate. The only refuse is some swamps that appear to be too wet for use, yet I apprehend that a number of them, if drained, would make excellent meadows. The timber is black oak, walnut, hickory, cherry, black ash, white ash, water ash, buckeye, black locust, honey locust, sugar-tree and elm. There is also some land, though comparatively but small, where the timber is chiefly white oak or beech; this may be called third rate. In the bottoms, and also many places in the uplands, there is a large quantity of wild apple, plum, and red and black haw trees. It appeared to be well watered, and a plenty of meadow ground intermixed with upland, but no large prairies or glades that I saw or heard of. In this route deer, bear, turkeys and raccoons appeared plenty, but no buffalo, and very little signs of elks.

"We continued our camp at the mouth of Canesadooharie for some time, where we killed some deer and a great many raccoons: the raccoons here were remarkably large and fat. At length we all embarked in a large birch bark canoe. This vessel was about four feet wide and three feet deep, and about five and thirty feet long; and though it could carry a heavy burden, it was so artfully and curiously constructed that four men could carry it several miles, or from one landing place to another, or from the waters of the lake to the waters of the Ohio. We proceeded up Canesadooharie a few miles, and went on shore to hunt; but to my great surprise, they carried the vessel that we all came in up the bank, and inverted it, or turned the bottom up, and converted it into a dwelling house, and kindled a fire before us to warm ourselves by and cook. With our baggage and ourselves in this house, we were very much crowded, yet our little house turned off the rain very well.

"We kept moving and hunting up this river until we came to the falls: here we remained some weeks, and killed a number of deer, several bears, and a great many raccoons. * * * They then buried their large canoe in the ground, which is the way they took to preserve this sort of a canoe in the winter season.

"As we had at this time no horses, every one got a pack on his back, and we steered an east course about twelve miles and encamped. The next morning we proceeded on the same course about ten miles to a large creek that empties into Lake Erie betwixt Canesadooharie and Cayahaga. Here they made their winter cabin in the following form: they cut logs about fifteen feet long, and laid these logs upon each other, and drove posts in the ground at each end to keep them together; the posts they tied together at the top with bark, and by this means raised a wall fifteen feet long, and about four feet high, and in the same manner they raised another wall opposite to this, at about twelve feet distance; they then drove forks in the ground in the centre of each end, and laid a strong pole from end to end on these forks; and from these walls to the poles, they set up poles instead of rafters, and on these they tied small poles in place of laths; and a cover was made of linn bark, which will run even in the winter season.

"As every tree will not run, they examine the tree first, by trying it near the ground, and when they find it will do, they fell the tree and raise the bark with the tomahawk, near the top of the tree, about five or six inches broad, then put the tomahawk handle under this bark, and pull it along down to the butt of the tree; so that sometimes one piece of bark will be thirty feet long. This bark they cut at suitable lengths in order to cover the hut.

"At the end of these walls they set up split timber, so that they had timber all around, excepting a door at each end. At the top, in place of a chimney, they left an open place, and for bedding they laid down the aforesaid kind of bark, on which they spread bear skins. From end to end of this hut, along the middle, there were fires, which the squaws made of dry split wood, and the holes or open places that appeared, the squaws stopped with moss, which they collected from old logs; and at the door they hung a bear skin; and notwithstanding the winters are hard here, our lodging was much better than I expected."

It appears that this Wyandot encampment consisted of eight hunters and thirteen squaws, boys and children. Soon afterwards, four of the hunters started upon an expedition against the English settlements, leaving Tontileaugo, three other Indians, and Smith, to supply the camp with food. The winter months passed in hunting excursions—the bear, even more than the deer, being an object of active and successful pursuit. The months of February and March, 1756, seem to have been occupied as follows:

"In February we began to make sugar. As some of the elm bark will strip at this season, the squaws, after finding a tree that would do, cut it down, and with a crooked stick, broad and sharp at the end, took the bark off the tree, and of this bark made vessels in a curious manner, that would hold about two gallons each; they made above one hundred of these kind of vessels. In the sugar-tree they cut a notch, sloping down, and at the end stuck in a tomahawk; in the place where they stuck the tomahawk, they drove a long chip, in order to carry the water out from the tree, and under this they set their vessel to receive it. As sugar-trees were plenty and large here, they seldom or never notched a tree that was not two or three feet over. They also made bark vessels for carrying the water that would hold about four gallons each. They had two brass kettles that held about fifteen gallons each, and other smaller kettles in which they boiled the water. But as they could not at times boil away the water as fast as it was collected, they made vessels of bark that would hold about one hundred gallons each for retaining the water; and though the sugar-trees did not run every day, they had always a sufficient quantity of water to keep them boiling during the whole sugar season.

"The way we commonly used our sugar while encamped

was by putting it in bear's fat until the fat was almost as sweet as the sugar itself, and in this we dipped our roasted venison. About this time, some of the Indian lads and myself were employed in making and attending traps for catching raccoons, foxes, wild-cats, &c.

"As the raccoon is a kind of water animal, that frequents the runs, or small water courses, almost the whole night, we made our traps on the runs, by laying one small sapling on another, and driving in posts to keep them from rolling. The under sapling we raised about eighteen inches, and set so that on the raccoon's touching a string, or a small piece of bark, the sapling would fall and kill it; and lest the raccoon should pass by, we laid brush on both sides of the run, only leaving the channel open.

"The fox-traps we made nearly in the same manner, at the end of a hollow log, or opposite to a hole at the root of a hollow tree, and put venison on a stick for bait; we had it so set that when the fox took hold of the meat the trap fell. While the squaws were employed in making sugar, the boys and men were engaged in hunting and trapping.

"About the latter end of March, we began to prepare for moving into town, in order to plant corn. The squaws were then frying the last of their bear's fat, and making vessels to hold it; the vessels were made of deer skins, which were skinned by pulling the skin off the neck, without ripping. After they had taken off the hair, they gathered it in small plaits round the neck, and with a string drew it together like a purse; in the centre a pin was put, below which they tied a string, and while it was wet they blew it up like a bladder, and let it remain in this manner until it was dry, when it appeared nearly in the shape of a sugar loaf, but more rounding at the lower end. One of these vessels would hold about four or five gallons. In these vessels it was they carried their bear's oil."

When all things were ready, the party returned to the falls of Canesadooharie, and thence, after building another canoe of elm bark, to the town at the mouth of the river.

By this time, Smith was thoroughly domesticated among his Indian captors. He found himself treated as an equal and often with disinterested kindness. His Indian name, by which they habitually addressed him, was Scoouwa. At length, he and his adopted brother, Tontileaugo, started for a westward journey to Sandusky Lake—Smith on horseback along the strand of Lake Erie, and the Indian in a canoe near the shore. Here we resume our extracts:

"After some time, the wind arose, and we went into the mouth of a small creek, and encamped. Here we stayed several days on account of high wind, which raised the lake in great billows. While we were here, Tontileaugo went out to hunt, and when he was gone, a Wyandot came to our camp: I gave him a shoulder of venison which I had by the fire, well roasted, and he received it gladly, told me he was hungry and thanked me for my kindness. When Tontileaugo came home, I told him that a Wyandot had been at camp, and that I gave him a shoulder of venison; he said that was very well, and I suppose you gave him also sugar and bear's oil, to eat with his venison. I told him I did not; as the sugar and bear's oil was down in the canoe, I did not go for it. He replied, you have behaved just like a Dutchman.[4] Do you not know that when strangers come to our

4) It is stated in a foot note that "the Dutch he called Skoharehaugo, which took its derivation from a Dutch settlement, Skoharey"—probably Scoharie. It will be remembered that these Caughnewagas were a mixed race of Mohicans and Iroquois—otherwise the name of a remote settlement in New York would be unknown to an Ohio Indian.

camp, we ought always to give them the best we have. I acknowledged that I was wrong. He said that he could excuse this, as I was but young, but I must learn to behave like a warrior, and do great things, and never be found in any such little actions.

"The lake being again calm, we proceeded, and arrived safe at Sunyendeand, which was a Wyandot town, that lay upon a small creek which empties into the little lake below the mouth of Sandusky.

"The town was about eighty rood above the mouth of the creek, on the south side of a large plain, on which timber grew, and nothing more but grass or nettles. In some places there were large flats, where nothing but grass grew, about three feet high when grown, and in other places nothing but nettles, very rank, where the soil is extremely rich and loose—here they planted corn. In this town, there were also French traders, who purchased our skins and fur, and we all got new clothes, paint, tobacco, &c.

"After I had got my new clothes, and my head done off like a redheaded woodpecker, I, in company with a number of young Indians, went down to the cornfield, to see the squaws at work. When we came there, they asked me to take a hoe, which I did, and hoed for some time. The squaws applauded me as a good hand at the business; but when I returned to the town, the old men hearing of what I had done, chid me, and said that I was adopted in the place of a great man, and must not hoe corn like a squaw. They never had occasion to reprove me for anything like this again; as I never was extremely fond of work, I readily complied with their orders.

"As the Indians, on their return from their winter hunt, bring in with them large quantities of bear's oil, sugar, dried venison, &c., at times they have plenty, and do not spare eating or giving—thus they make away with their provision as quick as possible. They have no such thing as regular meals, breakfast, dinner or supper; but if any one, even the town folks, would go to the same house several times in one day, he would be invited to eat of the best—and with them it is bad manners to refuse to eat when it is offered. If they will not eat, it is interpreted as a symptom of displeasure, or that the persons refusing to eat were angry with those who invited them.

"At this time, hominy, plentifully mixed with bear's oil and sugar, is what they offer to every one who comes in any time of the day; and so they go on until their sugar, bear's oil and venison is all gone, and then they have to eat hominy by itself without bread, salt or any thing else; yet still they invite every one that comes in, to eat whilst they have any thing to give. It is thought a shame not to invite people to eat, while they have any thing; but if they can, in truth, only say we have got nothing to eat, this is accepted as an honorable apology. All the hunters and warriors continued in town about six weeks after we came in; they spent this time in painting, going from house to house, eating, smoking, and playing at a game resembling dice, or hustle cap. They put a number of plum stones in a small bowl; one side of each stone is black, and the other white; they then shake or hustle the bowl, calling *hits*, *hits*, *hits*, *honesy*, *honesy*, *rego*, *rego;* which signifies calling for white or black, or what they wish to turn up; they then turn the bowl, and count the whites and blacks. Some were beating their kind of drum [described elsewhere as "a short hollow gum, closed at one end, with water in it, and parchment stretched over the end thereof, which they beat with one stick"] and singing; others were employed in playing on a sort of flute, made of hollow cane; and others playing on the jews harp. Some part of this time was also taken up in attending the council-house, where the chiefs, and as many others as chose, attended: and at night they were frequently employed in singing and dancing. Towards the last of this time, which was in June, 1756, they were all engaged in preparing to go to war against the frontiers of Virginia: when they were equipped, they went through their ceremonies, sung their war songs, &c. They all marched off, from fifteen to sixty years of age: and some boys, only twelve years old, were equipped with their bows and arrows, and went to war: so that none were left in town but squaws and children, except myself, one very old man, and another about fifty years of age, who was lame.

"The Indians were then in great hopes that they would drive all the Virginians over the lake, which is all the name they knew for the sea. They had some cause for this hope, because at this time the Americans were altogether unacquainted with war of any kind, and consequently very unfit to stand their hand with such subtle enemies as the Indians were. The two old Indians asked me if I did not think that the Indians and French would subdue all America except New England, which they said they had tried in old times. I told them I thought not; they said they had already drove them all out of the mountains, and had chiefly laid waste the great valley betwixt the North and South mountain, from Potomac to James River, which is a considerable part of the best land in Virginia, Maryland and Pennsylvania, and that the white people appeared to them like fools: they could neither guard against surprise, run, nor fight. These, they said, were their reasons for saying that they would subdue the whites. They asked me to offer my reasons for my opinion, and told me to speak my mind freely. I told them that the white people to the east were very numerous, like the trees, and though they appeared to them to be fools, as they were not acquainted with their way of war, yet they were not fools; therefore, after some time they will learn your mode of war, and turn upon you, or at least defend themselves. I found that the old men themselves did not believe they could conquer America, yet they were willing to propagate the idea in order to encourage the young men to go to war.

"When the warriors left this town we had neither meat, sugar or bear's oil left. All that we had then to live on was corn pounded into coarse meal or small hominy—this they boiled in water, which appeared like well thickened soup, without salt or anything else. For some time we had plenty of this kind of hominy; at length we were brought to very short allowance, and as the warriors did not return as soon as they expected, we were in a starving condition, and but one gun in the town and very little ammunition. The old lame Wyandot concluded that he would go a hunting in the canoe and take me with him, and try to kill deer in the water, as it was then watering time. We went up Sandusky a few miles, then turned up a creek and encamped. We had lights prepared, as we were to hunt in the night, and also a piece of bark and some bushes set up in the canoe, in order to conceal ourselves from the deer. A little boy that was with us held the light, I worked the canoe, and the old man who had his gun loaded with large shot, when we came near the deer fired, and in this manner killed three deer in part of one night. We went to our fire, ate heartily, and in the morning returned to town, in order to relieve the hungry and distressed.

"When we came to town the children were crying bitterly on account of pinching hunger. We delivered what we had taken, and though it was but little among so many, yet it was divided according to the strictest rules of justice. We immediately set out for another hunt, but before we returned a party of the warriors had come in, and brought with them on horseback a quantity of meat. These warriors had divided into different parties, and all struck at different places in Augusta county. They brought in with them a considerable number of scalps, prisoners, horses and other plunder. One of the parties brought in with them one Arthur Campbell. As the Wyandots at Sunyendeand and those at Detroit were connected, Mr. Campbell was taken to Detroit; but he remained some time with me in this town; his company was very agreeable and I was sorry when he left me. During his stay at Sunyendeand he borrowed my Bible, and made some very pertinent remarks on what he read. One passage, where it is said, 'It is good for a man that he bear the yoke in his youth.' He said we ought to be resigned to the will of Providence, as we were now bearing the yoke in our youth. Mr. Campbell appeared to be about sixteen or seventeen years of age.

"There was a number of prisoners brought in by these parties, and when they were made to run the gauntlet, I went and told them how they were to act. One John Savage was brought in, and a middle aged man of about forty years old. He was to run the gauntlet. I told him what he had to do; and after this I fell into one of the ranks with the Indians, shouting and yelling like them; and as they were not very severe on him, as he passed me I hit him with a piece of a pumpkin, which pleased the Indians much, but hurt my feelings.

"About the time that these warriors came in, the green corn was beginning to be of use, so that we had either green corn or venison, and sometimes both, which was comparatively high living. When we could have plenty of green corn, or roasting ears, the hunters became lazy, and spent their time, as already mentioned, in singing and dancing, &c. They appeared to be fulfilling the Scriptures beyond those who profess to believe them, in that of taking no thought of to-morrow; and also in love, peace and friendship together, without dispute. In this respect they shame those who profess Christianity.

"In this manner we lived until October; then the geese, swans, ducks, cranes, &c., came from the north and alighted on this little lake without number or innumerable. Sunyendeand is a remarkable place for fish in the spring, and fowl both in the fall and spring.

"As our hunters were now tired with indolence, and fond of their own kind of exercise, they all turned out to fowling, and in this could scarce miss of success; so that we had now plenty of hominy and the best of fowls; and sometimes, as a rarity, we had a little bread made of Indian corn meal, pounded in a hominy block, mixed with boiled beans, and baked into cakes under the ashes.

"This with us was called good living, though not equal to our fat roasted and boiled venison, when we went to the woods in the fall; or bear's meat and beaver in the winter; or sugar, bear's oil and dry venison in the spring.

"Sometime in October, another adopted brother, older than Tontileaugo, came to pay us a visit at Sunyendeand, and asked me to take a hunt with him on Cayahaga. As they always used me as a freeman, and gave me the liberty of choosing, I told him that I was attached to Tontileaugo—

had never seen him before, and therefore asked some time to consider this. He told me that the party he was going with would not be along, or at the mouth of this little lake, in less than six days, and I could in this time be acquainted with him, and judge for myself. I consulted with Tontileaugo on this occasion, and he told me that our old brother Tecaughretanego, (which was his name,) was a chief, and a better man than he was; and if I went with him I might expect to be well used; but he said I might do as I pleased, and if I stayed he would use me as he had done. I told him that he had acted in every respect as a brother to me; yet I was much pleased with my old brother's conduct and conversation; and as he was going to a part of the country I had never been in, I wished to go with him. He said that he was perfectly willing.

"I then went with Tecaughretanego to the mouth of the little lake, where he met with the company he intended going with, which was composed of Caughnewagas and Ottawas. Here I was introduced to a Caughnewaga sister, and others I had never before seen. My sister's name was Mary, which they pronounced *Maully*. I asked Tecaughretanego how it came that she had an English name. He said he did not know that it was an English name; but it was the name the priest gave her when she was baptized, and which he said was the name of the mother of Jesus. He said there were a great many of the Caughnewagas and Wyandots that were a kind of half Roman Catholics; but as for himself, he said, that the priest and him could not agree, as they held notions that contradicted both sense and reason, and had the assurance to tell him that the book of God taught them these foolish absurdities; but he could not believe that the great and good Spirit ever taught them any such nonsense; and therefore he concluded that the Indians' old religion was better than this new way of worshipping God.

"The Ottawas have a very useful kind of tents which they carry with them, made of flags, plaited and stitched together in a very artful manner, so as to turn the rain and wind well —each mat is made fifteen feet long and about five feet broad. In order to erect this kind of tent, they cut a number of long straight poles, which they drive in the ground, in the form of a circle, leaning inwards; then they spread the mats on these poles, beginning at the bottom and extending up, leaving only a hole in the top uncovered—and this hole answers the place of a chimney. They make fire of dry split wood in the middle, and spread down bark mats and skins for bedding, on which they sleep in a crooked posture, all round the fire, as the length of their beds will not admit of stretching themselves. In place of a door they lift up one end of a mat and creep in, and let the mat fall down behind them.

"These tents are warm and dry, and tolerably clear of smoke. Their lumber they keep under birch-bark canoes, which they carry out and turn up for a shelter, where they keep everything from the rain. Nothing is in the tents but themselves and their bedding.

"This company had four birch canoes and four tents. We were kindly received, and they gave us plenty of hominy and wild fowl boiled and roasted. As the geese, ducks, swans, &c., here are well grain fed, they were remarkably fat, especially the green necked ducks. The wild fowl here feed upon a kind of wild rice that grows spontaneously in the shallow water, or wet places along the sides or in the corners of the lakes.

"As the wind was high, and we could not proceed on our voyage, we remained here several days, and killed abundance of wild fowl, and a number of raccoons.

"When a company of Indians are moving together on the lake, as it is at this time of the year often dangerous sailing, the old men hold a council; and when they agree to embark, every one is engaged immediately in making ready, without offering one word against the measure, though the lake may be boisterous and horrid. One morning, though the wind appeared to me to be as high as in days past, the billows raging, yet the call was given *yohohyohoh*, which was quickly answered by all—*ooh-ooh*, which signifies agreed. We were all instantly engaged in preparing to start, and had considerable difficulties in embarking.

"As soon as we got into our canoes we fell to paddling with all our might, making out from the shore. Though these sort of canoes ride waves beyond what could be expected, yet the water several times dashed into them. When we got out about half a mile from shore, we hoisted sail, and as it was nearly a west wind, we then seemed to ride the waves with ease, and went on at a rapid rate. We then all laid down our paddles, excepting one that steered, and there was no water dashed into our canoes until we came near the shore again. We sailed about sixty miles that day and encamped some time before night.

"The next day we again embarked and went on very well for some time; but the lake being boisterous and the wind not fair, we were obliged to make to shore, which we accomplished with hard work and some difficulty in landing. The next morning a council was held by the old men.

"As we had this day to pass by a long precipice of rocks on the shore about nine miles, which rendered it impossible for us to land, though the wind was high and the lake rough, yet, as it was fair, we were all ordered to embark. We wrought ourselves out from the shore and hoisted sail (what we used in place of sail cloth were our tent-mats, which answered the purpose very well) and went on for some time with a fair wind, until we were opposite to the precipice, and then it turned towards the shore, and we began to fear we should be cast upon the rocks. Two of the canoes were considerably farther out from the rocks than the canoe I was in. Those who were farthest out in the lake did not let down their sails until they had passed the precipice; but as we were nearer the rock, we were obliged to lower our sails and paddle with all our might. With much difficulty we cleared ourselves of the rock and landed. As the other canoes had landed before us, there were immediately runners sent off to see if we were all safely landed.

"This night the wind fell, and the next morning the lake was tolerably calm, and we embarked without difficulty, and paddled along near the shore, until we came to the mouth of the Cayahaga, which empties into Lake Erie on the south side betwixt Canesadooharie and Presque Isle.

"We turned up Cayahaga and encamped, where we staid and hunted for several days; and so we kept moving and hunting until we came to the forks of Cayahaga.

"This is a very gentle river, and but few ripples, or swift running places, from the mouth to the forks. Deer here were tolerably plenty, large and fat; but bear and other game scarce. The upland is hilly, and principally second and third rate land; the timber chiefly black oak, white oak, hickory, dog-wood, &c. The bottoms are rich and large, and the timber is walnut, locust, mulberry, sugar-tree, red haw, black haw, wild apple-trees, &c. The west branch of this river interlocks with the east branch of Muskingum, and the east branch with the Big Beaver creek that empties into the Ohio about thirty miles below Pittsburgh.

"From the forks of Cayahaga to the east branch of Muskingum, there is a carrying place, where the Indians carry their canoes, &c., from the waters of Lake Erie into the waters of the Ohio.

"From the forks, I went over with some hunters to the east branch of Muskingum, where they killed several deer, a number of beavers, and returned heavy laden with skins and meat, which we carried on our backs, as we had no horses.

"The land here is chiefly second and third rate, and the timber chiefly oak and hickory. A little above the forks, on the east branch of Cayahaga, are considerable rapids, very rocky for some distance, but no perpendicular falls."

From the east branch of the Muskingum, the party went forty miles northeast to Beaver creek, "near a little lake or pond which is about two miles long and one broad, and a remarkable place for beaver." After various adventures in pursuit of beaver and other game, they went in February, 1757, to the Big Beaver, and in March returned to the forks of Cuyahoga. Here occurred a lesson upon profane swearing, which is not unworthy of repetition:

"I remember that Tecaughretanego, when something displeased him, said 'God damn it.' I asked him if he knew what he then said? He said he did, and mentioned one of their degrading expressions, which he supposed to be the meaning, or something like the meaning of what he had said. I told him that it did not bear the least resemblance to it; that what he had said was calling upon the Great Spirit to punish the object he was displeased with. He stood for some time amazed, and then said, if this be the meaning of these words, what sort of people are the whites? When the traders were among us, these words seemed to be intermixed with all their discourse. He told me to reconsider what I had said, for he thought I must be mistaken in my definition; if I was not mistaken, he said the traders applied these words not only wickedly, but oftentimes very foolishly, and contrary to sense or reason. He said he remembered once of a trader's accidentally breaking his gun lock, and on that occasion calling out aloud, 'God damn it'—surely, said he, the gun lock was not an object worthy of punishment for Owananeeyo, or the Great Spirit; he also observed the traders often used this expression when they were in a good humor and not displeased with any thing. I acknowledged that the traders used this expression very often, in a most irrational, inconsistent and impious manner; yet I still asserted that I had given the true meaning of these words. He replied, if so, the traders are as bad as Oonasharoona, or the underground inhabitants, which is the name they give to devils, as they entertain a notion that their place of residence is under the earth."

Making a "large chestnut canoe," the party "embarked," had an agreeable passage down the Cuyahoga and along the south side of Lake Erie, until they passed the mouth of Sandusky; then the wind arose, and they put in at the mouth of the Miami of the Lake, at Cedar Point, and sailed thence in a few days for Detroit. After remaining in the Wyandot and Ottawa villages opposite Fort Detroit until November, a number of families prepared for their winter hunt, and agreed to cross the lake together. Here occurs a description of the Island Region of Lake Erie:

"We encamped at the mouth of the river the first night, and a council was held whether we should cross through by the three islands, [meaning, of course, East Sister, Middle Sister and West Sister,] or coast round the lake. These islands lie in a line across the lake, and are just in sight of each other. Some of the Wyandots or Ottawas frequently make their winter hunt on these islands; though excepting wild fowl and fish, there is scarcely any game here but raccoons, which are amazingly plenty and exceedingly large and fat, as they feed upon the wild rice, which grows in abundance in wet places round these islands. It is said that each hunter, in one winter, will catch one thousand raccoons.

"It is a received opinion among the Indians, that the snakes and raccoons are transmigratory, and that a great many of the snakes turn raccoons every fall, and the raccoons snakes every spring. This notion is founded on observations made on the snakes and raccoons in this island.

"As the raccoons here lodge in rocks, the trappers make their wooden traps at the mouth of the holes; and as they go daily to look at their traps, in the winter season they commonly find them filled with raccoons; but in the spring, or when the frost is out of the ground, they say they find their traps filled with large rattle-snakes; and therefore conclude that the raccoons are transformed. They also say that the reason why they are so plenty in the winter, is, every fall the snakes turn raccoons again.

"I told them that though I had never landed on any of these islands, yet from the numerous accounts I had received, I believed that both snakes and raccoons were plenty there; but no doubt they all remained there both summer and winter, only the snakes were not to be seen in the latter; yet I did not believe that they were transmigratory. These islands are but seldom visited, because early in the spring and late in the fall it is dangerous sailing in their bark canoes; and in the summer they are so infested with various kinds of serpents (but chiefly rattle-snakes) that it is dangerous landing.

"I shall now quit this digression and return to the result of the council at the mouth of the river. We concluded to coast it round the lake, and in two days we came to the mouth of the Miami of the Lake, and landed on Cedar Point, where we remained several days. Here we held a council, and concluded we would take a driving hunt in concert and in partnership.

"The river in this place is about a mile broad, and as it and the lake form a kind of neck, which terminates in a point, all the hunters, (which were fifty-three,) went up the river, and we scattered ourselves from the river to the lake. When first we began to move, we were not in sight of each other, but as we all raised the yell, we could move regularly together by the noise. At length we came in sight of each other, and appeared to be marching in good order. Before we came to the point, both the squaws and boys in the canoes were scattered up the river and along the lake, to prevent the deer from making their escape by water. As we advanced near the point the guns began to crack slowly, and after some time the firing was like a little engagement. The squaws and boys were busy tomahawking the deer in the water, and we shooting them down on the land. We killed in all about thirty deer, though a great many made their escape by water.

"We had now great feasting and rejoicing, as we had plenty of hominy, venison, and wild fowl. The geese at this time appeared to be preparing to move southward. It might be asked what is meant by the geese preparing to move. The Indians represent them as holding a great council at this time concerning the weather, in order to conclude upon a day, that they may all at or near one time leave the northern lakes, and wing their way to the southern bays. When matters are brought to a conclusion, and the time appointed that they are to take wing, then they say a great number of expresses are sent off, in order to let the different tribes know the result of this council, that they may all be in readiness to move at the time appointed. As there was a great commotion among the geese at this time, it would appear from their actions, that such a council had been held. Certain it is, that they are led by instinct to act in concert, and to move off regularly after their leaders.

"Here our company separated. The chief part of them went up the Miami river, that empties into Lake Erie at Cedar Point, whilst we proceeded on our journey in company with Tecaughretanego, Tontileaugo, and two families of the Wyandots.

"As cold weather was now approaching, we began to feel the doleful effects of extravagantly and foolishly spending the large quantity of beaver we had taken in our last winter's hunt. We were all nearly in the same circumstances; scarcely one had a shirt to his back; but each of us had an old blanket which we belted round us in the day, and slept in at night, with a deer or bear skin under us for our bed.

"When we came to the falls of Sandusky, we buried our birch bark canoes as usual, at a large burying place for that purpose, a little below the falls. At this place the river falls about eight feet over a rock, but not perpendicularly. With much difficulty we pushed up our wooden canoes; some of us went up the river, and the rest by land with the horses, until we came to the great meadows or prairies that lie between Sandusky and Scioto.

"When we came to this place, we met with some Ottawa hunters, and agreed with them to take what they call a ring hunt, in partnership. We waited until we expected rain was near falling to extinguish the fire, and then we kindled a large circle in the prairie. At this time, or before the bucks began to run, a great number of deer lay concealed in the grass, in the day, and moved about in the night; but as the fire burned in towards the centre of the circle, the deer fled before the fire; the Indians were scattered also at some distance before the fire, and shot them down every opportunity, which was very frequent, especially as the circle became small. When we came to divide the deer, there were about ten to each hunter, which were all killed in a few hours. The rain did not come on that night to put out the outside circle of the fire, and as the wind arose, it extended through the whole prairie, which was about fifty miles in length, and in some places nearly twenty in breadth. This put an end to our ringhunting this season, and was in other respects an injury to us in the hunting business; so that upon the whole, we received more harm than benefit by our rapid hunting frolic. We then moved from the north end of the glades, and encamped at the carrying place.

"This place is in the plains, betwixt a creek that empties into Sandusky, and one that runs into Scioto; and at the time of high water, or the spring season, there is but about one half mile of portage, and that very level and clear of rocks, timber or stones, so that with a little digging, there may be water carriage the whole way from Scioto to Lake Erie.

"From the mouth of Sandusky to the falls, is chiefly first rate land, lying flat or level, intermixed with large bodies of clear meadows, where the grass is exceeding rank, and in many places three or four feet high. The timber is oak, hickory, walnut, cherry, black ash, elm, sugar tree, buckeye, locust and beech. In some places there is wet timber land

—the timber in these places is chiefly water-ash, sycamore or button-wood."

"From the falls to the prairies, the land lies well to the sun; it is neither too flat nor too hilly, and is chiefly first rate; the timber nearly the same as below the falls, excepting the water-ash. There are also here some plats of beech land, that appear to be second rate, as they frequently produce spicewood. The prairie appears to be a tolerably fertile soil, though in many places too wet for cultivation; yet I apprehend it would produce timber, were it only kept from fire.

"The Indians are of the opinion that the squirrels plant all the timber, as they bury a number of nuts for food, and only one at a place. When a squirrel is killed, the various kinds of nuts thus buried, will grow.

"I have observed that when these prairies have only escaped fire for one year, near where a single tree stood, there was a young growth of timber supposed to be planted by squirrels. But when the prairies were again burned, all this young growth was immediately consumed; as the fire rages in the grass to such a pitch that numbers of raccoons are thereby burned to death.

"On the west side of the prairie, or betwixt that and the Scioto, there is a large body of first rate land—the timber, walnut, locust, sugar-tree, buckeye, cherry, ash, elm, mulberry, plum-trees, spice-wood, black haw, red haw, oak and hickory."

After passing the winter on the Olentangy, a tributary of the Scioto, the old Indian and his young companion returned and proceeded down Sandusky, killing in the passage "four bears and a number of turkeys." We quote again:

"When we came to the little lake at the mouth of Sandusky, we called at a Wyandot town that was then there, called Sunyendeand, [he speaks as if it was a first visit, whereas we have devoted a large space to his former sojourn there.] Here we diverted ourselves several days by catching rock fish in a small creek, the name of which is also Sunyendeand, which signifies rock fish. They fished in the night with lights, and struck the fish with gigs or spears. The rock fish there, when they begin first to run up the creek to spawn, are exceedingly fat, sufficiently so to fry themselves. The first night we scarcely caught fish enough for present use for all that was in the town.

"The next morning I met with a prisoner at this place by the name of Thompson, who had been taken from Virginia. He told me if the Indians would only omit disturbing the fish for one night, he could catch more fish than the whole town could make use of. I told Mr. Thompson that if he knew he could do this, that I would use my influence with the Indians to let the fish alone for one night. I applied to the chiefs, who agreed to my proposal, and said they were anxious to see what the Great Knife (as they called the Virginian) could do. Mr. Thompson, with the assistance of some other prisoners, set to work, and made a hoop net of elm bark; they then cut down a tree across the creek, and stuck in stakes at the lower side of it to prevent the fish from passing up, leaving only a gap at one side of the creek; here he sat with his net, and when he felt the fish touch the net he drew it up, and frequently would haul out two or three rock fish that would weigh about five or six pounds each. He continued at this until he had hauled out about a wagon load, and then left the gap open, in order to let them pass up, for they could not go far on account of the shallow water.

Before day Mr. Thompson shut it up, to prevent them from passing down, in order to let the Indians have some diversion in killing them in daylight.

"When the news of the fish came to town, the Indians all collected and with surprise beheld the large heap of fish, and applauded the ingenuity of the Virginian. When they saw the number of them that were confined in the water above the tree, the young Indians ran back to the town, and in a short time returned with their spears, gigs, bows and arrows, &c., and were the chief part of that day engaged in killing rock fish, insomuch that we had more than we could use or preserve. As we had no salt or any way to keep them, they lay upon the banks, and after some time great numbers of turkey-buzzards and eagles collected together and devoured them."

But enough of our Ohio Crusoe. His remaining adventures, before his restoration to his friends in 1760, consisted of a trip to Detroit, another hunt up Sandusky and down Scioto, and a journey to Caughnewaga, "a very ancient Indian town about nine miles above Montreal," besides an imprisonment of four months in Montreal. This picture of northern Ohio, a century since, has the merit of novelty at least. That it is authentic, there can be no doubt, for in several historians of authority occur frequent and respectful reference to the narrative from whose pages we have drawn so copiously.

The geography of the last foregoing paragraphs, is less difficult of explanation than in the first portion of the chapter. The falls of Sandusky are doubtless the same as the rapids mentioned in the treaty of Greenville, near the site of Fremont, and the Sandusky plains, which were burnt over by the ring hunt, are in Marion, Wyandot and Crawford counties.

CHAPTER VIII.

THE SURRENDER OF THE WESTERN POSTS TO ENGLAND.

The fall of Fort Du Quesne, in 1758, terminated French dominion upon the Ohio, but the narrative of Forbes' expedition against that important stockade is incomplete, if the adventures of Charles Frederic Post, the Moravian envoy of Pennsylvania to the Ohio tribes, were entirely omitted. The Moravian annals first mention Post as laboring at Shekomeko, in 1743, near the present site of Poughkeepsie, in Eastern New York.[1] He married a baptized Indian woman, was imprisoned in 1745, on an unfounded charge of instigating the New York tribes to join the French, suggested by efforts to learn their dialects; resumed his missionary labors among the Connecticut Indians, and finally sojourned in Pennsylvania, when his influence with the Delaware chiefs was at length recognized by the colonial authorities as their most efficient mediation with the Western tribes. He was accordingly induced to make two expeditions into the heart of the enemy's country in the summer and autumn of 1758, and by his conferences with the representatives of eight nations, withheld them from an attack upon Forbes' expedition, and finally concluded a peace. His route ascended the Susquehanna, crossed to the Alleghany, opposite French creek, and thence to a town on the Big Beaver creek, called "Kushkushkee," containing ninety houses and two hundred Delaware warriors. The decisive conference was held, however, opposite Fort Du

1) History of Moravian Missions, Part ii, p. 37.

Quesne, whither the savages assured Post " they would carry him in their bosom, and he need fear nothing "—a pledge which was honorably redeemed. On the 24th of August, the Moravian, with his Indian protectors, reached the point opposite the fort, where followed a series of speeches, explanations and agreements. At this interview, though resulting in favor of an union with England, the Indians still complained bitterly of the disposition which the whites showed in claiming and seizing their lands. " Why did you not fight your battles at home, or on the sea, instead of coming into our country to fight them ?" they asked again and again, and were mournful when they thought of the future. " *Your* heart is good," they said to Post, "*you* speak sincerely ; but we know there is always a great number who wish to get rich ; they never have enough ; look ! we do not want to be rich, and take away what others have." " The white people think we have no brains in our head ; that they are big, and we a little handful ; but remember, when you hunt for a rattlesnake you cannot find it, and perhaps it will bite you before you see it."

The humble Moravian played no unimportant part in restoring to His British Majesty the key of western America —Fort Du Quesne,—and certainly warded an Indian attack upon Forbes' army.[2]

It is probable that French garrisons remained at Sandusky, and the forts on French creek, for a while after the occupation of Fort Du Quesne by the English ; but as the contest in Canada approached its crisis, the troops were gradually withdrawn.

We have already given the 8th of September, 1760, as

2) Perkins' Writings, vol. ii, pp. 216-17 ; see also Post's Journals in Craig's Olden Time, vol. i, pp. 98, 145

the date of the surrender of Canada to the English by the French Governor, Vaudrueil. Maj. Robert Rogers, a native of New Hampshire and an associate of Putnam and Stark, was ordered to take possession of the Western forts. He left Montreal on the 13th of September, with two hundred rangers, who were "half hunters, half woodsmen, trained in a discipline of their own, and armed, like Indians, with hatchet, gun and knife." Rogers is described as follows: "their commander was a man tall and vigorous in person and rough in feature. He was versed in all the arts of woodcraft, sagacious, prompt and resolute, yet so cautious withal that he sometimes incurred the unjust charge of cowardice. His mind, naturally active, was by no means uncultivated, and his books and unpublished letters bear witness that his style as a writer was not contemptible. But his vain, restless, grasping spirit, and more doubtful honesty, proved the ruin of an enviable reputation. Six years after his Western expedition, he was tried by a court martial for a meditated act of treason, the surrender of Fort Michillimacinac into the hands of the Spaniards, who were at that time masters of Upper Louisiana. Not long after, if we may trust his own account, he passed over to the Barbary States, entered the service of the Dey of Algiers, and fought two battles under his banners. At the opening of the war of independence, he returned to his native country, where he made professions of patriotism, but was strongly suspected by many, including Washington himself, of acting the part of a spy. In fact, he soon openly espoused the British cause, and received a colonel's commission from the crown. His services, however, proved of little consequence. In 1778, he was proscribed and banished, under the act of New Hampshire, and the remainder of his life was passed in such obscurity that it is difficult to determine when and where he died.[3]

On the 4th of November, Rogers left Presque Isle, and thence went slowly up Lake Erie in fifteen whale boats. From this point we prefer to give his own words. In 1765 he published in London a Journal of his Military Life, and also a " Concise Account of North America," from which we gather the particulars of his voyage along the southern coast of Lake Erie:

" We left Presque Isle," says Rogers, in his Journal, " the 4th of November, kept a western course, and by night had advanced twenty miles.

" The badness of the weather obliged us to lie by all the next day; and as the wind continued very high, we did not advance more than ten or twelve miles the 6th, on a course west-south-west.

" We set out very early on the 7th, and came to the mouth of Chogage River;[4] here we met with a party of Attawawa Indians, just arrived from Detroit. They were an embassy from Ponteack,[5] of some of his warriors, and some of the chiefs of the tribes that are under him; the purport of which was, to let me know that Ponteack was at a small distance, coming peaceably, and that he desired me to halt my detachment till such time as he could see me with his own eyes. His ambassadors had also orders to inform me that he was Ponteack, the king and lord of the country I was in.

3) Parkman's Pontiac, 145.

4) This is probably Geauga, or Grand River.

5) In a previous paragraph, Pontiac is described as the head of an Indian Confederacy of the lakes. "He puts on an air of majesty and princely grandeur, and is greatly honored and revered by his subjects," having certainly "the largest empire and greatest authority of any Indian chief that has appeared on the continent since our acquaintance with it."

"At first salutation, when we met, he demanded my business into his country, and how it happened that I dared to enter it without his leave. When I informed him that it was not with any design against the Indians that I came, but to remove the French out of his country, who had been an obstacle in our way to mutual peace and commerce, and acquainted him with my instructions for that purpose; I at the same time delivered him several friendly messages, or belts of wampum, which he received, but gave me no other answer than that he stood in the path I traveled in till next morning, giving me a small string of wampum, as much as to say, I must not march further without his leave. When he departed for the night, he inquired whether I wanted anything that his country afforded, and he would send his warriors to fetch it. I assured him that any provisions they brought should be paid for; and the next day we were supplied by them with several bags of parched corn, and some other necessaries. At our second meeting he gave me the pipe of peace, and both of us by turns smoked with it, and he assured me he had made peace with me and my detachment; that I might pass through his country unmolested and relieve the French garrison; and that he would protect me and my party from any insults that might be offered or intended by the Indians; and as an earnest of his friendship, he sent one hundred warriors to protect and assist us in driving one hundred fat cattle, which we had brought for the use of the detachment from Pittsburgh, by the way of Presque Isle. He likewise sent to the several Indian towns on the south side and west end of Lake Erie, to inform them that I had his consent to come into the country. He attended me constantly after this interview till I arrived at Detroit, and while I remained in the country, and was the means of preserving the detachment from the fury of the Indians, who had assembled at the mouth of the strait with an intent to cut us off.

"I had several conferences with him, in which he discovered great strength of judgment, and a thirst after knowledge. He endeavored to inform himself of our military order and discipline. He often intimated to me that he should be content to reign in his country in subordination to the King of Great Britain, and was willing to pay him such annual acknowledgment as he was able in furs, and to call him his uncle. He was curious to know our methods of manufacturing cloth, iron, &c., and expressed a great desire to see England, and offered me a part of his country if I would conduct him there. He assured me that he was inclined to live peaceably with the English while they used him as he deserved, and to encourage their settling in his country; but intimated that, if they treated him with neglect, he should shut up the way, and exclude them from it; in short, his whole conversation sufficiently indicated that he was far from considering himself as a conquered prince, and that he expected to be treated with the respect and honor due to a King or Emperor, by all who came into his country, or treated with him.[6]

"From this place we steered one mile west, then a mile south, then four miles west, then southwest ten miles, then five miles west and by south, then southwest eight miles, then west and by south seven miles, then four miles west, and then southwest six miles, which brought us to Elk River, as the Indians call it, where we halted two days on account of bad weather and contrary winds.[7]

"On the 15th we embarked and kept the following courses:

6) The particulars of this interview with Pontiac are from Rogers' "Account," &c.; what follows is from his Journal.

7) Forty-six miles to Cuyahoga River.

west-southwest two miles, west-northwest three miles, west-by-north one mile, west two miles; here we passed the mouth of a river,[8] and then steered west one mile, west-by-south two miles, west-by-north four miles, northwest three miles, west-northwest two miles, west-by-north ten miles, where we encamped at the mouth of a river twenty-five yards wide.[9]

"The weather did not permit us to depart till the 18th, when our course was west-by-south six miles, west-by-north four miles, west two miles; here we found a river about fifteen yards over, then proceeded west half a mile, west-southwest six miles and a half, west two miles and a half, northwest two miles, where we encamped and discovered a river sixteen yards broad at the entrance.[10]

"We left this place the next day, steering northwest four miles, north-northwest six miles, which brought us to Sandusky Lake; we continued the same course two miles, then north-northeast half a mile, northwest a quarter of a mile, north the same distance, northwest half a mile, north-by-east one furlong, northwest-by-north one quarter of a mile, northwest-by-west one mile, west-northwest one mile, then west half a mile, where we encamped near a small river, on the east side.

"The land on the south side of Lake Erie from Presque Isle, puts on a very fine appearance; the country level, the timber tall and of the best sort, such as oak, hickerie and locust; and for game, both for plenty and variety, perhaps exceeded by no part of the world.

"On the 20th we took a course northwest four miles and a half, southwest two, and west three, to the mouth of a river

8) Eight miles to Rocky River.
9) Twenty miles to Black River.
10) Huron River, in Erie county.

in breadth 300 feet.[11] Here we found several Huron sachems, who told me 'that a body of 400 Indian warriors was collected at the entrance into the great streight, in order to obstruct our passage.'

"On the 22d we encamped on a beach, after having steered that day northwest six miles, north-northwest four, to a river of the breadth of twenty yards,[12] then northwest-by-west two miles, west-northwest one, west four, and west-northwest five. It was with great difficulty we could procure any fuel here, the west side of the Lake Erie abounding with swamps. We rowed ten miles the next day, on a course northwest and-by-west to Point Cedar[13] and then formed a camp."

The rumors of intended hostility by the Indians, at the instigation of the French Commandant at Detroit, proved unfounded, and after some delay, Monsieur Beleter yielded the post on the 29th of November, 1760. Rogers remained in the vicinity of Detroit until December 23d, meanwhile making an excursion to Lakes St. Clair and Huron. From Detroit the Major went to the Maumee, and thence across by the Sandusky and Tuscarawas trail to Fort Pitt, and his journal of this overland trip is the first description of the route which has fallen under our notice. We shall renew our extracts, and accompany Major Rogers through the limits now constituting the State of Ohio:

"On the 23d of December I set out for Pittsburgh, marching along the west end of Lake Erie, till the 2d of January, 1761, when we arrived at Lake Sandusky.

"I have a very good opinion of the soil from Detroit to this place; it is timbered principally with white and black oaks, hickerie, locusts and maple. We found wild apples

11) Portage River, in Ottowa county.

12) Touissant creek, in Carroll township, Ottowa county.

13) Maumee Bay.

along the west end of Lake Erie, some rich savannahs of several miles extent, without a tree, but clothed with jointed grass near six feet high, which rotting there every year adds to the fertility of the soil. The length of Sandusky is about fifteen miles from east to west, and about six miles across it. We came to a town of the Windot Indians, where we halted to refresh.

"On January 3d, southeast-by-east three miles, east-by-south one mile and a half, southeast a mile through a meadow, crossed a small creek about six yards wide, running east, traveled southeast-by-east one mile, passed thro' Indian houses southeast three quarters of a mile, and came to a small Indian town of about ten houses. There is a remarkable fine spring at this place, rising out of the side of a small hill with such force that it boils above the ground in a column three feet high. I imagine it discharges ten hogsheads of water in a minute.[14] From this town our course was south-southeast three miles, south two miles, crossed a brook about five yards wide, running east-southeast, traveled south one mile, crossed a brook about four yards wide, running east-southeast, traveled south-southeast two miles, crossed a brook about eight yards wide. This day we killed plenty of deer and turkies on our march, and encamped.

"On the 4th we traveled south-southeast one mile, and came to a river about twenty-five yards wide, crossed the river, where are two Indian houses, from thence south-by-east one mile, south-southeast one mile and a half, southeast two miles, south-southeast one mile, and came to an Indian house, where there was a family of Windots hunting, from thence south-by-east a quarter of a mile, south five miles, came to the river we crossed this morning; the course of the river

14) Castalia, or Cold Spring, in Erie county.

here is west-northwest.[15] This day killed several deer and other game and encamped.

"On the 5th, traveled south-southwest half a mile, south one mile, south-southwest three quarters of a mile, south half a mile, crossed two small brooks running east, went a south-southwest course half a mile, south half a mile, southeast half a mile, south two miles, southeast one mile, south half a mile, crossed a brook running east-by-north, traveled south-by-east half a mile, south-southeast two miles, southeast three quarters of a mile, south-southeast one mile, and came to Maskongam creek,[16] about eight yards wide, crossed the creek, and encamped about thirty yards from it. This day killed deer and turkies in our march.

"On the 6th, we traveled about fourteen or fifteen miles, our general course being about east-southeast, killed plenty of game, and encamped by a very fine spring.[17]

"The 7th, our general course about southeast, traveled about six miles, and crossed Maskongam creek, running south, about twenty yards wide.[18] There is an Indian town about twenty yards from the creek, on the east side, which is called the Mingo Cabbins. There were but two or three Indians in the place, the rest were hunting. These Indians have plenty of cows, horses, hogs, &c.[19]

"The 8th, halted at this town to mend our mogasons and kill deer, the provisions I brought from Detroit being entirely

15) If the reader will follow the track of the Sandusky, Mansfield and Newark Railroad, eleven miles south from Monroeville, he will probably be on the route of Rogers, and will twice cross the Huron River.

16) Black Fork of Mohican, now called White Woman or Walhonding.

17) Who will identify this "fine spring," somewhere between Montgomery and Vermillion townships, in Ashland county?

18) Lake Fork of Mohican, near Jeromeville, Ashland county.

19) A prominent object on all early charts, but usually called "Mohican John's Town." The township is now called "Mohecan."

expended. I went a hunting with ten of the Rangers, and by ten o'clock got more venison than we had occasion for.

"On the 9th, traveled about twelve miles, our general course being about southeast, and encamped by the side of a long meadow, where there were a number of Indians hunting.[20]

"The 10th, about the same course, we traveled eleven miles, and encamped, having killed in our march this day three bears and two elks.

"The 11th, continuing near the same course, we traveled thirteen miles and encamped, where were a number of Wiandots and Six Nation Indians hunting.

"The 12th, traveled six miles, bearing rather more to the east and encamped. This evening we killed several beaver.

"The 13th, traveled about northeast six miles, and came to the Delaware's Town, called Beaver Town.[21] This Indian town stands on good land, on the west side of the Maskongam river, and opposite to the town on the east side is a fine river which discharges itself into it. The latter is about thirty yards wide, and the Maskongam about forty; so that when they both join they make a very fine stream, with a swift current running to the southwest. There are about 3000 acres of cleared ground round this place. The number of warriors in this town is about 180. All the way from the Lake Sandusky I found level land and a good country. No pine trees of any sort; the timber is white, black and yellow oak, black and white walnut, cyprus, chestnut and

20) Still called on the map of Ohio, "Long Prairie," in Plain township, Wayne county.

21) The Indian town of Tuscarora, opposite Sandy creek, at this time the residence of the leading Delaware chiefs. Here King Beaver resided in 1760, as also did the great war captain of the Delawares, Shingess, or King Shingask, whom we suppose to have been the same personage as Bockengehelas, who was living in 1804.

locust trees. At this town I staid till the 16th, in the morning, to refresh my party, and procured some corn of the Indians to boil with our venison.

"On the 16th, we marched nearly an east course about nine miles, and encamped by the side of a small river.

"On the 17th, kept much the same course, crossing several rivulets and creeks. We traveled about twenty miles, and encamped by the side of a small river.[22]

"On the 18th, we traveled about sixteen miles an easterly course and encamped by a brook.

"The 19th, about the same general course, we crossed two considerable streams of water, and some large hills timbered with chestnut and oak, and having traveled about twenty miles, we encamped by the side of a small river, at which place were a number of Delawares hunting.[23]

"On the 20th, keeping still an easterly course, and having much the same traveling as the day before, we advanced on our journey about nineteen miles, which brought us to Beaver creek, where are two or three Indian houses, on the west side of the creek, and in sight of the Ohio.

"Bad weather prevented our journeying on the 21st, but the next day we prosecuted our march. Having crossed the creek, we traveled twenty miles, nearly southeast and encamped with a party of Indian hunters.

"On the 23d, we came again to the Ohio, opposite to Fort Pitt, from whence I ordered Lieut. McCormack to march the party across the country to Albany, and after tarrying there until the 26th, I came the common road to Philadelphia, from thence to New York, where, after this long fatiguing tour, I arrived February 14, 1761."

22) Nimishillen creek, perhaps. 23) Little Yellow Creek, very likely.

CHAPTER IX.

CONSPIRACY OF PONTIAC.

THERE was a sullen submission to the new dominion of England through the Western wilderness. The French were subdued, and the Indians could not fail to respect the power of the British arms, but their jealousy of aggression on the one hand, or of no less unwelcome neglect on the other, still remained. Once more, as was the case ten years previously, an opportunity was afforded to the English to conciliate the natives, and avert for an indefinite period the horrors of a frontier war. It certainly behooved the colonies not to be less indulgent and considerate than the French had been. The latter had, from motives of policy, made frequent gifts to the tribes—treated their chiefs with consideration—supplied them with ammunition and clothing on reasonable terms, and by a frank and gay deportment won their good will.

If the reader will recall the interview between Rogers and Pontiac, narrated in the preceding chapter, he can readily appreciate not only the spirit of that chief, but also the dispositions of his followers. His lofty permission to Rogers, that the latter might "pass through his country unmolested," and his magnanimous protection of the detachment of Rangers from Indian attack, disclosed a proud consciousness that he was indeed "the King and Lord of the country." He was willing to recognize a slight protectorate in the English monarch, by an annual acknowledgment in furs and the style of "Uncle," yet this tenure, even less substantial than the slightest feudal relation, was not to impair the wild independence of the forest emperor.

The jealousies of the Ohio Indians were almost immediately excited by the encroachments of English emigrants. The Ohio Company was revived; Virginia multiplied her grants; traders and settlers pushed beyond the mountains, which, by the treaty of Easton, in 1758, had been fixed as the eastern limit of the Indian hunting grounds; and the savages were not slow to perceive that the professions with which both Braddock and Forbes had approached their frontier, that the English would protect the tribes from French aggression, were only intended to cover similar designs. While these apprehensions prevailed among the Delawares and Shawanese, the feeling among the Wyandots and Ottawas, as well as the more northern tribes, was even more distrustful. The parsimony of the English, as compared with the liberal and attractive gifts of the French, added to the discontent.

Soon a bitter revulsion of feeling prevailed through the entire west. The Delawares and Shawanese were irritated by the settlers from Virginia and Pennsylvania, while the more remote tribes meditated revenge for the neglect of the English, in particulars now become necessary to their comfort, and also by the frequent outrages of a lawless soldiery, who had replaced the French garrisons. There were not wanting French traders and voyagers to remind the Indians of a contrast so disadvantageous in all respects to the recent occupants, and to fan the flame of disaffection to the height of insurrection.

As early as the spring of 1761, Alexander Henry, an English trader, went to Michillimacinac for purposes of business, and he found the strongest feeling against the English, on account of their failure by word or deed to conciliate the

Indians. Having reached his destination, though in the disguise of a Canadian, he was discovered, and an Indian chief, supposed to be Pontiac himself, addressed him as follows:

"Englishman! Although you have conquered the French, you have not yet conquered us. We are not your slaves. These lakes, these woods, these mountains, were left to us by our ancestors. They are our inheritance, and we will part with them to none. Your nation supposes that we, like the white people, cannot live without bread, pork and beef. But you ought to know that the Great Spirit and Master of Life, has provided food for us upon these broad lakes and in these mountains."

He then spoke of the fact that no treaty had been made with them, no presents sent them; and while he announced their intention to allow Henry to trade unmolested, and to regard him as a brother, he declared that with his King the red men were still at war.[1]

On the 10th of February, 1763, the treaty of Paris was concluded, and extensive settlements in the conquered west were projected in the colonies at the moment that a wide spread conspiracy among the Indian tribes was on the eve of explosion.

The soul of this secret and formidable movement was Pontiac. Of his origin there are conflicting statements—one that he was a Catawba prisoner, adopted into the Ottawa tribe; while the more prevalent opinion is, that he was the son of an Ottawa father and an Ojibwa mother. All accounts unite that he was a chief of great genius and resources, possessing qualities unsurpassed by the most distinguished of his race.

1) Perkins' Writings, ii. 223; Travels of Alexander Henry in Canada from 1760 to 1776: New York, 1809.

Bancroft styles him "the colossal chief," whose "name still hovers over the northwest, as the hero who devised and conducted a great but unavailing struggle with destiny for the independence of his race." During the series of Indian wars against the English colonies and armies, from the Acadian war in 1747 to the general league of western tribes in 1763, he appears to have exercised the influence and power of an emperor, and by this name he was sometimes known. He had fought with the French, at the head of his Indian allies, against the English, in the year 1747. He had likewise been a conspicuous commander of the Indian forces in the defence of Fort Du Quesne, and took an active part in the memorable defeat of the British and provincial army under General Braddock, in 1755.

The voice of Pontiac appealed to savage superstition. He claimed to speak by the inspiration of the Great Spirit, and his messages were received with emotions of awe from Lake Michigan to the frontiers of North Carolina. "Why, says the Great Spirit, do you suffer these dogs in the red clothing to enter your country and take the land I have given you? Drive them from it! Drive them! When you are in distress, I will help you."

Thus in the winter of 1762–3 was silently organized a league, by which the confederated Indians were to environ the feeble and scattered garrisons, and by stratagem and force, simultaneously destroy them, and sweep the exposed frontiers with an indiscriminate massacre.

The catastrophe of May, 1763, is thus dramatized in the Historical Papers of J. H. Perkins. "The unsuspecting traders journeyed from village to village: the soldiers in the forts shrunk from the sun of the early summer, and dozed away the day; the frontier settler, singing in fancied security, sowed his crop, or, watching the sunset through the girdled trees, mused upon one more peaceful harvest, and told his children of the horrors of the ten years' war now, thank God! over. From the Alleghanies to the Mississippi the trees had leaved, and all was calm life and joy. But through that great country, even then, bands of sullen red men were journeying from the central valleys to the lakes of the Eastern hills. Bands of Chippewas gathered about Missillimacinac. Ottawas filled the woods near Detroit. The Maumee post, Presqu' Isle, Niagara, Pitt, Lingonier, and every English fort was hemmed in by mingled tribes, who felt that the great battle drew nigh which was to determine their fate and the possession of their noble lands. At last the day came. The traders every where were seized, their goods taken from them, and more than one hundred put to death. Nine British forts yielded instantly, and the savages drank, 'scooped up in the hollow of joined hands,' the blood of many a Briton. The border streams of Pennsylvania and Virginia run red again. 'We hear,' says a letter from Fort Pitt, 'of scalping every hour.' In Western Virginia, more than twenty thousand people were driven from their homes. Detroit was besieged by Pontiac himself, after a vain atttempt to take it by stratagem; and for many months that siege was continued in a manner and with a perseverance, unexampled among the Indians. It was the 8th of May when Detroit was first attacked, and upon the 3d of the following December it was still in danger. As late as March of the next year, the inhabitants were 'sleeping in their clothes,' expecting an alarm every night."

By midsummer, the only western posts which withstood the attacks of the savages, were Fort Pitt, defended by Capt. Ecuyer, with three hundred and fifty men, having two hundred women and children under their protection; Fort Lingonier, the outpost of Fort Pitt at the foot of the Alleghanies; and Detroit, where Maj. Gladwin and a garrison of one hundred and twenty-eight men were closely beleaguered by six hundred Indians, with the indomitable Pontiac at their head.

Sandusky "on Lake Jenandat" (as described in an old document) was the first to fall on the 16th of May.

On the 25th of May, the stockade at the mouth of St. Josephs on the eastern shore of Lake Michigan, was surprised by a party of Pottowatamies from Detroit; Schlosser, the commanding officer, seized; and all the garrison of fourteen men, except three, massacred.

On the 27th of May, Ensign Holmes, the commandant at Fort Miami, near the present site of Fort Wayne, on the Maumee River, was entreated to visit and bleed a sick squaw in a cabin three hundred yards distant, and on approaching the place, was shot down by Indians in ambush, while his sergeant, who followed, and the nine soldiers of the garrison, were made prisoners.

Fort Ouatanon, on the Wabash, just below Lafayette, in Indiana, yielded on the 1st of June, but the French in the vicinity generously ransomed the lives of the captives and gave them asylum in their houses.

On the 2d of June, Capt. Etherington and his subordinate officers were invited to witness a game of ball by rival parties of Chippewas, upon the plain adjoining the fort at Michillimacinac. The game, which somewhat resembled wicket, had proceeded with much animation from morning until noon, when, by apparent accident, a ball was tossed near the entrance of the fort; a rush was made within the enclosure, the war-whoop sounded, an officer, a trader, and fifteen men were killed, while the rest of the garrison of forty, and several Indian traders, were spared as captives.

Presque Isle, now Erie, a tenable structure, with a garrison of twenty-four men, and within prompt reach of relief, was surrendered, after a two days' defence, on the 22d of June.

Le Boeuf, still further inland, was burned on the night of the 18th of July, after successfully resisting an attack during the previous day, but the garrison fortunately escaped unnoticed through the darkness and the forest. On their way to Fort Pitt, they passed the ashes of Venango—fort and garrison having been involved in the same destruction.

Drake, in his Book of the Indians, adds to our enumeration "Le Bay, on Lake Michigan, near Green Bay."

Sandusky, on Lake Junandat, or Wyandot, was the only post within the present limits of Ohio. The particulars of its loss were furnished by Ensign Paully, its commandant, and by him transmitted to Sir Jeffrey Amherst, then Commander-in-Chief of the British forces. We give these details as compiled by Bancroft and Parkman.

On the 16th of May, Fort Sandusky was approached by a party of Indians, principally from the Wyandot village. Ensign Paully, the commanding officer, was informed that seven Indians were waiting at the gate to speak with him. They proved to be four Hurons or Wyandots and three Ottawas, and as several of them were known to him, he ordered them, without hesitation, to be admitted. Arrived at his quarters, two of the treacherous visitors seated themselves on each side of the commandant, while the rest were disposed in various parts of the room. The pipes were lighted and the conversation began, when an Indian, who stood in the door-way, suddenly made a signal by raising his head.

Upon this, the astonished officer was instantly seized, disarmed and tied by those near him, while at the same moment a confused noise of shrieks and yells, the firing of guns, and the hurried tramp of feet sounded from the area of the fort without. It soon ceased, however, and as Paully was led from the room, he saw the dead body of his sentry and the parade ground strewn with the corpses of his murdered garrison. The body of his sergeant lay in the garden, where he was planting at the time of the massacre. Some traders, who were stationed within or near the enclosure of the pickets, were also killed and their stores plundered. At nightfall, Paully was conducted to the margin of the lake, where several birch canoes lay in readiness; and as, amid thick darkness, the party pushed out from shore, the captive saw the fort, lately under his command, bursting on all sides into sheets of flame.

Paully was brought prisoner to Detroit, bound hand and foot, and solaced on the passage with the expectation of being burnt alive. On landing near the camp of Pontiac, he was surrounded by a crowd of Indians, chiefly squaws and children, who pelted him with stones, sticks and gravel, forcing him to dance and sing, though by no means in a cheerful strain. A worse infliction seemed in store for him, when happily an old woman, whose husband had lately died, chose to adopt him in place of the deceased warrior. Seeing no alternative but the stake, Paully accepted the proposal, and having been first plunged in the river, that the white blood might be washed from his veins, he was conducted to the lodge of the widow, and treated thenceforth with all the consideration due to an Ottawa warrior. This forced match took place about the 20th of May, and in July following a divorce occurred. One evening a man was seen running towards the fort at Detroit, closely pursued by Indians. On his arriving within gunshot distance, they gave over the chase and the fugitive came panting beneath the walls, where a wicket was flung open to receive him. He proved to be the commandant at Sandusky, who had seized the first opportunity to escape from the embrace of the Ottawa widow.

The tragedy at Sandusky did not long remain unavenged. On the 26th of July, a detachment of two hundred and sixty men, under the command of Capt. Dalzell, arrived at Sandusky on their coastwise route to the relief of Detroit. Thence they marched inland to the Wyandot village, which they burned to the ground, at the same time destroying the adjacent fields of standing corn. After inflicting this inadequate retribution of the scene of May 16th, Dalzell steered northward, and under cover of night effected a junction with the Detroit garrison.

Long and arduous were the hostilities at the forks of the Ohio and the straits of Detroit. The siege of Fort Pitt first reached a crisis favorable to the besieged. The Delawares and Shawanese, conscious of the strength of the garrison, endeavored to persuade Capt. Ecuyer to abandon the fort, offering safe conduct to the settlements for all within the inclosure. This overture was twice made and declined, and as often, furious but ineffectual assaults were made by the Indians. At length runners brought the intelligence that Bouquet, at the head of five hundred men, was advancing through the wilderness of Western Pennsylvania, and, as August approached, the Indians disappeared from before Fort Pitt for the purpose of harassing, and, if possible, cutting off the army of rescue and supply. The troops of Bouquet were the remains of two regiments of Highlanders, recently from active service in the West Indies—thoroughly disciplined and fortunate in their leader. Nothing interrupted their advance, until the 4th of August, when the advanced guard was suddenly attacked by the savages at Edge Hill, a mile east of the Bushy Run, and four days' march from Pittsburgh. The action continued two days, the enemy giving way before the bayonets of the Highlanders, but constantly renewing their treacherous ambuscades. As a last resort, Bouquet feigned a retreat; the Indians hurried to charge, when two companies, that had been purposely concealed, fell upon the flank of the savages, who were simultaneously attacked in front. This manœuvre decided the conflict in favor of the Americans, although their loss was fifty killed and sixty wounded.

The battle of Bushy Run is memorable in our border history, as well for the valor exhibited on both sides as for the important consequences. The Delawares and Shawanese, who were the instigators and principal resource of the confederation of 1763, never renewed the contest with the desperate devotion which they exhibited at Bushy Run. At Edge Hill the valley of the Ohio was virtually subjugated.

The genius of Pontiac prolonged the contest before the walls of Detroit. Although his original design of taking the fort by stratagem, on the 7th of May, was baffled, still he hoped to reduce the position by a close and vigorous siege. Having been advised of the approach of Lieut. Cuyler with ninety-six men and twenty-three batteaux laden with stores, along the northern shore of Lake Erie, a band of Wyandots was sent to surprise him, which they succeeded in doing on the night of May 28th, near Point Pelee. Most of the detachment were captured, although Cuyler with thirty men escaped, and, rowing all night, arrived at a small island. Cuyler now made for Sandusky, (as he says in a report,) which, of course, he found burned to the ground, and thence he returned to Niagara along the southern shore of Lake Erie.

However, in June, a schooner, with a reinforcement of sixty men, reached Detroit, and early on the morning of the 29th of July, the garrison were agreeably surprised by the arrival of Capt. Dalzell and his reinforcement of two hundred and sixty men. Dalzell immediately resolved to make a night sally against the besiegers. It proved unfortunate, the wily enemy being fully advised of the movement, and Dalzell's own life and the lives of twenty of his men were sacrificed in the inglorious retreat from the Indian ambuscade at Bloody Run. This victory encouraged the confederates, and Pontiac pressed the siege with a force increased to one thousand men.

Another month brought to the Ottawa chief the tidings of Bushy Run, and the occupation of Fort Pitt by Bouquet. Already it was apparent to Pontiac that the tide of success was turning against himself and the great purpose of the confederation, yet were his efforts unabated. Winter approached; the French commandant at Fort Chartres, on the Illinois, wrote to Pontiac that the Indians must expect no assistance from the French, and M. De Neyon went so far as to send belts, messages and peace pipes to the different western tribes, exhorting them to conclude a peace with the English. Finally, in the absence of any decisive success, the savages became disheartened, jealousies were revived, and Pontiac raised the siege of Detroit, repairing, with a number of his chiefs, to the Maumee, but still intent upon renewing hostilities in the spring.

On the 7th of October, 1763, a royal proclamation issued, which probably contributed to the pacification of the western border, by removing the causes of future outbreaks. It anticipated, in some degree, what has become the permanent

6*

Indian policy of the United States. The colonial governments were prohibited, "for the present," and until the royal pleasure should be further known, "to grant warrants of survey or pass patents for any lands beyond the heads or sources of any of the rivers which fall into the Atlantic ocean from the west or northwest." These western lands were declared to be under the sovereignty, protection and dominion of the crown for the use of the Indians, and individuals were warned not to settle them. Purchases from Indians of lands reserved to them within the colonies, where settlements had been permitted, were only to be conducted by the authorities of the colonies, and in no case to be made by individuals, but trade with the Indians was to be free and open to all, on taking out a license for that purpose from the Governor or Commander-in-chief of any of the colonies.

The historical department of the London Annual Register for 1764, alludes significantly to the terms of the old colonial charters, which had no other bound to the westward than the South sea, and adds that "nothing could be more inconvenient, or attended with more absurd consequences, than to admit the execution of the powers in those grants and distributions of territories in all their extent." The writer concludes that "where the western boundary of each colony ought to be settled is a matter which must admit of great dispute, and can, to all appearance, only be finally adjusted by the interposition of Parliament."

The proclamation in question was claimed by Washington, Chancellor Livingston and others, to have been a measure of temporary expediency, with reference to the Indian hostilities, which were pending. Such was the favorite construction among the colonists, and Virginia was not restrained from the issue of patents, very soon afterwards, for considerable tracts of land on the Ohio far beyond the Appalachian chain. If other and graver questions had not interposed, however, it cannot be doubted that this question of western lands would have led to serious difficulty with the mother country. As it was, the embarrassment was thrown upon the first epoch of our national independence, and threatened for a time to defeat the union of the States. At length, by a series of patriotic cessions, the wilderness of the west became the domain of the nation, and, as such, has been productive of more benefit to the citizens of the Atlantic States than if the untenable claims of their vague charters had been successfully asserted.

CHAPTER X.

THE EXPEDITIONS AGAINST THE WESTERN TRIBES UNDER BRADSTREET AND BOUQUET.

In the spring of 1764, the frontiers were again alarmed by savage incursions, and General Thomas Gage, who had succeeded Sir Jeffrey Amherst, in the command of the British forces in North America, resolved to send two expeditions into the heart of the enemy's country—one by the route of the lakes and another westward of Fort Pitt. The northern division was first upon the march under the command of Col. John Bradstreet. It consisted of eleven hundred men, chiefly provincial battalions from New Jersey, New York and Connecticut; that of Connecticut led by Col. Israel Putnam, and in July reached Niagara.[1] There were gathered the representatives of twenty or more tribes, suppliants for peace, and a grand council was held by Bradstreet and Sir William Johnson, at which the powerful Senecas were the first to bring in their prisoners and accept the terms dictated by the English negotiators.

Bradstreet had been ordered by Gage to chastise the Indians whenever they appeared in arms, but all hostile indications ceased on his advance. On the 12th of August, when within two days' march of Presque Isle, he was met by ten savages, who were probably Mingoes, or representatives of the New York tribes settled in Ohio and near Presque Isle,

1) Albany was the rendezvous of the troops, and the route to Niagara was by the Mohawk, Oneida Lake, Oswego River and Lake Ontario.

but who also assumed to speak for the Hurons of Sandusky, the Shawanese and the Delawares. They agreed that all prisoners should be delivered at Sandusky within twenty-five days; that six of the deputation should be retained as hostages, and the remaining four, accompanied by an English officer and a friendly Indian, should inform the chiefs of what they were required to do; that all claims to the forts and posts of the English in the west were to be abandoned, and leave given to erect as many forts and trading houses as might be necessary for the security of the traders, with a grant of as much land around each post as a cannon could throw a shot over; that if any Indian killed an Englishman he was to be delivered at Fort Pitt and there tried by English law, except that half of the jury were to be Indians of the same nation as the offender; and that if one tribe violated the peace the others would unite in punishing them.

There is reason to believe that the Delawares, Shawanese and Wyandots, had never authorized these Indians to stipulate for them, since the first two tribes continued their ravages after the treaty, and we find the Wyandots, when Bradstreet reached Sandusky, making their separate submission, and agreeing to follow him to Detroit for the purpose of concluding a treaty there. Parkman insists that the Indians who thus represented the Ohio tribes were only spies, and that Bradstreet was duped.[2] We notice among them the name of Cuyashota, which we suppose to have been that of the distinguished Seneca Chief, Guyasootha or Kayashuta, who was almost as prominent as Pontiac himself in organizing the conspiracy of the year before. The seat of his power and influence was on the upper Alleghany or near Presque Isle, and his concurrence gives a high sanction to

2) Conspiracy of Pontiac, 461.

Bradstreet's treaty of August 12, 1764. We shall afterwards find Kayashuta active in the surrender of prisoners to Col. Bouquet on the Muskingum, and the same chief, at a conference held in Pittsburgh, by George Croghan, four years afterwards, (May 4, 1768,) produced a copy of the treaty with Col. Bradstreet, and avowed its validity, and his constant adherence to its provisions.[3]

Bradstreet was so sanguine, not only that a binding treaty with the Ohio tribes had been concluded by him, but also of a ready compliance on their part with all the stipulations, that, on the 14th of August he wrote to Col. Bouquet, who was preparing to leave the Pennsylvania frontier on the southern expedition to the Ohio, requesting him to withdraw his troops. The latter, perceiving that the Delawares and Shawanese continued their depredations, declined to comply, and determined to prosecute his plan without remission, till he should receive further instructions from head quarters. Gen. Gage applauded his determination, "annulling and disavowing" the treaty at Presque Isle.

Bradstreet continued his route to Detroit, sparing the Sandusky villages, on a pledge that the Wyandots would make their submission at Detroit, where his army arrived safely on the 26th of August. A detachment was sent to take possession of Michillimacinac, and on the 7th of September a council was held at Detroit, which effectually pacified the northwestern tribes. Towards the head waters of the Maumee, however, were gathered many of the Ottawas and other immediate adherents of Pontiac, who were insolent and turbulent. An envoy of Bradstreet, Capt. Morris, as he approached the camp of the Indian leader, was confronted by

3) Craig's Olden Time, i. 344-67.

the chief with menace and insult, making a narrow escape of life from the hostile savages.

In respect to the subsequent movements of Col. Bradstreet, we have the authority of Hutchins,[4] the well-known historian of the contemporary expedition under Col. Bouquet, that the plan of the campaign had been, that "the two corps were to act in concert, and as that of Col. Bradstreet could be ready much sooner than the other, he was to proceed to Detroit, Michillimacinac and other places. On his return, he was to encamp and remain at Sandusky, to awe, by that position, the numerous tribes of western Indians, so as to prevent their sending any assistance to the Ohio Indians, while Col. Bouquet should execute his plan of attacking them in the heart of their settlements."

These instructions were promptly executed, and during the month of September Bradstreet returned to Sandusky. Here dispatches were received from Gen. Gage, condemning the indulgent treaty at Presque Isle in severe terms, and ordering him to advance upon the Indians living on the Scioto plains. At the same time, the journal of Morris, disclosing the hostile dispositions of the Indians upon the upper Maumee, reached Bradstreet, and it was probably apparent to him, that the Ottawas and Miamis, who were reported to have murdered their white prisoners, and who still rallied around Pontiac, were more properly an object of chastisement than the Scioto villages. It was true that the pledges for the return of prisoners which were made to him in August were not redeemed, but then it was to be considered that the Delawares and Shawanese, who held most of them, were

4) Thomas Hutchins, afterwards Geographer of the United States, and who accompanied Bouquet as "Assistant Engineer."

remote from Sandusky, and were already confronted by the army of Bouquet making a similar demand.

Under these circumstances, we think Parkman's strictures upon Bradstreet are unnecessarily severe. He admits that the water in the Sandusky River was low with drought, while the Cuyahoga route was circuitous and difficult of portage, and that sickness was prevalent in the camp, and, it might be added, the stormy season of lake navigation was at hand. Bradstreet passed a month in Sandusky Lake and up the river as far as navigable to Indian canoes, when, as he wrote to Colonel Bouquet, "he found it impossible to stay longer in those parts, absolute necessity requiring him to turn off the other way."

The return was unfortunate. As the boats of the army were opposite the iron-bound precipices west of Cuyahoga, a storm descended upon them, destroying several and throwing the whole into confusion. For three days the tempest raged unceasingly; and when the angry lake began to resume its tranquillity, it was found that the remaining boats were insufficient to convey the troops. A large body of Indians, together with a detachment of provincials, were therefore ordered to make their way to Niagara along the pathless borders of the lake. They accordingly set out, and, after many days of hardships, reached their destination; though such had been their sufferings, from fatigue, cold, and hunger, from wading swamps, swimming creeks and rivers, and pushing their way through tangled thickets, that many of the provincials perished miserably in the woods. On the fourth of November, seventeen days after their departure from Sandusky, the main body of the little army arrived safely at Niagara, and the whole, reëmbarking on Lake Ontario, proceeded towards Oswego. Fortune still seemed adverse; for a second tempest arose, and one of the schooners, crowded with troops, foundered in sight of Oswego, though most of the men were saved. The route to the settlements was now a short and easy one. On their arrival, the regulars went into quarters, while the troops levied for the campaign were sent home to their respective provinces.[5]

The expedition to the Muskingum was fortunate in its results, and also in having so intelligent an historian as Thomas Hutchins, and is therefore better known than any contemporary occurrence in the West. Its leader, distinguished by the success of Bushy Run, at the most critical period of the campaign of 1763, enjoyed the full confidence of Gage, the Commander-in-chief, and of the Pennsylvania and Virginia Governments. Besides five hundred regulars, Pennsylvania sent a thousand men, and Virginia replaced the desertions by a corps of volunteers.

It was October before the troops took up their march from Fort Pitt. Bouquet had previously seized three Indians, who sought a conference, but were probably spies, and on the 20th of September he sent one of them to the Delaware and Shawanese chiefs, demanding, that they should furnish two guides for an express to Col. Bradstreet, and threatening to avenge any molestation of the messengers, by putting the two captive Indians to death. He allowed twenty days for the trip to Detroit. This firm and determined conduct in opening the campaign, produced a favorable effect upon its prosecution. Two Indian runners were promptly sent to accompany the express.[6]

On the 3d of October, the army decamped from Fort Pitt, and next day reached the Ohio River at the beginning of the

5) Parkman's Pontiac, 476.

6) Hutchins' Account of Bouquet's expedition, 5 *et seq.*

narrows, following the course of the river along a flat gravelly beach for about six miles. When opposite the lower end of a considerable island, the army left the river—the distance from Fort Pitt being then about ten miles. Passing Logstown and crossing Big Beaver River near its junction with the Ohio, the course of the army was westward, apparently crossing the present boundary of Ohio near the line between Middleton and St. Clair townships in Columbiana county.

On the 9th, the army encamped on Yellow creek. During the day's march, (which was only five miles, from the necessity of cutting a road through some dense thickets) the path divided into two branches, that to the southwest leading to the lower towns upon the Muskingum, and at the forks stood several trees painted by the Indians in a hieroglyphic manner, denoting the number of wars in which they had been engaged, and the particulars of their success in prisoners and scalps. Crossing Yellow creek, one mile above, the next encampment was on a branch of Muskingum, fifty yards wide.

The country on the right bank of the Muskingum (designated Sandy creek at this point on modern maps) for ten miles east of the Nimischillen creek is described as "fine land, watered with small rivers and springs, where were several savannahs or cleared spots, which are by nature extremely beautiful, the second being, in particular, one continued plain of nearly two miles, with a fine rising ground, forming a semicircle round the right hand side, and a pleasant stream of water at about a quarter of a mile distant on the left."

Crossing, on Saturday, October 13, Nimischillen, (written by Hutchins, Nemenshehelas) and another small stream;

the army defiled between a high ridge on the right, and Sandy on the left, for a distance of seventy perches, passed a very rich bottom, and came to the main branch of Muskingum, about seventy yards wide, with a good ford. "A little below and above," adds Hutchins, "is Tuscarawas, a place exceedingly beautiful by situation, the lands rich on both sides of the river; the country on the northwest side being an entire level plain, upwards of five miles in circumference." He estimated, from the appearance of the "ruined houses," that the Indians who had inhabited these were as many as one hundred and fifty warriors.[7]

Thus, after a march of twelve days, or one hundred and ten miles, the army reached a point, which, more than any other, is noted in our ante-territorial annals. Here letters were received from Col. Bradstreet, by the messengers sent with Indian guides from Fort Pitt. They had been detained for a few days at a Delaware village, sixteen miles distant, but on the approach of the troops, they were set at liberty with a message to Colonel Bouquet, that the headmen of the Delawares and Shawanese were coming as soon as possible, to treat of peace with him.

The army encamped two miles further down the Muskingum on the 15th, where the river was a hundred yards wide and overlooked by a fine level country, extending from a high bank some distance back, producing stately timber, free from underwood, and with plenty of food for cattle; here a bower was erected at a short distance from the camp. At this place the Indian chiefs and warriors, who were assembled eight miles off, were notified to appear on the 17th. When

7) Three years before, in January, 1761, Rogers had found Tuscarora a populous town. It was probably deserted on the approach of Bouquet's army.

that day arrived, Colonel Bouquet, "with most of the regular troops, Virginia volunteers and light horse, marched from the camp to the bower erected for the congress; and soon after the troops were stationed, so as to appear to the best advantage, the Indians arrived, and were conducted to the bower. Being seated, they began in a short time to smoke their pipe or calumet, agreeable to their custom. This ceremony being over, their speakers laid down their pipes and opened their pouches, wherein were their strings or belts of wampum. The Indians present were—

Senecas—Kiyashuta, chief, with fifteen warriors.

Delawares—Custaloga, chief of the Wolf tribe; Beaver, chief of the Turkey tribe, with twenty warriors.

Shawanese—Keissinautchtha, a chief, and six warriors.

Kiyashuta, Turtle-Heart, Custaloga and Beaver were the chief speakers."

The submission of these savages was so unconditional and abject as completely to tame their eloquence. Not until the 20th was an answer vouchsafed to them. They were then required within twelve days to deliver at Wautamike, (an Indian village a short distance below the mouth of White-woman or Mohican river in Coshocton county,) all their prisoners, without exception, Englishmen, Frenchmen, women and children, whether adopted or not, as well as all negroes, furnishing at the same time clothing, provisions and horses for their journey to Fort Pitt.

The Delawares, at the close of their speeches on the 17th, had delivered eighteen white prisoners, and eighty-three small sticks expressing the number of captives yet to be delivered. The Shawanese deputy, in the absence of the chiefs of his tribe, sullenly assented to the terms prescribed. Kiyashuta addressed the Indians with an exhortation to comply faithfully with their engagements, and Col. Bouquet determined to march still further into the Indian country, believing that the presence of his army was the best security for a compliance with his requisitions. He was attended by the Indian deputations—Kiyashuta, as zealous now for peace as he had been resolute in the late war, volunteering as the guide.

Three days' march, or a distance of about twenty-one miles, brought the troops within a mile of the Coshocton forks of the Muskingum, which was fixed upon instead of Wakatamake as the most central and convenient place to receive the prisoners, "for," as Hutchins continues, "the principal Indian towns now lay around them, distant from seven to twenty miles, excepting only the lower Shawanese town situated on Scioto River, which was about eighty miles; so that from this place the army had it in their power to awe all the enemy's settlements and destroy their towns, if they should not punctually fulfill the engagements they had entered into. Four redoubts were built here opposite to the four angles of the camp; the ground on the front was cleared; a storehouse for the provisions erected, and likewise a house to receive and treat of peace with the Indians, when they should return. Three houses, with separate apartments, were also raised for the reception of the captives of the respective provinces, and proper officers to take charge of them, with a matron to attend the women and children; so that, with the officers, mess-houses, ovens, &c., this camp had the appearance of a little town in which the greatest order and regularity were observed."

Nothing of interest transpired before the 9th of November, except the arrival of Peter, a Caughnawaga chief, and twenty Indians of his nation, who brought letters from Col. Bradstreet, at Sandusky, announcing his speedy return to Niagara. At length all the prisoners were delivered, except one hundred in possession of the Shawanese, for whose surrender in the spring hostages were demanded and given. The number of prisoners thus surrendered was two hundred and six, of whom thirty-two males and forty-eight females and children were Virginians, and forty-nine males and sixty-seven females and children were Pennsylvanians.

On the 9th commenced the closing scenes in Indian council. The Senecas and the Wolf or Muncie tribe of Delawares were first treated with—Kiyashuta and ten warriors representing the former, and Custaloga and twenty warriors the latter. Most of their prisoners were already delivered, and they now brought forward only three, "the last of your flesh and blood," said they to the Americans, "that remained among the Senecas and Custaloga's tribe of Delawares." Then followed their figurative professions of peace. "We gather together," continued Kiyashuta, "and bury with this belt all the bones of the people that have been killed during this unhappy war, which the evil spirit occasioned among us. We cover the bones that have been buried, that they may never more be remembered. We again cover their place with leaves, that it may no more be seen. As we have been long astray, and the path between you and us stopped, we extend this belt that it may be again cleared, and we may travel in peace to see our brethren, as our ancestors formerly did. While you hold it fast by one end, and we by the other, we shall always be able to discover anything that may disturb our friendship."

In reply, Colonel Bouquet took the chiefs by the hand for the first time, and informed them that while he should wage no war against them, still a formal peace would be concluded by Sir William Johnson, to whom they were to send deputies fully authorized to treat. For this purpose hostages would be retained, but Capt. Pipe and Capt. John, who were seized at Fort Pitt, were set at liberty, greatly to the joy of their Delaware brethren.

A similar conference was held next day, with the Turkey and Turtle tribes of Delawares, King Beaver, their chief, and thirty warriors representing the former, and Kelappana, brother to their chief, with twenty-five warriors, the latter. Displeased at the absence of Nettowhatways, the chief of the Turtle Delawares, Col. Bouquet proclaimed that he was deposed from his chiefship, whereupon the tribe submissively named and installed his successor.

The 12th of November witnessed an interview between the fierce Shawanese and the English commanders. On the part of the Indians, Keissinautchtha and Nimwha, their chiefs, with the Red Hawk, Lavissimo, Bensivasica, Eweecunwee, Keigleighque and forty warriors, appeared. The Caughnawaga, Seneca and Delaware chiefs, with sixty warriors, were also present.

The Red Hawk was their speaker. "Brother," he said proudly, "when we saw you coming this road, you advanced toward us with a tomahawk in your hand; but we your younger brothers take it out of your hands and throw it up to God to dispose of as he pleases; by which means we hope never to see it more. And now, brother, we beg leave that you who are a warrior, will take hold of this chain (giving a string) of friendship, and receive it from us, who are also warriors, and let us think no more of war, in pity to our old men, women and children—intimating that it was compassion for them, not weakness of the nation, that closed the war."

In reply, Colonel Bouquet severely rebuked the Shawanese for their omission to restore their captives at the present conference, but sternly enjoined their delivery in the spring, and their humane treatment meanwhile. The engagements of the Indians in both respects were fully and honorably redeemed.

Hutchins reserves to the close of his narrative, the delineation of the scenes which were witnessed on the meetings of the prisoners with their relatives who had accompanied the march of the army. We copy what has also furnished a theme for the historic pencil of West.

"Language indeed can but weakly describe the scene, one to which the poet or painter might have repaired to enrich the highest colorings of the variety of human passions; the philosopher to find ample subject for the most serious reflection, and the man to exercise all the tender and sympathetic feelings of the soul. There were to be seen fathers and mothers recognizing and clasping their once lost babes, husbands hanging round the necks of their newly recovered wives, sisters and brothers unexpectedly meeting together, after a long separation, scarcely able to speak the same language, or for some time to be sure that they were the children of the same parents. In all these interviews, joy and rapture inexpressible were seen, while feelings of a very different nature were painted in the looks of others, flying from place to place, in eager inquiries after relatives not found; trembling to receive an answer to questions; distracted with doubts, hopes and fears on obtaining no account of those they sought for; or stiffened into living monuments of horror and woe, on learning their unhappy fate.

"The Indians too, as if wholly forgetting their usual savageness, bore a capital part in heightening this most affecting scene. They delivered up their beloved captives with the utmost reluctance—shed torrents of tears over them—recommending them to the care and protection of the commanding officer. Their regard to them continued all the while they remained in camp. They visited them from day to day, brought them wheat, corn, skins, horses, and other matters that were bestowed upon them while in their families, accompanied with other presents, and all the marks of the most sincere and tender affection. Nay, they did'nt stop here, but when the army marched, some of the Indians solicited and obtained permission to accompany their former captives to Fort Pitt, and employed themselves in hunting and bringing provisions for them on the way. A young Mingo carried this still further, and gave an instance of love, which would make a figure even in romance. A young woman of Virginia was among the captives, to whom he had formed so strong an attachment as to call her his wife. Against all the remonstrances of the imminent danger to which he exposed himself by approaching the frontier, he persisted in following her, at the risk of being killed by the surviving relatives of many unfortunate persons who had been captured or scalped by those of his nation.

"Among the captives, a woman was brought into camp at Muskingum, with a babe about three months old, at the breast. One of the Virginia volunteers soon knew her to be his wife. She had been taken by the Indians about six months before. He flew with her to his tent and clothed her and his child with proper apparel. But their joy, after the first transports, was soon dampened by the reflection that another dear child, about two years old, taken with the mother, had been separated from her, and was still missing, although many children had been brought in.

"A few days afterwards, a number of other persons were brought in, among them were several children. The woman was sent for, and one supposed to be hers was produced to her. At first sight she was not certain, but viewing the child with great earnestness, she soon recollected its features, and was so overcome with joy, that forgetting her sucking child, she dropped it from her arms, and catching up the new-found child, in ecstacy pressed it to her breast, and bursting into tears, carried it off unable to speak for joy. The father, rising up with the babe she had let fall, followed her in no less transport and affection.

"But it must not be deemed that there were not some, even grown persons, who showed an unwillingness to return. The Shawnees were obliged to bind some of their prisoners and force them along to the camp, and some women that had been delivered up, afterwards found means to escape, and went back to the Indian tribes. Some who could not make their escape, clung to their savage acquaintances at parting, and continued many days in bitter lamentations, even refusing sustenance."

On the 18th of November, the army broke up its cantonment at the Whitewoman and returned to Fort Pitt, which they reached on the 28th of the same month. This expedi tion was conducted with such skill and prudence as to avoid all disaster, except the loss of one man, who was killed and scalped by an Indian, when separated from camp. The Pennsylvania troops were under Lieut. Col. Francis and Lieut. Col. Clayton. Col. Reid was next in command to Col. Bouquet.

The provincial troops were discharged, and the regulars sent to garrison Fort Loudon, Fort Bedford and Carlisle. Col. Bouquet arrived at Philadelphia in January and received a conplimentary address from the Legislature, and also from the House of Burgesses of Virginia. Before these resolutions reached England, the King promoted him to be a Brigadier General. He was ordered to the command of the post at Mobile, and died within three years after his return from Muskingum, of a fever contracted at Pensacola.

CHAPTER XI.

OLD MAPS AND INDIAN TRAILS.

THE value of ancient maps to the student of history is almost incalculable. They furnish, at a glance, a complete summary of contemporary history as well as of geography. A collection of the old maps, published during the colonization and subsequent settlement of North America, might almost dispense with the printed page, and would certainly constitute its best elucidation. We have described the charts of Hennepin and La Hontan, whose ludicrous conceptions of western geography are yet full of interest, and the map now in question, nearly a hundred years later in date, is equally remarkable for its political features. The mere geography of the continent—the courses of streams and mountains and the outlines of lake and sea coast—are delineated with considerable correctness, but all other objects indicate an extraordinary contrast with the present situation of things. However difficult the task of description, still, so far as a few general details will avail, it may be well to attempt a verbal synopsis.

MAP OF THE BRITISH POSSESSIONS IN 1763

This map is published with the Annual Register for 1763, immediately after the cession by France to Great Britain, and delineates the "British Dominions in North America, with the limits of the Governments annexed thereto by the late treaty of peace and settled by proclamation—October 7th, 1763—Engraved by T. Kitchin. Geog'r."

What is now the State of Maine is put down as "York County," and included within New England. New York embraces Upper Canada, including the entire peninsula between Lakes Huron, Erie and Ontario, and with a fair presumption from the lines of boundary, that the colony was nominally extended across the peninsula of Michigan. This State is greatly shorn of its southern proportions, however, for the northern line of Pennsylvania is carried as far as the parallel of Buffalo, and thence eastwardly to Otsego Lake, near Cooperstown, whence it strikes south to the Delaware River. Virginia is extended west to the Mississippi as nearly as possible within the southern line of Kentucky and Virginia, and for a northern boundary, by the route of the National Road, or from Wheeling west to Quincy, Illinois. North Carolina, South Carolina and Georgia are also extended in strips of about the same width from the Atlantic to the Mississippi. West Florida is a narrow parallelogram between the Apalachicola and Mississippi Rivers, now divided in nearly equal instalments between Florida, Alabama, Mississippi and Louisiana, while East Florida is about the same as laid down on modern maps, except that it is now extended two and a half degrees west of the Apalachicola on the Gulf of Mexico. All the country west of the Mississippi is Louisiana.

The region afterwards organized as the Northwest Territory, except the portion lying south of the latitude of Wheeling and Columbus, which was included within the claim of Virginia, has no political classification, and seems to be recognized as Indian territory, subject generally to the crown of England.

The map is extremely meagre and inaccurate so far as the region which is now Ohio, is concerned. For instance, the mouth of the Great Miami River, at the North Bend of the

Ohio, is presented to be as much west of the longitude of Fort Wayne (then Fort Miami,) as it is actually east of that locality—an error of full one degree to the westward. The English trading post, fifty miles above Dayton, which was destroyed by the French in 1752, and is known in our history as Loramie station, is put down as "Pickawillany;" it is correctly represented as on the upper waters of the Great Miami or "G. Miamee" River. The "Sciota" River is correct, with a "Delaware town" near the present county of the same name; "Elk River" is also laid down in the proper place and direction, with a village of "Muskingum," situated on the western trail from Fort Pitt; and in the vicinity of the Cuyahoga River, (of which there is no trace,) there is a town called "Gwahago," doubtless intended for Cayahaga.

On reaching the southern shore of Lake Erie, the poverty of the map becomes still more conspicuous. The only village or settlement from Detroit to Niagara is "Sandoski," which is represented to be on the same line of longitude as the mouth of Elk or Muskingum River—that is, as far east as Cleveland. It stands on a bay, but no signs of a river. No stream in Northern Ohio is indicated, except the Maumee, which is faintly traced at the right point, and on which, at a reasonable distance from the mouth, stands "Miamis" or Fort Wayne.

Only ninety years since and such was the knowledge of the country now organized as the third State of the American Union. It is recorded in a work of the highest authority. Such a circumstance almost surpasses belief. As for "Sandoski," the fort was burned in May, 1763, and since it was never rebuilt, the map may refer to what had been and yet was a point of historical interest, or it might be a mode of designating the Indian villages which were known to adjoin the Lake Junandat or Sandusky. This, of course, must now rest altogether in conjecture.

Hutchins' Map of 1763 and Pownall's Map of 1776.

We shall refer to these publications only so far as they delineate our Ohio region. Their geographical outlines are hardly as disproportionate and imperfect as those of the London map already described, and they especially include many new details of the Indian villages and the natural features of the country.

A prominent object is the "Salt Springs." They are indicated on the Mahoning River, which were doubtless within the present township of Weathersfield, near Warren, in Trumbull county; on the Salt creek, east of the Scioto River, and within the present county of Jackson; on the Little Miami, apparently within Warren county, and on the Great Miami, near the site of Dayton. The first two localities are readily identified at the present time. Coal is noted near the Tuscarawas forks of the Muskingum and about midway of the right bank of the Hockhocking. Opposite Wheeling are "Ancient Sculptures;" in Jefferson county, at or about Mount Pleasant, is "petroleum:" on the Mad River, near the northwest angle of Greene county, is "limestone," and on the Hocking and Ohio Rivers, above their junction respectively, is "freestone." Hutchins also mentions a "lead mine" on Walnut creek, a stream which falls into the Scioto above Circleville.

We should infer from these maps that there were five Delaware villages within a few miles from each other on the Muskingum; one on Wills creek, where Cambridge, in Guernsey county, stands; one near the source of the Scioto, and in the present county of Delaware; one on the Killbuck, a tributary of the Mohican or White Woman, and apparently near the present Millersburg, in Holmes county, besides the settlement at the Tuscarawas forks of the Muskingum.

Near the source of the Hockhocking, "Beaverstown" is put down by Hutchins, and in his narrative he mentions King Beaver, a chief of the Turkey tribe of Delawares, as present at the Muskingum council. Our inference was that the village on the Hockhocking, which is apparently where Lancaster now stands, was inhabited by Delawares, but George Sanderson, Esq., in an address delivered before the Lancaster Institute, in March, 1844, states that the lands watered by the sources of the Hockhocking river, and now comprehended within the limits of Fairfield county, when first discovered by the early settlers at Marietta, were owned and occupied by Wyandots. He identifies the town, which in 1790, contained one hundred wigwams, and a population of 500 souls, with the present localities of Lancaster, and gives its name Tarhe, or in English, Crane-town, from the principal chief of the town. Another portion of the tribe, Mr. S. says, lived at Tobytown, nine miles west of Tarhetown, (now Royalton.) He adds that in 1795, the Wyandots ceded all their land on the Hockhocking River to the United States, and the Crane chief removed to Upper Sandusky.

On Pownall's map, (published but twelve years before the Marietta emigration,) this village is noted as "Hockhocking or French Margarets," and the situation is described as south of a "Big Swamp" and "Plains of Wild Rye"—indications of the scenery which suggested to Gov. St. Clair the name of Fairfield. This favors Wyandot occupation, for that nation were always intimately associated with the French. There is also evidence that Franklin and Hocking counties were formerly occupied by Wyandots, and Fairfield is in a line drawn from the Sandusky plains through the former counties.

The Shawanese, on both maps, are clustered along the Scioto, from the mouth northward to the Pickaway plains. Their villages also extended northeastwardly through the present counties of Clark, Champaign and Logan. Five are noted by Pownall, principally on the Scioto.

The Sandusky Bay and River were the principal seats of the Wyandots, who probably crossed the Scioto and occupied the valley of the Hockhocking.

The west branch of the Muskingum, known on our maps as the Whitewoman or Mohican, was assigned to the remnants of the old Connecticut tribe, whose name, otherwise evanescent, has been embalmed by the genius of Cooper. As we have seen from the diary of Smith, there was a Caughnawaga village (the Mohican was the origin of this tribe, but fused with Canadians and Iroquois, and lately resident near Montreal) about twenty miles above the Coshocton Forks, and still further north on the lake branch of the Mohican River, was the Mohican John's Town, near the (now) village of Jeromeville, in Ashland county. Thence these "Last of the Mohicans" were accustomed to range northward to the lake, and eastward over the comparatively vacant plains, now constituting the counties of the Western Reserve.

On the Cuyahoga River, near the falls, and adjoining the trail, which thence led to the Tuscarawas branch of the Muskingum, was a village of "Tawas," or Ottawas, the only reference to this tribe, except that on the site of Plymouth, Richland county, Hutchins notices the "ruins of a fort built by the Ottawas." There can be no doubt that they roamed the Sandusky peninsula and islands.

On Pownall, also, at the Falls of the Cuyahoga, is a Mingo town, mentioned on Hutchins as "Cayahaga." Here was doubtless a band of Cayuga Indians—the name of the New York tribe being, as we suppose, the origin of our "Cuyahoga" and "Geauga."

In the valley of the Mahoning, two towns are designated, which were probably colonies of the Seneca Indians. Their location seems to have been the present border of Mahoning and Trumbull counties.

Huron River is put down as "Bald Eagle Creek," and Black River, which we have supposed to be the Canesadooharie of Smith's diary, as "Gnahadahuyi."

Besides Fort Sandusky, and perhaps the affix of "French Margarets" to the Hockhocking town, we also find another indication of the French occupation of the Ohio, on the map of 1776. Near the Ottawa town on the Cayahaga, a French trading house is indicated. It has also been suggested (with little probability, however,) that the name of an Indian town on the Scioto near what is now Pike County—"Hurricane Tom's"—which is noted by Evans' map as early as 1755, was derived from some French trader. It was more likely the style of an Indian warrior.

The western border of the State is indefinitely assigned to the "Piques, or Tawichwis, or Mineamis, or Myamis" Indians, their principal town being near the present Piqua, although a small village of this tribe was at the mouth of the Little Miami River.

The rivers generally bear their present names. To the Ohio is added "or Palawa Thepiki or Fair River." The Islands of Lake Erie are, of course, imperfectly sketched, being called "Rattlesnake Islands." It is stated that the Indians were accustomed to cross the lake from island to island in canoes.

Indian Trails.

An interesting Appendix to Hutchins' History of Bouquet's expedition gives five different routes from Fort Pitt through the Ohio wilderness.

The First Route, which was N. N. W., after striking the Big Beaver, at a place called Kuskeeskees Town, forty-seven miles from Fort Pitt, ascended the east branch fifteen miles to Shaningo, and twelve miles to Pematuning, thence westward thirty-two miles to Mahoning on the west branch of Beaver, (probably Youngstown;) thence ten miles up said branch (Mahoning River) to Salt Lick (near the junction of Meander and Mosquito creeks in Weathersfield township, Trumbull county;) thence thirty-two miles to the Cuyahoga River (we suppose, just south of Ravenna—the name of Portage county thus derived,) and ten miles down Cuyahoga to Ottawatown, (Cuyahoga Falls.) The distance from Fort Pitt by the above route, was one hundred and fifty-six miles.

Second Route, W. N. W. was twenty-five miles to the mouth of Big Beaver, ninety-one miles to Tuscaroras, (the junction of Sandy and Tuscaroras Creeks at the south line of Stark county;) fifty to Mohikon John's Town (Mohican township, near Jeromeville or Mohicanville on the east line of Ashland county;) forty-six to Junandat or Wyandot Town (Castalia or the source of Cold creek in Erie county;) four to Fort Sandusky (at mouth of Cold creek, near Venice on Sandusky Bay;) twenty-four to Junqueindundeh (now Fremont, on Sandusky River, and in Sandusky county.) The distance from Fort Pitt to Fort Sandusky was two hundred and sixteen miles; to Sandusky River, two hundred and forty miles.

Third Route, W. S. W., was one hundred and twenty-eight miles to the Forks of the Muskingum, (at Coshocton;) six to Bullet's Town, on the Muskingum, (probably in Virginia township;) ten to Waukatamike, (near Dresden, Muskingum county, we will suppose;) twenty-seven to King Beaver's Town, near the sources of the Hockhocking, (see above for the probabilities whether this was the site of Lancaster, Fairfield county;) forty to the lower Shawanese town, on the river Scioto, (Circleville, we presume, but the route must have been circuitous;) twenty to Salt Lick Town, near the sources of Scioto, (this is difficult to understand, but on Hutchins' map, a small pond, situated the proper distance to the northeast, is written "Source," and seems to be the point designated;) thence one hundred and ninety miles northeast to Fort Miamis (now Fort Wayne, Indiana, on the Maumee River)—the distance from Fort Pitt to Fort Miamis being four hundred and twenty-six miles.

Fourth Route, down the Ohio, was twenty-seven miles to mouth of Big Beaver, twelve to Little Beaver; ten to Yellow Creek; eighteen to Two Creeks (just below Wellsburg, on Virginia side;) six to Wheeling; twelve to Pipe Hill (near Pipe Creek, quite likely;) thirty to Long Reach (probably opposite the township of Grandview, in Washington county, where the Ohio River is without a bend for a considerable distance;) eighteen to foot of Reach (near Newport;) thirty to mouth of Muskingum; twelve to Little Kanawha River; thirteen to mouth of Hockhocking River; forty to mouth of Letort's creek (opposite Letart township, Meigs county;) thirty-three to Kiskeminetas (an Indian village, otherwise called "Old Town," on the Ohio bank, perhaps in Cheshire township, Gallia county;) eight to mouth of Big Kenawha or New River; forty to mouth of Big Sandy; forty to Scioto River; thirty to Big Salt Lick River (Brush creek, in Adams county?) twenty to an island (opposite Manchester, in Adams county;) fifty-five to mouth of Little Miami; thirty to Big Miami or Rocky River, (no stoppage at Cincinnati, as now;) twenty to Big Bones, ("so called from the bones of an elephant found there;") fifty-five to Kentucky River; fifty to Falls of Ohio; one hundred and thirty-one to Wabash River; sixty to Cherokee (Tennessee) River, and forty to Mississippi. Total, from Fort Pitt, eight hundred and forty.

CHAPTER XII.

SUBMISSION AND FATE OF PONTIAC.

In the spring of 1765, late in April, Sir William Johnson was seated in council at German Flats, far in the interior of New York, and around him gathered the representatives of all the Western tribes. What the armies of 1764 had accomplished on the waters of Muskingum and Sandusky, was then consummated by the negotiations of the sagacious superintendent. At this meeting, two propositions were made; one to fix some boundary line, west of which the Europeans should not go; and the savages named as this line, the Ohio or Alleghany and Susquehannah; but no definite agreement was made, Johnson not being empowered to act. The other proposal was, that the Indians should grant to the traders who had suffered in 1763, a tract of land in compensation for the injuries then done them, and this the Indians agreed to do.

With the returning deputies of Senecas, Shawanese and Delawares, George Croghan, Sir William Johnson's sub-commissioner, embarked at Pittsburgh on the 15th of May, 1765, intending to visit the Wabash and Illinois, secure the allegiance of the French who inhabited their valleys, and conclude a treaty with Pontiac and his Ottawa and Miami adherents, whose submission was yet withheld.[1] His voyage down the Ohio in two batteaux was not eventful—the Journal affording a panorama of "rich and fertile bottoms;"

1) See Croghan's Journal in Craig's Olden Time, vol. i., p. 403.

hills now withdrawn beyond these bottoms, and anon "pinching close on the river," and "islands mostly lying high out of the water." About a mile below Big Beaver creek, a deserted Delaware town, "built for that nation by the French in 1756," was noticed—some of the stone chimneys yet remaining on the north side of the river. About two miles below where Steubenville stands, still on the north side of the Ohio, and near the mouth of Indian Cross creek, they passed a Seneca village, the chief of which joined the party. This place is usually designated Mingo Town, and although most of the Indians might have been Senecas, yet doubtless many from the other New York tribes were among its inhabitants. Here was afterwards the residence of Logan.

Croghan, on the 19th of May, encamped at the mouth of Little Conhowa River, and "here" he says "buffaloes, bears, turkeys, with all other kind of wild game, are extremely plenty." Five days from Pittsburgh, he came to the "mouth of Hochocen or Bottle River," passing within twenty miles above "five very fine islands; the country being rich and level, with high steep banks to the rivers." From this place, an Indian runner was despatched to the Plains of Scioto, with a letter to the French traders from the Illinois residing there with the Shawanese, requiring them to join him at the mouth of Scioto, that they might take the oath of allegiance to the British crown, be properly licensed to trade, and also accompany Croghan to the French settlements on the Wabash and Illinois.

Thirty miles below Hockhocking, an encampment was made at Big Bend, now within Meigs county. Here was such abundance of buffalo, bears, deer, and all sorts of game, that the party killed whatever was needed "out of the boats;" and still a country fine and level, with high banks, and an abundance of creeks falling into the Ohio. They passed "a place called Alum Hill, from the great quantity of that mineral found there by the Indians." Discovering some Cherokees near their encampment on the evening of the 22d, a good guard was kept the first part of the night, but nothing more was seen of them.

At the mouth of Scioto the journalist was enraptured. "The soil on the banks of the Scioto," he writes, "for a vast distance up the country, is prodigious rich, the bottoms very wide, and in the spring of the year, many of them are flooded, so that the river appears to be two or three miles wide. Bears, deer, turkeys, and most sorts of wild game, are very plenty on the banks of the river. On the Ohio, just below the mouth of Scioto, on a high bank, near forty feet, formerly stood the Shawanese town, called the Lower Town, which was all carried away, except three or four houses, by a great flood in the Scioto. I was in the town at the time; though the banks of the Ohio were so high, the water was nine feet on the top, which obliged the whole town to take to their canoes and move with their effects to the hills. The Shawanese afterwards built their town on the opposite side of the river, which, during the French war they abandoned for fear of the Virginians, and removed to the plains on Scioto. * * In general, all the lands on the Scioto River, as well as the bottoms on Ohio, are too rich for anything but hemp, flax, or Indian corn."

During the next three days, which were passed in camp at Scioto, the French traders arrived from the Shawanese towns, and on the 28th the party proceeded. The river being wider and deeper, with no islands, they "drove all night." On the 30th, the Great Miami was passed, and about forty miles below, they "arrived at the place where the elephant's bones are found." Under date of May 31, Croghan writes: "Early in the morning we went to the great Lick, where these bones are only found, about four miles from the river, on the south-east side. In our way we passed through a fine timbered clear wood; we came into a large road which the buffalos have beaten, spacious enough for two wagons to go abreast, and leading straight into the Lick. It appears that there are vast quantities of these bones lying five or six feet under ground, which we discovered in the bank at the edge of the Lick. We found here two tusks above six feet long; we carried one, with some other bones, to our boats, and set off. This day we proceeded down the river about eighty miles, through a country much the same as already described, since we passed the Scioto."

Passing the Falls of the Ohio and the Five Islands, the mouth of the Wabash was reached on the 6th of June, and is thus described: "At the mouth of the Ouabache we found a breast-work erected, supposed to have been done by the Indians. The mouth of this river is about two hundred yards wide, and in its course runs through one of the finest countries in the world, the lands being exceedingly rich and well-watered; here hemp might be raised in immense quantities. All the bottoms, and almost the whole country abounds with great plenty of the white and red mulberry tree. These trees are to be found in great plenty in all places between the mouth of the Scioto and the Ouabache; the soil of the latter affords this tree in plenty as far as Ouicatanon, and some few on the Miami River. Several large fine islands lie in the Ohio, opposite the mouth of the Ouabache, the banks of which are high, and consequently free from inundations; hence we proceeded down the river about six miles to encamp, as I judged some Indians were sent to waylay us, and came to a

8

place called the Old Shawnese Village, some of that nation having formerly lived there."

Letters were sent on the following day to Lord Frazer, an English officer on the Illinois, and to Monsieur St. Ange, the French commandant at Fort Chartres, and some speeches to the Indians there, informing them of the late peace, and that Croghan was coming to conclude matters with them. All these plans were interrupted, however, on the 8th of June. At day break, the English and their allies were attacked by a party of Indians, consisting of eighty warriors of the Kickapoos and Musquattimes, who killed two of the whites and three Indians, wounding Croghan and all the rest of the party, except two whites and one Indian. The survivors were made prisoners and plundered. In answer to the remonstrance of a Shawanese deputy, who was shot through the thigh, the marauders confessed that their "fathers, the French, had spirited them up, telling them that the Indians were coming with a body of southern Indians to take their country from them and enslave them; that it was this that induced them to commit the outrage."

Seven days' travel, at first through heavy woods, but principally "prodigious rich bottoms," clear woods and "some large meadows, where no trees for several miles together are to be seen, but with buffalos, deer and bears in plenty," brought captives and captors to Port Vincent, (now Vincennes,) which is described as a village of eighty or ninety French families, settled on the east side of the Wabash, and the inhabitants, as "an idle, lazy people, or parcel of renegades from Canada," who secretly exulted at the misfortunes of the English, and fell to bartering trifles for the valuables of which the prisoners had been plundered—ten of Croghan's half johannes, which a savage had appropriated, being extorted for a pound of vermillion. Two hundred and ten miles from Port Vincent, they came to Ouicatanon, (now Lafayette,) where fourteen French families lived in the fort, which stood north of the river. A glowing description is given of the "spacious and beautiful meadows," with their growth of "fine wild grass, and wild hemp ten or twelve feet high."

On the 25th of July, "after settling all matters happily with the natives," as Croghan indefinitely says, he started for the Miamis, and on the first of August was received with distinction at a Twightwee or Miami village, situated on both sides of the St. Josephs River, a quarter of a mile from its junction with the Miami, now Maumee. At this village, consisting of forty or fifty Indian cabins and nine or ten French Houses, the English flag was hoisted by the savages, some English prisoners surrendered, and peace established. Among these Indians Pontiac had taken refuge, but his mood was now submissive. The Indian chief and the English commissioner smoked the calumet together and interchanged belts of peace. "He would no longer," Pontiac said, "stand in the path of the English. Yet they must not imagine that in taking possession of the French forts they gained any right to the country; for the French had never bought the land, and lived upon it by sufferance only." The impression upon Croghan by this interview with the Ottawa chief is thus stated in a letter to Sir Wm. Johnson: "Pontiac is a shrewd, sensible Indian, of few words, and commands more respect among his own nation than any Indian I ever saw."

The scene of this interview was not far from Fort Miamis, which stood on the east side of the junction of the St. Josephs and the Maumee, and was then "somewhat ruinous," and we presume was without a garrison.

Followed by Pontiac and other chiefs, Croghan descended

the Miami River in a canoe. The banks were high and the country overgrown with lofty timber of various kinds—the land level and the woods clear. "About ninety miles from the Miamis or Twightwee," quoting again from the Journal, "we came to where a large river that heads in a large lick, falls into the Miami River; this they call the Forks (Auglaise at Defiance.) The Ottawas claim this country, and hunt here, where game is very plenty. From hence we proceeded to the Ottawa village. This nation formerly lived at Detroit, but is now settled here on account of the richness of the country, where game is always to be found in plenty. Here we were obliged to get out of our canoes and drag them eighteen miles, on account of the rifts which interrupt the navigation, (the rapids at Providence, between Lucas and Henry counties, undoubtedly.) At the end of these rifts we came to a village of Wyandots, who received us very kindly, and from thence we proceeded to the mouth of this river, where it falls into Lake Erie."

On the 17th of August, Croghan arrived at Detroit. We shall further digress by repeating his account of that position: "Fort Detroit is a large stockade, inclosing about 80 houses, and stands close on the north side of the river on a high bank; commands a very pleasant prospect for nine miles above and nine miles below the fort; the country is thickly settled with the French, their plantations are generally laid out about three or four acres in breadth on the river, and about eighty in depth; the soil good, producing plenty of grain. All the people here are generally poor wretches, and consist of three or four hundred French families, a lazy, idle people, depending chiefly on the savages for subsistence; though the land, with little labor, produces plenty of grain, they scarcely raise as much as will supply their wants, in imitation of the Indians, whose manners and customs they have entirely adopted and cannot subsist without them. The men, women and children speak the Indian tongue perfectly well. In the last Indian war, the most part of the French were concerned in it, (although the whole settlement had taken the oath of allegiance to his Britannic Majesty;) they have, therefore, great reason to be thankful to the English clemency in not bringing them to deserved punishment. Before the Indian war, there resided three nations of Indians at this place; the Putawatimes, whose village was on the west side of the river, about one mile below the fort; the Ottawas, on the east side, about three miles above the fort, and the Wyandots, whose village lays on the east side, about two miles below the fort. The former two nations have removed to a considerable distance, and the latter still remain where they were, and are remarkable for their good sense and hospitality. They have a particular attachment to the Roman Catholic religion, the French, by their priests, having taken uncommon pains to instruct them."

On the 27th, a meeting was held with the Ottawas and the other tribes of Detroit and Sandusky, when Croghan, with much flourish of Indian rhetoric, addressed them as follows:

"Children, we are glad to see so many of you here present at your ancient council-fire, which has been neglected for some time past; since the high winds have blown and raised heavy clouds over your country. I now, by this belt, rekindle your ancient fire and throw dry wood upon it, that the blaze may ascend to heaven, so that all nations may see it, and know that you live in peace and tranquillity with your fathers, the English.

"By this belt I disperse all the black clouds from over

your heads, that the sun may shine clear on your women and children, that those unborn may enjoy the blessings of the general peace, now so happily settled between your fathers, the English, and you, and all your younger brethren to the sun-setting.

"Children, by this belt I gather up all the bones of your deceased friends, and bury them deep in the ground, that the buds and sweet flowers of the earth may grow over them, that we may not see them any more.

"Children, with this belt I take the hatchet out of your hands, and pluck up a large tree, and bury it deep, so that it may never be found any more; and I plant the tree of peace, which all our children may sit under and smoke in peace with their fathers.

"Children, we have made a road from the sunrising to the sunsetting. I desire that you will preserve that road good and pleasant to travel upon, that we may all share the blessings of this happy union."

On the following day Pontiac spoke in behalf of the several nations assembled at the council:

"Father, we have all smoked out of this pipe of peace. It is your children's pipe, and as the war is all over, and the Great Spirit and Giver of Light, who has made the earth and everything therein, has brought us all together this day for our mutual good, to promote the good works of peace, I declare to all nations, that I have settled my peace with you before I came here, and now deliver my pipe to be sent to Sir Wm. Johnson, that he may know I have made peace, and taken the king of England for my father in the presence of all the nations now assembled, and whenever any of those nations go to visit him, they may smoke out of it with him in peace. Fathers, we are obliged to you for lighting up our old council fire for us, and desiring us to return to it; but we are now settled on the Miami River, [Miami of the lakes or Maumee] not far from hence; whenever you want us you will find us there ready to wait on you. The reason why I choose to stay where we are now settled, is, that we love liquor, and to be so near this as we formerly lived, our people would be always drunk, which might occasion some quarrels between the soldiers and our people. This, father, is all the reason I have for not returning to our old settlements; and where we live is so nigh this place, that when we want to drink we can easily come for it. [Gave a large belt with wampum tied to it.]

"Father, be strong and take pity on us, your children, as our former father did. It is just the hunting season of your children. Our fathers, the French, formerly used to credit his children for powder and lead to hunt with. I request, in behalf of all the nations present, that you will speak to the traders now here to do the same. My father, once more I request that you tell your traders to give your children credit for a little powder and lead, as the support of our families depends upon it. We have told you where we live, not far from here, that whenever you want us, and let us know, we will come directly to you. [A belt.]

"Father, you have stopped up the rum barrel, when we came here, until the business of this meeting was over. As it is now finished, we request you may open the barrel, that your children may drink and be merry."

A year afterwards, Pontiac visited Sir William Johnson at Oswego, where was held, on the 23d of July, another Congress of Ottawas, Pottawattamies, Hurons and Chippewas, with ceremonials and results similar to those of the council at Detroit.

Thenceforth we have only vague memorials of Pontiac. About the year 1769, when more than usual distrust prevailed among the savages, the English traders on the Illinois were disturbed by the appearance of Pontiac on a visit to the French garrison and village on the present site of St. Louis. St. Ange, then in command of that post, was highly esteemed by Pontiac, and a citizen of St. Louis, Pierre Chouteau, who lived to a great age, was accustomed to describe the appearance of the distinguished chief on that occasion. He wore the full uniform of a French officer, the gift of Marquis of Montcalm toward the close of the French war. He remained at St. Louis for two or three days, when, hearing that a large number of Indians were assembled at Cahokia, on the opposite side of the river, and that some drinking bout or other social gathering was in progress, he told St. Ange that he would cross over to see what was going forward. St. Ange endeavored to dissuade him, reminding him of the little friendship that existed between him and the British. Pontiac's answer was, "Captain, I am a man! I know how to fight. I have always fought openly. They will not murder me; and if any one attacks me as a brave man, I am his match." He went off, was feasted, drank deeply, and, when the carousal was over, strode down the village to the adjacent woods, where he was heard to sing the medicine songs, in whose magic power he trusted as the warrant of success in all his undertakings. In the meanwhile, an English trader, named Williamson, bribed a Kaskaskia Indian with a barrel of rum, and the promise of a greater reward, if he would succeed in killing Pontiac. The assassin stole near Pontiac, in the forest, and watching his moment, glided behind him, and buried a tomahawk in his brain.

This murder roused the vengeance of all the tribes friendly to Pontiac, and the Illinois were nearly exterminated in the retributive war which was waged against them.

Pontiac was buried by his friends, the French officers and residents, with warlike honors, near the fort at St. Louis. "For a mausoleum," says his accomplished biographer, "a city has risen above the forest hero; and the race whom he hated with such burning rancor, trample with unceasing footsteps over his forgotten grave."

CHAPTER XIII.

ENGLISH NEGOTIATIONS WITH THE WESTERN TRIBES—THE CLAIM TO KENTUCKY.

The English government, as we have seen, never failed to assert the right of the New York tribes to treat the Ohio valley as their conquest, and before the cession by France in 1763, the English claim of sovereignty rested chiefly upon a series of treaties with the chiefs of the Six Nations in 1684, in 1701, and especially on the 14th of September, 1726, by which their lands were conveyed to England, in trust, "to be protected and defended by his majesty, *to and for the use of the grantors and their heirs.*"

At Lancaster, in 1744, however, it was sought to obtain a different and far more important concession from these Indians. Deputies from Pennsylvania, Virginia and Maryland met the chiefs of the Six Nations, and after a scene of debauchery in the highest degree disgraceful to its English instigators, the Indians were persuaded to give a deed "recognizing the King's right to all lands that are, *or by his Majesty's appointment shall be*, within the colony of Virginia."

Here was a claim to an indefinite extent of the Ohio valley by purchase, but it was very justly obnoxious to the Ohio Indians—to the Delawares and Shawanese especially, whose villages were within the nominal limits of the colony of Virginia, and who indignantly denied any proprietary right in the Indians of New York.

Nevertheless, on this unsubstantial basis rested the grant

of 1748 to the Ohio Company of five hundred thousand acres, to be *principally* located on the south side of the Ohio River, between the Monongahela and Kenhawa Rivers. The exploration of Gist, in 1750–1, and the mere designation of a road to the Monongahela seem to have been the only effective steps towards a realization of this design.

The Virginians were very sensible that some form of assent by the Ohio Indians was indispensable. Great efforts were therefore made to procure it, and at length representatives of the western tribes were assembled at Logstown, seventeen miles below Pittsburgh, on the 9th of June, 1752.

This was a favorable moment for the designs of the English colonists, since the savages, even to the remote Twightwees, were then inimical to the French and favorably disposed towards the English, but the Virginia commissioners, Messrs. Fry, Lomax and Patton, had no easy task. They produced the Lancaster Treaty, and insisted upon the right of the crown, under its grant, to sell the western lands; but "No," the chiefs said, "they had not heard of any sale west of the warriors' road, which ran at the foot of the Alleghany ridge." The commissioners then offered goods for a ratification of the Lancaster treaty; spoke of the proposed settlement by the Ohio Company; and used all their persuasions to secure the land wanted. Upon the 11th of June, the Indians replied. They recognized the treaty of Lancaster, and the authority of the Six Nations to make it, but denied that they had any knowledge of the western lands being conveyed to the English by said deed; and declined, upon the whole, having any thing to do with the treaty of 1744. They were willing to give special permission to erect a fort at the fork of the Ohio, "as the French have already struck the Twigtwees," but the Virginians wanted much more, and finally, by the influence of Montour, the interpreter, who was probably bribed, the Indians united, on the 13th of June, in signing a deed confirming the Lancaster treaty in its full extent, and consenting to a settlement southeast of the Ohio.

The dissatisfaction of the Ohio savages with the proceedings at Logstown, is very apparent from the fact that in September, 1753, William Fairfax met their deputies at Winchester, Virginia, where he concluded a treaty, with the particulars of which we are unacquainted, but on which, it is stated, was an endorsement that *he had not dared to mention to them either the Lancaster or Logstown treaty;* a sad commentary upon the modes taken to obtain those grants.

All attempts to secure any practical results from those treaties were postponed by the outbreak and continuance of hostilities, and it was not until after the pacification of 1765, that the occupation of the lands west of the Alleghanies, otherwise than by the Indians, was agitated in any considerable degree.

The royal proclamation of October 7, 1763, our readers have not forgotten, forbade all private settlement or purchase of lands west of the Alleghanies, but as soon as peace was restored by the treaty of German Flats, settlers crossed the mountains and took possession of lands in Western Virginia and along the Monongahela. The Indians remonstrated—the authorities issued proclamations warning off intruders—orders were forwarded by Gen. Gage to the garrison of Fort Pitt to dislodge the settlers at Redstone, but all was ineffectual. The adventurous spirits of the frontier were not alone in their designs upon the wilderness. The old Ohio Company sought a perfection of their grant—the Virginia volunteers of 1754, who had enlisted under a proclamation offering liberal bounties of lands, were also clamorous—individual grants were urged—Sir William Johnson was ambitious of being the governor of an armed colony south of the Ohio, upon the model proposed by Franklin in 1754, and the plan of another company, led by Thomas Walpole, a London banker of eminence, was submitted to the English ministry.

Notwithstanding such a fever of land speculation, it was still felt, that a better muniment of title was requisite, than the obsolete pretensions of Lancaster and Logstown, and Gen. Gage having represented very emphatically the growing irritation of the Indians, Sir William Johnson was instructed to negotiate another treaty. Notice was given to the various colonial governments, to the Six Nations, the Delawares, and the Shawanese, and a Congress was appointed to meet at Fort Stanwix, now Rome, New York. It assembled on the 24th of October, 1768, and was attended by representatives from New Jersey, Virginia, and Pennsylvania; by Sir William and his deputies; by the agents of those traders who had suffered in the war of 1763; and by deputies from all of the Six Nations, the Delawares, and the Shawanese. The first point to be settled, was the boundary line, which was to determine the Indian lands of the west from that time forward; and this line the Indians, upon the 1st of November, stated should begin on the Ohio, at the mouth of the Cherokee (or Tennessee) River; thence go up the Ohio and Alleghany to Kittaning: thence across to the Susquehannah, &c.; whereby the whole country south of the Ohio and Alleghany, *to which the Six Nations had any claim*, was transferred to the British. One deed, for a part of this land, was made on the 3d of November, to William Trent, attorney for twenty-two traders, whose goods had been destroyed by the Indians in 1763. The tract conveyed by this, was between the Kenhawa and Monongahela, and was by the traders named Indiana. Two days afterwards, a deed for the remaining western lands was made to the King, and the price agreed on, paid down. There were also given two deeds of lands in Pennsylvania, one to Croghan, and the other to the proprietaries of that colony. These deeds were made upon the express agreement, that no claim should ever be based upon previous treaties, those of Lancaster, Logstown, &c.; and they were signed by the chiefs of the Six Nations, for themselves, their allies and dependents, the Shawanese, Delawares, Mingoes of Ohio, and others; but the Shawanese and Delaware deputies present, did not sign them.[1]

"Such," adds Perkins, "was the treaty of Stanwix, whereon rests the title by purchase to Kentucky, Western Virginia, and Pennsylvania. It was a better foundation, perhaps, than that given by previous treaties, but was essentially worthless; for the lands conveyed, were not occupied or hunted on by those conveying them. In truth, we cannot doubt that this immense grant was obtained by the influence of Sir William Johnson, in order that the new colony, of which he was to be governor, might be founded there. The fact that such an extent of country was ceded voluntarily—not after a war, not by hard persuasion, but at once, and willingly,—satisfies us that the whole affair had been previously settled with the New York savages, and that the Ohio Indians had no voice in the matter."

The efforts to organize an immense land company, which should include the old Ohio Company, and the more recent Walpole scheme, besides recognizing the bounties of the Virginia volunteers, were apparently successful by the royal sanction of August 14, 1774, but previously there were

1) Perkins' Writings, vol. ii., p. 232.

immense private appropriations of the region south of the Ohio. Prominent among those interested in such speculations, was George Washington.[2] His impression in favor of the country had been fully confirmed by a trip down the Ohio in 1770, his journal of which affords a glimpse of that beautiful stream, similar to the description of Croghan five years before. Washington was accompanied by Capt. William Crawford, whose death at the stake is one of the most appalling traditions of the west. They descended the river to the mouth of the Great Kenhawa, ascending that stream fourteen miles. On his return, after describing the Seneca or Mingo Town, which we have already identified as Logan's residence, Washington makes the following significant observations: "The Indians who reside upon the Ohio, the upper parts of it at least, are composed of Shawanese, Delawares, and some of the Mingoes, who, getting but little part of the consideration that was given for the lands eastward of the Ohio, view the settlements of the people upon this river with an uneasy and jealous eye, and do not scruple to say, that they must be compensated for their right, if the people settle thereon, notwithstanding the cession of the Six Nations. On the other hand, the people of Virginia and elsewhere, are exploring and marking all the lands that are valuable, not only on the Redstone and other waters on the Monongahela, but along the Ohio, as low as the Little Kenhawa; and by the next summer, I suppose they will get to the Great Kenhawa at least." Well might Washington

2) *Sparks' Washington*, vol. ii., pp. 346-7. He had patents for 32,373 acres —9,157 on the Ohio, between the Kenhawas, with a river front of 13½ miles —23,216 acres on the Great Kenhawa, with a river front of forty miles. Besides these lands, he owned, fifteen miles below Wheeling, 587 acres, with a front of two and a half miles. He considered the land worth $3.33 per acre.—*Sparks' Washington*, xii., 264, 317.

make this prediction, for on reaching the mouth of the Kenhawa, "at the beginning of the bottom above the junction of the rivers, and at the mouth of a branch on the east side (he) marked two maples, an elm and hoop-wood tree, as a corner of soldiers' land, intending to take all the bottom from (thence) to the rapids in the Great Bend, into one survey. (He) also marked at the mouth of another run lower down on the west side, at the lower end of the long bottom, an ash and hoop-wood for the beginning of another of the soldiers' surveys to extend up so as to include all the bottom in a body on the west side." Most certainly, Washington's own example was on the most liberal scale of appropriation.

As early as 1768, the Shawanese indicated their jealousy of the settlement of Kentucky—a region which, though often the theatre of desperate conflicts with the Cherokees and Catawbas, whose seats were further south, was still a most desirable range for hunting; and they complained of the frequent voyages of the English down the Ohio River. At a conference with the Ohio tribes, held by George Croghan, at Pittsburgh, in May, 1768, Nymwha, one of the Shawanese chiefs, who submitted so reluctantly to the army of Bouquet, thus expressed himself: "We desired you not to go down this river in the way of the warriors belonging to the foolish nations to the westward; and told you that the waters of this river, a great way below this place, were colored with blood; you did not pay any regard to this, but asked us to accompany you in going down, which we did, and we felt the smart of our rashness, and with difficulty returned to our friends, (alluding adroitly to Croghan's unlucky capture at the mouth of the Wabash in 1765.) We see you now about making batteaux, and we make no doubt you intend going down the river again, which we now tell you is disagreeable to all nations of Indians, and now again desire you to sit still at this place.

"They are also uneasy to see that you think yourselves masters of this country because you have taken it from the French, who, you know, had no right to it, as it is the property of us Indians. We often hear that you intend to fight with the French again; if you do, we desire you will remove your quarrel out of the country, and carry it over the great waters, where you used to fight, and where we shall neither see or know any thing of it."

Still, at a later period in the conference, when the dissatisfied speaker was rebuked by the Seneca and Delaware envoys, these bold expressions were materially modified, and the Shawanese envoys desired Croghan to "forget what they first spoke and help them to some council wampum, as they were very poor." Subsequently, as each year increased the European occupation of Kentucky, there can be no doubt of the increased alienation of the fierce denizens of the Scioto.

The peaceful Delawares met the encroachments upon their hunting grounds, by slowly retiring before the advancing column of emigration—concentrating their villages, more and more, within the wilderness north of the Ohio, and it was not until 1774 that the smothered flame of hostility, which had been long kindled among the Shawanese, burst forth. The wanton murders of Logan's family immediately leagued the bands of Mingoes or Senecas with their neighbors on the Scioto, in the work of vengeance. But, until we have recalled some events hitherto omitted, we shall postpone the consideration of the border war of 1774, otherwise called Dunmore's war.

CHAPTER XIV.

THE MORAVIAN MISSIONS ON THE MUSKINGUM.

THE most critical period in the history of the American colonies, namely, from 1764 to 1776, was not particularly eventful within the present limits of Ohio. Sandusky was a blackened ruin, and no effort was made by the English to extend their settlements in this region of the West. The contest between the speculators and settlers from Virginia and Pennsylvania on one side, and the Shawanese and Senecas on the other, which interrupted the peace of the Ohio valley in 1774, was confined to the western districts of those colonies, including the hunting grounds of the Indians within the State of Kentucky. The Wyandots and Ottawas were at that time too far removed from the scene of action, and too much under the influence of the English garrison at Detroit, to break the truce concluded by Pontiac on the 27th of August, 1765.

The progress of English emigration, like the French colonization, seemed to avoid Ohio. There were settlements on the Wabash, sooner than on the Scioto or the Miamis—a circumstance attributable, perhaps, to the vicinity of the Mississippi, and the contrast in number and force of the Delawares, Wyandots, and Shawanese of Ohio and the unfortunate Illinois, whose power had been broken, and their towns desolated in revenge for the assassination of Pontiac. Then the open prairies may have been more attractive than the heavy forests, which usually intercepted the sun between Lake Erie and the Ohio. Traders of course, found their way along the lake and river coasts, but no stockades were founded, no efforts made by associations or individuals to secure proprietary rights on the northern border of the Ohio River.

It was a sentiment of religious devotion, which first ventured within the existing limits of the State of Ohio, and has invested its first permanent settlement with an interest, similar to the Puritan advent in New England, and the Canadian missions of the Jesuits. If the first European settlement was by the French, when they established a fort at Sandusky in 1750, yet, as we have seen, that locality was abandoned by the English after the massacre and conflagration of 1763, and it was reserved for a few German missionaries to establish a permanent colony on the Muskingum. Of course we refer to the Moravians, who have been characterized as "the most remarkable Christian society that has arisen on the European continent since the era of the Protestant reformation."

As early as 1761, Charles Frederick Post, the indefatigable and sagacious Moravian, whose success as an ambassador to the Ohio Indians in 1758, has been noticed, penetrated to the Muskingum, and obtained permission from the Delawares, who had recently removed thither, to settle on the east side of the Muskingum, at the junction of its two forks, the Sandy and Tuscarowas. On the spot designated by the Indians, Post built a log cabin, and then returned to Bethlehem to seek a suitable associate, who might teach the Indian children to read and write, while the former preached to the savages. This companion he found in John Heckewelder, who, at the age of nineteen, was released from an apprenticeship to a cedar cooper, for the purpose of joining Post on his benevolent errand.

In March, 1762, they started on their hazardous journey. Narrowly escaping the snows of the Alleghanies, and the swollen streams, but encouraged by the hospitality of Col. Bouquet and Capt. Hutchins, then stationed at Fort Pitt, the adventurers crossed the Beaver River, assisted by the canoes and services of the Indians residing there, who also gave them some venison and bear's fat—White Eyes, a chief, adding a gift of "a few chickens." Four days after, on the 11th of April, they arrived at their destination, after a pilgrimage of thirty-three days. They entered their cabin "singing a hymn."

Heckewelder, in his memoirs, says that "no one lived near on the same side of the river; but on the other, a mile down the stream, resided a trader, named Thomas Calhoon, a moral and religious man. Farther south was situated the Indian town, called Tuscarora; consisting of about forty wigwams. A mile still farther down the stream, a few families had settled; and eight miles above, there was another Indian village." The locality called Tuscarora town, was on the south (or west, according to Heckewelder) side of the river, just above where Fort Laurens was afterwards built, and immediately contiguous to the present village of Bolivar, in Tuscarowas county.

Although the Indians had allowed Post to erect his cabin, during his absence they had become suspicious, fearing that the missionary scheme was a mere pretence, in order to enable the white people to obtain a footing in the Indian country, and that in course of time a fort would be erected. When they observed Post marking out three acres of ground for a corn-field, and beginning to cut down trees, they were alarmed, and sent him word to appear before them at the council house on the following day, and meanwhile to desist from doing any further work on the premises. On his appearance before them at the time appointed, the speaker, in the name of the council, delivered the following address:

"Brother! Last year you asked our leave to come and live with us, for the purpose of instructing us and our children; to which we consented; and now being come, we are glad to see you.

"Brother! It appears to us that you must since have changed your mind; for instead of instructing us or our children, you are cutting down trees on our land; you have marked out a large spot of ground for a plantation, as the white people do every where; and by and by another and another may come and do the same, and the next thing will be that a fort will be built for the protection of those intruders; and thus our country will be claimed by the white people, and we driven farther back, as has been the case ever since the white people came into this country. Say, do we not speak the truth?"

In answer to this address, Post said:

"Brothers! What you say I told you, is true, with regard to my coming to live with you, namely, for the purpose of instructing you; but it is likewise true that an instructor must have something to live upon, otherwise he cannot do his duty. Now, not wishing to be a burden to you, so as to ask of you provision for my support, knowing that you already have families to provide for, I thought of raising my own bread; and believed that three acres of ground were little enough for that. You will recollect that I told you last year that I was a messenger from God, and prompted by him to preach and make known his will to the Indians; that they also by faith might be saved, and become inheritors of his heavenly kingdom. Of your land I do not want a foot, neither will my raising a sufficiency of corn and vegetables for me and my brother to subsist on, give me or any other person a claim to your land."

Post having retired, to give the chiefs and council time to deliberate, was addressed as follows at a second interview:

"Brother! Now as you have spoken more distinctly, we may perhaps be able to give you some advice. You say that you are come at the instigation of the Great Spirit to teach and to preach to us. So also say the priests at Detroit, whom our Father, the French, has sent among his Indian children. Well, this being the case, you, as a preacher want no more land than those do; who are content with a garden lot to plant vegetables and pretty flowers in, such as the French priests also have, and of which the white people are all fond.

"Brother! As you are in the same station and employ with those preachers we allude to, and as we never saw any one of those cut down trees and till the ground to get a livelihood, we are inclined to think, especially as those men without laboring hard look well, that they have to look to another source than that of hard labor for their maintenance. And we think that if, as you say, the Great Spirit urges you to preach to the Indians, he will provide for you in the same manner as he provides for those priests we have seen at Detroit. We are agreed to give you a garden spot, even a larger spot of ground than those have at Detroit—it shall measure fifty steps each way, and if it suits you, you are at liberty to plant therein what you please."

Post agreed, as there was no remedy, and Capt. Pipe

stepped off the boundaries of the lot, stakes were driven at the corners, and Post told that now he might go on.[1]

We have given this transaction as narrated by Heckewelder, and it illustrates the jealousy of the Indians, even towards one who possessed their confidence, whenever the right of their lands was in question.

Next came the danger of starvation. No flour could be procured from Fort Pitt, the reserved stock having been destroyed by an inundation; a famine prevailed among the Indians, who saved every grain of maize for planting; potatoes were also very scarce; although wild ducks were abundant, they had no canoe to hunt them; the wild geese flew near the centre of the river; pheasants and squirrels were worthless in summer; and their food consisted chiefly of fish and the few vegetables of the surrounding forests. They lived mostly on nettles which grew in the bottoms, but they had brought some tea and coffee, their only luxury, although drank without milk or sugar. Upon such a diet, the labor of clearing their little garden, chopping the wood very short, so as to drag or roll it from the enclosure, and of loosening the ground with pickaxes, reduced their strength daily.

"One day," says Heckewelder, "some chiefs came to request my assistance for a few days in making a fence round their land. I gladly accepted the invitation, being desirous of doing anything to secure their good will; and I did my best to be of service to them. At the same time, I was enabled to restore my health and strength; for as long as I stayed with them, I could eat enough to satisfy the cravings of hunger. Thus I found myself suddenly transferred, as it were, to a land of plenty, and where I had opportunities to cultivate the acquaintance of the Indian

1) Heckewelder's Narrative, p. 98.

youth, and to secure the favor of the tribe by my industry. During my stay with them, I received the name of "Pisela-tulpe," Turtle; by which I was afterwards known among the Delawares."

Late in the summer an Indian conference was to be held at Lancaster, and Post was desired by the Governor of Pennsylvania to attend and bring with him as many of the Western Delawares as possible, "but above all King Beaver, and the great war-chief *Shingask*, generally called by the whites, King Shingas. King Beaver, and probably Conecogeauge, or White Eyes, were among those who accompanied Post, but the great war-chief was unwilling to place himself in the power of the Governor of Pennsylvania, who had set a high price on his scalp. It had been arranged at Bethlehem, by the Elders of the Congregation, that if Post returned to Lancaster, Heckewelder should not remain alone in the wilderness; but the brave youth, unwilling to abandon the enterprise, resolved not to leave the lonely cabin on the Muskingum. In order to bring cedar wood for the purpose of making tubs and like articles for the Indians, and to procure game, a canoe was constructed; and a number of old sermons and religious books were also left with Heckewelder, although he was cautioned not to read or write in the presence of the Indians, "for," said his more experienced friend, "they are suspicious of those white people whom they see engaged in reading or writing, especially the latter, believing that it concerns them or their territory." With these provisions for the comfort and contentment of his comrade, Post departed, and for a short time, Heckewelder did not lack for food, frequently bringing down five or six wild duck at a shot, and securing them by the aid of his canoe. In respect to his spiritual food, "I kept," he writes, "my books and papers in the garret, from a window of which I could see whether any one was approaching the cabin. Here I whiled away many an hour, far from civilization, alone with my books, my thoughts and my God."

Before many days were over, his canoe was lost by the carelessness or dishonesty of the Indian boys, who often borrowed it to spear fish, or to pursue the deer on the river by torchlight. The young hermit's distress for food returned; he was often entirely destitute; the nettles had become too large and hard to use; the vegetables in his garden were stolen, and in consequence of exposure in wading through the Muskingum to visit Calhoon, the trader, he was attacked by ague and fever.

A short time before, the wife of the chief Shingask, (Bog meadow) had died of a fever, or, as the Indians supposed, by the enchantment of a malicious sorcerer. As soon as she had breathed her last, her death was announced by the shrieks and howlings of women appointed for the purpose, and the funeral ceremony is thus described by Heckewelder. "Mr. Calhoon and myself, two Indian men and two Indian women, carried her to the grave. The body was dressed in the most superb Indian style; and being covered with ornaments and painted with vermillion, was placed in the coffin; at the upper end of which an opening had been made, that the soul might go in and out, until it had found a new home. A number of female mourners formed part of the funeral procession; which was conducted amid a dead silence. On arriving at the grave, the deceased was passionately entreated to stay with the living; after which the coffin was lowered, the grave filled up, and a red pole driven in at its head. So far the whole was sufficiently solemn; but what followed, showed that the living were more thought of than the dead. A great feast was made, and presents to the value of two hundred dollars were distributed amongst the attendants: Mr. Calhoon and myself received each of us, a black silk handkerchief and a pair of leggins; but none were better rewarded than the women who had acted as chief mourners. For three weeks after the funeral, a kettle with provisions was carried out every evening and placed upon the grave in order to refresh the departed spirit on its way to the new country. During that time the lamentations of the women-mourners were heard every evening, though not so loud or so violent as before."

At length, his paroxysms of fever growing more violent, and his weakness rendering him unable to ford the river, Heckewelder remained in the cabin—destitute and disconsolate. He declined an invitation to remove to Mr. Calhoon's house, although, as he says, he would gladly have accepted the kind offer, but he "had promised Post to remain at the cabin, as otherwise the Indians would have stolen every thing." His journal continues: "Whilst I was in this miserable condition, I was once visited by an Indian of my acquaintance; and I begged him to make me a little bark canoe; in return for which I promised to give him a knife. He did so, and I soon made my first trial with it, passing down the river to visit Mr. Calhoon. He hardly recognized me, so much had hunger and fatigue changed my appearance. I was received in the most friendly manner, and food was immediately set before me. I told him of my new acquisition, and that I intended to use my canoe to visit him and the Indians in the village, in order to procure some food, until I should be sufficiently recovered to hunt. 'Very well,' said he, 'never pass me by in your expeditions. I shall cheerfully share with you.' I then preferred my first request for a knife to give the Indian as I had promised. The good-natured trader immediately told me to send the man to his store, so that he might have his choice, as he was the best Indian that he had ever known; and that I need not pay him any thing for it. I had in fact not one cent in my possession, but had permission from Post, in case of necessity, to draw upon the trader for what was absolutely necessary. At this time I was frequently reduced to such distress, that the least morsel of food, if offered, would have been acceptable. But although I could make out to live, I was unable to do any thing, towards effecting the object for which I had come. Indeed it soon became evident that our enterprise was to be a complete failure.

"Post had hardly been gone three weeks, when the rumor was spread, that he never intended to return; nay, more, that even were he to attempt it, he would not be allowed by the tribe to do so; that his sole purpose was to deliver the Indian country into the hands of the white people, and that this was the secret of his pretended missionary efforts. It was also reported that a war would soon break out between the English and Indians, in which the latter would be assisted by their old allies, the French. All this I had written to Post; having found means to send him the information by a Mr. Denison from Detroit, who was traveling to Philadelphia. He returned answer, that he had already heard the unwelcome news, and that, in the pass things had come to, I could do no better than to return as speedily as possible. Gladly would I have followed his advice, but my horse was lost, or had been stolen, for upwards of three months. I was too weak to travel on foot; and Mr. Calhoon's pack-horse drivers, who had intended to set out for Pittsburgh with furs, were all laid up with the fever. I was therefore under the necessity of waiting for their recovery; and in the meantime I put my trust in the Lord.

"Meanwhile I was twice warned by friendly Indians to leave their country; and every time I visited Tuscarora, I saw strangers among the real inhabitants, and perceived that I was the object of their scrutiny. But I remained in happy ignorance of my dangerous situation, until, one afternoon, one of Mr. Calhoon's men called from the opposite bank of the Muskingum, requesting me to lock my door and cross the river immediately, as Mr. Calhoon wished to speak with me on business of great importance. Having wrapped up a few articles of dress in my blanket, I paddled across. As soon as I arrived at Mr. C.'s, he told me privately that an Indian woman, who frequently came to his store, and who made shirts which he kept for sale, had asked him that day whether the white man, who lived above on the other side of the river, were his friend; and that on his answering in the affirmative, she had said: 'Take him away; don't let him remain one night longer in his cabin; he is in danger there.'

"The next morning I wished to return, to see whether any thing had taken place at the cabin, and, if possible, to fetch a few necessary articles which had been left behind in the hurry of my departure. Mr. Calhoon, however, would not let me go, but sent two of his strongest men to see how things stood. One of them, James Smith, was a man of such uncommon strength, that the Indians considered him a Manitto, and would hardly be anxious to engage him personally. They reported that the house had been broken open during the night, and that, judging from appearances there, two persons had been in. There were signs of a late fire on the hearth, and they had evidently been waiting for me. Of course my return was out of the question; the attempt would have been actual foolhardiness. I never saw my lonely cabin again, remaining under the hospitable roof of the trader. Meanwhile, as I afterwards heard, emissaries of the Senecas and Northern Indians, were busily engaged in exciting the Delawares to take up the hatchet against the English; and soon after my departure, war broke out, and more than thirty white people of my acquaintance lost their lives.

"About this time, the Indian chiefs, whom Post had accompanied to Lancaster, returned home; and we soon perceived that, from some cause or other, their friendship had considerably cooled. One of them, however, King Beaver, remained favorably disposed; but all he could do was to give me several friendly hints to hasten my departure. Fortunately, Mr. Calhoon's men were now restored to health, and determined to set out on their journey to Pittsburgh. My kind host lent me a young horse to ride on; and in return I offered what assistance I could give his men in loading and unloading at the encampments.

"We now took an affectionate leave of each other. His conduct had been that of a Christian indeed; and his kindness will be remembered by me as long as I live. He would have left the country with me; but property of great amount had been entrusted to him, and this he considered himself bound to guard as long as possible. After my return to Bethlehem, I learned through the public papers that he and his brother, together with their servants, had been ordered by the Delaware chiefs to leave their country; as they were unable any longer to protect them. They set out for Pittsburgh, but were attacked on the road, at the Beaver River, by a party of warriors, and only two saved their lives, Mr. C. himself, who outstripped his pursuers in the race, and James Smith, who had strangled his antagonist.

"On the third day after our departure from Muskingum, we met Post and the Indian agent, Captain McKee; who were returning to the Indian country, totally ignorant of the real state of affairs. In spite of our earnest remonstrances, they insisted on proceeding, not considering the danger so imminent. They were soon undeceived on their arrival; and their lives were in danger. The agent was protected by the friendship of the chiefs; but Post, whom the Indians suspected of secret designs against them, as they were at a loss to explain his missionary movements, had to fly for his life, and was conducted to a place of safety, through a secret forest-path, by one of his former fellow-travelers, to Lancaster.

"Having taken leave of Post, I hastened after my companions, who had proceeded in the meantime. At a distance of five miles I expected to find their tents; and seeing the smoke of an encampment curling above the trees, I rode on, but was much surprised to find myself suddenly in the midst of a war-party. The sight of the Indian captives and of the scalping pole, with its savage decorations, was not calculated to encourage me. I was, however, suffered to pass on; and on riding five miles further, I found my company, by whom I was informed that I had fallen in with a party of Senecas, who had just returned from an expedition against the Cherokees."

In the third week of October, Mr. Heckewelder arrived at Pittsburgh, and when he finally reached Bethlehem, fatigue and disease had so altered his appearance that he was not at first recognized by his brethren.[2]

Years afterwards, the young enthusiast, who accompanied Post to the solitary cabin on the banks of the Muskingum, and returned to his brethren at such imminent hazard of his

2) Life of Heckewelder, by Rev. Edward Roundthaler, 45-58.

life, was instrumental in establishing a mission in Ohio, and in later years became widely known as a useful envoy of the United States to the Indian tribes, and as the author of several works of much historical value.

No less prominent in the history of the Moravian mission in Ohio—indeed, its effectual founder—was the Rev. David Zeisberger. This devoted missionary, encountering many discouragements at the missionary stations founded on the Alleghany, or Upper Ohio, in 1768, and on the Beaver in 1770, was agreeably surprised, in the spring of 1771, to receive an invitation from a council of Delaware Indians on the Muskingum, to remove a colony of missionaries and Christian Indians to that river. Next year, the invitation was with much earnestness renewed, the Wyandots joining in it. Zeisberger was encouraged to make a journey of exploration, accompanied by a few Indian brethren, and on the 16th of March, 1772, (according to Loskiel,) discovered a large tract of land, situated not far from the banks of the Muskingum, with a good spring, a small lake, good planting grounds, much game, and every other convenience for the support of an Indian colony. This place was about seventy miles from Lake Erie, and thirty miles from Gekelemukpechink, where resided the Delaware chiefs, upon whose invitation the Moravians had come. Thither Zeisberger repaired, and informed the council that the converted Indians had thankfully accepted of their invitation, desiring that the tract of land he had just now discovered might be given to them. In answer to this request, he heard with great pleasure that this was the very spot of ground destined by the chiefs in council for them. They also determined, in a solemn manner, that all the lands from the entrance of the Gekelemukpechink creek into the river Muskingum to Tuscarora, should belong to the converted

Indians, and that no other Indians should be permitted to settle upon them: further that all Indians dwelling on the borders of this country, should be directed to behave peaceably towards them and their teachers, and neither disturb their worship, nor prevent people from going to them to hear the word of God.

"Zeisberger," adds Loskiel, "praised the Lord for his gracious help in the execution of this important commission, and having again visited the above mentioned country, took possession of it in the name of the Christian Indians, who were uncommonly rejoiced by the account of his success given on his return to Friedenstadt.

"Five families, consisting in all of twenty-eight persons, were now appointed to begin the new settlement, and were willing to undertake it. Brother Zeisberger set out with them on the 14th of April, and after a safe but tedious journey, arrived May 3d at the new land on the Muskingum. The day following they marked out their plantations, erected field huts, and were all diligently employed in clearing land and planting.

"Brother Zeisberger began immediately to preach the Gospel in this new settlement, to which he gave the name of Schoen-brunn, (the Beautiful Spring.)"[3]

Our present purpose simply is to record the general fact of the settlement on the Muskingum in 1772–3, by the Moravians and their Indian disciples—hoping, however, that the brief narrative has already enlisted the sympathy of the reader with these unselfish colonists. Having thus introduced them, we propose to enlarge upon the previous history of this remarkable sect, whose labors of love have been attested in the darkest recesses of the pagan world. The Moravian

3) Loskiel's History of the Moravian Missions in North America; London translation, 1794; part iii., p. 74.

missionaries were more successful than any other class in subduing the intractable soul of the American savage to the Gospel. Indeed, their aptitude for these beneficent toils has been illustrated with equal distinctness wherever their missions have extended.

Our notice of their movements in Ohio would perhaps be more cursory, if they had been confined to the southeastern section of the State, but as, ten years afterwards, the Cuyahoga and Huron Rivers were the scene of temporary settlements, it seems to be requisite that the character of this extraordinary brotherhood, and their exertions among the North American Indians should constitute the theme of another chapter.

CHAPTER XV.

THE SOCIETY OF UNITED BRETHREN.

THE Christian society, generally called Moravians, which has since extended its branches to so many nations and supplied at once the most industrious citizens to civilized communities, and the most diligent and successful missionaries to heathen and savage hordes, has been described by different writers under the various denominations of *Moravians*, from the district of Moravia,[1] in Germany, which they once inhabited; of *Herrnhutters*, from Herrnhutt, in Saxony, where in 1722, they found a refuge from persecution within the domains of the celebrated Court Zinzendorf, who became their bishop; and of *The United Brethren of the Protestant Episcopal Church*, which is the title recognized by themselves.

According to the society's own account, however, they derive their origin from the Greek Church, in the ninth century, when by the instrumentality of Methodius and Cyrillus, two Greek monks, the kings of Bulgaria and Moravia, being converted to the faith, were, together with their subjects, united in communion with the Greek Church.[2] Methodius was their

1) The ancient province of Moravia adjoined Hungary on the northwest, and was surrounded by that country, Bohemia and Austria. It lies northwest from Vienna; and Olmutz, the prison of Lafayette, is its principal town.

2) Another version is, that in the ninth century a sister of the King of Bulgaria being carried a prisoner to Constantinople, became a Christian; and through her means, on her return to her native land, a Christian church was established in her country, of which the King of Moravia and the Duke of Bohemia became members.

first bishop, and for their use Cyrillus translated the Scriptures into the Sclavonian language.

The antipathy of the Greek and Roman Churches is well known, and by much the greater part of the brethren were in process of time compelled, after many struggles, to submit to the see of Rome. A few, however, adhering to the rites of their mother Church, united themselves, in 1470, to the Waldenses and sent missionaries into many countries. In 1547 they were called *Fratres Legis Christi*, or Brethren of the Law of Christ: because, about that period, they had thrown off all reverence for human compilations of the faith, professing simply to follow the doctrines and precepts contained in the Word of God.

There being at this time no bishops in the Bohemian Church, who had not conformed to the Church of Rome, three preachers of the United Brethren were, about the year 1467, ordained by Stephen, a bishop of the Waldenses in Austria; and these, on their return to their own country, ordained ten bishops or seniors, from among the rest. In 1523, the United Brethren commenced a friendly correspondence, first with Luther, and afterwards with Calvin, and other leaders among the reformers. A persecution which was brought upon them on this account, and some religious disputes which took place among themselves, threatened for awhile the society with ruin; but the disputes were, 1570, put an end to, by a synod, which decreed that differences about non-essentials should not destroy their union; and the persecution ceased in 1557, when the United Brethren obtained an edict for the public exercise of their religion. This toleration was renewed in 1609, and liberty granted them to erect new churches. But a civil war, which, in 1612, broke out in Bohemia, and a violent persecution which followed it in 1621, occasioned the dispersion of their ministers, and brought great distress upon the brethren in general. Some of them fled to England, others to Saxony and Brandenburg; whilst many, overcome by the severity of the persecutions, conformed to the Church of Rome. One colony of these, who retained their original principles and practice, was, in 1722, conducted by a brother named Christian David, from Fulneck, in Moravia, to Upper Lasatia, where they put themselves under the protection of Nicholas Lewis, Count of Zinzendorf, and built a village on his estate, at the foot of a hill, called Hutberg, or Watch Hill. They called their settlement Herrnhut, "the watch of the Lord." The Count, who soon after their arrival, removed from Dresden to his estate in the country, showed every mark of kindness to the poor emigrants; but being a zealous member of the church established by law, he endeavored for some time to prevail upon them to unite themselves with it by adopting the Lutheran faith and discipline. This they declined; and the Count, on a more minute inquiry into their ancient history and distinguishing tenets, not only desisted from his first purpose, but became himself a convert to the faith and discipline of the United Brethren.

The Synod, which, in 1570, put an end to the disputes which then tore the church of the Brethren into factions, had considered as non-essentials the distinguishing tenets of their own society, of the Lutherans and of the Calvinists. In consequence of this, many of the reformers of both these sects had followed the Brethren to Herrnhut, and been received by them into communion; but not being endued with the peaceable spirit of the church which they had joined, they started disputes among themselves, which threatened the destruction of the whole establishment. By the indefatigable exertions of Count Zinzendorf, these disputes were allayed; and statutes being, in 1727, drawn up and agreed to for the regulation both of the internal and of the external concerns of the congregation, brotherly love and union were again established; and no schism whatever, in point of doctrine, has since that period disturbed the church of the United Brethren.

In 1735, their eminent benefactor, Zinzendorf, was ordained a Bishop, and congratulated on the event by Dr. Potter, then Archbishop of Canterbury in England, and continued to discharge the duties of that station until his death in 1760.

The United Brethren allow to their Bishops no eminence of rank or authority. The form of government is essentially representative, the source of power being the Synod of the whole Unity. This Assembly meets at intervals of from ten to twenty years; the time of holding the Synod being determined by lot. To this synod every congregation may send a deputy, as also every provincial conference. The place of meeting is either at Herrnhut, or at Bertherlsdorf in Saxony. All questions of importance are determined by lot; and the resolutions of the Synod, copies of which are sent to the different congregations, are binding on every member of the Unity. At the close of the sessions, all of the assembled deputies vote for members of the General Conference of Elders of the Unity; who are to carry out the measures of the Synod, and manage the affairs of the church until a new Synod is assembled, at the commencement of which they resign their offices. The members of this Conference are also determined by lot, from among those who have received the highest number of votes. By this Conference inferior ones are appointed in the different provinces of the church; of which there are two in America, the members of which meet at Bethlehem in Pennsylvania, and at Salem in North Carolina. The provincial conferences appoint ministers to the different congregations, with the consent of the respective committees of these latter.

As to the tenets of the Moravians, they adhered to the Augsburgh Confession of Faith, composed by the German Reformers in the year 1530, and they professed a strictly literal obedience to the primitive ordinances of Christianity. Finding no warrant in Scripture for the common practice of transferring Sabbatical honor to the first day of the week, they dedicated Saturday to contemplative quiet, and entire cessation from bodily labor; and yet assembled on Sunday to commemorate the death and resurrection of Christ. Like the Quakers, they renounced all war and violence; like the *Tunkers*,[3] they established a community of goods; they taught industry as a branch of religion—regarding its offices and its fruits alike, as occasions or instruments of fulfilling the will of God; and they retained the primitive practices of washing feet, saluting with the kiss of holy love, and solving doubts by appealing to Heaven through the intervention of lots. This last practice was employed in particular, as a test of the propriety of contracting intended marriages.[4]

3) For twenty years after the settlement of Bethlehem, in 1742, this so cialism prevailed, when the members were allowed to purchase their tene ments on payment of a slight ground rent.

4) Madame de Stael thus particularizes on this subject, (2 *Germany*, 276): "When a young man chooses to take a companion, he addresses himself to the female superintendents of girls or widows, and demands of them the person he wishes to espouse. They draw lots in the church, to know whether he ought to marry the woman whom he prefers; and if the lot is against him, he gives up his demand. The Moravians have such a habit of resignation, that they do not resist this decision; and as they only see the women at church, it costs them less to renounce their choice."

There is no doubt that such was the case in their original constitution; but the custom is now changed, and the consent of the elders can always be obtained, where the marriage is suitable, and the conduct of the parties has been free from impropriety.

The men and women, before marriage, lived separately from each other, in assemblies where the most perfect equality prevailed; and in each of these assemblies, one of the members, in rotation, was appointed to pass the night in watching and prayer. Silent assiduity in business, gentleness of manner, plainness of apparel, and the utmost personal and domestic neatness were universally cultivated by the members of this society. It was a fundamental principle of their faith, that the true dignity and highest worth of a human being, consist not in requiring and receiving service from his fellows, but in rendering it to them. The Moravians have been termed by Madame de Stael, *the monks of Protestanism*, for though they rejected vows, their society was entirely ecclesiastical, every thing being accomplished by religious influence, and all affairs subjected to the superintendence and direction of the elders of the church.

Madame De Stael has left to us the following pleasing description of a Moravian village:[5]

"I was sometime ago at Dentendorf, a little village near Erforth, where a Moravian community is established. This village is three leagues distant from every great road; it is situated between two mountains, upon the banks of a rivulet; willows and lofty poplars environ it; there is something tranquil and sweet in the look of the country, which prepares the soul to free itself from the turbulence of life. The buildings and the streets are marked by perfect cleanliness; the women, all clothed alike, hide their hair, and bind their heads with a riband, whose color indicates whether they are married, maidens or widows; the men are clothed in brown, almost like Quakers. Mercantile industry employs nearly all of them; but one does not hear the least noise in the vil-

5) See her "Germany;" Philadelphia edition, 1814; vol. ii., p. 276.

lage. Everybody works in regularity and silence; and the internal action of religious feelings lulls to rest every other impulse.

"Instead of bells, wind instruments, of a very sweet harmony, summon them to divine service. As we proceeded to church, by the sound of this imposing music, we felt ourselves carried away from the earth; we fancied that we heard the trumpets of the last judgment, not such as remorse makes us fear them, but such as a pious confidence makes us hope them; it seemed as if the divine compassion manifested itself in this appeal, and pronounced beforehand the pardon of regeneration.

"The church was dressed out in white roses, and blossoms of white thorn; pictures were not banished from the temple; and music was cultivated as a constituent part of religion; they only sang psalms; there was neither sermon, nor mass, nor argument, nor theological discussion; it was the worship of God in spirit and in truth. The women, all in white, were ranged by each other without any distinction whatever; they looked like the innocent shadows who were about to appear together before the tribunal of the Divinity.

"The burying ground of the Moravians, is a garden, the walks of which are marked out by funeral stones: and by the side of each is planted a funeral shrub. All these grave stones are equal; not one of these shrubs rises above the other; and the same epitaph serves for all the dead. 'He was born on such a day; and on such an other, he returned into his native country.' Excellent expression to designate the end of our life! The ancients said 'he lived;' and thus threw a veil over the tomb, to divest themselves of its idea; the Christians place over it the star of hope.

"On Easter-day, divine service is performed in the burying ground, which is close to the church, and the resurrection is announced in the middle of the tombs. All those who are present at this act of worship, know the stone is to be placed over their coffin; and already breathe the perfume of the young tree, whose leaves and flowers will penetrate into their tombs.

"The communion of the Moravians cannot adapt itself to the social state, such as circumstances ordain it to be; but as it has been long and frequently asserted that Catholicism alone addressed the imagination, it is of consequence to remark that what truly touches the soul in religion is common to all Christian churches. A sepulchre and a prayer exhaust all the power of the pathetic: and the more simple the faith, the more emotion is caused by the worship."[6]

But the characteristic of the Moravians which has led to this extended notice of the sect, is their missionary zeal. "Their missionaries," it has been observed, "are all of them volunteers; for it is an inviolable maxim with them to persuade no man to engage in missions. They are all of one mind as to the doctrines they teach, and seldom make an attempt, where there are not half a dozen of them in the

6) This picture, by the author of Corinne, is repeated in its leading features at Bethlehem and Litiz, which, with Nazareth, are still Moravian villages. In Howe's Pennsylvania, (p. 515) Bethlehem is thus described: "The town has always elicited the admiration of travelers by its substantial, neat and orderly appearance. The principal buildings and other objects of interest are the spacious church, capable of containing about 2,000 persons, the only one in the place; the Brother's house and Sister's house, where those who choose to live in a state of single-blessedness, and still earn an independent support, can do so; the corpse house and cemetery; the museum of the Young Men's Missionary Society, containing a cabinet of minerals and a collection of curiosities, sent in by the missionary brethren from all parts of the world; the celebrated female seminary; the water works on the Manockisy, said to have been in operation more than 90 years, (prior to 1843,) and which furnished the model for those in Philadelphia.

mission. Their zeal is calm, steady, persevering. They would reform the world, but are careful how they quarrel with it. They carry their point by address, and the insinuations of modesty and mildness, which commend them to all men, and give offence to none. The habits of silence, quietness, and decent reserve, mark their character. If any of their missionaries are carried off by sickness or casualty, men of the same stamp are ready to supply their place." Perhaps by no class of Protestant Christians was so much missionary merit acquired as by the Moravian brethren. In the education of their own children, not less than in their exertions to instruct adult heathens, the members of this society were preëminently successful. One main cause, doubtless, was, that they regarded tuition, whether children in years, or children in understanding, as a process calculated alike for the benefit of the instructors and the pupils: and were primarily careful to apply to themselves, and practically demonstrate in their intercourse with others, the influence of the doctrines and precepts which they communicated.

"As early as 1727," says Loskiel, "which was soon after the restoration of the Unity of the Brethren, they began to

"All the property belongs to the Society, who lease out the lots only to members of their own communion. Each individual, when of age, becomes a subscriber to the rules of the Society, with the right of withdrawing himself at pleasure; in which case, however, he is required to dispose of his property, if a householder, and remove from the town. Each member pursues his occupation on his own private account; but if any particular trade should suffer by too great competition, the Society will not permit a new competitor in the same trade, although a member of the Society, to locate himself in the place. This secures to all a competence." The same love of music in their worship—having an organ and a full band of instruments. The grave-yard, as described by De Stael. The bodies of the dead lie in a corpse-house three days before interment. When a member dies, they have a peculiar ceremony: four musicians ascend to the tower of the church with trumpets, and announce the event by performing a dirge.

take the conversion of the Heathen in general into the most earnest consideration." The first missionaries went to St. Thomas, an island in the West Indies, in 1732; next year to Greenland, and in 1734, a party of Moravians, who had started for Georgia, changed their minds on reaching Holland, and went to Pennsylvania. Another company left Herrnhut in November, 1734, and on the invitation of the Society in England for propagating the Gospel, proposed to emigrate to Savannah. Oglethorpe, the founder of Georgia, had previously corresponded with Count Zinzendorf, and been liberal in his encouragement of the Moravians. A free passage; provisions in Georgia for a whole season; land for themselves and their children, free for ten years, then to be held for a small quit-rent; the privileges of native Englishmen; freedom of worship—these were the promises made by the trustees of the colony, accepted and honorably fulfilled. Count Zinzendorf dismissed his brethren to their Georgia destination, with written instructions, in which he particularly recommended, that they should submit themselves to the wise direction and guidance of God in all circumstances, seek to preserve liberty of conscience, avoid all religious disputes, and always keep in view that call, given unto them by God himself, to preach the Gospel of Jesus Christ to the Heathen, and further, that they should endeavor as much as possible to earn their own bread.

According to Loskiel, the first detachment of Moravians arrived in Georgia in the spring of 1735, but their number was increased by a larger company during the summer. Before embarking, they all disclosed to the trustees their determination not to engage in war, and received a pledge that they should be exempted from military service.

On one of these voyages, probably the latter, the Wesleys,

John and Charles, emigrated to Savannah. They had already attracted attention in England for their zealous piety, and were induced by the trustees to join the infant colony—Charles as secretary to Oglethorpe, and John with fervent longings to become an apostle to the Indians. "Our end in leaving our native country," said they, "is not to gain riches and honor, but singly this—to live wholly to the glory of God." With such sentiments, their attention could not fail to be drawn to the walk and conversation of their Moravian companions. The journal of John Wesley, now known to Christendom as the founder of a numerous sect, contains the following testimony:

"I had long before observed the great seriousness of their behavior. Of their humility they had given a continual proof by performing those servile offices for the other passengers, which none of the English would undertake: for which they desired and would receive no pay, saying, 'It was good for their proud hearts, and their Saviour had done more for them.' And every day had given them occasion of showing a meekness which no injury could move. If they were pushed, struck or thrown down, they rose again and went away; but no complaint was found in their mouth. There was now an opportunity of trying whether they were delivered from the spirit of fear, as well as from that of pride, anger and revenge. In the midst of the psalm wherewith their service began, a storm arose, the sea broke over us, split the mainsail in pieces, covered the ship, and poured in between the decks as if the great deep had already swallowed us up. A terrible screaming began among the English. The Germans calmly sang on. I asked one of them afterwards, 'Was you not afraid?' He answered, 'I thank God, no!' I asked, 'But were not your women and children afraid?' He replied mildly, 'No; our women and children are not afraid to die.'" At the time when the danger seemed most imminent, and the vessel was expected immediately to founder, an infant was brought to Wesley to be baptized. "It put me in mind," he says, "of Jeremiah's buying the field when the Chaldeans were on the point of destroying Jerusalem, and seemed a pledge of the mercy God designed to show us even in the land of the living."

Of the manners of the Germans in Georgia, Wesley subsequently gives this representation: "They were always employed, always cheerful themselves, and in good humor with one another." He adds, "They met this day to consult concerning the affairs of their church; Mr. Spangenburg being shortly to go to Pennsylvania, and Bishop Nitschman to return to Germany. After several hours spent in conference and prayer, they proceeded to the election and ordination of a Bishop. The great simplicity as well as solemnity of the whole almost made me forget the seventeen hundred years between, and imagine myself in one of those assemblies where form and state were not, but Paul, the tent-maker, or Peter, the fisherman, presided yet with the demonstration of the Spirit and of power."

After their arrival, a spot for their village was chosen and called Ebenezer. "In a few years, the produce of raw silk by the Germans amounted to ten thousand pounds a year; and indigo also became a staple. In earnest memorials, they long deprecated the employment of negro slaves, pleading the ability of the white man to toil even under the suns of Georgia. Their religious affections bound them together in the unity of brotherhood; their controversies were decided among themselves; every event of life had its moral, and the fervor of their worship never disturbed their healthy tranquillity of judgment. They were cheerful and at peace."[7] A school house for the children of the Creek nation was established—the good will of the Indians was secured, and they frequently came to hear the *great word*, as they expressed it—the Rev. Peter Boehler, of the University of Jena, was chosen and ordained minister of the Georgia colony, in 1737, and arrived there in the year following, and everything seemed auspicious, until the outbreak of hostilities with the Spaniards subjected the Moravians to peculiar trials.

In 1739, war was declared by England against Spain. An act of Parliament was passed at the same time for naturalizing all foreign Protestants settled in any of the British colonies in America. If this act was meant to gratify or retain the Moravian settlers in Georgia, its efficacy was completely defeated by the contemporary proceedings of the English inhabitants of this province. About a year before, when a provincial force was hastily assembled to encounter an apprehended invasion of the Spaniards, the Moravians were summoned to join their fellow-colonists in defending their adopted country. This summons they mildly but firmly refused to obey; declaring that no human power or motive could induce them to take the sword, and appealing to the pledge they had received from the trustees, of exemption from military service. The magistrates were constrained to admit the force of the appeal; but so much jealousy and displeasure were expressed on this account by the bulk of the planters against the Moravians, that several of these sectaries, unwilling to remain among a people in whom their presence excited unfriendly sentiments, abandoned the province and retired to the peaceful domain of the Quakers in Pennsylvania, where already a numerous society of

7) Bancroft's United States.

the Moravian brotherhood was collected. The rest, under the direction of their pastor, Boehler, continued to reside in Georgia; being desirous of discharging the pecuniary debt which they had contracted to the trustees, and unwilling to forsake their missionary labors. But in the present year, they again received a summons to join the provincial militia; and declining to resume the former controversy, they bade farewell to Georgia, surrendered their flourishing plantations without a murmur, and reunited themselves to their brethren who were established in Pennsylvania. One of their number, John Hagen, returned in 1740 to Georgia, at the request of George Whitefield, for the purpose of prosecuting the work which had been commenced among the Creeks. The Indians were in an unfavorable mood, and, according to Loskiel, Hagen, "finding their hearts and ears shut against him, and that no fruits were to be expected, was obliged to desist and return sometime after to Pennsylvania." Nevertheless, Georgia was not entirely abandoned by the Moravians, for in 1751, when the original prohibition of slavery in that colony was annulled, Bancroft represents some of the brethren as "acquiescing" in the change. After the departure of Oglethorpe, he says, "slavers from Africa sailed directly to Savannah, and the laws against them were not rigidly enforced. Whitefield, who believed that God's Providence would certainly make slavery terminate for the advantage of the Africans, pleaded before the trustees in its favor, as essential to the prosperity of Georgia; even the poorest people desired the change. The Moravians still expressed regret, moved partly by a hatred of oppression, and partly by antipathy to the race of colored men. At last, they too began to think that negro slaves might be employed in a Christian spirit, and it was agreed that, if the negroes are treated in a Christian manner, their change of country would prove to them a benefit. A message from Germany served to hush their scruples. "If you take slaves in faith, and with the intent of conducting them to Christ, the action will be not a sin, but may prove a benediction."[8]

In 1739, the brethren at Herrnhut resolved to extend their missions in North America. An incident which occurred in 1736 served to animate the purpose which the Moravian Society in Europe had cherished for some time, of attempting the instruction of the Indians. In the winter of that year Conrad Weisser, a Pennsylvanian colonist of German descent, and interpreter between the provincial government and the Indians, was dispatched by the Governor of Pennsylvania to treat with the Six Nations and dissuade them from making war, which they were preparing to do, on an Indian tribe within the territory of Virginia. In performing this journey of nearly five hundred miles, Weisser, forcing his way mostly on foot through deep snow and thick forests, was nearly exhausted by toil and hardship, when he

8) The trustees, at the outset, adopted a rule that forbade the introduction of slaves. Bancroft quotes some pregnant sentences from the publications of 1734 in favor of this feature of colonial policy. For instance: "Slavery, the misfortune, if not the dishonor of other plantations, is absolutely proscribed. Let avarice defend it as it will, there is an honest reluctance in humanity against buying and selling and regarding those of our species as our wealth and possessions." "The name of slavery is here unheard, and every inhabitant is free from unchosen masters and oppression." And the testimony of Ogelthorpe, who yet had once been willing to employ negroes, and once, at least, ordered the sale of a slave, explains the motive of the prohibition. "Slavery," he relates, "is against the gospel, as well as the fundamental law of England. We refused, as trustees, to make a law permitting such a horrid crime." "The purchase of negroes is forbidden," wrote Van Reck, "on account of the vicinity of the Spaniards;" and this was doubtless the governmental view. The colony was also "AN ASYLUM TO RECEIVE THE DISTRESSED. It was necessary, therefore, not to permit slaves in such a country; for slaves STARVE THE POOR LABORER."

met two Indians, who exhorted him not to be faint, but to take courage—adding that the sufferings endured by a man in his mortal body cleansed the imperishable soul from sin. On his return, Weisser related this occurrence to Spangenberg, a Moravian Bishop, by whom it was reported to his brethren in Europe. They were greatly struck with it, and determined to spare no pains to instruct those blind but thinking heathens in the knowledge of a better way to that expiation of which they obscurely felt the necessity, and impart to them the experience of the only fountain capable of cleansing the human soul from sin.

Ranch, a Moravian missionary, arriving at New York from Europe, in the year 1740, commenced a course of apostolic labor among the Mohican Indians inhabiting the borders of Connecticut and New York. The sachem, or chief of the tribe, declared of himself and his people, that they were all helplessly sunk in misery, drunkenness and every vice and crime that could defile and degrade human nature; and protested that the missionary would confer an inexpressible benefit upon them if he could teach them how to lead a wiser and happier life. They listened with profound astonishment to the first promulgation of the doctrines of Christianity, but soon rejected them with unanimous derision. Ranch, however, was not to be discouraged; he persisted in his pious labors without any other visible fruit except increased unpopularity and ridicule among the Indians; till one day the chief, who was himself the worst man of the tribe, earnestly requested him once more to explain how the blood of a Divine Redeemer could possibly expiate and obliterate the defilement of the human soul. Ranch declared that the most valuable gift in the world could not have afforded him a gratification comparable to the delight with which that question inspired him. He who so felt was formed to conquer in this glorious and happy field. Appearances of mental conversion and a considerable reformation of manners ensued among the tribe. But now was aroused the jealousy of a numerous band of European traders, who derived a guilty gain from the dependence to which the savages were reduced by their vices and poverty. Some of them threatened to shoot Ranch if he remained longer in the country; others assured the Indians that the missionary's instructions tended to delude them, and that his real purpose was to carry their children beyond seas and sell them for slaves. The abused and ignorant people, as credulous of this falsehood as they had been slow to believe divine truth, began to regard the missionary with rage and detestation, and meanwhile were copiously supplied with strong liquor by those perfidious counsellors, for the purpose of exciting them to wreak their erring fury on their benefactor.

Ranch overcame this opposition by a wisdom and virtue equal to every emergency. He softened the resentment of some of the white settlers and traders by the mild courtesy of his manners, and gained the protection of one of them by teaching his children to read and write. To the Indians he behaved with an unabated tenderness and confidence, which powerfully appealed to their remaining virtue—to that sense of good which is never wholly obliterated while human life endures. They were struck with the new proof which he afforded of the efficacy of the principles which he had preached, in shielding their professor from evil and fear, and rendering him always secure and happy; they were astonished that a man, whom they studiously endeavored to insult by contumely, and terrify by menace, should persist in following them with patience, benedictions, tears, and every other demonstration of affectionate and disinterested regard; and one of them, who had made an attempt to take the missionary's life, contemplating him as he lay stretched in placid slumber on the floor of the Indian's own hut, was constrained to acknowledge to himself, "This *cannot* be a bad man; he fears no evil; not even from us who are so savage; but sleeps comfortably, and places his life in our hands." The Indians at length became generally convinced that evil could not be meditated by a man who was himself so completely exempted from the suspicion of it; his influence was restored and augmented, and his ministry attended with happy effects. All the Moravian missionaries were charged by their ecclesiastical superiors to study rather the confirmation of the faith than the increase of the numbers of professed converts. Ranch's first congregation consisted of ten baptized Indians, whose devotion, simple yet profound, enthusiastic yet sincere and sustained, excited the grateful delight of their pastor and his associates, and the wonder and admiration of the wildest of the surrounding savages. Meanwhile, from the increasing resort of members of the Moravian brotherhood to Pennsylvania, there were formed the principal settlements of the society at places which obtained the names of Nazareth and Bethlehem; and from which, with all convenient speed, missionaries, animated with the same spirit as Ranch, carried the benefit of their instructions and example among the Delaware Indians, with the usual varieties of success which ever attend the preaching of the gospel, and which are far more strikingly manifested in tribes and nations to which the tidings are delivered for the first time than in societies which have been long nominally christianized, and where habit blunts the force of impressions and veils the significance of language.

In the year 1742, Count Zinzendorf, who was chief bishop

or warden of the society of Moravian brethren, having visited their settlements in America,[9] traveled, along with Conrad Weisser, Peter Boehler, and other associates, into the Indian territories and preached to a great variety of tribes. Some of the fiercest warriors of the Six Nations, who, from a recent quarrel among themselves, had been roused to a state of high and dangerous excitement at the time when he casually met them, were exceedingly struck with the mixture of simplicity, authority and benevolence that characterized his address to them, and after some consultation, thus replied to it:—"Brother, you have made a long voyage over the seas, to preach to the white people and to the Indians. *You* did not know that we were here, and *we* knew nothing of you. This proceeds from above. Come, therefore, to us, both you and your brethren; we bid you welcome, and take this fathom of wampum in confirmation of the truth of our words." After a short but successful ministry in America, Zinzendorf returned to Europe in 1743, leaving a numerous and increasing body of missionaries to pursue the labors thus felicitously begun. It was a rule with these missionaries to earn their own livelihood by bodily labor for behoof of the objects of their pious concern; and this rule their Christian moderation enabled them generally to practice, although their savage employers could afford only a slender recompense of their toil; but whenever they could not subsist in this manner, they were supplied with the necessaries of life by the society at Bethlehem. They lived and dressed in the Indian style; and one of them, Frederick Post, did not scruple to marry a baptized Indian woman. In addition to the inevitable

9) Zinzendorf was accompanied in his tour of the Indian villages by his daughter *Benigna*—a word worth preserving, perhaps, by those who think that there is virtue in a name.

drudgery and privation which they incurred, they were frequently exposed to insult and danger from the savages who rejected the boon of the gospel with contempt, and heard its testimony against the corruption of human nature with indignation. Gideon Mack, one of the missionaries, having been waylaid by an Indian who presented his gun and desired him to prepare to die, for insulting the Indians by talking perpetually of their need of Christ, replied calmly, "If Christ does not permit you, you cannot shoot me." The savage, struck with the language and demeanor of his intended victim, dropped his gun, retired in silence, and soon after embraced the faith which, he perceived, was calculated to form the highest style of character.

A curious objection, which reminds us of incidents and reproaches that attended the first promulgation of the gospel upon earth, was raised by some Indians, who, observing their friends greatly moved by the discourses of the missionaries, exclaimed that these men must be sorcerers, and in league with evil spirits, for that nothing but magic could produce such effects. The most formidable opposition was created by a number of white traders, who were concerned at the influence which the missionaries exerted in persuading the savages to abstain from purchasing the spirituous liquors, to avoid contracting debts, and to exchange hunting for agriculture. They were aided by some weak and ignorant or bigoted colonists of New York and New England, who looked on the Moravian society as a branch of the Church of Rome, and were convinced that the spread of their tenets and influence would promote the interests of France among the Indian race. Several of the missionaries were seized as Roman Catholic teachers by the inhabitants of Connecticut, and detained in custody some days, till they were liberated by command of the provincial governor. But in New York, which abounded with traders, hostile to the conversion of the Indians, and contained a number of clergymen and laymen devoted exclusively to the Church of England, the opposition grew daily stronger, and was inflamed by the fluctuating politics of the Six Nations. Some of the colonists assured their savage neighbors that the Moravian brethren were not *legally* entitled to undertake the pastoral office which they exercised—a statement which the Indians were totally unable to comprehend; others, and especially certain persons engaged in the Indian trade, attempted to debauch the new converts and seduce them to resume the vices they had forsaken; and the provincial magistrates committed several of the missionaries to prison, as enemies of the British government and corrupters of its Indian allies. The most respectable inhabitants of the province, who had at first imbibed prejudices against the missionaries, were speedily disabused, and not only encouraged them to persevere in their useful labors, but openly declared of them, that they were, of all men, the best instruments of the security of the colonists and the happiness of the Indians. At length, however, in consequence of a report that a number of the Indian converts had wholly detached themselves from their previous friendly connection with Britain, the public rage was kindled to such a pitch that an act of the New York Assembly was passed, prohibiting any member of the Moravian society from preaching or residing among the tribes connected with the province. This policy was little calculated to soothe or conciliate the Indians, who had generally conceived a high regard for the missionaries—of whom some now quitted the province, and others, lingering in it with the hope of being yet permitted to resume their pious labors, were afterwards thrown into prison and treated with great severity. The Indians who seemed most attached to them, became the objects of a strong aversion and jealousy to many of the colonists, who loudly and fiercely importuned the government to send troops to destroy them. Not long after the departure of the missionaries, a number of converted Indians of the confederacy of the Six Nations, forsaking their country and kindred, followed their teachers to Pennsylvania, and established themselves at Bethlehem.

In the mean time, and for several years after, Spangenberg, Nitchsman, Cammerhoff, and a great many other pastors supplied by the Moravian brotherhood, were actively and successfully engaged in proselyting and civilizing the savage tribes adjacent to the colonial settlements of Pennsylvania, Delaware and New Jersey. They collected various Indian societies, in which the duties of morality were practised, the habits of civilized life studied and pursued, and the profession of Christianity embraced with a sincerity which was tried and attested by severe suffering and patient virtue. The Indian converts and their children were taught to read; and some portions of the Christian Scriptures were translated into various dialects of the Indian tongue. So far from pretending to any superiority over their converts, the missionaries appeared at once their teachers and their servants; and at all the settlements, not only participated in their rural labors, but appropriated to themselves the heaviest part of every drudgery, in consideration of the incompetence of Indian constitutions for steady and continuous toil. The progress of these beneficent exertions was interrupted by the outbreak of the last war with France, and by the ravages which the Indian allies of the French inflicted on the borders of Pennsylvania. Many of the Pennsylvania colonists were progressively incensed to such a degree, by the devastation of their country, the massacre of their friends, and the danger of their families, that they conceived an incurable hatred and jealousy against the whole Indian race.

A sect of fanatics sprung up in Pennsylvania about the year 1755, who clamorously demanded the total extirpation of the aboriginal tribes, lest the vengeance of Heaven should fall upon the Christians for not destroying the heathen, as the Israelites by divine command had been directed to destroy the Canaanites of old. The general delusion was increased by the publication of a letter, which was said to have been intercepted by the British forces, purporting to have been written by a French officer at Quebec to one of his friends, and extolling the Moravian brethren as the secret partizans and useful agents of France. This letter, whether the offspring of French or of English artifice, produced all the effect that its fabricators designed. A universal cry was raised through the British colonies that the Moravian settlers were *snakes in the grass*, and the most dangerous because the most perfidious enemies of Britain. The persons and settlements of these calumniated men, in Pennsylvania, were now exposed to the greatest danger; and the provincial government, though sincerely inclined to protect them, was evidently incapable of withstanding the headlong rage with which the great body of the people imprecated vengeance on the Moravian brethren and their Indian flocks. The mildness and patience with which this injustice was endured by the objects of it was insufficient to quell the popular fury, which was on the point of venting itself in some notable outrage, when, to the general surprise, a sudden attack was made by the Indian allies of France on a Moravian settlement, situated near Mahoning creek, (a small tributary of the Lehigh river, and not far from Bethlehem,) in which a number of the brethren and of their Indian associates were slain. This circumstance, concurring with the willingness of some of the Moravian settlers to prepare for defensive war against the enemy, and the liberal contributions of others to relieve the wants of their fellow-colonists, who had suffered from hostile rage, produced a great and sudden abatement of the public jealousy and displeasure. The blessings of tranquillity and security were now enjoyed in the Moravian settlements till the year 1763, when all the hatred and fear that the Indian race had ever excited in Pennsylvania, were revived with augmented violence by the great Indian war which broke out at that period, and the dreadful desolation of the frontiers of this province which attended the first explosion of its fury. A general attack was now projected by a great number of the inhabitants on the Indian inhabitants of the province, of whom many were forced to fly; some were conveyed to Philadelphia by order of the government, which tendered its protection, and some were cruelly slain.

Near the Susquehanna, and at no great distance from the town of Lancaster, was a spot known as the Manor of Conestoga, where a small band of Indians, chiefly of Iroquois blood, had been seated from the first settlement of the province, and always remained on good terms with the English. On the east bank of the river, some distance above Conestoga, stood the town of Paxton, which had been devastated by the Indians in 1755. The relatives of those slain at that time rebuilt the village, but were inimical to the race of their persecutors, and suspicious of the band at Conestoga. They organized into a body of rangers, and were active in defending the borders. At length, deeming their suspicions confirmed, they fell upon the Conestoga Indians, and a horrid massacre ensued, the victims being principally women and children. Those who by absence escaped the fury of the Paxton men, fled to Lancaster, and were placed in jail for security, which was broken open soon after by a party of the assassins, and the butchery completed. The provincial authorities were impotent to prevent or redress these outrages, and the Moravians next became objects of distrust and persecution.

About three months before the massacre at Conestoga, a party of drunken rangers, fired by the general resentment against the Moravian Indians, murdered several of them, both men and women, whom they found sleeping in a barn. Not long after, the same party of rangers were, in their turn, surprised and killed, some peaceful settlers of the neighborhood sharing their fate. This act was at once ascribed, justly or unjustly, to the vengeance of the converted Indians, relatives of the murdered; and the frontier people, who, like the Paxton men, were chiefly Scotch and Irish Presbyterians, resolved that the objects of their suspicion should live no longer. At this time the Moravian converts consisted of two communities, those of Nain and Wecquetank, near the Lehigh, and to these may be added a third, at Wyalusing, near Wyoming. The latter, from its distant situation, was, for the present, safe; but the two former were in imminent peril, and the inhabitants in mortal terror for their lives, stood day and night on the watch.

At length, about the tenth of October, 1764, a gang of armed men approached Wecquetank, and encamped in the woods at no great distance. They intended to make their attack under favor of the darkness; but before evening, a storm, which to the missionaries seemed providential, descended with such violence, that the fires of the hostile camp were extinguished in a moment, the ammunition of the men wet, and the plan defeated.

After so narrow an escape, it was apparent that flight was the only resource. The terrified congregation at Wecquetank broke up on the following day, and under the charge of their missionary, Bernard Grube, removed to the Moravian town of Nazareth, where it was hoped they might remain in safety.

By order of the provincial assembly, the Christian Indians were removed to Philadelphia, as the last means to secure their protection. Their total number, including the missionaries, was about one hundred and forty. Insulted by the populace and soldiery, the unfortunate exiles only found sympathy and kindness from the Quakers. Attended by these kindred sectarians, the Moravians and converts proceeded to Province Island below the city, where they were lodged in some deserted barracks, and their wants provided for, by the authorities and the society of Friends.

Immediately after the Conestoga murders at Lancaster jail, which did not take place until some weeks after the removal of the Moravian converts to Philadelphia, the rioters prepared to march upon the city and finish their work by killing the Indians whom it had taken under its protection. Such was the consternation that it was determined to send the refugees to New York, and place them under the protection of the Indian Superintendent, Sir William Johnson. Passing through Trenton, they reached Amboy, when a message was received from Governor Colden, of New York, forbidding the Indians to come to that province. Similar letters were received from Gen. Gage and the city authorities, the latter threatening heavy penalties to the owners of vessels if they should transport the Indians from New Jersey.

Thus disappointed in their hopes of escape, the hapless Indians remained several days lodged in the barracks at Amboy, where they passed much of their time in religious services. A message, however, soon came from the Governor of New Jersey, requiring them to leave that province ; and they were compelled reluctantly to retrace their steps to Philadelphia. A detachment of one hundred and seventy soldiers had arrived, sent by Gen. Gage, on the requisition of Governor Penn ; and under the protection of these troops the exiles began their backward journey. On the 24th of January they reached Philadelphia, where they were lodged at the barracks within the city, the soldiers, forgetful of former prejudices, no longer refusing them entrance.

Again came tidings of danger from the country, and vigorous preparations for defence were made, even Quaker non-resistance yielding to the imminence of the occasion. The insurgents having advanced to Germantown, within seven miles of Philadelphia, Governor Penn fled for safety and counsel to the house of Dr. Franklin ; and Pennsylvania seemed to be on the brink of civil war. Franklin, however, and some other popular individuals, undertook to meet and expostulate with the insurgents ; and in the conference that ensued, exerted their sense, address and influence so effectually as to prevail with them to relinquish their ferocious purpose and return to their homes. To improve this happy success, Franklin immediately after composed and published a pamphlet in defence of the Indians, which produced a considerable effect in soothing the passions of his countrymen and restoring tranquillity.

From the year 1763, till the revolt of America from the dominion of Britain, no general or considerable opposition resisted the exertions of the Moravian brethren to disseminate among the objects of their care the principles, habits, and benefits of piety, morality and civilization. The chief settlements were Bethlehem and Nazareth, in the county of Northampton, where their modes of life and worship still attract the attention of the traveler. Here and at Litiz, a beautiful Moravian village, eight miles north of Lancaster, are institutions for the instruction of girls, which have been long and justly celebrated. We are not aware that any other Moravian communities, preserving the peculiarities described so attractively by Madame de Stael, have survived on this continent except at these three villages. Bethlehem was first settled in 1740, Nazareth soon after, and Litiz in 1756.

To return to the Moravian traditions prior to the revolution. The counties of Carbon, Lehigh, Schuylkill and Northumberland lie west of Bethlehem, and within their limits, as now delineated on the map, were numerous Moravian missionary stations between 1745 and 1765. These were the principal sufferers during the tumults of 1764, which have just been described. The settlement of Nain was about a mile from Bethlehem, and Wecquetank, described above as near the Lehigh, is supposed to have been situated near the eastern corner of Schuylkill county, on the border of Carbon. Gnadenhutten, settled in 1746, was in Carbon county, about half a mile above the junction of Mahoning creek and the Lehigh River. Here the first murder of Moravians took place. Still further west, at Shamokin, now Sunbury, in Northumberland county, was a station in 1747. It is supposed that none of these are now in existence.

The Wyalusing station is even more closely related to our Ohio mission than those already enumerated. It was established by Zeisberger, in 1763, and was called Friedenshutten or Tents of Peace. The site was on the Susquehanna river, in Bradford county, and near the southern border of New York. The Iroquois gave permission to occupy even a larger tract of land than was desired, but soon after, in 1768, sold the whole country to Pennsylvania. At length, in 1772, the entire community moved to the station on the Beaver River, and thence, after a few days, proceeded to Shoenbrun, on the Muskingum. They were accompanied by Rev. John Ettwein and Rev. John Heckewelder—the veteran Zeisberger having gone to the Beaver to escort the party. The hospitable Delawares were informed of the arrival of the Susquehanna party, and the brethren were congratulated, in full council, with all the ceremony of Indian compliment.

The wandering settlement of western Pennsylvania is even more closely related to the colony at Shoenbrun. In 1768, Zeisberger penetrated to a spot in the now county of Venango, on the left bank of the Alleghany, not far from the mouth of Tiouesta. Here the mission of Goshgoshunk was established, but soon after removed to fifteen miles further up, near Hickory town. There was a Delaware village, forty miles north of Pittsburgh, in what is Butler county, called Kaskaskunk, where resided Glikhikan, who became first the friend of the Moravians, and afterwards a convert to Christianity. On his first interview with Zeisberger, he was struck by the fulfillment of a vision, which occurred to him years before. He had dreamed that he came to a place where a number of Indians were assembled in a large room. They wore their hair plain, and had no rings in their noses. In the midst of them, he discovered a short white man, and the Indians beckoning to him to come in. He entered, and was presented by the white man with a book, who desired him to read. On his replying, "I cannot read," the white man said: "After you have been with us some time you will learn to read it." From this time he frequently told his hearers that there were certainly white people somewhere, who knew the right way to God, for he had seen them in a dream. Therefore, when he came hither, and saw the Indians and the short white man, Brother Zeisberger, exactly answering to the figure of him he saw in his dream, he was much astonished. He now frequently went to Lawunakhannek, the mission where Zeisberger and his converted Delawares were, and conversed earnestly with the brethren." Heckewelder says (Narrative, p. 109) that the name of the chief signified "the *stud* or *foremost sight of a gun-barrel;* that he was admired and dreaded by all who knew him, on account of his superior courage as a warrior, for his talents in council, and his unequaled manner of delivering himself as a natural orator or speaker."

Glikhikan was influential, and the missionaries were invited, in 1770, to come to the Big Beaver, whither they went in April of that year, settling about twenty miles from its mouth. About this time, Glikhikan left Kaskaskunk, (about forty miles north of Pittsburgh) and, avowing himself a Christian convert, henceforth lived with the brethren. The new station on the Beaver was called Friedenstadt, the town of Peace, whither the new disciple came. An old Delaware chief, Pakanke, to whom Glikhikan had been chief captain and speaker, was greatly concerned at this defection. Meeting the latter soon afterwards, he railed as follows: "And even you have gone over from this council to them. I suppose you mean to get a white skin. But I tell you, not even one of your feet will turn white, much less your body. Was you not a brave and honored man, sitting next to me in council, when we spread the blanket and considered the belts of wampum lying before us. Now you pretend to despise all this, and think to have found something better. Some time or other you will find yourself deceived." Glikhikan made but a short and meek reply, and his accuser afterwards was so much mollified, by a current superstition, that hostility to the missionaries was the cause of an epidemic sickness among his people, that he went to hear the brethren preach, declared his conviction and recommended his children to receive the gospel. Glikhikan was baptized by the name of Isaac, and was henceforth very prominent in the history of the Ohio mission.

In 1773, the Christian Indians on the Beaver River resolved also to emigrate to Ohio, and on the 13th of April, the village of Freidenstadt was evacuated, one part of the congregation traveling across the country by land, and the other, led by John Heckewelder, descending the Big Beaver and Ohio, and ascending the Muskingum to Shoenbrun in twenty-two canoes.

The first settlement by Zeisberger consisted of twenty-eight persons; the emigration from the Susquehanna was two hundred and forty-one in number; and if we suppose the population of the village on the Beaver now transplanted to the Muskingum to have been one hundred, the number on the Muskingum in 1773 was 369. The Mohicans built ten miles below Schoenbrun, calling the village Gnadenhutten.

When the pilgrimage of 1772, from the distant Wyalusing, was happily ended, and the Indians in council had welcomed the new arrival, David Zeisberger and John Heckewelder summoned the congregation together. John Ettwein, about to invoke the blessing of Heaven and depart to Bethlehem, stood near while the rules of the congregation (the phrase is Heckewelder's) as agreed to and approved by the national assistants, were read and accepted by the whole congregation. It was a scene not wholly unlike the first compact of the Puritan community in the cabin of the Mayflower. An August sky was above them—the waters of the Elk Eye glided gently by—the "beautiful spring" reflected the motionless group; and the voice of prayer and praise hallowed the adoption of the following homely frame of civil and religious obligation—the first act of Ohio legislation—the constitution of 1772.[10]

1. We will know of no other God, nor worship any other but him who has created us, and redeemed us with his most precious blood.

2. We will rest from all labor on Sundays, and attend the usual meetings on that day for divine service.

3. We will honor father and mother, and support them in age and distress.

4. No thieves, murderers, drunkards, adulterers and whoremongers shall be suffered among us.

5. No one shall be permitted to dwell with us without the consent of our teachers.

6. No one that attendeth dances, sacrifices, or heathenish festivals, can live among us.

7. No one using *Trchappich* (or witchcraft) in hunting, shall be suffered among us.

8. We will renounce all juggles, lies and deceits of Satan.

9. We will be obedient to our teachers, and to the helpers (national assistants) who are appointed to see that good order be kept, both in and out of town.

10. We will not be idle and lazy—nor tell lies of one another—nor strike each other—we will live peaceably together.

10) It is taken from Heckewelder's narrative.

11. Whosoever does any harm to another's cattle, goods or effects, &c., shall pay the damage.

12. A man shall have only one wife—love her and provide for her and the children. Likewise a woman shall have but one husband, and be obedient to him; she shall also take care of the children, and be cleanly in all things.

13. We will not permit any rum, or spirituous liquor, to be brought into our town. If strangers or traders happen to bring any, the helpers (national assistants) are to take it into their possession, and take care not to deliver it to them until they set off again.

14. None of the inhabitants shall run in debt with traders, nor receive goods on commission for traders, without consent of the national assistants.

15. No one is to go on a journey or long hunt without informing the minister or steward of it.

16. Young people are not to marry without the consent of their parents, and taking their advice.

17. If the stewards or helpers apply to the inhabitants for assistance, in doing work for the benefit of the place, such as building meeting and school houses, clearing and fencing lands, &c., they are to be obedient.

18. All necessary contributions for the public ought cheerfully to be attended to.

"The above rules were made and adopted at a time when there was a profound peace; when, however, six years afterwards (during the revolutionary war) individuals of the Delaware nation took up the hatchet to join in the conflict, the national assistants proposed and insisted on having the following additional rules added, namely:

19. No man inclining to go to war—which is the shedding of blood—can remain among us.

20. Whosoever purchases goods or articles of warriors, *knowing* at the time that such have been stolen or plundered, must leave us. We look upon this as giving encouragement to murder and theft.

"According to custom, these rules were, at the commencement of every year, read in public meeting; and no new member or applicant could be permitted to live in the congregation without making a solemn promise that he or she would strictly conform to them. When any person residing in the congregation gave offence, or caused disturbance, it was the duty of the national assistants first to admonish such person or persons in a friendly manner; but where such admonition proved ineffectual, then to consult together for the purpose of publicly putting him, her or them, out of the soci ety, and dismissing such altogether from the place. Next to these rules, other necessary and proper regulations were made and adopted; for instance, respecting the daily meetings and the duty of church wardens, schools, attending to visitors, and the attention to be paid to the poor, sick and needy, or distressed—and also with regard to contributions to be made from time to time for the benefit of the congregation at large, as also individuals in the same, unable to support themselves, or furnish the necessary attire for the deceased, so that the corpse of the poorest person in the community was dressed as decent as the wealthy."

Our narrative of Moravian antecedents has been minute, but not, as we submit, disproportionate. We should expect that the historian of Massachusetts would not stint the chapters devoted to the tale of Puritan suffering in England, which at length freighted the Mayflower. The annalist of Pennsylvania could devote no less space to the traditions of Fox, Penn and their associates; and who could object to a general memoir of the Huguenots of France, in writing a history of North Carolina, or of the Jesuit organization, in a narrative of Canadian colonization? Such a relation the Moravians bear to Ohio, and the theme is in all respects too attractive, not to have yielded to the temptation of fullness in detail. Indeed, the principal embarrassment has been, not to seek, but how to decline, the materials for the present episode.[11]

We have the authority of James Patrick, Esq., of New Philadelphia, that the present site of Shoenbrun is about two miles south of New Philadelphia, in Tuscarawas county; seven (Heckewelder says ten) miles farther south, was Gnadenhutten, in the immediate vicinity of the present village

11) This sketch of the Moravians, prior to their occupation of Ohio in 1772, has been mostly compiled from Loskiel's History of the Missions in North America, Graham's Colonial History of the United States, Bancroft's History, Heckewelder's Narrative, Howe's Pennsylvania, the Religious Encyclopedia and John Wesley's Journal. The work of Loskiel appears to be the fountain from which subsequent writers have drawn. The best compilation of his work is Graham's Colonization of America, to whose paraphrase this chapter is greatly indebted. Parkman's Conspiracy of Pontiac has also supplied some particulars of the excitement in Pennsylvania in 1764, which were not attainable elsewhere. Graham's work has never been appreciated. The author was a Scotchman, who never visited this country, but being a lover of civil and religious freedom, as well as a consummate scholar and jurist, his attention was turned to the early planting of the American States; and by an intelligent and assiduous investigation of the historical archives of England, France, Holland and Germany, he was enabled to produce and perfect a work, accurate, liberal, authoritative and attractive. Himself strongly religious by temperament and habit, the Moravian annals seemed to have impressed his sensibilities in a remarkable degree, and a transcript of the historian Loskiel forms an interesting portion of his work. It is a singular fact that an Italian (Botta) was one of the earliest and most estimable historians of the American Revolution, while the colonization of the continent was first satisfactorily narrated by another foreigner—neither Graham or Botta having ever formed any personal associations, as a visitor or resident, with a country whose history afforded the theme of their enthusiastic and successful labors.

of that name; and about five miles further below, was Salem, afterwards established a short distance from the village of Port Washington. The first and last mentioned were on the west side of the Tuscaroras, now near the margin of the Ohio canal. Gnadenhutten is on the east side of the river.

But at the moment that the first permanent colonization of the State seemed to be progressing thus auspiciously, the storm of Indian hostility was filling the horizon. We hasten to record the events of 1774.

CHAPTER XVI.

DUNMORE'S EXPEDITION IN 1774. THE STORY OF LOGAN.

THE name of Logan is closely associated with the hostilities of 1774, usually called Dunmore's war, from the fact that Lord Dunmore, then Governor of Virginia, commanded one division of the army, by whose invasion it was terminated. We shall precede our narrative of its events, by a few memorials of the remarkable person above mentioned.

When Count Zinzendorf, the Moravian bishop, visited his Pennsylvania brethren in 1742, he followed the course of the Susquehannah River to Shomokin, a populous Indian town, and thence crossed to the residence of Catharine Montour, near the head of Seneca Lake in New York. He was accompanied by Conrad Weisser, the Indian agent of Pennsylvania, and four converted Indians. At Shomokin, they were hospitably entertained by Shikellimus, a Cayuga chief, who is described as the "first magistrate and head-chief of all the Iroquois Indians living on the banks of the Susquehannah as far as Onondago." Afterwards Shikellimus was converted to Christianity, and the missionaries "considered him a candidate for baptism, but hearing that he had been already baptised by a Roman Catholic priest in Canada, they only endeavored to impress his mind with a proper idea of the importance of this sacramental ordinance, upon which he destroyed a small idol, which he wore about his neck."[1]

1) Loskiel's North American Missions, part ii., p. 120.

Shikellimus died in 1749, attended in his last moments by David Zeisberger.

There is no doubt that Logan was the second son of this chief—his name being a tribute of respect to James Logan, Secretary of the Province of Pennsylvania, who was highly esteemed by Shikellimus. Heckewelder wrote to Jefferson that "about the year 1772, Logan was introduced to him by an Indian friend, as son to the late reputable chief, Shikellimus, and as a friend to the white people." Heckewelder was favorably impressed by the "superior talents" and correct sentiments of Logan.[2]

After reaching manhood, Logan lived for a while in Pennsylvania, within the present limits of Mifflin county, and the following anecdotes of him during this period, are preserved in Day's Historical Collections of that State, but the dates of their occurrence are not given.

William Brown, with two companions, had been hunting bear, and was separated from his two companions in the pursuit of one which they had started. In his own words, he was traveling along, looking about on the rising ground for the bear, when he suddenly came upon a spring, and laid down to drink. Suddenly he saw reflected on the opposite side, the shadow of a tall Indian. Brown sprung to his feet, seized his rifle, but the Indian knocked up the pan of his gun, threw out the priming, and extended his open palm in token of friendship. This was Logan, and the two became firm allies. Further down the stream, was the camp of another hunter, Samuel Maclay, and thither Logan conducted his new acquaintance. In a few days, Brown and Maclay visited Logan at his camp, which was in the same

2) Jefferson's Notes on the State of Virginia. Philadelphia, 1801; appendix, p. 39.

neighborhood—the Kishacoquilas valley—and situated near what is now known as Logan's spring, in Mifflin county. Here Maclay and Logan shot at a mark for a dollar a shot. Logan lost four or five rounds, and acknowledged himself beaten. When the white men were about to leave, he went into his hut, and brought out as many deer skins as he had lost dollars, and handed them to Mr. Maclay, who refused to take them, alleging that he was Logan's guest, and did not come to rob him; that the shooting had been only a trial of skill, and the bet merely nominal. Logan drew himself up with great dignity, and said "me bet to make you shoot your best—me gentleman, and me take your dollar if me beat." There was, of course, no alternative than to take the skins. So sensitive was Logan, that he would not accept even a horn of powder in return.

Mr. Brown, who was an associate judge of Mifflin county from its organization till his death at the age of ninety-one or two, soon afterwards settled in the vicinity. When his little daughter was just beginning to walk, her mother expressed her regret that she could not get a pair of shoes to give more firmness to her little step. Logan stood by, but said nothing. He soon after asked Mrs. Brown to let the little girl go up and spend the day at his cabin. The cautious heart of the mother was alarmed at such a proposition; but she knew the delicacy of an Indian's feelings—and she knew Logan, too—and with secret reluctance, but apparent cheerfulness, she complied with his request. The hours of the day wore slowly away, and it was nearly night, when her little one had not returned: but just as the sun was going down, the trusty chief was seen coming down the path with his charge; and in a moment more the little one trotted into her mother's arms, proudly exhibiting a beautiful pair of moccasins on her little feet—the produce of Logan's skill. It is no wonder that Judge Brown should call the kind and noble hearted Logan "the best specimen of humanity (he) ever met with, either white or red." "Poor Logan!" he is reported to have said on the same occasion, the tears coursing down his cheeks, "he soon after went into the Alleghany, and I never saw him again."[3]

We have already assumed that the Mingo town upon the Ohio River at the mouth of Indian Cross Creek, was the residence of Logan, but it could not have been founded by him. In 1765, George Croghan, in his journal of a voyage to the Wabash, describes a Seneca village, "on a high bank on the north side of the river at a place called Two Creeks, about fifteen miles from Yellow Creek," and says that the chief of this village offered his services to go with him to the Illinois country, which were not refused, from a fear of giving offence, although Croghan "had a sufficient number of deputies already." Washington, in his journal of a tour to the Ohio in 1770, after descending Long Island (now opposite Island Creek township in Jefferson county), and Big Stony Creek, a mile or two below the island on the west side, adds: "About seven miles from the last mentioned creek, and about seventy-five from Pittsburg, we came to the Mingo town, situate on the west side of the river, a little above Cross creeks: this place contains about twenty cabins and seventy inhabitants of the Six Nations. It is made probable by the communication of Heckewelder, published by Jefferson, that this village did not become the residence of Logan until after Washington's visit. Heckewelder says that when he met Logan in 1772, on the Beaver River, the latter expressed an *intention* to settle on the Ohio River below Big Beaver, but was then encamped at the mouth of Beaver. In April, 1773, when

3) Historical Collections of Pennsylvania, by Sherman Day, p. 467.

Heckewelder was on his way to the Muskingum, with the Moravian emigration from Freidenstadt, he called at "Logan's settlement, receiving every civility from such of the family as were at home." We assume, therefore, that the Mingo town in question, composed of Indians from the different New York tribes, but principally of Senecas, was known for some years before Logan's emigration to the Ohio in 1772, but that, almost immediately on his arrival, he became so prominent among the Indians of the frontier, that the village was called after his name. David Zeisberger, the friend of his father Shikellimus, and who had known Logan from boyhood, speaks of him as "a man of quick comprehension, good judgment and talents." There is evidence, also, that he was a person of distinguished appearance.

We will now endeavor, from a mass of conflicting testimony, to narrate the circumstances which transformed Logan from the firm friend to the bitter enemy of the whites.

In the winter of 1773–4, one Dr. John Connolly, a nephew of George Croghan, determined to assert the claims of Virginia upon Fort Pitt and its vicinity. He issued a proclamation to the inhabitants, to meet at Redstone, now Brownsville, on the 24th and 25th of January, 1774, and organize themselves as a Virginia militia. Before the time appointed, Connolly was arrested by Arthur St. Clair, who then represented the Pennsylvania proprietors at Pittsburgh, and the assemblage at Redstone dispersed without definite action. As soon as Connolly was released from custody, however, he renewed his efforts to establish the exclusive authority of Virginia. He came to Pittsburgh on the 28th of March, with an armed band of followers, and in the name and by the authority of Lord Dunmore, proclaimed the jurisdiction of Virginia—rebuilding Fort Pitt, which was called Fort Dunmore. He was recognized as Captain Commandant of a district called West Augusta, and almost immediately exhibited a tyrannical spirit to all who were in the Pennsylvania interest, while he seemed not unwilling to involve the frontier in an Indian war—one motive for the latter policy being, as suggested by Arthur St. Clair and others, to cloak his extravagant civil expenditure, with the indefinite item of frontier defence. At any rate, his letters to the Virginians, who were scattered in exploring parties along the south bank of the Ohio, contributed materially to the outbreak of hostilities.[4] On the 21st of April, Connolly wrote that the Shawanese were not to be trusted, and that the whites ought to be prepared to revenge any wrong done them. Already the Indians were accused of stealing horses from the encampments and settlements of the Virginians, and on the 16th of April, a canoe, belonging to William Butler, a leading Pittsburgh trader, had been attacked near Wheeling by three Cherokees, and one white man had been killed. The alarm spread down the river, and a party of Virginian surveyors and explorers organized, with Capt. Michael Cresap at their head, and repaired to Wheeling, to determine what course to pursue. George Rogers Clark, who was of this band, has left a statement that Cresap dissuaded them from an intention to attack a town called Horsehead Bottom, on the Scioto and near its mouth, and proposed the return to Wheeling.[5] Here, according to Clark, two letters were received from Connolly—one requesting the men to keep their position for a few days, as war was

4) For the facts relative to Connolly's conduct, &c., see American Archives, fourth series, i., 252 to 288, 435, 774, &c.

5) Clark's letter was originally published in the Louisville News Letter, and is quoted in the Hesperian, February, 1839, p. 309.

apprehended, and messengers were then at the Indian towns to ascertain their purpose, and a second letter (we suppose the same above mentioned as dated April 21,) addressed to Capt. Cresap, informing him that the messengers had returned from the Indians: that "war was inevitable, and the country should be covered with scouts until the inhabitants could fortify themselves." Clark continues: "The reception of this letter was the epoch of open hostilities with the Indians. A new post was planted, a council was called, and the letter read by Cresap, all the Indian traders being summoned on so important an occasion. Action was had, and war declared in the most solemn manner: and the same evening two scalps were brought into the camp."

These were probably the scalps of friendly Indians, who had been despatched by William Butler, the Pittsburgh trader, to look after the cargo of the canoe, which the Cherokees had attacked. Ebenezer Zane, who was settled at Wheeling, has testified that he opposed the project of killing these Indians, but his good counsel was lost. The party, or some of them, went up the river. On being asked at their return, what had become of the Indians, they coolly answered that "they had fallen overboard into the river." The traders were brought back in safety, but Zane says that he examined the canoe, "found much blood and bullet holes," and inferred the tragic condition of affairs.

We resume Clark's narrative. "The next day some canoes of Indians were discovered on the river, keeping the advantage of an island to cover themselves from our view. They were chased fifteen miles down the river, and driven ashore; a battle ensued; a few were wounded on both sides: one Indian only taken prisoner. On examining their canoes, we found a considerable quantity of ammunition and other warlike stores.

On our return to camp, a resolution was adopted to march the next day, and attack Logan's camp on the Ohio, about thirty miles above us. We did march about five miles, and then halted to take some refreshment. Here the impropriety of executing the attempted enterprise was argued. The conversation was brought forward by Cresap himself. It was generally agreed that those Indians had no hostile intentions; as I myself and others present had been in their camp about four weeks past, on our descending the river from Pittsburg. In short, every person seemed to detest the resolution we had set out with. We returned in the evening, decamped, and took the road to Redstone."

We suppose that Col. Ebenezer Zane, in his statement, dated Feb. 4, 1800, alludes to the same affair as Clark here relates, in the following paragraph: "On the afternoon of the day this action (killing the two Indians above Wheeling) happened, a report prevailed that there was a camp of Indians on the Ohio, below or near the Wheeling. In consequence of this information, Captain Cresap with his party, joined by a number of recruits, proceeded immediately down the Ohio for the purpose, as was then generally understood, of destroying the Indians above mentioned. On the succeeding day, Captain Cresap and his party returned to Wheeling, and it was generally reported by the party that they had killed a number of Indians. Of the truth of this report I had no doubt, as one of Cresap's party was badly wounded, and the party had a fresh scalp, and a quantity of property, which they called Indian plunder. At the time of the last mentioned transaction, it was generally reported that the party of Indians down the Ohio, were Logan and his family, but I have reason to believe that this report was unfounded.

If we are correct in supposing that Clark and Zane refer

to the same transaction, Doddridge is an authority to the additional facts that the battle was fought at the mouth of Captina creek, at the southeast border of Belmont county, and that one of Cresap's party was severely wounded.[6]

"Two days afterwards," says Clark, or "within a few days," according to Zane and Doddridge, or on the 4th of May, according to a third account, occurred the tragedy opposite the mouth of Yellow creek. One Baker was settled on the Virginia side, and a party of thirty-two persons had gathered in the neighborhood. On the north, or Indian side of the Ohio, was an Indian encampment, from which a party of five men, one woman, (some accounts say two) and a little child crossed to Baker's. Here rum was offered them by the direction of Greathouse, and three of the men were made drunk. The other two men and the woman refused to drink and were shot down, while the intoxicated Indians were tomahawked. This was done by only five or six of Greathouse's party, the rest protesting against it as an atrocious murder, but not preventing the deed. The child, a very young female infant, was spared by the humanity of some one of the party.

The Indians in the camp at Yellow creek, hearing the firing at the house, sent a canoe with two men in it to inquire what had happened. These two Indians were both shot down as soon as they landed on the beach. A second and larger canoe was then manned with a number of Indians in arms; who, attempting to reach the shore some distance below the house, were received with a well directed fire from the party, which killed the greater number of them, and compelled the survivors to retire. A great number of shots were exchanged

6) Doddridge's Notes, p. 226. The subject is fully presented in the appendix to Jefferson's Notes.

across the river, but without damage to the white party, not one of whom was even wounded. The Indian men who were murdered were all scalped. The surviving Indians escaped down the river.

In the course of these bloody transactions, several relatives of Logan were killed—probably his brothers and a sister. His own language, in the earliest copy of his celebrated speech which is extant, was that "Col. Cresap cut off, in cold blood, all the relations of Logan, not sparing women and children;" but Jefferson's version reads, "not sparing *my* women and children."

It is related by Henry Jolly, many years associate judge of Washington county, Ohio, (whose narrative of the affair at Yellow creek we have partially adopted) that a short time before, in an Indian council, Logan had strongly recommended peace. He reminded the Indians of some aggressions on their own part, and that the only effect of hostilities would be that the "Long Knife," or Virginians, would come like the trees in the woods, and the Indians would be driven from the good lands they possessed. His advice was adopted, the hatchet grounded—when the fugitives from Yellow creek arrived with the appalling intelligence of the slaughter of his own relatives.[7]

Our first specific account of Logan's retaliation is as late as the 12th of July. Doubtless, in the six or eight weeks previous, efforts were making to renew the confederation of the Ohio Indians against the English. Loskiel mentions that the Delawares were urged by the Senecas and Shawanese to join in hostilities—but they refused, as a nation, to take up the hatchet. They were called *Shwonnoks*, or white people, in derision, greatly exasperating the young Delawares, many

7) See Appendix No. V, for further particulars of these massacres.

of whom probably fell into the war-path as volunteers. But even among the Shawanese there was a peace party. Their great chief, Cornstalk, was influential in saving the lives of some Pittsburgh traders from the fury of the Mingoes, and sent them in safety to their homes. It is said that Connolly, as if determined to precipitate a general war, attempted to seize the Shawanese Indians, three in number, who had escorted the traders through the wilderness, and when restrained by his uncle, Col. Croghan, sought to intercept them on their return, and that one was severely wounded by the whites. If so, all friendly dispositions would vanish of course. There is no doubt that before August had arrived, the Shawanese, and all the Mingo bands, were in the field, recruited by a few Delawares and Cherokees.

Logan was determined that his blow for vengeance should fall where it would produce the greatest consternation, and with a chosen band of eight warriors, he penetrated to the settlements on the head waters of the Monongahela, where many scalps and several prisoners were taken, with which, by the signal conduct of their chief, the party were enabled to elude pursuit and return in safety.

Among these prisoners was William Robinson, with whom Logan was very friendly during the journey to an Indian town near Dresden, on the Muskingum River—"speaking English well," as Robinson testifies in an affidavit annexed to Jefferson's Notes on Virginia. Arrived at the village, Logan made an extraordinary effort to save the life of Robinson. He spoke nearly an hour, and very eloquently; but the council was resolved to torture the prisoner. He was at length rescued, while bound at the stake—Logan cutting his thongs, throwing a belt of wampum around him, and leading him in safety to his wigwam, where he was adopted in place of a brother who was killed at Yellow creek.

About the 21st of July, Logan came to Robinson, and brought a piece of paper, and told him to write a letter for him. Some ink was prepared from gunpowder, and Logan dictated the following letter:

"CAPTAIN CRESAP:—What did you kill my people on Yellow creek for? The white people killed my kin at Conestoga, a great while ago; and I thought nothing of that. But you killed my kin again, on Yellow creek, and took my cousin prisoner. Then I thought I must kill too, and I have been three times to war since; but the Indians are not angry: only myself. CAPTAIN JOHN LOGAN."

This document was afterwards found tied to a war-club, in a house on the north fork of Holston creek, in Fincastle county, the family having been cut off by the Indians.[8]

While the war was thus carried to the heart of the Alleghany range, the Virginians, in their turn, gathered in July at Wheeling, descended the Ohio to the mouth of Captina, or as some say, Fish creek, and thence struck westwardly to the Indian town of Wappatomica, on the Muskingum. They were commanded by Col. McDonald, and baffling an attempt to surprise them, destroyed several villages, and returned with three chiefs as prisoners. This foray only added to the general irritation.

In August, the governor of Virginia determined to raise a large force and carry the war into the enemy's country. The plan of the expedition was soon arranged. Three complete regiments were to be raised west of the Blue Ridge, under the command of General Andrew Lewis, while an

8) American Pioneer, vol. i., pp. 7–24—an interesting compilation of facts in respect to Logan.

equal force from the interior should be commanded by Lord Dunmore in person. The armies were to form a junction at the mouth of the Great Kenhawa, and proceed together under Dunmore to the Indian towns in Ohio.

On the 1st of September, a part of General Lewis' division, consisting of two regiments under the orders of Col. Charles Lewis, his brother, and Col. William Fleming, of Botetourt, assembled at Camp Union, (now Lewisburgh, Va.) where they were joined by an independent regiment of backwoods volunteers, under the orders of Col. John Fields, a distinguished officer, who, together with most of those now assembled, had served under Braddock. Here they remained, awaiting the arrival of Col. Christian, who was busily engaged in collecting another regiment. By the junction of Field, Lewis' force amounted to about eleven hundred men, accustomed to danger, and conducted by the flower of the border officers. General Lewis, as well as his brother, had been present at Braddock's defeat, and were subaltern officers in two companies of Virginia riflemen, who formed the advance of the English army.

Having waited several days at Lewisburgh for Colonel Christian, without hearing from him, Gen. Lewis determined no longer to delay his advance. On the 11th of September he left Lewisburgh, and without any adventure of importance, arrived at the concerted place of rendezvous. Dunmore had not yet arrived, and Lewis remained several days in anxious expectation of his approach. At length he received dispatches from the governor, informing him that he had changed his plan, and had determined to move directly upon the Scioto villages, at the same time ordering Lewis to cross the Ohio and join him.

Although not much gratified at this sudden change of a

plan which had been deliberately formed, Lewis prepared to obey, and had issued directions for the construction of rafts, boats, &c., with which to cross the Ohio; when, on the morning of the 10th of October, two men were fired upon, while scouting about a mile and a half from the camp. One was killed, but the other escaped to the camp, bearing the alarm that a body of Indians was at hand.

General Andrew Lewis immediately ordered his brother, Col. Charles Lewis, with one hundred and fifty of the Augusta troops, to march to the right some distance from the Ohio, while Col. Fleming, with one hundred and fifty of the Botetourt, Bedford and Fincastle troops, was ordered to the bank of the Ohio on the left. Col. Charles Lewis had not marched half a mile, when, about sunrise, he was attacked by a large Indian force, and in "about the second of a minute," Col. Fleming's division was also engaged. The two commandants fell mortally wounded, and the Augusta or Lewis' division was forced to give way before the heavy fire of the enemy. The former were shortly reinforced by eight companies led by Col. Field, and the Indians retreated in turn, until the right wing was in line with Fleming's divission, who were still engaged on the bank of the Ohio. The action was fiercely contested. "The close underwood and many steep banks and logs, greatly favored the retreat of the Indians." The savages made the best use of these advantages, while small detachments were employed in throwing the dead into the Ohio River, and removing their wounded. The closing scenes of the engagement are thus described by a Virginia officer, whose letter from camp bears date October 17, 1774. "After twelve," he writes, "the action in a small degree abated, but continued, except at short intervals, sharp enough until after one o'clock. The long retreat of the Indians, gave them a most advantageous spot of ground, from whence it appeared to the officers so difficult to dislodge them, that it was thought most advisable to stand as the line was then formed, which was about a mile and a quarter in length, and had sustained a constant and equal weight of the action from wing to wing. A scattered fire continued until near sunset, and as soon as it was dark, the Indians effected a safe retreat.

Another letter (Staunton, Virginia, November 4, 1774,) says that Lewis' division retreated about a quarter of a mile. After the reinforcement, "they continued fighting until noon, and were never above twenty yards apart from the Indians, often within six and sometimes closer, tomahawking one another." "Our men," the writer adds, "got upwards of twenty scalps, eighty blankets, about forty guns, and a great many tomahawks."

The foregoing narrative of the battle of Point Pleasant, is derived from contemporary publications,[9] but the current version is somewhat different. It describes the battle as "raging until four o'clock in the afternoon, without any decisive result"—that the Indians were at length entrenched behind a breastwork of logs formed from one river to another, and enclosing the Virginians within the point, (*when* could it have been constructed without interruption from the adjacent camp?) and that the savages did not give way, until three companies under the command of Captain Evan Shelby,[10] had been detached by Gen. Lewis to ascend a small stream which empties into the Kenhawa a short distance above its mouth, and which at that time had high and

9) See letters in American Archives, fourth series, i., 808–18.

10) Father of Isaac Shelby, afterwards Governor of Kentucky, and then a lieutenant in his father's company.

bushy banks, and attack the Indians in the rear. All accounts agree that the latter withdrew during the night across the river, while the Virginians were indisposed to molest them.

It is a tradition of the border, that Logan, Cornstalk, Ellenipsico, Red Hawk and many other celebrated chiefs were present, and were often heard loudly encouraging their warriors. Cornstalk, the well known Shawanese chieftain, and leader of the allied forces, was particularly conspicuous. His voice rang above the din of the battle, "Be strong! Be strong!" and he is said to have buried his hatchet in the brain of a warrior, who exhibited a disposition of flight.

In this desperate conflict the Virginians lost half their commissioned officers and 52 men killed. It is not an unreasonable statement that the whole number of killed and wounded was one-fourth of the force engaged. The Indian loss is unknown, but 33 is the highest estimate of the number found dead on the field, and many were thrown into the river. One statement makes their loss in killed and wounded 233. The force on both sides was nearly equal—about eleven hundred.

Soon after the battle, three hundred Fincastle troops, under the command of Col. Christian, reached Point Pleasant, and the Virginians, eager with the purpose of revenging their deceased brethren, dashed across the Ohio, in obedience to Dunmore's orders, leaving a garrison at the scene of the late engagement.

Meanwhile, Lord Dunmore's division, about as numerous as that of General Lewis, had passed the mountains at the Potomac Gap, and came to the Ohio somewhere above Wheeling. About the 6th of October, a talk was had with the chiefs of the Six Nations and the Delawares, some of whom had been to the Shawanese towns on a mission of peace, but they reported unfavorably. Dunmore descended the Ohio to the mouth of the Hockhocking, where he ordered a block-house, called Fort Gower, to be erected. He was at this point when the battle at Point Pleasant occurred, and Abraham Thomas, late of Miami county, has stated that by laying his ear close to the surface of the river, on the day of the battle, he could distinctly hear the roar of musketry twenty-eight miles distant. Leaving a garrison with some stores at Fort Gower, Dunmore's army ascended the Hocking to the site of Logan, the present seat of Hocking county, where he left the stream and marched westward to the left bank of Sippo creek, about seven miles southeast of Circleville. Near this place he was met by a flag and a white man named Elliott, who bore a message of submission from the Shawanese chiefs. The governor complied with their request to send in an interpreter, with whom they could communicate, and ordered an encampment on Sippo creek. It was called Camp Charlotte, and was situated on the southwest quarter of section 12, township 10, range 21, upon a pleasant piece of ground, in view of the Pickaway plains. Another express was now started to intercept the march of General Lewis, but that gallant officer and his men were solicitous for another opportunity to attack the Shawanese, and they pressed forward in pursuit of the enemy, until, on the 24th of October, they encamped on the banks of the Congo creek, in Pickaway township, Pickaway county, within striking distance of the Indian towns. The principal Shawanese village stood where the village of Westfall is now situated, on the west bank of the Scioto, and on the Ohio canal, near the south line of Pickaway county. This was the head quarters of the confederated tribes, and was called Chillicothe, and because there were other towns either at that time or soon after, of the same name, it was known as *Old* Chillicothe.[11]

It was with the utmost difficulty that the Virginians could be restrained from falling upon the Indian towns. They were infuriated, not only by the border tragedies of the summer, but by the more recent carnage at Point Pleasant. They charged Dunmore with the design of forming an alliance with a confederacy of Indians to assist Great Britain against the colonies in the crisis of the revolution, which all foresaw. The dissatisfaction and disappointment with the negotiation for peace was almost a mutiny. Lewis, smarting with the death of his gallant brother, refused to obey the command for a halt. Dunmore went in person to enforce his orders, and drew his sword upon General Lewis, threatening him with instant death if he persisted in farther disobedience. Regarded historically, however, the conduct of the English governor in granting peace to a prostrate and supplicant enemy, cannot be blamed. The slaughter of the Indians, under such circumstances, would have been wanton massacre. Dunmore probably hastened a peace with the savages, from an anxiety to return to the sea-coast, where the stability of his government was already precarious, but beyond that there seems to be no reason to suspect sinister designs on his part.

On the opposite bank of Scioto, in the Indian town, there was now but one voice—peace at any cost. When Cornstalk returned from the battle of Point Pleasant, he called a council of the nation to consult what should be done, and upbraided them for not suffering him to make peace, as he is said to have desired, on the evening before the battle. "What," said he, "will you do now? The Big Knife is coming on

11) Whittlesey's Discourse, 1840, p. 24.

us, and we shall all be killed. Now you must fight or we are undone." But no one answering, he said, "then let us kill all our women and children and go and fight until we die." Still no answer was made; when, rising, he struck his tomahawk in a post of the council-house, and exclaimed, "I'll go and make peace," to which all the warriors grunted, "Ough! ough!" and the chiefs immediately followed the example of their great leader. The appearance and oratory of Cornstalk, when he appeared before Lord Dunmore, is thus described by Col. Wilson, one of the staff:

"When he arose, he was no wise confused or daunted, but spoke in a distinct and audible voice, without stammering or repetition, and with peculiar emphasis. His looks, while addressing Dunmore, were truly grand and majestic, yet graceful and attractive. I have heard many celebrated orators, but never one whose powers of delivery surpassed those of Cornstalk on this occasion."

As Dunmore approached the Scioto, the Indians had besought him to send an interpreter, and John Gibson was sent forward by Lord Dunmore. He has stated in an affidavit annexed to Jefferson's Notes, "that on his arrival at the towns, Logan, the Indian, came to where the deponent was sitting with the Cornstalk and the other chiefs of the Shawanese, and asked him to walk out with him; that they went into a copse of wood, where they sat down, when Logan, after shedding abundance of tears, delivered to him the speech, nearly as related by Mr. Jefferson in his notes on the State of Virginia; that he, the deponent, told him then that it was not Col. Cresap, who had murdered his relations, and that although his son, Capt. Michael Cresap, was with the party that killed a Shawanese chief and other Indians, yet he was not present when his relations were killed at Baker's, near the mouth of Yellow creek, on the Ohio; that this deponent, on his return to camp, delivered the speech to Lord Dunmore; and that the murders perpetrated as above were considered as ultimately the cause of the war of 1774, commonly called Cresap's war."

Of this speech or message, there are, besides that of Jefferson, two versions—one contained in a letter from Williamsburgh, Virginia, dated February 4, 1775, and preserved in the American Archives, volume 1, page 1020, and another, which was published in New York, on the 16th of February, as an extract of a letter from Virginia. Jefferson adopted the latter. Probably Gibson noted down the expressions of Logan, as uttered by him in his simple English, and on his return to Lord Dunmore's camp, the officers, in taking copies, may have modified an occasional expression. The different versions are presented for comparison:

WILLIAMSBUGH. (Feb. 4, 1775.)	NEW YORK. (Feb. 16, 1775.)	JEFFERSON. (1781–2.)
I appeal to any white man to say, that he ever entered Logan's cabin, but I gave him meat; that he ever came naked but I clothed him.	I appeal to any white man to say, if ever he entered Logan's cabin hungry, and I gave him not meat; if ever he came cold and naked, and I gave him not clothing.	I appeal to any white man to say, if ever he entered Logan's cabin hungry, and he gave him not meat; if ever he came cold and naked, and he clothed him not.
In the course of the last war, Logan remained in his cabin an advocate for peace. I had such an affection for the white people, that I was pointed at by the rest of my nation. I should have even lived with them, had it not been for Col. Cresap, who, last year, cut off in cold blood all the relations of Logan, not sparing women and children. There runs not a drop of my blood in the veins of any human creature. This called on me for revenge. I have sought it—I have killed many,	During the course of the last long and bloody war, Logan remained in his tent an advocate for peace. Nay, such was my love for the whites, that those of my own country pointed at me as they passed by, and said, "Logan is the friend of white men." I had even thought to live with you, but for the injuries of one man. Colonel Cresap, the last spring, in cool blood and unprovoked, cut off all the relations of Logan, not sparing even my women and children. There runs not a drop	During the course of the last long and bloody war, Logan remained idle in his cabin, an advocate for peace. Such was my love for the whites, that my countrymen pointed as they passed, and said, "Logan is the friend of white men." I had even thought to have lived with you, but for the injuries of one man. Colonel Cresap, the last spring, in cold blood and unprovoked, murdered all the relations of Logan, not even sparing my women and children. There runs not

and fully glutted my revenge. I am glad that there is a prospect of peace, on account of the nation; but I beg you will not entertain a thought that any thing I have said proceeds from fear! Logan disdains the thought. He will not turn on his heel to save his life. Who is there to mourn for Logan? No one.

of my blood in the veins of any human creature. This called on me for revenge. I have sought it. I have fully glutted my vengeance. For my country, I rejoice at the beams of peace. Yet, do not harbor the thought that mine is the joy of fear. Logan never felt fear. He will not turn on his heel to save his life. Who is there to mourn for Logan? Not one.

a drop of my blood in the veins of any living creature. This called on me for revenge. I have sought it. I have killed many. I have fully glutted my vengeance. For my country, I rejoice at the beams of peace. But do not harbor a thought that mine is the joy of fear. Logan never felt fear. He will not turn on his heel to save his life. Who is there to mourn for Logan? Not one.

Of this production, Jefferson says: "I may challenge the whole orations of Demosthenes and Cicero, and of any more eminent orator, if Europe has furnished any more eminent, to produce a single passage, superior to the speech of Logan, a Mingo chief, to Lord Dunmore when governor of Virginia." It was cited in refutation of the hypothesis, that the soil and climate of America tended to impair the vigor, mental and bodily, of the human race. Elsewhere he styles it a "morsel of eloquence." Certainly no specimen of the kind has been more widely circulated, or highly appreciated.

At the subsequent conference at Camp Charlotte, Logan did not attend, and the Mingoes were not parties to the peace there concluded, although their pledge to observe a peace had been communicated to Lord Dunmore. Little is known of this treaty, except that the Shawanese agreed not to hunt south of the Ohio, nor molest travelers. A strong block-house, strengthened with pickets, was erected at the mouth of the Kenawha, and a hundred men left as its garrison. Fort Dunmore or Pittsburgh, received a few troops—also Fort Fincastle at Wheeling. Lord Dunmore was to have returned to Pittsburgh in the spring, to meet the Indians, and form a definite peace, but the Revolutionary movements prevented. The army, which numbered about 2500 men, returned to Fort Gower, and thence proceeded to Western Virginia, where they were disbanded.

Of the future fate of Logan, we shall repeat all the evidence within our reach. Heckewelder, in a letter to Jefferson, thus speaks of him after the close of the war: "His expressions from time to time, denoted a deep melancholy. Life (said he) had become a torment to him: he knew no more what pleasure was; he thought it had been better if he had never existed. Report further states, that he became in some measure delirious, declared he would kill himself, went to Detroit, and on his way between that place and Miamis, was murdered. In October, 1781, (while as prisoner on my way to Detroit,) I was shown the spot where this should have happened."

Mr. Benjamin Sharp, in 1842 a resident of Warren county, Missouri, communicated to the "American Pioneer," a narrative of the capture of two of his sisters, with their husbands and families, by a band of British and Indians, at Riddle's station, on the Licking in Kentucky, some time in 1778. They were taken prisoners to Canada, but afterwards returned in safety at the close of the Revolutionary War. Mr. Sharp proceeds: "The celebrated Logan was with this party: my brother-in-law, Captain John Dunkin, an intelligent man, had several conversations with him on this trip. He said Logan spoke both English and French: he told Captain Dunkin that he knew he had two souls, the one good and the other bad; when the good soul had the ascendant, he was kind and humane; and when the bad soul ruled, he was perfectly savage, and delighted in nothing but blood and carnage. The account that Captain Dunkin gave of his death, was, that his brother-in-law killed him as they returned home from a council held at Detroit, on account of some misusage he had given his sister at the council."

Henry C. Brush, Esq., of Tiffin, Seneca county, has stated on the authority of Good Hunter, an aged and familiar acquaintance of Logan, that his last years were truly melancholy. He wandered about from tribe to tribe, a solitary and lonely man; dejected and broken hearted by the loss of his friends, and the decay of his tribe, he resorted to the stimulus of strong drink, to drown his sorrow. He was at last murdered in Michigan, near Detroit. He was, at the time, sitting with his blanket over his head, before a camp fire, his elbow resting on his knees, and his head upon his hands, buried in profound reflection, when an Indian, who had taken some offence, stole behind him, and buried his tomahawk in his brains.

Thus closed the mournful episode of the sorrows, the vengeance and the fate of Logan. Although his motive was personal—the paroxysm of private grief,—and therefore not so imposing as the patriotic impulse of a Pontiac or a Tecumseh, yet the appeal to our sympathies is irresistible; while the genius of Logan has irradiated the history of his race in the annals of the New World.

CHAPTER XVII.

THE RELATION OF THE WESTERN TRIBES TO THE REVOLUTIONARY CONTEST.

THERE is no passage in the history of the struggle between England and her American colonies, which suggests more impressively the special guidance and aid of Providence, than the relations of the Indian tribes. One familiar with the border wars of 1755 and 1763, would immediately anticipate a third combination of all the tribes against the inhabitants of the American frontier; and if so, while the Atlantic campaigns exhausted the resources of the colonies, the most disastrous consequences were more than probable. There can be no doubt that the British agents, even prior to the battle of Lexington, urged the Indians to side with them, and assist in subduing their rebellious children.

The first mention of the subject is in the address of the Massachusetts Congress to the Iroquois, in April, 1775, in which they say, that they hear the British are exciting the savages against the colonies, and they ask the Six Nations to aid the Americans or be neutral; and in June following, when James Wood visited the Western tribes, and invited them to a council, which he did under the direction of the Virginia House of Burgesses, he found that Governor Carleton had already offered the alliance of England.[1]

It is not surprising that both parties should estimate highly

1) Perkins' Western Annals, p. 153. American Archives, fourth series, iv., p. 110.

the military power of the savages, and their ability to turn the impending scale of the contest. At the Revolutionary period, Col. George Morgan supposed that the Indians of New York, Ohio, and the vicinity of the Lakes, could bring 10,000 warriors into the field, and if a general confederacy had been organized, the concurrence of attack—by the savage hordes on one side and the British armies on the other—might have been decisive of the result.

In their efforts to secure an Indian alliance, the English had many advantages. Although Sir William Johnson died suddenly in June, 1774, his son-in-law, Col Guy Johnson, had succeeded him as Superintendent. His influence, and that of Sir William's son and heir, John Johnson, were hostile to the colonies, and with them coöperated the celebrated Joseph Brant. Such powerful advocacy was seconded by liberal presents, and the English emissaries practiced with equal success the artful tactics by which the French effected the powerful combination of 1755, the first fruits of which was the defeat of Braddock. On the other hand, the Americans were poor and distressed to provide means for the army of Washington, and the Indians were prompt to perceive the disadvantageous contrast. Besides, the Americans were the immediate aggressors on the hunting domains of the savages, and their expulsion, with English aid, seemed practicable and in all respects desirable.

The battle of Lexington was fought on the 20th of June, 1775. In July, of that year, Col. Guy Johnson held a Congress at Oswego with thirteen hundred and forty warriors, and thenceforth all the Six Nations, except the Oneidas and Tuscaroras, were in close alliance with the British. Joseph Brant, at the head of his fierce Mohawks, was foremost in the league.

How was it in the valley of the Ohio? Dr. John Connolly, whose forcible occupation of Pittsburgh the year before we have noticed, determined to show his loyalty to the crown of England, by effecting a union of the northwestern Indians with British troops, and, leading them from Detroit, traverse the frontiers to eastern Virginia, where it was arranged that he should join Lord Dunmore. But Connolly, on his return from a visit to Gen. Gage at Boston, where this scheme was unquestionably concocted, was arrested at Hagarstown, Maryland, and detained a close prisoner until 1781. Thus, at the outset, the west was fortunate in its relief from the intrigues of an active and unscrupulous partizan of the British crown.[2]

Detroit soon became a centre of British influence, but it is a remarkable coincidence that the efforts of officers and agents stationed there to array the Indian tribes against the Americans, encountered an obstacle similar to the disagreement of the Oneidas and Tuscaroras to the confederacy of the New York tribes. A majority of the Delawares, and a numerous party of the Shawanese, were in favor of neutrality in the puzzling contest between the colonies and Great Britain. To strengthen, and, if possible, extend this disposition, Congress, in July, 1775, organized three Indian departments; a northern one, including the Six Nations and all north and east of them, to the charge of which Gen. Schuyler, Oliver Wolcott and three others were appointed; a middle department, including the western Indians, who were to be looked to by Messrs. Franklin, Henry and Wilson; and a southern department, including all the tribes south of Kentucky, over which commissioners were to preside under the appointment of the South Carolina Committee of Safety. The commis-

2) See Appendix No. VI, for further particulars of Connolly's scheme.

sioners were to keep a close watch upon the nations in their several departments, and upon the king's superintendents among them. These officers they were to seize, if they had reason to think them engaged in stirring up the natives against the colonies, and in all ways were to seek to keep them out of the contest. A series of conferences was held, and Heckewelder has preserved in his narrative a report of the talk at Pittsburgh in October or November, which the Delaware chiefs carried back to the Muskingum:[3]

"The commissioners, having first informed the chiefs that disputes had arisen between the king of England and the people of this country, and that their quarreling with each other, could not affect them in any wise, provided they did not interfere and take a part in it, they next proceeded to state the cause from whence the dispute had originated, calling the same a family dispute, a quarrel between a parent and his child, which they described as follows: 'Suppose a father had a little son whom he loved and indulged while young, but growing up to be a youth, began to think of having some help from him, and making up a small pack, he bid him carry it for him. The boy cheerfully takes this pack up, following his father with it. The father finding the boy willing and obedient, continues in this way; and as the boy grows stronger, so the father makes the pack in proportion larger,—yet as long as the boy is able to carry the pack, he does so without grumbling. At length, however, the boy having arrived at manhood, while the father is making up the pack for him, in comes a person of an evil disposition and learning who was to be the carrier of the pack, advises the father to make it heavier, for surely the son is able to carry a large pack. The father listening rather to the bad adviser,

3) Heckewelder's Narrative of Indian Missions, 136, *et seq.*

than his own judgment and the feelings of tenderness, follows the advice of the hard-hearted adviser, and makes up a heavy load for his son to carry. The son now grown up, examining the weight of the load he is to carry, addresses the parent in these words: 'Dear father, this pack is too heavy for me to carry, do pray lighten it; I am willing to do what I can, but am unable to carry *this* load.' The father's heart by this time having become hardened, and the bad adviser calling to him to whip him if he disobeys and refuses to carry the pack, now in a peremptory tone, orders his son to take up the pack and carry it off, or he will whip him; and already takes up a stick to beat him. 'So,' says the son, 'am I to be served thus, for not doing what I am unable to do? Well, if entreaties avail nothing with you, father, and it is to be decided by blows, whether I am able or not to carry a pack so heavy, then I have no other choice left me, but of resisting your unreasonable demand by my strength; and thus, by striking each other, learn who is the strongest.' " The foregoing parable was intended to make the colonial dispute clear to the savage pack-carriers, and was probably concocted by that adept in allegory, Benjamin Franklin. It was not unappreciated by those to whom it was directed.

This Pittsburg conference was attended by Delawares, Senecas, and a portion of the Shawanese. One of the Delaware chiefs, Captain White Eyes, boldly advocated the American cause, to the great annoyance of some Senecas, who were in the British interest, and had come to Pittsburg to induce the Delawares to follow the example of the New York tribes. These Seneca Indians reminded White Eyes, in a haughty tone, that the Delawares were subordinate to the Six Nations, when Captain White Eyes, (as reported by Heckewelder,) "long since tired of this language, with his usual spirit and an air of disdain, rose and said, 'he well knew that the Six Nations considered his nation as a conquered people, and their inferiors.' 'You say (said he) that you had conquered me,[4] that you had cut off my legs—had put a petticoat on me, giving me a hoe and cornpounder in my hands, saying, Now woman! your business henceforward shall be to plant and hoe corn, and pound the same for bread for us men and warriors. Look (continued White Eyes) at my legs; if as you say, you had cut them off, they have grown again to their proper size! the petticoat I have thrown away, and have put on my own proper dress! the corn hoe and pounder I have exchanged for these fire-arms, and I declare that I am a man.' Then waiving his hand in the direction of the Alleghany River, he exclaimed, 'and all the country on the other side of that river is *mine*.'"

This spirited declaration by White Eyes was seized as a pretext for a separation of the war party among the Delawares, who were mostly the Monsie or Wolf tribe. These, led by the Monsie chief, Newalike, and Captain Pipe, left the Muskingum, where the peace chiefs lived, and withdrew towards Lake Erie, into the more immediate vicinity of the English and their allies. The Delaware chiefs, who sustained White Eyes' course in the council, were, Netawatwes, who was deposed by Col. Bouquet because he refused to attend the conferences on Muskingum in 1764, and whose son and nephew had been recently converted to Christianity, Gelelemend or Killbuck, and Machingwi Puschiis or Big Cat and others, who (says Heckewelder,) did every thing in their power to preserve peace among the nations, by sending embassies, and exhorting them not to take up the hatchet, or to join

4) It must be remarked that the Indian orators always speak in the singular number, though meaning the nation.

either side, to which, however, the Sandusky Wyandots insolently replied, "that they advised their cousins, the Delawares, to keep good shoes in readiness to join the warriors." This message being returned to them by the Delaware council, with the admonition "to set down and reflect on the misery they had brought upon themselves by taking an active part in the late war between the English and the French," was also carried to the Wyandots near Detroit, but having been delivered by White Eyes in the presence of the English Governor, the latter treated the Delaware deputies with much indignity.

Another Delaware chief, whose influence was decidedly for peace, was Welapachtschiechen,[5] or Captain John. He was from the Hockhocking, and had been detained as a prisoner at Fort Pitt by Col. Bouquet, but in April, 1776, was converted to Christianity, and declined his chiefship.

Heckewelder enumerates the Christian Indians at the close of 1775, as four hundred and fourteen persons, and there is no doubt that we owe to their pacific principles and example, that the powerful Delaware tribe, with the exceptions already mentioned, were restrained from joining the hostile league, which soon embraced all the Ohio Indians, except a few Shawanese. It was the influence of a missionary, Kirkland, which concluded the treaty at German Flats on the 28th of June, 1775, by which the Oneidas and Tuscaroras gave to the Americans their pledge of neutrality;[6] and on the western border, it was a missionary, Zeisberger, who, by his timely colonization of the Muskingum in 1772,

5) Meaning "erect posture."

6) James Dean, the founder of Westmoreland, Oneida county, New York, no less than Samuel Kirkland, was influential in securing the friendship of the Oneidas. We have compiled (Appendix No. VII,) the allusions to his efforts and adventures, which occur in the American Archives, fourth series.

was indirectly influential, three years afterwards, in removing the keystone of a hostile league of all the tribes from the Cherokees to the Chippewas, against the struggling colonies. It is our firm belief, that if God had not placed those devoted messengers of the gospel in the interior of New York, and on the Muskingum of central Ohio, respectively, at the precise period, and in the precise circumstances of the case, that an indomitable host of Indian warriors would have penetrated to the heart of the Atlantic States, simultaneously with the lowest depression of the American army. At a later period, even the Delawares were swept into the vortex of hostilities, but fortunately the French alliance had then been consummated, invigorating the army and the country—the rumor of which was most potential upon the Indian tribes and European colonists of the Wabash, the Illinois, the Mississippi, and even the lakes.

If we mistake not, Samuel Kirkland sleeps in the valley of the Oriskany, and the grave of David Zeisberger is visible near the Muskingum—spots alike worthy of patriotic commemoration. Few who bore arms in the revolutionary struggle, contributed more than they to its fortunate progress and consummation.

Fortunately also for the United States, Col. George Morgan of Princeton, New Jersey, was appointed Indian agent for the middle department, with his headquarters at Pittsburgh, in April, 1776. He is described in Hildreth's Pioneer History, as "a man of unwearied activity, great perseverance, and familiar with the Indian manners and habits; having for several years had charge of a trading post in the Illinois, after that country was given up by the French, which was owned by a commercial house in Philadelphia. His frank manners, soldierly bearing, generosity, and, above all, his strict honesty in all his dealings with them, won their fullest confidence; and no white man was ever more highly esteemed than was Col. Morgan, by all the savages who had any intercourse with him. He was a native of Philadelphia, and at the time of his appointment, held the post of Colonel in the army of the United States." As we shall see hereafter, this praise is not exaggerated. The Delawares gave the name of Tamenend to Col. Morgan, which, according to Heckewelder, was the highest praise they could confer.

For nearly two years, the judicious and conciliatory course of Morgan prevented a general attack upon the frontier. It was a gloomy period, nevertheless, but marked by more apprehension of danger, than was in fact experienced. The friendly dispositions of the Delawares and some of the Shawanese and Wyandots, led them to advise the agent at Pittsburgh, of the hostile expeditions from the vicinity of Detroit and Lake Erie, and vigilant measures in abandoning or protecting an exposed situation, were usually successful. It was known that the British were making extraordinary efforts to mature a formidable Indian campaign, but the explosion yet lingered. Still there were not wanting instances of savage barbarity, which suggested measures of retribution, and in the spring of 1777, Patrick Henry, then governor of Virginia, had resolved to send an expedition under the command of Col. David Shepherd, and Maj. Henry Taylor, to invade the country west of the Ohio, and especially to chastise a mongrel band of Indians, only sixty or eighty in number, whose village on the head waters of the Scioto was called Pluggy's Town, from the name of their chief. Governor Henry, in a letter to Col. Morgan, dated March 12, 1777, was explicit in thus defining the destination of the party, which was to consist of three hundred men. The Wyandots were not yet in arms, though understood to be fully committed to Governor Hamilton of Detroit. But the agent at Pittsburgh, even then, was conscious that the utmost circumspection was requisite, or calamitous consequences would be precipitated, and, jointly with John Nevill, he replied in terms, of which an extract will forcibly indicate the feverish condition of the border. After assuring Gov. Henry that the most effectual measures to aid the expedition, if undertaken, should be pursued, Colonel Morgan and his colleague added:

"We nevertheless wish we were left more at liberty to exercise our judgments, or to take advice on the expediency and practicability of the undertaking at this critical time: for although we are persuaded, from what has already passed between Col. Morgan and our allies, the Delawares and Shawanese, that they would wish us success therein; yet we apprehend the inevitable consequences of this expedition will be a general Indian war, which we are persuaded it is the interest of the State at this time to avoid, even by the mortifying means of liberal donations to certain leading men among the nations, as well as by calling them again to a general treaty. And if the State of Pennsylvania should judge it prudent to take some steps to gratify the Six Nations in regard to the encroachments made on their lands on the northwestern frontier of that State, of which they have so repeatedly complained, we hope and believe it would have a salutary effect. The settlement of the lands on the Ohio, below the Kenhawa and at Kentucky, gives the western nations great uneasiness. How far the State of Virginia may judge it wise to withdraw or confine those settlements for a certain term of years or during the British war, is too delicate a matter for us to give an opinion; but we have reason to think that the measures we have (though perhaps out of the strict line of our duty) presumed to hint at, would not only tend greatly to the happiness of this country, but to the interest of the whole State; more especially if measures can be taken to treat the different nations in all respects with justice, humanity, and hospitality; for which purpose, and to punish robberies and murders committed on any of our allies, some wholesome orders or acts of government may possibly be necessary; for parties have been formed to massacre some who have come to visit us in a friendly manner, and others who have been hunting on their own lands, the known friends to the commonwealth. These steps, if continued, will deprive us of all our Indian allies, and multiply our enemies. Even the spies who have been employed by the county-lieutenants of Monongahela and Ohio, seem to have gone on this plan, with a premeditated design to involve us in a general Indian war; for on the 13th of March, at day-break, five or six of these spies fired on three Delaware Indians on this side the Delaware town, between that and Wheeling, and out of the country or track of our enemies. Luckily all the Indians escaped, only one of them was wounded, and that slightly in the wrist."

Col. Morgan, in the same letter, anticipates no attack from Detroit or Sandusky, there being no garrison at the latter place, and but sixty-six soldiers at Detroit, from whence by land to Fort Pitt is near three hundred miles, impassable by artillery, and all that country (he is) told could not furnish to an enemy of one thousand men, sufficient provisions or horses, for such an expedition.

If the Shawanese, or any portion of the tribe, were disposed to be allies of the Americans, as Morgan intimates, an event soon occurred, which extinguished any such sentiment. The revolutionary annals of the Ohio valley have many dark stains, but none of deeper dye than the massacre of the heroic Cornstalk. That magnanimous chief, after the treaty of 1774 with Dunmore, had been the steadfast friend of neutrality among the belligerent whites. Perhaps he had the sagacity to perceive that the future of his race could not be altered by any issue of the controversy—that the rapacity of Europeans, not of a party, was the proper object of patriotic dread. In the spring of 1777, Cornstalk, accompanied by Red Hawk (the reader will remember the Shawanese orator at the council held by Col. Bouquet, in 1764,) came on a friendly visit to the fort at Point Pleasant, communicated the hostile disposition among the Ohio tribes, and expressed his sorrow that the Shawanese nation, except himself and his tribe, were determined to espouse the British side, and his apprehension that he and his people would be compelled to go with the stream, unless the Long Knives could protect them.

Upon receiving this information, the commander of the garrison, Captain Arbuckle, seized upon Cornstalk and his companion as hostages for the peaceful conduct of his nation, and set about availing himself of the advantage he had gained by his suggestions. During his captivity, Cornstalk held frequent conversations with the officers, and took pleasure in describing to them the geography of the west, then little known. One afternoon, while he was engaged in drawing on the floor a map of the Missouri territory, its water courses and mountains, a halloo was heard from the forest, which he recognized as the voice of his son, Ellinipsico, a young warrior, whose courage and address were almost as celebrated as his own. Ellinipsico entered the fort and embraced his father most affectionately, having been uneasy at his long absence, and come hither in search of him.

The day after his arrival, two men belonging to the fort, whose names were Hamilton and Gilmore, crossed the Kenhawa, intending to hunt in the woods beyond it. On their return from hunting, some Indians, who had come to view the position at the Point, concealed themselves in the weeds near the mouth of the Kenhawa, and killed Gilmore while endeavoring to pass them. Col. Stewart (who was at the post in the character of a volunteer) was standing on the opposite bank of the river at the time, and was surprised that a gun had been fired so near the fort in violation of orders.

Hamilton ran down the bank, and cried out that Gilmore was killed. Captain Hall commanded the company to which Gilmore belonged. His men leaped into a canoe and hastened to the relief of Hamilton. They brought the body of Gilmore, weltering in blood and the head scalped, across the river. The canoe had scarcely reached the shore, when the cry was raised, "Kill the red dogs in the fort!" Captain Hall placed himself in front of his soldiers, and they ascended the river's bank, pale with rage, and carrying their loaded firelocks in their hands. Colonel Stewart and Captain Arbuckle exerted themselves in vain to dissuade the men, exasperated to madness by the spectacle of Gilmore's corpse, from the cruel deed which they contemplated. They cocked their guns, threatening those gentlemen with instant death if they did not desist, and rushed into the fort.

The interpreter's wife, who had been a captive among the Indians, and felt an affection for them, ran to their cabin and informed them that Hall's soldiers were advancing, with the intention of taking their lives, because they believed that the Indians who killed Gilmore had come with Cornstalk's son on the preceding day. This the young man solemnly denied, declaring that he had come alone, and with the sole object of seeking his father. When the soldiers came within hearing, the young warrior appeared agitated. Cornstalk encouraged him to meet his fate composedly, and said to him, "My son, the Great Spirit has sent you here that we may die together." He turned to meet his murderers the next instant, and receiving seven bullets in his body, expired without a groan.

When Cornstalk had fallen, Ellinipsico continued still and passive, not even raising himself from his seat. He met death in that position with the utmost calmness. The Red Hawk made an attempt to climb the chimney, but fell by the fire of some of Hall's men.

The day before his death, Cornstalk had been present at a council of the officers, and had spoken to them on the subject of the war, with his own peculiar eloquence. In the course of his remarks, he expressed something like a presentiment of his fate; "When I was young," he said, "and went out to war, I often thought each would be my last adventure, and I should return no more. I still lived. Now I am in the midst of you, and if you choose, you may kill me. I can die but once. It is alike to me whether now or hereafter."

His atrocious murder was dearly expiated. The warlike Shawanese were thenceforth the foremost in excursions upon the frontier, particularly the scattered and exposed stations of Kentucky.

CHAPTER XVIII.

BORDER WAR OF THE REVOLUTION.

WE have forborne, with some effort of self-denial, to enlarge upon the early explorations and occupation of Kentucky by the whites. We have paused on the margin of the Ohio as the boundary of our subject, as well as of the state whose introductory annals constitute our special theme; but with a full consciousness of the fascinating interest which invests pioneer life in Kentucky. The solitary wanderings of Boone and Kenton as early as 1769, in the valleys of the Kentucky and Licking, where immense herds of buffalo sought the Saline springs—the adventures of Knox and his band of forty hunters who crossed the Appalachian chain in 1770, and explored the wild and broken region lying upon the northern boundaries of Tennessee—Boone's repulse by the Indians, when, in 1773, he attempted to remove five families besides his own, from the Yadkin in North Carolina to the banks of the Kentucky—the settlements of the McAfees, Thomas Bullett, Hancock, Taylor, James Douglas, Colonel Floyd and others also in 1773—the foundation of Harrodsburg by the solitary log cabin of James Harrod in 1774—the claim of Richard Henderson to the lands lying between the Kentucky and Cumberland Rivers, by a grant from the Cherokee Indians, and under which, notwithstanding the protest of Virginia afterwards successfully enforced, the colony of Transylvania was organized on the 23d of May, 1775—the arrival of four American women, Mrs. Boone, Mrs.

McGary, Mrs. Denton, and Mrs. Hogan, at Boonesborough in September, 1775—the rapid increase of emigration thenceforth—the appointment of George Rogers Clark, and one Gabriel Jones, in June, 1776, at a little Congress assembled in Boonesborough, to represent Kentucky in the Assembly of Virginia—at length, after a year's suspense and apprehension, excited by occasional outbreaks of Indian hostility, the frightful scenes of 1777, when the Shawanese once more, as in 1774, ravaged the settlements:—this succession of events, although of thrilling interest, we must dismiss with the most cursory allusion.

As we have said, the murder of Cornstalk terminated all uncertainty, and precipitated the savages over the Kentucky and Virginia border. At the close of 1777, only three settlements existed in the interior of Kentucky—Harrodsburg, Boonesborough and Logan's—and of these three, the whole military population, did not exceed one hundred and two in number. It was a year of siege, of struggle, of suffering—but the gloomy months elicited some extraordinary instances of heroism and humanity. We read of James Ray, a lad of sixteen, loading an old horse with the game which he shot by day, remote from Harrodsburg, and silently stealing into the besieged fort at night, whence, however, he would again emerge before the next dawn, thus for weeks saving the distressed garrison from starvation—of Benjamin Logan, breaking from the shelter of a block house, into a tempest of rifle balls, to rescue a wounded comrade who had been surprised by an ambush of savages: and of a journey of four hundred miles, through a wilderness swarming with war parties of Indians, and across the mountains to the settlements, to obtain ammunition for his beleaguered companions, successfully accomplishing his hazardous errand. Such, and similar occurrences, which tradition fondly cherishes, are the romance of history.

The month of September witnessed the siege of Wheeling. Here, where the Zanes had settled in 1770, Fort Fincastle (so called from the western county of Virginia,) was established by Lord Dunmore in 1774. The name was changed in 1776, to Fort Henry, in honor of Patrick Henry, then Governor of Virginia, and this fort was the central point between Fort Pitt and the stockade at the mouth of Kenhawa. In the early autumn of 1777, Colonel Hand, who commanded at Fort Pitt, was informed that a large body of the northwestern Indians was preparing to attack the posts of the Upper Ohio. On the evening of September 26, smoke was seen by those near Wheeling, down the river, and was supposed to proceed from the burning of the block house at Grave Creek, and the people of the vicinity, taking the alarm, repaired to the fort. Here were assembled forty-two fighting men, well supplied with rifles and muskets, but with a scanty supply of gunpowder. Early on the 27th, two men, who were sent out for horses, for the purpose of alarming neighboring settlements, and had proceeded some distance from the fort, met a party of six savages, by whom one of them was shot. The commandant, Col. Shepherd, learning from the survivor, that there were but six of the assailants, sent a party of fifteen men in pursuit. These were led into an ambush, where, completely surrounded, all but three were killed. Still another band of thirteen men rushed from the fort to the assistance of their comrades, and shared their fate. It was now sunrise, and four hundred Indians, led by Simon Girty, soon invested the fort, which was defended by only twelve men and boys.

Fort Henry stood immediately upon the bank of the Ohio,

about a quarter of a mile above the mouth of Wheeling creek. Between it and the steep river hill on the east, were twenty or thirty log huts, which the Indians occupied, and challenged the garrison to surrender. Colonel Shepherd refused, and the attack commenced. From sunrise until noon, the fire on both sides was constant, when that of the assailants slackened. Within the fort, the only alarm was for the want of powder, and then it was remembered that a keg was concealed in the house of Ebenezer Zane, some sixty yards distant. It was determined to make an effort to obtain it, and the question, "Who will go?" was proposed. Then occurred an incident which is related as follows by Mr. G. S. McKiernan, in the American Pioneer:[1]

"At this crisis, a young lady, the sister of Ebenezer and Silas Zane, came forward and desired that she might be permitted to execute the service. This proposition seemed so extravagant that it met with a peremptory refusal; but she instantly renewed her petition in terms of redoubled earnestness, and all the remonstrances of the Colonel and her relatives failed to dissuade her from her heroic purpose. It was finally represented to her that either of the young men, on account of his superior fleetness and familiarity with scenes of danger, would be more likely than herself to do the work successfully. She replied that the danger which would attend the enterprise was the identical reason that induced her to offer her services, for, as the garrison was very weak, no soldier's life should be placed in needless jeopardy, and that if she were to fall her loss would not be felt. Her petition was ultimately granted, and the gate opened for her to pass out. The opening of the gate arrested the attention of several Indians who were straggling through

1) Vol. ii., p. 309.

the village. It was noticed that their eyes were upon her as she crossed the open space to reach her brother's house; but seized, perhaps, with a sudden freak of clemency, or believing that a woman's life was not worth a load of gunpowder, or influenced by some other unexplained motive, they permitted her to pass without molestation. When she reäppeared with the powder in her arms, the Indians, suspecting, no doubt, the character of her burden, elevated their firelocks and discharged a volley at her as she swiftly glided towards the gate; but the balls all flew wide of the mark, and the fearless girl reached the fort in safety with her prize. The pages of history may furnish a parallel to the noble exploit of Elizabeth Zane, but an instance of greater self-devotion and moral intrepidity is not to be found anywhere."[2]

The assault was resumed with much fierceness, and continued until evening. A party of eighteen or twenty Indians, armed with rails and billets of wood, rushed forward and attempted to force open the gate of the fort, but were repulsed with the loss of six or eight of their number. As darkness set in, the fire of the savages grew weaker, though it was not entirely discontinued until next morning. Soon after nightfall, a considerable party of Indians advanced within sixty yards of the fort, bringing with them a hollow maple log, which they had converted into a cannon by plugging up one of its ends with a block of wood. To give it additional strength, a quantity of chains, taken from a blacksmith's shop, encompassed it from end to end. It was heavily charged with powder, and then filled to the muzzle with

2) "Elizabeth Zane afterwards lived about two miles above Bridgeport, on the Ohio side of the river, near Martinsville, in Belmont county. She was twice married—first to Mr. McLaughlin, and, secondly, to Mr. Clark." —*Howe's Ohio Historical Collections*, 61.

pieces of stones, slugs of iron, and such other hard substances as could be found. The cannon was graduated carefully to discharge its contents against the gate of the fort. When the match was applied, it burst into many fragments, and although it made no effect upon the fort, it killed and wounded several of the Indians who stood by to witness its discharge. A loud yell succeeded the failure of this experiment, and the crowd dispersed.

Late in the evening, Francis Duke, a son-in-law of Col. Shepherd, arrived from the forks of Wheeling, and was shot down by the Indians before he could reach the gate of the fort. Early next morning, Col. Swearingen, with fourteen men from Cross creek, and Major Samuel McCullough, with forty mounted men from Short creek, succeeded in reaching the inclosure, except Major McCullough himself, who was not permitted to pass the gateway. After a perilous pursuit, Putnam-like, he baffled the Indians, by dashing his horse down an almost perpendicular precipice of one hundred and fifty feet descent, with Wheeling creek at its base, and so made his escape.

After the escape of Major McCullough, the Indians concentrated at the foot of the hill, and soon after set fire to all the houses and fences outside of the fort, and killed about three hundred head of cattle belonging to the settlers. They then raised the siege and disappeared.

This band were principally Wyandots, with some Mingoes and Shawanese, and their loss is estimated at from sixty to one hundred. The total number of Americans killed was twenty-six, and four or five were wounded. During the investiture of the fort, not a man within the walls was killed, and only one slightly wounded.

This attack upon Fort Henry indicates decisively that the

Wyandots, Ottawas, Mingoes and Shawanese were engaged in open hostilities against the Americans in the autumn of 1777; and about the same time, the Delawares began to waver in their resolution to observe a neutrality. A report was circulated that Col. Hand, who had recently been appointed to the command at Pittsburgh, was about to march, with a body of American troops, to attack Goschocking, the Delaware town at the forks of the Muskingum. Captain Pike's party was immediately on the alert, and he declared that he would join the Wyandots to repel the Americans. Very soon, however, friendly speeches were received from the commandant at Pittsburgh and Col. Morgan, assuring the Delawares that they had nothing to fear. Notwithstanding these assurances, the American officers were unable to restrain a party of freebooters from the Ohio settlements, who were proceeding in October to destroy the Delaware towns, when they were encountered by a party of Wyandots, and defeated with great slaughter. It can be readily conceived that such an outrage would exasperate the Delawares and make it almost impossible to prevent an offensive alliance with the Wyandots and Shawanese. The war-party increased daily. During the winter of 1777–8, Alexander McKee, Matthew Elliott and Simon Girty[3] made their appearance in

3) These names will occur so frequently that some other than incidental notice of them may be expected.

Alexander McKee had been an Indian agent of the British government; and, when here mentioned, had been permitted to go at large on parol, which he forfeited by leaving Pittsburgh at this time.

Mathew Elliott was an Indian trader, and we first hear of him in 1774, as an envoy to Lord Dunmore from the submissive Shawanese. He continued to traverse the Indian country as a trader, but after the war between England and the colonies, he received a commission as a British captain. He concealed this fact, however, and was once taken prisoner by a party of Sandusky warriors, but was of course liberated at Detroit. On his return to Pittsburgh he endeavored to deceive the inhabitants and authorities with

the Muskingum towns, with the false intelligence that the English were completely victorious, and that the Americans, driven to the westward, were about to wage an indiscriminate war against the Indians. This redoubled the activity of Captain Pipe, and great consternation prevailed among the Delawares. The peace-chief, White Eyes, saw, with much concern, that an overwhelming majority of his nation, under the influence of McKee and his associates, were resolved upon war, but he did not lose his self-possession. Knowing that his conduct was closely watched by his astute rival, Captain Pipe, White Eyes called a general council of the nation, in which, when assembled, he proposed to delay hostilities against the Americans for ten days, in order to obtain further information, either from Tamenend, (Col. Morgan) Col. Gibson, or some other friend. Pipe, thinking that the

regard to his real character, by boasting of his ingenuity in having procured his liberation from the British. In the winter of 1777, McKee and Elliott seemed to have absconded from Pittsburgh, and were thenceforth the avowed emissaries of the British, as we find above.

There were three Girtys—Simon, George and James. They were taken prisoners from Pennsylvania about 1755, and adopted into different tribes. Simon became a Seneca; and, although a white savage, was not incapable of humane conduct, and was scrupulously exact in the redemption of his word. James was adopted by the Shawanese, and seems to have been an unmitigated monster. George was adopted by the Delawares, and belonged to that small fragment of the tribes who were constantly engaged in the campaigns against the settlements. The trio were desperate drunkards.

Early in the Revolutionary struggle, the Girtys, like their Indian brethren, were undecided how to act. Even in the summer of 1777, James Girty was the medium of speeches and presents from the Americans, to atone for the murder of Cornstalk; while Simon Girty acted as interpreter for the United States on many occasions. About 1777, however, both brothers had been seduced by the British emissaries, and are known to border tradition as renegades. This is hardly just. They should not be regarded otherwise than as Indians of their respective tribes. Such had been their training—their education. They were white savages—nothing else—and the active partizans of Great Britain for the rest of the century.

moment had arrived to destroy the influence of White Eyes, or "place him in the back ground," as Heckewelder expresses it, summoned the warriors together, and proposed "to declare every man an enemy to the nation who should throw an obstacle in the way that might tend to prevent the taking up arms against the American people." White Eyes, seeing the blow aimed against himself, once more assembled his men and told them, "That if they meant in earnest to go out, (as he observed some of them were preparing to do) they should not go without him. He had taken peace measures in order to save the nation from utter destruction. But if they believed that he was in the wrong, and gave more credit to vagabond fugitives, whom he knew to be such, than to himself, who was best acquainted with the real state of things—if they had determined to follow their advice, and go out against the Americans, he would go out with them, but not like the hear hunter, who sets the dogs on the animal to be beaten about with his paws while he keeps at a safe distance. No! he would himself lead them on, place himself in the front, and be the *first* who should fall. They only had to determine what they meant to do, for his own mind was fully made up not to survive the nation; and he would not spend the remainder of a miserable life in bewailing the total destruction of a brave people who deserved a better fate."

This spirited address of White Eyes had the desired effect; all declared that they would wait until the ten days were expired, and many added that they never would go to war against the American people unless they had him for a leader.

It so happened that our old friend, John Heckewelder, had been dispatched in February, 1778, by the Moravians of Bethlehem, with instructions to repair to Pittsburgh, and, if possible, to the Muskingum, and ascertain the condition and prospects of the Ohio missionaries and their flocks. He bore a passport from Henry Laurens, the President of Congress, and, upon his arrival at Pittsburgh, found the officer in command, Col. Hand, and the Indian agent, Col. Morgan, extremely solicitous lest the machinations of McKee, Elliott and Girty should result in the total alienation of the Delawares. They had sought in vain for a trusty messenger to bear their pacific messages—the risk of death from the numerous war parties of Indians being so imminent. The devoted Heckewelder, "after due consideration during a night," determined to undertake the hazardous journey. He was accompanied, he says, "by a white man, brother John Shabosch, who had married an Indian sister, and whose family resided at Gnadenhutten." We shall continue the narrative of their subsequent adventures in the words of Heckewelder himself:

"Accordingly, in the morning," as his narrative proceeds, "we made known our resolution to Cols. Hand and Gibson, whose best wishes for our success we were assured of, and leaving our baggage behind, and turning a deaf ear to all entreaties of well-meaning friends, who considered us lost if we went, we crossed the Alleghany River, and at eleven o'clock in the night, after the third day, reached Gnadenhutten, after having several times narrowly escaped falling in with war-parties. Indeed, in one instance, we were encamped on the Big Beaver, near its mouth, when a party of warriors in that very night were murdering people on Raccoon creek, not many miles distant from where we were, though we were ignorant of the circumstances at that time. We had traveled all day and night, only leaving our horses time to feed. We crossed the Big Beaver, which had overflowed its banks, on a raft we had made of poles. Other large creeks on the way we swam with our horses—never attempting to kindle a fire, fearing lest we might be discovered by the warriors perceiving the smoke. When arrived within a few miles of Gnadenhutten, we distinctly heard the beat of a drum, and on drawing near, the war-song of an Indian party: all which being in the direction of the town, we naturally concluded that the Christian Indians must have moved off; wherefore we proceeded with caution, lest we should fall into the hands of the warriors. However, the people still there informed us that the war-party consisted of Wyandots from Sandusky, who arrived that evening, and were encamped on the bluff two miles below the town, on the opposite side of the river; and who probably would the next morning travel along the path we had just come.

"Fatigued as we were, after our journey, and without one hour of sound sleep, I was now requested by the inhabitants of Gnadenhutten, to proceed immediately to Goschoching, about thirty miles distant. At that place, all was trouble and confusion; and many were preparing to go off to fight the American people, in consequence of the advice given them by McKee, Elliott and Girty; who had told them that the Americans were embodying themselves at this time, for the purpose of killing every Indian they should meet with, be he friend or foe. We were further informed that Captain White Eyes had been threatened with death, if he persisted in vindicating the character of the American people: many believing the stories propagated by McKee and his associates, had, in consequence already shaved their heads, ready to lay on the war-plume, and turn out to war, as soon as the ten days, which White Eyes had desired them to wait, should have expired; and to-morrow being the ninth day, and no message having arrived from their friends at Pittsburgh, they were now preparing to go; and further, that this place, Gnadenhutten was now breaking up, and its inhabitants were to join the congregation at Lichtenan: they having been assured that they were not safe, even for one day, from an attack by the Americans, while they remained here. Finding the matter so very urgent, and admitting of not even a day's delay, I consented to proceed. After enjoying a few hours' repose, and furnished with a trusty companion and a fresh horse, between three and four in the evening, the national assistant, John Martin, being called on for the purpose, we sat out, swimming our horses across the Muskingum River, and taking a circuit through the woods, in order to avoid the encampment of the war party, which was close to our path. Arriving about ten o'clock in the forenoon, within sight of Goschoching, a few yells were given by a person who had discovered us, to notify the inhabitants that a white man was coming. This immediately drew the whole body of the Indians into the street; but although I saluted them in passing, not a single person returned the compliment; which, as my conductor observed, was no good omen. Even Captain White Eyes and the other chiefs, who had always befriended me, now stepped back, when I reached out my hand to them. This strange conduct would have disheartened me, had I not observed among the crowd, some men well known to me as spies of Captain Pipe, watching the actions of these peace-chiefs. I was therefore satisfied, that they were acting from policy, and not from any ill will against me personally. Indeed, on looking round, I thought I could read joy in the countenances of many of them, on seeing me among them at so critical a juncture, when they had been told but a few days before, that nothing short of their destruction had been determined upon by the long knives (the Virginians or American people.) Yet as no one would reach out his hand to me, I inquired into the cause: when Captain White Eyes, boldly stepping forward, replied: 'That by what had been told them by McKee and his party, they no longer had a single friend among the American people: if, therefore, this be so, they must consider every white man who came to them from that side as an enemy, who came but to deceive them, and to put them off their guard, in order to give an enemy an opportunity to take them by surprise.' I replied that the imputation was unfounded, and that were I not their friend, they would have never seen me here. 'Then,' continued White Eyes, 'will you tell us the truth with regard to what I ask?' On my having assured him of this, he asked me: 'Are the American armies all cut to pieces by the English troops? Is General Washington killed? Is there no more a Congress; and have the English hung some of them, and taken the rest to England to hang them there? Is the whole country beyond the mountains in the possession of the English; and are the few thousand Americans, who have escaped them, now embodying themselves on this side of the mountains for the purpose of killing all the Indians in this country, even our women and children? Now do not deceive us, but speak the truth; is all this true that I have been saying to you?'

"I declared before the whole assembly, that not one word of what he had just now told me was true; and held out to him, as I had done before, the friendly speeches sent for them by me; which he however refused to accept, probably from prudential considerations. I thought by the countenances of most of the bystanders, that the moment bade fair for their listening at least to the contents of these speeches, and accidentally catching the drummer's eye, I called to him to beat the drum for the assembly to meet, for the purpose of hearing what their American brethren had to say to them. There was a general smile of approbation; and White Eyes, thinking the favorable moment had arrived, asked the assembly, 'Shall we, my friends and relations, listen once more to those who call us their brethren?' The question was answered almost by acclamation: the drum was beat, and the whole body repaired to the council house. The speeches, all of which were of the most pacific nature, were read and interpreted to them: when Captain White Eyes rose, and in a long address, took particular notice of the good disposition of the American people towards the Indians; observing that they had never as yet called on them to fight the English, knowing that wars were destructive to nations; and that they (the Americans) had, from the beginning of the war to the present time, always advised the Indians to remain quiet, and not to take up the hatchet against either side. A newspaper containing the capitulation of General Burgoyne's army, being found enclosed in the packet, White Eyes again rose, and holding the paper unfolded with both his hands, so that all could have a view of it, said, 'See, my friends and relatives, this document contains great events; not the song of a bird, but the truth.' Then stepping up to me, he gave me his hand; saying, 'you are welcome with us, brother.' Every one present immediately followed his example."

But for the expedition of Heckewelder, and the foregoing interview, the spring of 1778 would have inevitably recruited the Indian allies of Great Britain with the Delawares of Ohio. It is interesting, also, to mark the reverberation of the victory at Saratoga (its date was October 17, 1777,) in the western wilderness. The surrender of Burgoyne, which, in the old world, led to the recognition of American Independence by France, and the presentiment in England that the colonies were lost, was not without its salutary influence upon the savage denizens of the Ohio and the other tributaries of the mighty Mississippi.

The affair at Saratoga was of some use to the Indian agent at Pittsburgh. The Spanish Governor of Louisiana, addressed a letter written in his own language, to Colonel Morgan, which was dated August 9th, 1777, but only received "by due course," on the 24th of February, 1778. Unluckily, the agent knew no Spanish, and on forwarding it to Congress, not a member of that honorable body could read it, nor (as the Colonel reluctantly confessed in his reply) could any person be found capable and worthy of trust to translate it. As it was, Col. Morgan replied to Don Bernardo de Galvez in sturdy English, detailing with much patriotic unction, what White Eyes had justly denominated the "great event" of Burgoyne's surrender.

CHAPTER XIX.

THE CONQUEST OF ILLINOIS BY GEORGE ROGERS CLARK. INDIAN SIEGES OF FORT LAURENS.

During the years 1777-8 the conviction had been forced upon Congress, that Detroit must be taken, or the English governor of that post checked in some manner, or a heavy blow would fall upon the colonial cause from the depths of the Western wilderness, which, in connection with the pressure of the seaboard might be fatal to the United States. Early in the spring of 1778, preparations for an invasion of the enemy's territory were commenced. Col. Morgan was instructed to make an estimate of the quantity of provisions necessary for the support of three thousand men for three months. "The stock to be laid in amounted to 610,000 lbs. of flour, 732,000 lbs. beef, requiring 3,812 horses for the transport of the flour, and 2,440 head of cattle, which were to be driven on foot and slaughtered as needed. It also required 136 horses to transport the single article of salt. The food for the horses and cattle was to be chiefly furnished by the native growth of grass, vines, &c., found in abundance at that day during the summer months on the rich lands of the West. The whole expense of this expedition was estimated at $609,538. The cattle cost at that time £10, or $33.33 a head: the horses cost £25, or $83.25 each. Flour was fifty shillings a hundred, or sixpence a pound, equal to sixteen dollars a barrel. The price of a common woodman's axe was thirty shillings, or five dollars, and the price of a pack saddle was the same. Salt was six pounds a bushel or twenty dollars. These were specie prices, not estimated in a depreciated currency."[1]

A similar division of the army of invasion was proposed, as was made by Dunmore in 1774. Fifteen hundred men were to march through Green Briar, down the Big Kenawha to Fort Randolph, at the junction with the Ohio, and the same force was to assemble at Fort Pitt and descend the Ohio to that post. In fact, the former detachment was never levied, and Gen. McIntosh, who was appointed to the command of the expedition, had never a greater force than fifteen hundred men, if so many. In the spring of 1778, he crossed the mountains with a body of five hundred troops. Soon after, he built a fort which bore his name, on the alluvian plain near the mouth of Big Beaver, intended to cover any excursion into the Indian country. It was a regular stockade, with four bastions, each mounted with a six-pounder.

The summer wore away, and on the 17th of September, a council with the Delawares was held at Pittsburg, and their consent to march through their territory obtained. Of this conference, Col. Morgan, who was absent at Philadelphia when it was held, says in a letter written soon afterwards: "There never was a conference with the Indians so improperly or so villainously conducted as the late one at Pittsburg." The assurances given to the Delawares were so wantonly neglected, that Col. Morgan had great difficulty in preventing a total alienation of the tribe. To conciliate their chiefs, they were encouraged to visit Congress in the spring of 1779.

In October, 1778, General McIntosh assembled one thousand men at the newly erected fort at the mouth of Beaver, and marched into the enemy's country. The design upon

1) Hildreth's Pioneer History.

Detroit had been relinquished, and the first object of the expedition was to attack the Wyandots and other Indians near Sandusky. After marching about seventy miles beyond Fort McIntosh, the troops halted on the west bank of the Tuscarawas River, a little below the mouth of Sandy creek. Here, on a elevated plain, it was concluded to build a stockade, which was named Fort Laurens. After its completion, a garrison of 150 men was placed in it, and left in the charge of Col. John Gibson, while the rest of the army returned to Fort Pitt. So unexpected and rapid were the movements of Gen. McIntosh, that the Indians were not aware of his presence in their country, until the fort was completed.

Fortunately for the safety of the frontiers—fortunately for the Republic, while this languid and inefficient campaign disappointed the hopes of Congress on the upper Ohio, George Rogers Clark was achieving the happiest results in the region of the Wabash and the Illinois. This hero of Kentucky divides the military honors of the Northwestern Territory, with Anthony Wayne alone. The men were not unlike—the same combination of energy and sagacity.

Clark was born in Albemarle county, Virginia, in 1743: was in Dunmore's expedition of 1774, and among the earliest emigrants to Kentucky; in 1776, had the boldness to urge upon the people of the border to demand assistance from Virginia or independence of her dominion, and obtained five hundred pounds of gunpowder for immediate defence, which the province transported to Fort Pitt: was authorized, in January, 1778, to raise a body of troops for the reduction of the English posts of Kaskaskia and St. Vincents; and, returning to the west with his instructions and twelve hundred pounds of depreciated currency, was able to recruit only a force of two hundred men. With three companies and several private adventurers, Clark at length commenced his descent of the Ohio, which he navigated as far as the falls, where he took possession of and fortified Corn Island, opposite the spot now occupied by Louisville. At this place he had appointed Capt. Joseph Bowman to meet him with such recruits as had reached Kentucky by the southern route, and as many men as could be spared from the stations. Here, also, he announced the real destination of the expedition. Having waited until his arrangements were all completed, and those chosen who were to be of the invading party, on the 24th of June, during a total eclipse of the sun, he left his position and fell down the river. His plan was to follow the Ohio as far as the old French fort, Massac, or Massacre, about sixty miles from the mouth of the river; and thence to go by land direct to Kaskaskia. His troops took no other baggage than they could carry in the Indian fashion, and for his success he trusted entirely to surprise. If he failed, his plan was to cross the Mississippi and throw himself into the Spanish settlements on the west of that river. Before commencing his march, Clark received two items of information which were of much service in his subsequent operations. One of these was the alliance of France with the colonies; this at once made the American side popular with the French and Indians of Illinois and the lakes, France having never lost her hold upon her ancient subjects and allies. The other item was, that the inhabitants of Kaskaskia, and the other old towns, had been led by the British to believe that the Long Knives, or Virginians, were the most fierce, cruel, and blood-thirsty savages that ever scalped a foe. With this impression on their mind, Clark saw that proper management would readily dispose them to submit from fear, if surprised, and then to become friendly from gratitude, when treated with unlooked-for clemency.

At midnight of the sixth day after leaving the Ohio, July 3, they reached the precincts of Kaskaskia, having marched two days without food, and determined forthwith to take the town or die in the attempt. The town was strongly fortified, and contained about two hundred and fifty well-built houses; but the approach of the invaders was unknown; the people and the garrison were alike slumbering in security; and both town and fort were taken—the latter being carried by surprise, although the defences were sufficiently strong to resist a thousand men. The commanding officer, Phillip Rocheblave, was made prisoner; and among his papers, falling into the hands of Col. Clark, were the instructions which he from time to time had received from the British governors of Quebec, Detroit and Michillimacinac, urging him to stimulate the Indians to war by the proffer of large bounties for scalps. Rocheblave was sent a prisoner to Williamsburgh, Virginia, and with him were forwarded the papers taken from his portfolio.

On the day after the fall of Kaskaskia, Captain Joseph Bowman, at the head of thirty mounted men, was sent to attack three other towns upon the Mississippi, the first of which, called Parraderuski, distant fifteen miles from Kaskaskia, was surprised, and taken without opposition—the inhabitants at once assenting to the terms of the conqueror. The next town was St. Phillips, distant nine miles farther up. The force of Captain Bowman was so small, that he wisely determined to make a descent upon St. Phillips in the night, that his strength, or rather his weakness, might be concealed. The precaution ensured success; and the inhabitants, with whom the whole affair was conducted in the night, acceded to the terms prescribed. From St. Phillips, Bowman directed his course upon the yet more considerable town of Cahokia, distant between forty and fifty miles. This town contained about one hundred families, and was also approached secretly, and entered in the night. Captain Bowman, with his troops, rode directly to the quarters of the commander, and demanded the surrender of himself and the whole town, which was immediately complied with. Taking possession of a large store-house, well fortified, the bold dragoon immediately established his quarters therein, and awaited the morning's dawn, which would disclose to the people the diminutive force to which they had surrendered. Enraged at the discovery, one of the enemy threatened to bring a body of one hundred and fifty Indians against the little American squadron and cut them off. But he was secured, and in the course of ten days upwards of three hundred of the inhabitants became so reconciled to their change of masters as to take the oath of allegiance to the United States. Leaving a small guard at Cahokia, Captain Bowman returned to Kaskaskia.

But St. Vincents, the most important western post except Detroit, still remained unconquered, nor could Clark, with his small force, hope to obtain possession of it, as he must of necessity be for some time near the Mississippi, to organize a government for the colonies he had taken, and treat with the Indians of the northwest. But the French priest of Kaskaskia volunteered to bring over the inhabitants of St. Vincents (now Vincennes) to the cause of the Americans without fighting. Hardly believing it possible, Clark dismissed him on this embassy. The British governor was absent, and M. Gibault succeeded entirely. In two or three days after his arrival, the inhabitants threw off the British government, and, assembling in a body in the church, took the oath of allegiance to Virginia. A commandant was chosen, and the American flag displayed over the fort, to the astonishment of the Indians. The savages were told by their French friends, "that their old Father, the king of France, was come to life again, and was mad with them for fighting for the English; that if they did not wish the land to be bloody with war, they must make peace with the Americans."[2]

But Clark's skill in Indian diplomacy was no less remarkable than his gallantry. By an attentive study of the Indian character, he had learned to combine dignity and firmness with that respectful and ceremonious behavior which pleases the pride and vanity of the savage. The following speech to the tribes of the Wabash was well adapted to convey a conception of the causes of the war between the United States and England:

"The Big Knife is very much like the red people; they don't know how to make blankets, and powder and cloth; they buy these things from the English, from whom they are sprung. They live by making corn, hunting and trade, as you and your neighbors, the French, do. But, the Big Knife, daily getting more numerous, like the trees in the woods, the land became poor and hunting scarce; and having but little to trade with, the women began to cry at seeing their children naked, and tried to learn how to make clothes for themselves; women made blankets for their husbands and children; and the men learned to make guns and powder. In this way we did not want to buy so much from the English; they then got mad with us, and sent strong garrisons through our country (as you see they have done among you on the lakes, and among the French;) they would not let our women

2) Perkins' Western Annals, p. 189.

spin, nor our men make powder, nor let us trade with any one else. The English said we should buy everything of them, and since we had got saucy, we should give two bucks for a blanket[3] which we used to get for one: we should do as they pleased, and they killed some of our people to make the rest fear them.

"This is the truth, and the real cause of war between the English and us; which did not take place for some years after this treatment. But our women became cold and hungry, and continued to cry; our young men got lost for want of counsel to put them on the right path. The whole land was dark, the old men held down their heads for shame, because they could not see the sun; and thus there was mourning for many years over the land. At last the Great Spirit took pity on us, and kindled a great council-fire that never goes out, at a place called Philadelphia; he then stuck down a post, and put a war tomahawk by it and went away. The sun immediately broke out, the sky was blue again, and the old men held up their heads and assembled at the fire; they took up the hatchet and sharpened it, and put it into the hands of our young men, ordering them to strike the English as long as they could find one on this side the great waters. The young men immediately struck the war-post and blood was shed. In this way the war began, and the English were driven from one place to another until they got weak, and then they hired you red people to fight for them. The Great Spirit got angry at this, and caused your old father, the French king, and other great nations, to join the Big Knife and fight with them against all their enemies. So the English have become like a deer in the woods; and you may see that it is the Great Spirit that has caused your waters to be

3) The skin of a buck was "legal tender," in the wilderness, for a dollar.

troubled, because you have fought for the people he is mad with. If your women and children should now cry, you must blame yourselves for it, and not the Big Knife. You can now judge who is in the right; I have already told you who I am; here is a bloody belt and a white one, take which you please. Behave like men, and don't let your being surrounded by the Big Knife cause you to take up one belt with your hands, while your hearts take up the other. If you take the bloody path, you shall leave the town in safety, and may go and join your friends, the English; we will then try like warriors, who can put the most stumbling blocks in each others' way, and keep our clothes longest stained with blood. If, on the other hand, you take the path of peace, and be received as brothers to the Big Knife with their friends, the French—should you then listen to bad birds that may be flying through the land, you will no longer deserve to be counted as men, but as creatures with two tongues, that ought to be destroyed."[4]

This speech was not without the desired effect, and the season passed in a series of successful negotiations with the Indians, and the civil organization of the country of Illinois, which the legislature of Virginia hastened to create. Thanks were also voted "to Col. Clark and the brave officers and men under his command, for their extraordinary resolution and perseverance in so hazardous an enterprize, and for the important services thereby rendered their country."

This summer campaign aroused Governor Hamilton to unusual exertions. He projected a powerful Indian expedition against the Virginia frontier early in the spring. With this design, he left Detroit in the autumn, and after personally adjusting his arrangements on the Maumee and Sandusky,

4) See Butler's History of Kentucky, p. 68.

proceeded to St. Vincents, on the Wabash, in order to act more efficiently as soon as the winter should break up. He arrived at St. Vincent with seventy-nine British soldiers and upwards of four hundred Indians in the month of December, and found that post occupied by *two men*, Captain Helm and one Henry. Butler, the historian of Kentucky, relates that Helm was not disposed to yield, even to such odds as five hundred to two; so loading his single cannon, he stood by it with a lighted match, and, as the British came nigh, bade them stand, and demanded to know what terms would be granted the garrison, as otherwise he should not surrender. The governor, unwilling to lose time and men, offered the usual honors of war, and could scarce believe his eyes when he saw the threatening garrison was only one officer and a private.

Hamilton, instead of pressing forward to attack Clark, determined to wait until spring, and allowed his Indians to scatter. This was fatal, for his energetic antagonist correctly supposing that his only chance of escape was to strike the first blow, immediately despatched a boat with forty-six men and the artillery found at Kaskaskia, up the Wabash River, to wait below the town for further orders. He then commenced his march with one hundred and seventy men, of whom two French companies made a part, for St. Vincents.

The march was commenced on the 7th of February. The prairies were flooded and it was "still raining." When the troops arrived at the Wabash, they found the country between the Great and Little Wabash, "although a league asunder," inundated. Making a canoe, the men were ferried over, and continued their march through "rain and water." On the 18th they heard Hamilton's morning guns, and guided their course accordingly. On the 19th, Bowman records (we are quoting from a diary of Captain Joseph Bowman) that there had been "no provision of any sort for two days," but this "hard fortune" was slightly relieved on the 20th, when "one of the men killed a deer which was distributed in the camp very acceptably." On the 21st they came to a body of water a league in extent, and which Clark, on sounding, found "as deep as to his neck." The troops were half starved, and without provisions for men or horses, a delay of twenty-four hours (the time requisite to transport themselves in their few canoes,) would be unendurable; and so Clark "put some water in his hand, poured on powder, blackened his face, gave a war-whoop and marched into the water without saying a word." He had directed those immediately near him to do the same, and all followed. An acre of solid ground, called Sugar Camp, was soon reached, where they passed the night, the weather now growing suddenly and sharply cold. The next morning another inundated plain was to be forded, before reaching the table of land, on which stood the town and fort of St. Vincents. The strength of the men was sorely tried by this last struggle. The water was colder than the day before, and no less deep, but the "low men and the weakly hung to floating logs until taken off by the canoes, while the strong and tall got out and built fires." Fortunately, an Indian canoe, containing a quarter of buffalo, some corn, tallow, kettle, &c., was seized. "This was a grand prize," says Clark himself, "and was invaluable. Broth was immediately made and served out to the most weakly, with great care; most of the whole got a little; but a great many gave their part to the weakly, jocosely saying something cheering to their comrades. This little refreshment and fine weather by the afternoon gave new life to the whole. Crossing a narrow deep lake in the canoes, and marching some distance, we came to a copse of timber called the Warrior's Island. We were now in full view of the fort and the town, not a shrub between us, at about two miles distance."

As Clark and his men emerged in sight of the garrison, they availed themselves of a stratagem to convey an exaggerated impression of their force. Clark thus describes this artifice: "We moved on slowly in full view of the town, but as it was a point of consequence to us to make ourselves appear formidable, we, in leaving the covert that we were in, marched and countermarched in such a manner that we appeared numerous. In raising volunteers in the Illinois, every person that set about the business had a set of colors given them, which they brought with them, to the amount of ten or twelve pair. These were displayed to the best advantage; and as the low plain we marched through was not a perfect level, but had frequent raisings in it seven or eight feet higher than the common level, (which was covered with water,) and as these raisings generally run in an oblique direction toward the town, we took the advantage of one of them, marching through the water under it, which completely prevented our being numbered; but our colors showed considerably above the heights, as they were fixed on long poles procured for the purpose, and at a distance made no despicable appearance; and as our young Frenchmen had, while we lay on the Warrior's Island, decoyed and taken several fowlers, with their horses, officers were mounted on these horses, and rode about more completely to deceive the enemy. In this manner we moved, and directed our march in such a way as to suffer it to be dark before we had advanced more than half way to the town. We then suddenly altered our direction, and crossed ponds where they could not have suspected us, and about eight o'clock gained the heights back of the town."

All night of the 22d, and with brief intervals, until the morning of the 24th, a brisk fire upon the fort was sustained. Negotiations ensued, and towards night Hamilton surrendered, and the post was delivered to the Virginians on the following day. The assailants had only one man wounded—within the fort, seven were wounded through the ports.

It was the good fortune of Col. Clark, also to intercept and capture a valuable convoy of provisions and stores, coming to St. Vincents from Detroit. The surrender of St. Vincents or Fort Sackville, was most timely. Hamilton, instead of guiding the savage elements of a general border war, was sent a prisoner to Williamsburgh, where the Virginia council were about to confine him in irons on bread and water, as a punishment of his barbarism in offering scalp-bounties, when Washington interposed against such a step, as not in accordance with the terms of his surrender.

This imputation upon the British Governor, whom Clark, in his proclamation to the people of Vincennes, just before the attack on the fort, had not scrupled to call the "hair-buyer Hamilton," is also supported by the evidence of one Daniel Sullivan, who, in March, 1778, returned to Pittsburgh with a statement of his discoveries at Detroit and in the Indian country. Captured by the Delawares when a boy, and living with them for nine years, he was well suited for such a service, and asserted positively that Governor Hamilton instigated the Indians to massacre the white inhabitants of the frontiers of Virginia and Pennsylvania, paying them very high prices for all the scalps they would bring. In justice to the British commander, it should be mentioned however, that when Daniel Boone and twenty-eight of his neighbors were captured at Blue Licks in February, 1778, it was evidently the interest of the Shawanese captors, to take them alive to Detroit, and although scalps were marketable there, yet it is reasonable to suppose that the British officers discriminated in favor of prisoners. On this occasion, Boone informs us that he was treated with much humanity by Governor Hamilton, who desired to ransom him, but the Indians prized their prisoner too highly to consent.

We recall our attention from these remote but highly important transactions of the Illinois expedition, to an Indian siege of Fort Laurens. This post had been erected as a part of McIntosh's design upon Detroit, but also, very probably, to check the incursions of the Sandusky Indians upon the settlements south of the Ohio River, and to protect the Delawares who were still disposed for peace. The usual approach from Fort McIntosh, the nearest military station, was by the old Indian trail from the valley of Yellow Creek, across to Sandy and down that stream. In January, 1779, Col. John Gibson and his garrison of one hundred and fifty men were closely besieged by the Indians. Of the incidents which preceded and accompanied this siege, we recognize a manuscript narrative by Henry Jolly, Esq., late judge of Washington county, Ohio, who was one of the garrison, as the most satisfactory. He says:

"When the main army left the fort to return to Fort Pitt, Captain Clark remained behind with a small detachment of United States troops, for the purpose of marching in the invalids and artificers who had tarried to finish the fort, or were too unwell to march with the main army. He endeavored to take the advantage of very cold weather, and had marched three or four miles, when he was fired upon by a small party of Indians very close at hand, I think, twenty or thirty paces. This discharge wounded two of his men slightly. Knowing as he did, that his men were unfit to fight Indians in their own fashion, he ordered them to reserve their fire and to charge bayonet, which being promptly executed, put the Indians to flight, and after pursuing a short distance, he called off his men, and retreated to the fort, bringing in his wounded." In other accounts of this affair, it is stated that ten of Captain Clark's men were killed. "During the cold weather, while the Indians were lying about the fort, although none had been seen for a few days, a party of seventeen men went out for the purpose of carrying in firewood, which the army had cut before they left the place, about forty or fifty rods from the fort. Near the bank of the river, was an ancient mound, behind which lay a quantity of wood. A party had been out for several preceding mornings, and brought in wood, supposing the Indians would not be watching the fort in such cold weather. But on that fatal morning, the Indians had concealed themselves behind the mound, and as the soldiers passed round on one side of the mound, a part of the Indians came round on the other, and enclosed the wood party, so that not one escaped."

The statements hitherto published of this affair are, that the Indians enticed the men from the fort to search for horses, by taking off their bells and tinkling them, but Mr. Hildreth is certain that no horses were left at the fort, as they must either have starved or been stolen by the Indians.

Stone, in his Life of Brant, states that toward evening of the day on which this detachment of seventeen men was cut off, the whole force of the Indians, painted, and in the full costume of war, presented themselves in sight of the garrison, by marching in single files, though at a respectful distance, across the prairie, and their number, according to a count from one of the bastions, was eight hundred and forty-seven; but Col. Morgan was told by the Delaware chiefs that the party consisted of one hundred and eighty Indians, composed of Wyandots, Mingoes, Munsies and four Delawares, and that the sons of Catherine Montour were among them.

After the display of strength above mentioned, the Indians took a position upon an elevated piece of ground at no great distance from the fort, though on the opposite side of the river. In this situation they remained several weeks, in a state rather of armed neutrality than of active hostility. Some of them would frequently approach the fort, and hold conversation with those upon the walls. They uniformly professed a desire for peace, but protested against the encroachments of the white people upon their lands—more especially was the erection of a fort so far within the territory claimed by them as exclusively their own, a subject of complaint. There was with the Americans in the fort, an aged friendly Indian named John Thompson, who seemed to be in equal favor with both parties, visiting the Indian encampment at pleasure, and coming and going as he chose. They informed Thompson that they deplored the continuance of hostilities, and finally sent word by him, to Col. Gibson, that they were desirous of peace, and if he would present them with a barrel of flour and some meat, they would send in their proposals the next day. In fact, the garrison was short of provisions, which the Indians suspected, and perhaps their request was a ruse to ascertain the resources of the besieged, but Colonel Gibson sent the flour and meat promptly, and said that he could spare the provisions very well, as he had plenty more. The Indians soon after disappeared. They had, indeed, continued the siege as long as they could obtain subsistence, and raised it only because of the lack of supplies.

The situation of the garrison was now becoming deplorable.

For two weeks the men had been reduced to half a pound of sour flour, and a like quantity of offensive meat, per diem; and for a week longer they were compelled to subsist upon raw hides, and such roots as could be found in the adjacent woods. A runner was sent to Fort McIntosh with a statement of their distress, and requesting an immediate supply of provisions. The inhabitants south of the Ohio volunteered their aid, and General McIntosh headed the escort. But still they came near being immediately reduced to short allowance again, by an untoward accident causing the loss of a great portion of the supplies. These were transported through the wilderness upon pack-horses. The garrison, overjoyed at the arrival of succors, on their approach to within about a hundred yards of the fort, manned the parapets, and fired a salute of musketry. The horses, which were probably young in the service, became frightened, began to rear and plunge, and broke from their guides. The example was contagious, and in a moment more, the whole cavalcade of pack-horses were bounding into the woods at full gallop, dashing their burdens to the ground and scattering them in all directions—the greater portion of which could never be recovered. Of the provisions saved, the officers very incautiously dealt out two days' rations per man, the whole of which was devoured by the famishing soldiers, to the imminent hazard of the lives of all, and the severe sickness of many. Leaving the fort again, General McIntosh assigned the command to Major Vernon, who remained upon the station several months. He, in turn, was left to endure the horrors of famine, and in the summer of 1779, Fort Laurens was threatened with another siege by forty Shawanese, twenty Mingoes and twenty Delawares, but by the interference of the friendly Delaware chiefs, they were persuaded to abandon the siege without firing a gun, and the fort was soon after relinquished. It is worthy of notice, that while there were only four Delawares (as distinguished from Munsies) at the attack in January, twenty were present on the last occasion, thus indicating that the influence of Capt. Pipe and the war party of the tribe was on the increase.

In October, 1778, the distinguished peace-chief of the Delawares, Captain White Eyes, or Koquethagaeehlon, who had accompanied the army of General McIntosh to Tuscaroras, died suddenly of small-pox. Thenceforth the efforts of Killbuck, Big Cat, and another chief, whose Indian name was Tetepachsi, to resist the current against the Americans became less effective than before the death of their able coadjutor. In the summer of 1779, their friend, Col. Morgan, or Tamenend, resigned his post of Indian agent at Pittsburgh, and the desertion of Fort Laurens exerted an unfavorable influence. The American agents, about the same time, began to urge the Delawares to change their former attitude of neutrality, and to wage war against the Indian allies of the English. This was bad policy under the circumstances of the Ohio frontier, for, as the tribe was situated, any change of attitude must have been unfavorable to the Americans. Very soon, therefore, the few Delawares, who remained friendly to the colonies, were compelled to take refuge at or near Fort Pitt, and at length the Delaware nation may be said to have openly joined the combination of the Ohio Indians with the British.

Fortunately, this hostile demonstration had been postponed to a period when the defection was less disastrous than it would have been at any former period of the war. The pacification of the remote tribes on the Wabash and Illinois, and the favorable dispositions of the French residents there and elsewhere—the destruction of the Seneca towns in the lake and Genesee region of New York, by the army under Sullivan, in the autumn of 1779, and a similar excursion from Pittsburgh, by Colonel Daniel Brodhead, (who had succeeded General McIntosh in February, 1779,) at the head of six hundred men, during which he destroyed many villages of the Seneca Indians on the head waters of the Alleghany, ravaged five hundred acres of standing corn, and captured a booty of skins valued at three thousand dollars—these were events which tended essentially to relieve the valley of the Ohio, at least for a season.

Upon Brodhead's return to Pittsburgh, September 14, he found deputies from the Delawares, Wyandots, and the Maquichee branch of the Shawanese, with whom a conference was held three days afterwards. The only Indian names mentioned in the report of this council are Doonyontat, a Wyandot chief, Kelleleman, a Delaware, and better known as Killbuck, and Keeshmatree, the Maquichee or Shawanese chief, and his counsellor, Nimwha. On this occasion, the professions of amity were as ample and rhetorical as usual.

For a year or two, the settlements of the upper Ohio felt the beneficial effect of these events, but, as we shall see, the main body of the Shawanese, with their British and Indian allies, continued to scourge the Kentucky station, but not without a full retribution. We shall devote a separate chapter to the narrative of these Shawanese campaigns.

CHAPTER XX.

THE KENTUCKY CAMPAIGNS AGAINST THE SHAWANESE.

The assassination of Cornstalk and his companions at Point Pleasant, in 1777, effectually concurred with other causes of irritation to inflame the Shawanese against the Americans, and for the residue of the revolutionary period the tribe was implacably hostile. There is some evidence that the Maquichee tribe were occasionally inclined to peace, but this exception, so far as it existed, was probably attributable to the influence of the Moravian missionaries, who interchanged visits with those chiefs living near the Muskingum. The tribe at large, irritated by the encroachments on their Kentucky hunting grounds, were determined to extirpate the infant settlements; and for this purpose the channels of the prominent tributaries to the Ohio offered great facilities. The canoes of their war-parties floated down the Scioto and the Miamis, and silently ascended the Licking and Kentucky rivers until within striking distance of the scattered stations.

At this time the Shawanese were divided into four tribes or bands—the Maquichee, or Mequachake, the Chillicothe, the Kiskapocoke, and the Piqua. In the first tribe, to which the priesthood was confided, the office of chief was hereditary—in the others it was conferred according to merit. It is reasonable to suppose that the Shawanese living near Wappatomica, on the Muskingum, (if any remained there after it was destroyed by McDonald's party in the summer of 1774) and in the Scioto towns, which were only saved from destruction by submission to Lord Dunmore on the approach of his army, were less prompt to renew hostilities than the inhabitants of the more remote towns on the Little Miami and the Mad River. Cornstalk himself resided east of the Scioto River, on the right bank of Sippo creek, just above the junction of Congo creek, (now Pickaway township and county) while on the opposite bank stood Grenadier Squaw Town, so called from the residence of his sister, a woman six feet high and well proportioned; and notwithstanding the injuries inflicted upon the family of Cornstalk by the whites, it is probable that the Shawanese on the Scioto sympathized, in some degree, with the peaceful dispositions of the neighboring Delawares. This opinion is corroborated by the fact that all the retaliatory expeditions from Kentucky, during and after the revolutionary period, passed by the mouth of Scioto, and were designed to chastise the Shawanese bands who were seated in the Miami and Mad River valleys, and within the present counties of Greene, Miami, Champaigne and Logan. The principal villages in the Miami region were Chillicothe, standing near the mouth of Massie's creek, three miles north of Xenia: Piqua, memorable as the birth-place of Tecumseh, and situated on the north bank of Mad River, seven miles west of Springfield, in Clark county: and Upper and Lower Piqua, in Miami county, where the tribe at length concentrated in great numbers.[1]

In the spring of 1778, while Clark was mustering his expedition to the Illinois, Daniel Boone, equally noted as the pioneer hunter of Kentucky, was a captive in the Shawnee town of Chillicothe. He and twenty-seven others had been seized in February, while making salt at Blue Licks, and his

1) See Appendix No. VII, for further particulars of the Shawanese villages.

companions had been admitted to ransom or detained as British prisoners at Detroit—but not so fortunate was Boone. Although Governor Hamilton had taken a great fancy to him, and sought to obtain his release upon the usual terms, the Indians refused to part with the hero of the woods. They took him back to Chillicothe, where he was formally adopted as a son of the tribe, and consigned to the lodge of an Indian woman, in place of a deceased warrior. Until June, he adapted himself, with extraordinary address, to his new position, and so far won the favor and confidence of the Indians that he was suffered to accompany a party to the Salt Lick, in the Scioto valley, within the present county of Jackson. There they remained ten days and returned to Chillicothe, where Boone found four hundred and fifty warriors, armed and painted for an expedition against his own Boonesborough. Instantly, but silently, he resolved to escape, which was effected on the 16th of June, under the pretence of chasing a deer that bounded past the village. The weary journey of one hundred and fifty miles was successfully accomplished, but his flight seemed to have postponed the march of the war-party, for neither in June or July did they appear. On the 1st of August, Boone started with nineteen men, among them Simon Kenton, to look after the enemy. He approached their town on Paint Creek, but found it deserted, and meeting a small band of warriors, in full paint, marching southwardly, the suspicion flashed upon his mind that Boonesborough would be speedily attacked. They immediately retraced their course, and only reached the borough a day before it was surrounded by five hundred savages, with British and French flags flying and led by one Captain Du Quesne, a Canadian. A day passed in parley before the fort, and active preparation for defence within. On the 9th of August, Boone and eight of the garrison consented to advance sixty yards into the plain for a further consultation with the British commandant, but this interview was rudely interrupted by an attempt to seize the Kentuckians—a treachery which was instantly checked by a fire from the alert rifles of the garrison, and the sudden and safe retreat of Boone's party within the walls. Of course the attack commenced immediately, and lasted for ten days, but to no purpose. On the 20th, the Indians were forced unwillingly to retire, having lost thirty-seven of their number, and wasted a vast amount of powder and lead. The garrison picked up from the ground, after their departure, one hundred and twenty-five pounds of their bullets.

The adventures of Simon Kenton, in the autumn of 1778, afford us another glimpse of the scene of Boone's captivity, and of other Shawanese villages. Colonel John Bowman was then meditating an expedition against the Shawanese villages, particularly Chillicothe; (Oldtown, Greene county,) and Kenton, accompanied by Alexander Montgomery and George Clark, undertook to explore the route to Chillicothe, and the vicinity and position of the town. This was effectually done, and all risk would have been avoided if the three spies had not yielded to the temptation of running off a drove of horses which they found enclosed in a pound. It was late at night, but the noise of the operation alarmed the Indians in the adjacent village. Kenton and his companions were pursued, and although they reached the northern bank of the Ohio River with the stolen animals, yet, before its passage could be effected, they were overtaken, Montgomery killed and Kenton made prisoner, Clark escaping.

The Indians were greatly exasperated at their captive, abusing him as a "tief!—a hoss steal—a rascal!" and he received no indulgence at their hands, except that he was not struck dead with a tomahawk. With his hands tied behind him, and his feet lashed under the horse's belly, he was compelled to ride a restive colt through the thickets of the forest, while at night the prisoner was extended upon his back and closely bound to the earth in a painful posture. Arrived at Chillicothe, he ran the gauntlet, but as Kenton saw an Indian in the line with a drawn knife, ready to plunge it into his breast, he broke through the lines and ran towards the council-house with a crowd of several hundred at his heels. Just before reaching that refuge, he was thrown down by an Indian who was in his path and terribly bruised by the blows of his pursuers. Immediately a council was held, and soon Kenton saw, from the manner of speakers and auditors, that he was doomed to die. When the vote was taken, those who were for his torture struck the war club, which was passed from hand to hand, violently on the ground—their number far exceeding those who simply passed the club to a neighbor in token of mercy. Then arose a debate upon the time and place of the tragedy, and it was resolved that he should be immediately taken to Wapatomika (now Zanesfield, Logan county.) On his way thither, he passed through the Indian towns of Piqua (now Boston, seven miles west of Springfield, Clark county,) and Machecheek, (now West Liberty, Logan county,) running the gauntlet at each town, and baffled at Machecheek in an attempt to escape. Soon after his arrival at Wapatomika, Simon Girty came to see him, and soon discovered that Kenton had been his companion and friend at Fort Pitt and in Dunmore's expedition. McDonald thus describes the scene which ensued: "Girty threw himself into Kenton's arms, embraced and wept aloud over him—calling him his dear and esteemed friend. This hardened wretch, who had been the cause of the death of hundreds, had some of the sparks of humanity remaining in him, and wept like a child at the tragical fate which hung over his friend. 'Well,' said he to Kenton, 'you are condemned to die, but I will use every means in my power to save your life.'

"Girty immediately had a council convened, and made a long speech to the Indians to save the life of the prisoner. As Girty was proceeding through his speech, he became very animated; and under his powerful eloquence, Kenton could plainly discover the grim visages of his savage judges relent. When Girty concluded his powerful and animated speech, the Indians rose with one simultaneous grunt of approbation, saved the prisoner's life, and placed him under the power and protection of his old companion, Girty."[2]

The British had a trading post at Wapatomika, from which Girty provided Kenton with clothing, and also furnished him with horse and gun. The two friends were constantly together, roaming the woods and passing from village to village. While they were at Solomon's Town, a short distance from Wapatomika, a party of warriors returned to the latter place from an expedition against Wheeling, in which they had been defeated by the whites with considerable loss, and demanded the life of Kenton. Another council was summoned, and Kenton was again sentenced to death, notwithstanding all the efforts and eloquence of Girty. The latter could only obtain a reprieve until the prisoner could be taken to Upper Sandusky, where the Indians were soon to assemble and

2) For the above and following particulars of Simon Kenton, see Sketches, by John McDonald, p. 196—an interesting series of pioneer biography. Its author is recently deceased, but his contribution to the history of the State should preserve his memory. See McClung's Western Adventure, p. 80.

receive their annuities and presents from the British agents. As the Indians passed from Wapatomika to Upper Sandusky, they reached a village upon the headwaters of Scioto, where Kenton for the first time beheld the celebrated Mingo chief, Logan, who walked gravely up to the place where Kenton stood, and the following short conversation ensued: "Well, young man, these young men seem very mad at you?" "Yes sir, they certainly are." "Well, don't be disheartened, I am a great chief; you are to go to Sandusky; they speak of burning you there; but I will send two runners to-morrow to speak good for you." McClung adds that Logan's form was striking and manly, his countenance calm and noble, and he spoke the English language with fluency and correctness. Kenton's spirits instantly rose at the address of the benevolent chief, and he once more looked upon himself as providentially rescued from the stake.

On the following morning, two runners were despatched to Sandusky, as the chief had promised, and until their return, Kenton was kindly treated, being permitted to spend much of his time with Logan, who conversed with him freely, and in the most friendly manner. In the evening, the two runners returned and were closeted with Logan. Kenton felt the most burning anxiety to know what was the result of their mission, but Logan did not visit him again until next morning. He then walked up to him, accompanied by Kenton's guards, and giving him a piece of bread, told him that he was instantly to be carried to Sandusky; and without uttering another word, turned upon his heel and left him.

At Upper Sandusky, Kenton was finally rescued from a death of torture by the interposition of Peter Druyer, a Canadian Frenchman, who was a Captain in the British service, and acted as Indian agent and interpreter. It was to this influential personage, probably, that Logan's message had been conveyed. He offered the Indians one hundred dollars in rum and tobacco, if they would allow him to take Kenton to Detroit for examination by the British governor, promising to return him when they should require. A slight additional remuneration, afterwards paid to the Indians, completed the ransom of Kenton, who accompanied Captain Druyer to Detroit, and about a year afterwards, escaped and returned to Kentucky.

In the summer of 1779, Col. John Bowman with one hundred and sixty Kentuckians, marched against Chillicothe. There are conflicting accounts of this expedition, some of which exhibit a partisanship in favor of Captain Benjamin Logan, at the expense of his commanding officer. The following narrative of the expedition is authenticated by the recollection of the late Col. Robert Patterson of Dayton, who was present, and we prefer to adopt it.

The mouth of Licking was the point of rendezvous. Towards the close of the second night, after the commencement of the march from the opposite shore, the party approached the town of Chillicothe undiscovered. An attack was ordered to be made at daylight, but before the officers and men had arrived at the places assigned them, the enemy became alarmed, and a fire commenced on both sides. The whole population of the village took refuge in several strong cabins, in the heart of the town, and prepared for a vigorous defence. The Kentuckians, having no arms but tomahawks and rifles, dared not attack these entrenchments, and they contented themselves with firing the deserted cabins, some thirty or forty in number, after stripping them of kettles, blankets and other articles. They also collected one hundred and thirty-three horses in the adjacent woods, and then commeneed their march homeward. The party had not gone more than nine or ten miles, before the Indians appeared in considerable force in their rear, and began to press hard upon that quarter. Bowman selected his ground, and formed his men into a square; but the Indians declined a close engagement, only keeping up a scattered fire, and it was soon discovered that their object was to retard their march until they could procure reinforcements from the neighboring villages.

As soon as a strong position was taken by Col. Bowman, the Indians retired, and he resumed the line of march, when he was again attacked in the rear. He again formed for battle, and again the Indians retired. Thus harrassed, the troops began to waver, when Benjamin Logan, John Bulger, James Harrod and George Michael Bedinger, at the head of a body of mounted men, scoured the woods in every direction, forcing the Indians from their coverts, and cutting down as many as they could overtake. This decisive step completely dispersed the enemy, and the weary and dispirited troops continued their retreat unmolested. Their loss was nine killed and a few wounded. The Indian loss was unknown, but a prominent chief, Blackfish, was disabled (some accounts say mortally wounded) by a shot through the knee.[3] Bowman crossed the Ohio at the mouth of the Little Miami, when the men dispersed to their several homes.

In the autumn of 1779, a number of keel boats were ascending the Ohio River under the command of Major Rogers, and had advanced as far as the mouth of Licking without accident.[4] Here they were drawn ashore by a strat-

3) Butler says that Blackfish was killed, and that Red Hawk continued the battle, and was also killed.—*History of Kentucky*, 109.

4) They were on their return from New Orleans, where they had been sent by the Governor of Virginia, for the purpose of procuring supplies to

agem. At first a few Indians only appeared, standing upon a sand bar near the mouth of the Licking, while a canoe, with three other Indians was paddling towards them as though to receive them on board. Rogers immediately ordered the boats to be made fast to the Kentucky shore, while the crews, to the number of seventy men well armed, cautiously advanced in such a manner as to encircle the spot where the enemy had been seen. When Rogers had, as he supposed, completely surrounded the enemy, and was preparing to rush upon them, from several quarters at once, he was thunderstruck at beholding several hundred savages suddenly spring up in front, rear, and upon both flanks. They instantly poured in a close discharge of rifles, and then throwing down their guns, fell upon the survivors with the tomahawk. Major Rogers and forty-five of his men were killed almost instantly. The survivors made an effort to regain the boats, but the five men who had been left in charge of them, had immediately put off from shore in the hindmost boat, and the enemy had already gained possession of the others. Disappointed in the attempt, they turned furiously upon the enemy, and aided by the approach of darkness, forced their way through their lines, and with the loss of several severely wounded, at length effected their escape to Harrodsburgh.

Among the wounded was Capt. Robert Benham. Shortly after breaking the enemy's lines, he was shot through both hips, and the bones being shattered, he instantly fell. Fortunately, a large tree had lately fallen near the spot where he lay, and with great pain, he dragged himself into the top and lay concealed among the branches. The Indians, eager

support the military posts on the upper Ohio and Mississippi.—*Butler's History of Kentucky*, 102.

in the pursuit of others, passed him without notice, and by midnight all was quiet. On the following day, the Indians returned to the battle ground, in order to strip the dead and take care of the boats. Benham, although in danger of famishing, permitted them to pass without making known his condition, very correctly supposing that his crippled legs would only induce them to tomahawk him upon the spot, in order to avoid the trouble of carrying him to their town. He lay close, therefore, until the evening of the second day, when perceiving a raccoon descending a tree near him, he shot it, hoping to devise some means of reaching it, when he could kindle a fire and make a meal. Scarcely had his gun cracked, however, when he heard a human cry, apparently not more than fifty yards off. Supposing it to be an Indian, he hastily reloaded his gun and remained silent, expecting the approach of an enemy. Presently the same voice was heard again, but much nearer. Still Benham made no reply, but cocked his gun, and sat ready to fire as soon as an object appeared. A third halloo was quickly heard, followed by an exclamation of impatience and distress, which convinced Benham that the unknown must be a Kentuckian. As soon, therefore, as he heard the expression, "Whoever you are, for God's sake, answer me!" he replied with readiness, and the parties were soon together. Benham, as we have already observed, was shot through both legs! the man who now appeared, had escaped from the same battle *with both arms broken!* Thus each was enabled to supply what the other wanted. Benham having the perfect use of his arms, could load his gun and kill game with great readiness, while his friend, having the use of his legs, could kick the game to the spot where Benham sat, who was thus enabled to cook it. When no wood was near them, his companion would rake up brush with his feet, and gradually roll it within reach of Benham's hands, who constantly fed his companion, and dressed his wounds, as well as his own—tearing up both of their shirts for the purpose. They found some difficulty in procuring water at first, but Benham at length took his own hat, and placing the rim between the teeth of his companion, directed him to wade into the Licking, up to his neck, and dip the hat into the water. The man who could walk, was thus enabled to bring water by means of his teeth, which Benham could afterwards dispose of as was necessary. When the stock of squirrels and other small game in the neighborhood was exhausted, the man on his legs would roam away and drive up a flock of wild turkeys, then abundant in those woods, until they came within range of Benham's rifle. Thus they lived for six weeks, when, on the 27th of November, they discovered a boat on the Ohio and were taken to Louisville. Both thoroughly recovered from their wounds.[5]

It will be seen that the leading events of 1779—the abortive expedition of Bowman, and the surprise of the party under Rogers—were not likely to discourage Indian incursions ; and in June, 1780, occurred a most formidable invasion of Kentucky. A body of six hundred men, Canadians and Indians, commanded by Colonel Byrd, a British officer, and accompanied by either two or six cannon, marched up the valley of the Licking. They first appeared on the 22d of June, before Riddle's station, on the south fork of that river. There was no alternative but a surrender, as the cannon would have speedily prostrated the palisades. Martin's Station, on the same stream, was next taken, and then, to the infinite relief and astonishment of the settlers, the invaders retreated.

5) Butler's Kentucky, 105.

An expedition for the destruction of the Shawanese towns, which were well known to be the places of rendezvous for these war-parties, was immediately proclaimed by General George Rogers Clark, and within a month a thousand men flocked to his standard—a fact conclusive of the rapid settlement of Kentucky, notwithstanding the discouragements of an Indian war. One division of the army, under Col. Benjamin Logan, descended the Licking, while another division, commanded by Clark, ascended the Ohio from the falls. The present site of Cincinnati was the point of rendezvous.

The late Abraham Thomas, of Miami county, has published a statement which presents a forcible contrast to the scene now visible opposite the mouth of Licking. His own words are: "In ascending the Ohio, Daniel Boone and myself acted as spies on the Kentucky side of the river, and a large party on the Indian side was on the same duty; the latter were surprised by the Indians, and several killed and wounded. After making our destination, and before the boats crossed over to the Indian side, Boone and myself were taken into the foremost boat and landed above a small cut in the bank opposite the mouth of Licking. We were desired to spy through the woods for Indian signs. I was much younger than Boone, ran up the bank in great glee, and cut into a beech tree with my tomahawk, which I verily believe was the first tree cut into by a white man on the present site of Cincinnati. We were soon joined by other rangers, and hunted over the other bottom (the second table of land, probably;) the forest every where was thick set with heavy beech and scattering underbrush of spicewood and paw-paw. We started several deer, but seeing no sign of Indians, returned to the landing." Here was erected a small stockade for stores.

On the 2d of August, General Clark took up his line of march, which was as follows: the first division under his own command, took the front position; the centre was occupied by artillery, military stores and baggage; the second, commanded by Col. Logan, was placed in the rear. The men were ordered to march in four lines, at about forty yards distant from each other, and a line of flankers on each side, about the same distance from the right and left line. There was also a front and rear guard, who only kept in sight of the main army. In order to prevent confusion, in case of an attack of the enemy on the march, a general order was issued, that in the event of an attack in front, the front was to stand fast, and the two right lines to wheel to the right, and the two left lines to the left, and form a complete line, while the artillery was to advance forward to the centre of the line. In case of an attack on either of the flanks or side lines, these lines were to stand fast, and likewise the artillery, while the opposite lines wheeled and formed on the two extremes of those lines. In the event of an attack being made in the rear, similar order was to be observed as in an attack in front.

On the 6th of August, at 2 o'clock in the afternoon, the army reached Chillicothe and found the town in flames, the Indians having deserted and fired it that morning. After destroying several hundred acres of corn, on the 7th the march was resumed at 4 o'clock in the direction of Piqua, on the Mad River, twelve miles distant. After proceeding a mile, the men were drenched by a thunder-storm of rain. As soon as it ceased, near dark, the army encamped, kindled fires—discharging and reloading their guns by single companies successively. On the 8th, shortly after noon, they approached Piqua. The Indian road from Chillicothe to

Piqua, which the army followed, crossed the Mad River about a quarter of a mile below the town, and as soon as the advanced guard crossed into a prairie of high weeds, they were attacked by the Indians, who had concealed themselves within the weeds. The ground on which the attack was made, as well as the manner of it, left no doubt that a general engagement was intended. Col. Logan was therefore ordered, with about four hundred men, to file off to the right, and march up the river on the east side, and to continue to the upper end of the town, so as to prevent the Indians from escaping in that direction. Another detachment, under Cols. Lynn, Floyd and Harrod, was ordered to cross the river and encompass the town on the west side; while Gen. Clark, with the troops under Col. Shaughter, and such as were attached to the artillery, marched directly towards the town. The prairie in which the Indians were concealed, who commenced the attack, was only about two hundred yards across to the timbered land, and the division of the army destined to encompass the town on the west side found it necessary to cross the prairie to avoid the fire of a concealed enemy. The Indians evinced great skill and judgment, and to prevent the western division from executing the duties assigned to them, they made a powerful effort to turn their left wing. This was discovered by Lynn and Floyd, and to prevent being outflanked, they extended the line of battle west more than a mile from the town, and which continued warmly contested on both sides until about 5 o'clock, when the Indians disappeared, except a few in the town. The field-piece, which had been entirely useless before, was now brought to bear upon the houses, when a few shot dislodged the Indians within them.

Piqua was built in the manner of the French towns, and

extended along the margin of the river for more than three miles; the houses, in many places, being more than twenty poles apart. Col. Logan, therefore, in order to surround the town on the east, as was the order, marched fully three miles, while the Indians turned their whole force against those on the opposite side of the town; and Logan's party were not in the action at all. It is said that the sudden cessation of the Indian fire was caused by the withdrawal of Simon Girty and three hundred Wyandot and Mingo Indians under his command.

Piqua was also burned to the ground, and all the cornfields in the vicinity devastated. On the 10th of August, the army commenced their return march, and from the mouth of Licking dispersed to their homes. The Kentuckians lost seventeen lives during the expedition.

The effect of this blow was to reduce the Indians to the necessity of extraordinary efforts to support their women and children during the ensuing year—greatly to the relief of the Kentucky settlements.

The summer of 1782 was a disastrous season for Kentucky. Not only the Shawanese, but all the northwestern tribes who were accessible to British influence, scourged the channel and valley of the Ohio. A party of Wyandots, having committed some shocking outrages near Estell's station, were pursued by Capt. Estell and twenty-five men, and a severe conflict occurred near the present town of Mount Sterling, in Montgomery county, Kentucky. The parties were of equal strength, but Capt. Estell divided his force for the purpose of attacking the enemy in rear. This was fatal: the Indian chief instantly charged across a stream that divided the combatants, and overpowered the Kentuckians. Captain Estell and eight of his party were killed, and four mortally wounded. In August, another Kentucky settlement, called Hoy's station, was visited by the Indians, by whom two lads were carried into captivity. This band was also pursued by Captain Holder, with a party of seventeen men, who, coming up with the Indians, were likewise defeated with a loss of seven killed and two wounded.

On the 14th of August, Bryant's station, five miles from Lexington, was invested by five hundred Indians and Canadians, led by the notorious Simon Girty. Fortunately there were assembled at this post a body of borderers who had collected for the purpose of marching to the relief of a neighboring station, and were fully armed, and when the Indians assaulted the station on the third day, they were repulsed with a loss of eighty killed and many wounded, and the same night abandoned the siege. They were pursued on their retreat by Colonels Todd, Trigg and Boone, and Major Harland, at the head of only one hundred and seventy-six men. It was known that Col. Logan was on the way to Bryant's station with considerable reinforcements, but the infuriated Kentuckians could not be restrained. The Indians drew the pursuers into an unfortunate position on the 19th, when the severe battle of Blue Licks ensued, in which the Kentuckians were routed with the loss of seventy-six men; among whom were Colonels Todd and Trigg, Major Harland, and a son of Colonel Boone. The battle lasted only fifteen minutes. The retreat from the field was still more disastrous. The scene of action was on the banks of the main fork of Licking River, at the great bend, forty-three miles from Lexington.

It was a sad day, and was long remembered as a tragic anniversary. The cry for revenge rang from Kenhawa to the falls of Ohio, and once more a thousand volunteers flocked to the plain opposite the mouth of Licking. Clark led the expedition, and Col. Logan, as in 1780, was in command of a division. The army suffered greatly from hunger—their supply of provisions being scanty and the requisite discipline not suffering any diversion to obtain game. The route was across the Mad River, not far from the present site of Dayton; thence up the east side of the Miami, crossing that river about four miles below the Piqua towns. Shortly after gaining the bottom, on the west side of the river, a party of Indians on horseback, with their squaws, came out of a trail that led to some Indian villages near the present site of Greenville. The men took to flight, leaving their women and a female captive in the hands of the Kentuckians. On arriving at Piqua, that and the adjacent villages were deserted, and so suddenly, that fires were burning, meat roasting, and corn still boiling in their kettles. The provisions were a most acceptable treat to the Kentuckians, who were nearly famished, but the escape of their enemies excited deep and universal chagrin. The work of destruction was repeated as on former occasions. The station of a French trader, Loramie, was also destroyed at the mouth of the creek, which henceforth bore his name—the same locality as the English Pickawillany, which was destroyed by the French in 1752. During this expedition five Indians were killed, and the loss of the Kentuckians was only two.

The only other expedition of any importance, which preceded the territorial organization, (except an abortive expedition in 1785, under Col. Edwards,) was led by Col. Benjamin Logan, in 1786. In the autumn of that year, Gen. Clark projected and raised the forces for a campaign against the Indians on the Wabash, and Col. Logan was detached from the army at the falls of the Ohio, to raise a considerable force with which to proceed against the Indian villages on the head waters of Mad River and the Great Miami. We have an interesting narrative of this incursion, in the papers of the late Gen. William Lytle, of Cincinnati, who, although a lad of sixteen, was present as a volunteer.

The Indian towns on the Mad River would have been completely surprised, had not one of Logan's men deserted to the enemy. As it was, eight of the Machacheek villages were burned—numerous cornfields destroyed—70 or 80 warriors taken prisoners, and about twenty others killed, among them a distinguished chief, Moluntha, by a treacherous act of one of the officers. Logan was accompanied by Daniel Boone, Simon Kenton, Robert Patterson, and other familiar names of border history. The famous Grenadier Squaw was among the captives—also a young Indian, who was afterward adopted by Gen. Logan, and became a distinguished Indian ally of the Americans. He was known as Captain Logan, although his Indian name was Spemica Lawba, or "High Horn."

Here we close our outline of the Kentucky and Shawanese campaigns. Each successive year of hostilities had removed the line of battle westward; for, while in 1774, the banks of the Kenhawa and the Scioto were the scene of action, the valley of the Little Miami was the destination of Bowman and Clark, in 1779 and 1780, and the Great Miami of the expedition of 1782. Logan, in 1786, penetrated further north than any preceding invader. It was not until the treaty of Greenville, in 1795, that this warlike tribe finally submitted to destiny, and acquiesced in a permanent peace.

CHAPTER XXI.

THE MORAVIAN MISSIONS ON THE MUSKINGUM, FROM 1772 TO 1782.

It is with a decided sensation of relief that we turn from the repulsive reiteration of Indian massacre, and its swift retaliation, which constitutes so marked a feature of American border history, to the narrative of the Moravian Mission. While elsewhere on the Ohio and its tributaries, war assumed its most hideous and demoniac form, the Muskingum yielded the peaceable fruits of righteousness. Shoenbrun, the Beautiful Spring, and Gnadenhutten, the Tents of Grace, were the abodes of a Christian community, where the regeneration of the gospel was abundantly and admirably illustrated. The annals of this colony of Indian converts have been faithfully reported by the missionaries, Heckewelder and Zeisberger, and also by George Henry Loskiel, historian of the Mission of the United Brethren of North America. Our purpose is only to preserve a transcript of these memorials.

Hitherto, a description of the temporary residence of Post and Heckewelder at Tuscaroras, during the summer of 1762, and the subsequent emigration from the Susquehanna and Beaver Rivers of Pennsylvania, in 1772 and 1773, have constituted our only direct reference to the devoted Germans and their aboriginal congregation. Although Post's pioneer mission was rudely interrupted by the general border war of 1763, familiarly known as the conspiracy of Pontiac, yet the attempt was not entirely fruitless. The Indians appreciated its self-devotion, and when the Delaware Council at Gekelemukpechink forwarded their invitation to Zeisberger to occupy the Muskingum, it was unquestionably prompted by the favorable impressions which had been communicated ten years previously.

The village of Shoenbrun, principally occupied by converted Delawares, was situated at the first settlement, on the east bank of the Muskingum,[1] about two miles below New Philadelphia in Tuscarawas county; while the Mohican village of Gnadenhutten was seven miles south of Shoenbrun on the same side of the river. At each place, a chapel was built—that at Shoenbrun forty feet by thirty-six—of squared timber, roofed with shingles, and surmounted by a cupola and bell. Heckewelder describes the towns as regularly laid out, with wide and clean streets, and fenced to exclude cattle; presenting a neat and orderly appearance, which excited the astonishment of their savage visitors. Besides the missionaries already named, John Jacob Schmick arrived in August, 1777, and was installed over the congregation at Gnadenhutten.

The indefatigable Zeisberger, before the close of 1773, had twice visited the Shawanese villages. He was accompanied by the converted Delaware chief, Glikhikan, or Isaac by baptism, and another native missionary or national assistant. Their first destination was Wakatameki, (probably at the mouth of the creek still so called, near Dresden, in Muskingum county,) where they were hospitably received by a Shawanese Indian, whose father had been an acquaintance of Zeisberger in 1755, in the Wyoming valley of Pennsylvania. The son of Paxnous, their present host, spoke the Del-

1) In 1779, Schoenbrun, after a temporary desertion, was rebuilt on the opposite or west side of the Muskingum.

aware language fluently, and accompanied the missionaries on their farther journey, which extended to the "chief town of the Shawanese." Here the party were entertained with civility by a heathen teacher of great influence, who assembled the Indians, and gave Zeisberger an opportunity to address them in Delaware, a language generally understood by those present. The exhortation made a profound impression, and before his departure, the missionary received a message from the chief and council of the town, avowing a determination to receive the word of God, and live in conformity with it," concluding with a request that the believing Indians and their teachers would come and live with them. Zeisberger promised to communicate their message to his brethren at Bethlehem, but the outbreak of Dunmore's war in the following year, prevented the establishment of a mission. On his second visit to the Shawanese country, in September, 1773, Zeisberger found the head-chief of the tribe very much exasperated against the whites, although his reception of the missionary was kind. On meeting the latter and his companions, he gave them his hand, adding in a loud tone, "This day, God has so ordered, that we should see and speak to each other face to face."

Our impression that this chief was the noted Cornstalk, and that the "chief town" which the missionaries visited, was the "Old Chillicothe" of the Scioto plains, is strengthened by the circumstance mentioned in Loskiel, that "in May, 1775, the chief of a large Shawanese town spent six days agreeably at Gnadenhutten, accompanied by his wife, a captain, several councillors, in all, above thirty persons." Again, in Loskiel's narrative of 1776, we find the following paragraph: "In Gnadenhutten, arrived about this time, a chief of the Shawanese, commonly called Cornstalk, with a retinue of upwards of an hundred persons, men, women, and children. His behavior was courteous, and he showed a particular friendship for the missionary Jacob Schmick, to whom he addressed the following speech through his interpreter, an old mulatto, who had lived twenty years among the Shawanese: "I greatly rejoice to see you and your wife. I shall never forget the kindness you have shown me during my last visit. Therefore, I consider you and your wife as my parents and declare and own you anew as such." Brother Schmick answered: "This is doing us too much honor. We shall be satisfied if you will consider me as your brother, and my wife as your sister." He seemed pleased, and taking the missionary by the hand, thanked them, and said: "I will acquaint all my friends that we have established this bond of friendship." The next spring, the magnanimous chief was murdered: but the foregoing circumstances are sufficient to indicate that his well known inclination to preserve the neutrality of his tribe during the revolutionary war, was, in a great degree, attributable to Moravian influence.

Very soon, indeed, after the erection of this chapel in the wilderness, the happy effects of the Muskingum mission were apparent among the Ohio Delawares. A chief called Echpalawehund, having announced his resolution to renounce heathenism and live with the brethren, much confusion prevailed at Gekelemukpechink. He was prominent and influential, and a party arose among the Indians demanding that the missionaries should be banished from the country, as disturbers of the peace and hostile to their customs and sacrifices. Another party held a council of three days and resolved that they would change their manner of living; prohibit drunkenness; exclude rum traders; appoint six men to preserve good order; and thus give no one a pretext for leaving the town. A year afterward, however, these good resolutions were so completely forgotten that Echpalawehund abandoned the tribe for the communion of Gnadenhutten.

Another prominent Delaware chief, known to the whites as Captain John—the same detained by Col. Bouquet at Fort Pitt, in 1764—joined the brethren in 1776. He was from Achsinink, or Assiningk, ("solid rock,") on the Hockhocking River,[2] and his wife was a white woman, born in Virginia, but from childhood a captive among the Indians. He resigned his station as chief and became a zealous Christian. Among the converts were also a son and nephew of the old and venerable chief, Netawatwes.

Netawatwes, or Nettowhatways, was the chief of the Turtle Tribe of Delawares, who absented himself at the general submission of the Delawares and Shawanese, in 1764, and whose recusancy Col. Bouquet sought to punish by deposing him from his chieftainship. Although the Indians seemed to acquiesce in this deposition, and even proceeded to appoint a successor, yet Netawatwes regained his former position and influence immediately on the retirement of the invaders, and in 1772 and afterwards resided at Gekelemukpechink.[3] He had warmly concurred in the original invitation to Zeisberger, and welcomed the subsequent emigration under Heckewelder and Rothe, but when it was proposed that the missionary, Schmick, should take charge of the settlement at Gnaden-

2) Doubtless the well known "standing stone," now called Mt. Pleasant, near Lancaster, Fairfield county. It is a sandstone formation. The base is a mile and a half in circumference; the apex about thirty by one hundred yards, resembling, at a distance, a huge pyramid.

3) He was called King Newcomer by the whites; and the village of his residence was probably on the site of Newcomers Town, in Tuscarawas county. For further particulars of this chief, and other prominent Delawares, see Appendix No. VIII.

hutten, Loskiel reports that "Netawatwes was of opinion that they had teachers enough, for the new one would teach nothing but the same doctrine," although he afterwards agreed to his coming.

Towards the close of 1774, a warm debate sprung up among the Delawares. Although the believing Indians had been hospitably received, yet there had been no act of adoption or guaranty by the tribe. Glikhikan, whose former rank as a warrior and an orator was not forgotten, often attended the Indian council at Gekelemukpechink, by the invitation of its leading members. Here he often enforced the doctrines and duties of the gospel, but was not unmindful of the material interests of his brethren. At first he encountered the opposition of old Netawatwes, whose jealousy of the whites had now overcome his prepossessions in favor of the missionaries; but, on the other hand, was powerfully supported by the eloquence of Captain White Eyes, who "demanded (in the words of Loskiel) that the Christian Indians should enjoy perfect liberty of conscience, and their teachers safety and protection; adding, that it was but right that the believers should live separate from the rest, and be protected by the chiefs and council against every intruder. But finding that his remonstrances would not avail, he separated himself entirely from the chiefs and council. This occasioned great and general surprise, and his presence being considered, both by the chiefs and people, as indispensable, a negotiation commenced, and some Indian brethren were appointed arbitrators (Glikhikan among them, doubtless). The event was beyond expectation successful, for chief Netawatwes not only acknowledged the injustice done to Captain White Eyes, but changed his mind with respect to the believing Indians and their teachers, and remained their constant friend to his death. He likewise published this change of sentiment to the whole council, in presence of the deputies from Shoenbrun and Gnadenhutten. Captain White Eyes then repeated the proposal which they had formerly rejected; and the council agreeing to it, an act was made in the name of the whole Delaware nation to the following effect: "From this time forward we solemnly declare that we will receive the word of God, and that the believing Indians and their teachers shall enjoy perfect liberty throughout the Indian country, with the same rights and privileges enjoyed by other Indians. The country shall be free to all, and the believers shall have their right and share in it, as well as the unbelievers. Whoever wishes to go to the brethren, and to receive the gospel, shall be at liberty to join them, and none shall hinder him.

"Netawatwes expressed great joy at this act and declaration, and concluded his speech with these words: 'I am an old man, and know not how long I may live in this world. I therefore rejoice that I have been able to make this act of which our children and grandchildren will reap the benefit; and now I am ready to go out of the world whenever God pleases.' He sent, moreover, the following message to chief Pakanke, in Kaskaskunk, (on the Beaver River, in Pennsylvania, to whom Glikhikan had been a favorite counsellor.) 'You and I are both old, and know not how long we shall live. Therefore let us do a good work before we depart, and leave a testimony to our children and posterity, that we have received the word of God. Let this be our last will and testament.' Pakanke accepted the proposal, and he and other chiefs made it known by solemn embassies in all places where it was necessary. For a still greater security, a treaty was set on foot with the Delamattenoos, (Wyandots) who had given this part of the country to the Delawares about thirty years before, by which a grant was procured insuring to the believing Indians an equal right with the other Delawares to possess land in it. And that this transaction might be duly ratified in the Indian manner, and the act remain unrepealed, the Christian Indians sent a formal embassy to the chiefs and council of the Delaware nation, to return their humble thanks for it. The deputies repeated the whole declaration of the council concerning the believing Indians and their teachers, and Netawatwes confirmed it to be their own act and deed in presence of all the people; adding that they had called the Indian congregation and their missionaries into this country, and that all the words now repeated by the deputies had been spoken and ratified by this council. Then the deputies proceeded to return thanks in the name of both congregations, delivering several belts of wampum, which were forwarded to the neighboring nations. They were made without ornaments, and immediately known by their plainness to be the belts of the Christian Indians. Thus this important business was concluded and confirmed in due form."

We regard this transaction as corroborating so fully our opinions of the prominence of the Moravian mission, at the outbreak of the American Revolution, and the corresponding influence of the missionaries, not only among the Delawares but with the other Ohio tribes—an influence which was potently exercised to preserve their relation of neutrality between the parties to that struggle—that we shall cite Heckewelder in reiteration and confirmation of the European annalist:

"In other respects," he says, "this year (1774) had been remarkable to the Christian Indians. First, the chiefs of the nation, both on the Muskingum and at Cushcushkee,[4] had unitedly agreed and declared that the brethren should have full liberty to preach the gospel to the nation wherever they chose; and this resolution they also made publicly known. And secondly, these seeing that their friends and relations pursued agriculture, and kept much cattle, they enlarged the tract of land first set apart to them by moving their people off to a greater distance. And consulting their uncles, the Wyandots, on the subject, (they being the nation from whom the Delawares had originally received the land) these set apart, granted and confirmed, all that country lying between Tuscaroras (old town) and the great bend below Newcomerstown,[5] a distance of upwards of thirty miles on the river, and including the same, to the Christian Indians. Two large belts of wampum were on this occasion delivered by the Wyandots, and the chiefs of the Delaware nation, to the Christian Indians, who, in return, thanked them for the gift, both verbally and by belts and strings of wampum."

"Meanwhile," says Loskiel, "Gekelemukpechink was forsaken by its inhabitants, and a new town built on the east side of the Muskingum, opposite to the influx of the Walhanding. This town was called Goschhocking, and chief Netawatwes chose it for his future residence."

Under these auspicious circumstances, the year 1775 commenced, and proved a season of external repose and internal prosperity to the mission. "The rest enjoyed by the Indian congregation, in the year 1775, was peculiarly pleasing,"

4) A town on the Beaver River.

5) In a communication by John Heckewelder, in 1822, to the Secretary of War, the limits of this grant are thus described—"to extend from the mouth of One Legged creek to the great bend in the river below Gakalamukpeking, old town, a distance of about thirty miles on the river, and from which tract two small Indian villages were removed, besides single families, so as to open the country at once to the Christian Indians entirely."

says Loskiel, "and much favored the visits of strangers, who came in such numbers that the chapel at Schoenbrun, which might contain about five hundred hearers, was too small." At the close of this year their number amounted to four hundred and fourteen persons. All were in the enjoyment of the comforts, almost the luxuries, of civilization; the lives and deaths of the aboriginal converts, as reported to us, were very exemplary; while the children were zealously taught in schools, into which the missionary Zeisberger had introduced a spelling-book, published in the Delaware language.

In April, 1776, Zeisberger and Heckewelder founded another settlement within two miles of Goschocking, and called it Lichtenau. This spot had been selected by the chiefs themselves, according to Heckewelder, "that they, as well as their children, might have an opportunity of hearing the gospel preached—a wish which the old and principal chief, Netawatwes, had repeatedly informed them of, both by public and private messages."

The external relations of the mission, (to adopt a favorite expression of the Moravian historians) have been incidentally included in our narrative of the efforts of the Delaware peace-chiefs to preserve the neutrality of the nation. As Netawatwes and the other chiefs at the forks of the Muskingum, were the protectors of the missionaries, and concurred in the pacific dispositions of the Christian Indians, their interests and sympathies in that respect were identical; and the American people unquestionably owe to the locality and labors of the Moravian teachers at this critical period, that a general combination of the western Indians was postponed until 1780—a date when the French alliance and the increase of population on the southern bank of the Ohio, concurred to arrest its most disastrous consequences.

Netawatwes died at Pittsburgh towards the close of 1776. "Ever since his sentiments had changed in favor of the gospel, he was a faithful friend of the brethren, and being one of the most experienced chiefs in his time, his council proved often most serviceable to the mission. The wish he uttered as his last will and testament, that the Delaware nation might hear and believe the word of God, preached by the brethren, was frequently repeated in the council by his successor, and then they renewed their covenant to use their utmost exertions to fulfill this last wish of their old worthy and honored chief. Upon such an occasion, Captain White Eyes, holding the Bible and some spelling-books in his hand, addressed the council with great emotion, and even with tears: 'My friends,' said he, 'you now have heard the last will and testament of our departed chief. I will therefore gather together my young men and their children, and kneeling down before that God who created them, will pray unto him, that he may have mercy upon us, and reveal his will unto us. And as we cannot declare it unto those who are yet unborn, we will pray unto the Lord our God, to make it known to our children and children's children.' "[6]

The year 1777, already noticed as the period when the Shawanese joined the Indians of the lakes against the Americans, brought severe trials to the Moravian colony. The inhabitants of Shoenbrun were mostly Delawares, and were constantly tempted by the Muncie, or war party of the nation, to abandon the missionaries. Newallike, a Muncie chief hitherto belonging to the congregation at Schoenbrun, and who had accompanied the emigration from the Susquehanna,

6) Loskiel's North American Missions, part iii., 116. The quotations from Loskiel, in the present chapter, are numerous, and often made without special reference to the author, except by inverted commas. Heckewelder's Narrative will be specially alluded to.

was the first to apostatize, and his example was followed by so many that finally Zeisberger gathered the faithful remnant together and abandoned Schoenbrun—thus increasing the population of Gnadenhütten and Lichtenau. Soon afterwards, the missionaries Heckewelder and Youngman returned to Bethlehem.

Thenceforth the efforts of the Wyandots and Shawanese to involve the Delawares at Goschocking in the warfare against the colonies, were urgent and incessant. The messages of the Wyandots, and the deference with which they were received, confirm the impression that the Delawares recognized the Wyandots as the original lords of the soil, and that they were denizens of Ohio by the grace of their northern neighbors. Still, this tradition was not offensively suggested, nor did it impair the independence of the Delawares. In July, 1777, Loskiel informs us that an embassy of twenty deputies from the Hurons arrived in Goschocking. They offered the war-belt three times successively, demanding the assistance of the Delawares to make war against the colonies, and declaring that all the nations on Lake Erie were united as one man to fight against the Americans; but the Delaware chiefs returned the war-belt and answered that they could not comply with their demand, having promised at the treaty of peace made after the last war, that as long as the sun should shine and the rivers flow, they would not fight against the white people; that therefore they had no hand left to take up the war-belt. The ambassadors returned, greatly displeased with the answer, and the Moravians anticipated nothing less than an attack by the Indian allies of the English.

Early in August, they were alarmed by intelligence, that a body of two hundred Wyandots led by Pomoacan, the

Half King of Upper Sandusky, were on the way to Lichtenau. "After mature consideration," to resume the narrative of Loskiel, "the brethren resolved to show no signs of fear, but to gain these savages, by giving them a kind reception. Oxen and pigs were killed, and other food provided, and the liberality of the Indian Brethren and Sisters in contributing to these preparations, was truly remarkable, for they considered it as the only means of saving the lives of their beloved teachers. August the 8th, the warriors arrived in Goschocking, and upon their meeting a number of the Christian Indians from Lichtenau, carrying provisions for them, their surprise and pleasure were equally great. The good humor which this occasioned, was improved by the assistants, who soon after sent a solemn embassy to the Half King and other chiefs of the Hurons. Isaac Glikhikan thus addressed them:

"'Uncle! we, your cousins, the congregation of believing Indians at Lichtenau and Gnadenhutten, rejoice at the opportunity to see and speak with you. We cleanse your eyes from all the dust, and whatever the wind may have carried into them, that you may see your cousin with clear eyes and a serene countenance. We cleanse your ears and hearts from all evil reports which an evil wind may have conveyed into your ears, and even into your hearts on the journey, that our words may find entrance into your ears and a place in your hearts.' Here he delivered a string of wampum and proceeded: 'Uncle! hear the words of the believing Indians, your cousins, at Lichtenau and Gnadenhutten. We would have you know, that we have received and believed in the word of God for thirty years and upwards, and meet daily to hear it, morning and evening. You must also know, that we have our teachers dwelling among us, who instruct us and our children. By this word of God, preached to us by our teachers, we are taught to keep peace with all men, and to consider them as friends; for thus God has commanded us, and therefore we are lovers of peace. These our teachers are not only our friends, but we consider and love them as our own flesh and blood. Now, as we are your cousin, we most earnestly beg of you, Uncle, that you also would consider them as your own body, and as your cousin. We and they make but one body, and therefore cannot be separated, and whatever you do unto them, you do unto us, whether it be good or evil.' Hereupon, another string of wampum, several fathoms in length, was delivered. The Half King replied, that these words had penetrated his heart, and that he would immediately consult with his warriors about them. This being done, he returned the following answer to the deputies: 'Cousins! I am very glad, and feel great satisfaction that you have cleansed my eyes, ears, and heart from all evil, conveyed into me by the wind on this journey. I am upon an expedition of an unusual kind; for I am a warrior, and am going to war, and therefore many evil things and evil thoughts enter into my head, and even into my heart. But thanks to my cousin, my eyes are now clear, so that I can behold my cousin with a serene countenance. I rejoice, that I can hear my cousins with open ears, and take their words to heart.' He then delivered a string of wampum, and repeating all the words of the deputies relating to the missionaries, he expressed his approbation of them, and added: 'Go on as hitherto, and suffer no one to molest you. Obey your teachers, who speak nothing but good unto you, and instruct you in the ways of God, and be not afraid that any harm shall be done unto them. No creature shall hurt them. Attend to your worship, and never mind other affairs. Indeed you see us going to war; but you may remain easy and quiet, and need not think much about it,' &c.

"During these transactions, the brethren at Lichtenau were under great apprehensions, fearing the event. The deputies had therefore agreed, that as soon as they should perceive that the Half King spoke in an angry tone, they would send a messenger full speed to Lichtenau, before he concluded his speech, that the whole congregation might take flight. So much the greater was the joy of all, when the affair took so favorable a turn, and every one felt himself excited to thank and praise the Almighty Saviour of his people, for having heard the numberless sighs and prayers offered up to him at this critical juncture. The word of Scripture for the day was: '*Sing aloud unto God our strength: make a joyful noise unto the God of Jacob.*'—Ps. lxxxi, 1. This was done with one accord, and with a full heart.

"The same day, Half King, the chief captain, and eighty-two warriors came to Lichtenau. They were first shown into the school-house, where the missionaries Zeisberger and William Edwards received them. They shook hands with all they met, and the Half King spoke as follows: 'We rejoice to see our father, and to take him by the hand: from this time forth we will consider you as our father, and you shall own and consider us as your children, nor shall any thing ever disturb your minds in this respect, but our covenant shall remain firm forever. We will also acquaint the other nations with the proceedings of this day, and they will doubtless rejoice.' Zeisberger answered this friendly compliment in a proper manner, after which the missionaries and some Indian brethren dined with the Half King and his officers, under a hut made of green boughs: the other warriors seated themselves in the shade in front of the place, and were so richly provided with food, that after having made a hearty meal, each could carry a large portion with him to Goschocking, to which place they all returned in the evening. "The Half King then sent messengers to the English governor in Detroit, and to the chiefs in the Huron country, to give them an account of the covenant made with the believing Indians, adding that he and his warriors had acknowledged the white brethren to be their father and would ever own them as such."

During the first alarm, the missionary Schmick and his wife were persuaded by the Indians to fly to Pittsburgh, whence they returned to Bethlehem, leaving Zeisberger and William Edwards in charge of the congregations. The band of Indians under Half King increased to two hundred, composed, according to Loskiel, of "Hurons, Iroquois, Ottawas, Chippeways, Shawanose, Wampanos, and Potawontakas," besides some Canadian French. It was a full fortnight before the inhabitants of Lichtenau were relieved of their presence in the vicinity.

For a period of four years, the mission experienced no serious annoyance from the Ohio savages: but the friendship of the Hurons, and the fact that their war-parties usually traversed the Moravian villages on their march to Pennsylvania and Virginia, exposed Gnadenhutten and Lichtenau to the danger of attack by the American borderers. On one occasion these villages were deserted, and the inhabitants fled up the Walhonding, alarmed by a false report, that an armed band of Virginians were marching against the Delaware towns: while in October, 1777, a party which had actually started upon such an expedition, was cut off by the Half King of the Hurons.

As long as the Delaware chiefs at Goschocking were determined to preserve their neutrality, Lichtenau, only two miles distant, was the principal seat of the mission. Indeed, in April, 1778, Gnadenhutten was abandoned on account of the annoyances of "freebooters belonging to the whites," and the whole community concentrated at Lichtenau. But in 1779, the neighborhood of Goschocking became less desirable. After the death of Captain White Eyes, in the autumn of 1778, the English party among the Delawares rapidly increased—with the evacuation of Fort Laurens by the Americans, the peace-chiefs and their few adherents were compelled to retire to the vicinity of Pittsburgh; and thus, late in the summer of 1779, the Christian Indians stood alone, within the present limits of Ohio, in the resolution to observe a neutrality between the contending whites. The inhabitants of Goschocking thenceforth sought to molest their peace-loving neighbors in various ways; and their robberies, drunkenness and other outrages became so insupportable to the congregation, that Gnadenhutten was at length reöccupied; Shoenbrun rebuilt, although on the opposite side or west side of the Muskingum, and Lichtenau itself, on the 30th of March, 1780, was, in turn abandoned, and a new settlement, called Salem, established about five miles below Gnadenhutten.

In May, 1780, Loskiel mentions the arrival of "the single sister, Sarah Ohneberg, who afterwards married John Heckewelder." Their eldest daughter, Mary Heckewelder, was born at Salem on the 16th of April, 1781, and is generally supposed to have been the first born of white American children, north of the Ohio. In July, 1781, an arrangement of religious teachers was effected, by which David Zeisberger superintended the whole mission, but particularly served the congregation at Schoenbrun, assisted by John George Youngman; while Gottlob Senseman and William Edwards were stationed at Gnadenhutten, and John Heckewelder and Michael Young at Salem. The missionary Shebosch, who was married to an Indian convert, also returned from Bethlehem in November, 1780.

It was the peculiar hardship of these inoffensive religionists, that every act of benevolence or humanity on their part, was sure to excite distrust and hostility in some quarter. If a war-party from the lakes halted near their towns, and in obedience to universal Indian usage, were furnished with a meal of victuals: or if, on their return, the missionaries interposed to ransom a prisoner, the rumor ran through the settlements that the Moravian Indians were leagued with the hostile savages. On the other hand, the English emissaries, McKee, Elliott and Girty, made frequent and bitter complaints that Zeisberger and his companions were in the habit of sending runners to the American commandant at Pittsburgh, when informed that the Indians were meditating an expedition upon some particular point of the Virginia border. There is no doubt that such was frequently the case. So far, the Moravians deviated from a strict neutrality, yet their motive was the simple suggestion of humanity —in no sense political—and it is a melancholy reflection that such acts of disinterested kindness were so ill-requited, as we shall see in the sequel. Still, it is due to the impetuous settlers of the upper Ohio, to add, that whatever appeared like a complication of the Christian Indians with the savage enemy, was so notorious as to provoke exaggeration, while the evidence of an opposite or friendly disposition was diligently guarded by Morgan, McIntosh or Brodhead—the American officers at Pittsburgh—as confidential communications

In the summer of 1781, there was an illustration of the different sentiments with which the Moravians were regarded by the American officers and the militia under their command. Colonel Daniel Brodhead, then stationed at Pittsburgh, led an expedition against Goschocking, the Delaware town on the east bank of Muskingum, and on his march thither, halted about five miles below Salem. Here he addressed a note to Heckewelder, requesting a supply of provisions, and that the missionary would visit his camp. Heckewelder hastened to comply, and personally received from the American officer assurances that his troops should not molest the Moravian Indians, who had conducted themselves, he proceeded to say, in a manner that did them honor, and that neither the English or Americans could with justice reproach them with improper conduct in their situation. While Col. Brodhead was speaking, however, an officer hastily entered to inform him that a body of militia were about "breaking off for the purpose of destroying the Moravian settlements up the river," and it was with great difficulty that the commanding officer, aided by Col. David Shepherd of Wheeling, could restrain the men from adding such an outrage to the other acts of inhumanity which attended this Coshocton campaign, and which will hereafter occupy our attention.

Immediately after this Coshocton campaign, a deeply interesting interview occurred between a distinguished Delaware chief, and the inhabitants of the Moravian villages. Heckewelder calls him "the head war chief of the Delaware nation," and we are satisfied that he is the same individual of whom we first hear in the French and English war as "Shingess;" next, in 1762, as Bog Meadow or King Shingas; now in 1781, as Pachgantschihilas; again in 1785, at an Indian Council near the mouth of the Great Miami, as Pacanchichilas, and long afterwards as the Bockingehelas, whom many of the early settlers of Ohio recollect to have been living in 1804, at a great age. This chief, on the present occasion, was accompanied by eighty warriors, who silently surrounded Gnadenhutten before day break. As they approached, the town was hailed, and their leader demanded the delivery of Gellelemend or Killbuck and the other peace-chiefs of the Delawares. He was informed that they had gone to Pittsburgh some time before, and after a strict search, the Indians were satisfied that they were not in the town. The nation now being at war, these peace-chiefs had become subordinate to the war-chiefs, and Pachgantschihilas was determined to remove them where they could exercise no function, until their services were required to conclude a peace.

The Delaware chief then demanded that deputies from the three Moravian towns should be assembled, and he proceeded to address them, according to Heckewelder, as follows:

"Friends and kinsmen! Listen to what I have to say to you. You see a great and powerful nation divided. You see the father fighting against the son, and the son against the father. The father has called on his Indian children to assist him in punishing his children, the Americans, who have become refractory. I took time to consider what I should do—whether or not I would receive the hatchet of my father to assist him. At first I looked upon it as a family quarrel, in which I was not interested. However, at length it appeared to me that the father was in the right, and his children deserved to be punished a little. That this must be the case, I concluded from the many cruel acts his offspring had committed from time to time on his Indian children; in encroaching on their lands, stealing their property, shooting at, and murdering without cause, men, women and children! Yes! even murdering those who at all times had been friendly to them, and were placed for protection under the roof of their father's house—the father himself standing sentry at the door at the time![7]

"Friends and relatives!—Often has the father been obliged to settle and make amends for the wrongs and mischiefs done to us by his refractory children, yet these do not grow better. No! they remain the same, and will continue to be so as long as we have any land left us. Look back at the murders committed by the Long Knives (Virginians) on many of our relations, who lived peaceable neighbors to them on the Ohio! Did they not kill them without the least provocation? Are they, do you think, better now than they were then? No, indeed not, and many days are not elapsed since you had a number of these very men near your doors, who panted to kill you, but fortunately were prevented from so doing by the Great Sun,[8] who, at that time, had, by the Great Spirit, been ordained to protect you.

"Friends and relatives!—You love that which is good, and wish to live in peace with all mankind, and at a place where you may not be disturbed whilst praying. You are very right in this, and I do not reproach you in having made the choice. But, my friends and relatives, does the place you are at present settled at answer this purpose? Do you not live in the very road the contending parties pass over when they go to fight each other? Have you not discovered the footsteps of the Long Knives almost within sight of your

7) The allusion here is to the slaughter of the Conestoga Indians, of Pennsylvania, by a mob of whites, although they had taken refuge in Lancaster jail.

8) A name given by the Indians to Col. Brodhead.

towns, and seen the smoke arising from their camps? Should not this be sufficient warning to you, and lead you to consult your own safety? We have long since turned our faces towards your habitations, in the expectation of seeing you come from where you now are to us, where you would be out of danger; but you were so engaged in praying that you did not discover our anxiety for your sakes.

"Friends and relatives!—Now listen to me and hear what I have to say to you. I am myself come to bid you rise and go with me to a secure place. Do not, my friends, covet the land you now hold under cultivation. I will conduct you to a country[9] equally good, where your fields shall yield you abundant crops, and where your cattle shall find abundant pasture; where there is plenty of game; where your women and children, together with yourselves, will live in peace and safety; where no Long Knife shall ever molest you. Nay, I will live between you and them, and not even suffer them to frighten you. There you can worship your God without fear. Here, where you are, you cannot do this. Think on what I have now said to you, and believe that if you stay where you now are, one day or the other, the Long Knives will, in their usual way, speak fine words to you, and at the same time murder you."

In the course of an hour, the Christian Indians replied to the foregoing address with thanks for the kind expressions of their friends and relatives, but stating that they were unwilling to believe that their American brethren, against whom they had never committed a hostile act, should inflict such injuries upon them. They hinted that their only danger

9) Here Heckewelder adds in a note, "the Miami country." There is reason to believe that after this chief led his band from Tuscaroras, (the upper forks of Muskingum) he emigrated, perhaps not immediately, to the Miami, or Maumee River, near the junction of the Auglaize.

grew out of the fact that war-parties, like the present, by going or returning through their villages, might draw an enemy upon them—otherwise they had no fears. As to the invitation to leave their settlements, they objected that they were much too heavy (in possession of too much property, provisions, etc.,) to think of rising and going with their friends and relatives.

Pachgantschihilas, after another consultation with his captains, repeated his former warning, but disclaimed any purpose of compelling the Moravians to leave their settlements. He requested, in conclusion, that any who chose to avoid the dangers which he anticipated, might be free to accept his protection, to which the missionaries assured him there would be no objection. The next day, the chief and his warriors proceeded to Salem, where a feast had been prepared for them under the direction of Glikhikan, who came forth to greet and welcome his guests. The warriors approached gravely and decorously, without a yell or shout. When they arrived in the centre of the village, opposite the chapel and the residence of Heckewelder, Pachgantschihilas ordered a halt, and publicly pronounced a warm eulogy upon the believing Indians. He then dismissed them to the entertainment which had been provided in a grove of sugar-maple, while the chief himself, accompanied by two Shawanese and two Delaware war-captains, repaired to the house of Heckewelder, in whom he recognized the youthful pall-bearer at the funeral of his favorite wife, nineteen years before, at Tuscaroras. Here, where also were assembled the national assistants of the mission, he repeated his friendly assurances, and soon after departed with his warriors, having first proclaimed from the centre of the street, in a tone audible to all the inhabitants, that "if at any time they should hear it said that Pachgantschihilas was an enemy to the believing Indians, they should consider such words as lies."

It was from the English quarter that the first serious interruption to the peaceful pursuits of the Moravian community proceeded. The tory leaders of the Ohio savages, McKee, Elliott and Simon Girty, were extremely hostile, and are charged with having instigated several attempts to assassinate or seize the missionaries. Baffled in these, by the vigilance and devotion of the Christian Indians, they represented to the British commandant at Detroit, Col. Depeyster, that the missionaries were partizans and spies of Congress, and that their influence was extremely prejudicial to the British interest. That officer was induced to insist upon their removal from the vicinity of Pittsburgh, and early in 1781, his wishes were communicated to the great council of the Six Nations, assembled at Niagara, by whom a message was sent to the Ottawas and Chippewas to the following effect: "We herewith make you a present of the Christian Indians on the Muskingum to make broth of;" an expression well understood to mean: "We desire you to put those people to death." But those two nations, being a branch of the Delaware stock, and ranking as their grandchildren, replied: "We have no cause for doing this." The Wyandots, at first, were even more disinclined to assume the ungrateful task, because the Detroit division of the tribe held the relation of guardian or protector to the Christian Indians among themselves, who were the converts of Catholic missionaries, and they knew no sectarian distinction between the Catholic Wyandot and the Protestant Delaware or Mohican, while Pomoacan, or the Half King, at Upper Sandusky, had hitherto avowed and conducted himself as a friend and champion of the Muskingum mission. But Captain Pipe and his followers were now the neighbors of Half King, at Upper Sandusky, and the latter was persuaded to lead a body of two hundred warriors against the Moravian towns. Heckewelder, after the arrival of some reinforcements, states the whole force at three hundred men, and classifies them as Wyandots from Upper Sandusky, commanded by Half King; another band of Wyandots from Detroit and Lower Sandusky, commanded by Kuhn, a head war-chief of the latter place; a party of Delawares from Upper Sandusky, led by the war-chiefs Pipe and Wingemund; about forty Muncies, also from Upper Sandusky (probably under the apostate Newalike); two Shawanese captains, named by the traders John and Thomas Snake, with a few warriors from the Scioto; several straggling Indians of the Mohegan and Ottawa tribes, and Elliott, whose rank in the British service was Captain, with his attendant Michael Herbert and Alexander McCormick, the bearer of a British flag, and a small train of unarmed Wyandots, men and women, with horses, who had come to assist in removing the booty.

When this formidable band approached Salem, the Half King sent a message to the Christian Indians, desiring them to fear nothing, adding that he came himself to see that no injury should be done to them; but having good words to speak, he wished to know which of their settlements would be most convenient for a meeting. Now, as Gnadenhutten was in every respect the most proper place, it was accordingly fixed upon. The warriors, therefore, pitched their camp, on the 11th of August, on the west side of Gnadenhutten, and were treated in the most liberal manner.

On the 20th of August, the Half King appointed a meeting of the believing Indians and their teachers, and delivered the following speech:

"Cousins! ye believing Indians in Gnadenhutten, Schoenbrun and Salem! I am much concerned on your account, perceiving that you live in a dangerous spot. Two powerful, angry and merciless gods stand ready, opening their jaws wide against each other; you are setting down between both, and thus in danger of being devoured and ground to powder by the teeth of either one or the other, or of both. It is, therefore, not advisable for you to stay here any longer. Consider your young people, your wives and your children, and preserve their lives, for here they must all perish. I therefore take you by the hand, lift you up, and place you in or near my dwelling, where you will be safe and dwell in peace. Do not stand looking at your plantations and houses, but arise and follow me. Take also your teachers with you, and worship God in the place to which I shall lead you, as you have been accustomed to do. You shall likewise find provisions, and our father beyond the lake (meaning the governor of Detroit) will care for you. This is my message, and I am come purposely to deliver it."

He then delivered a string of wampum, and the missionaries and Indian assistants of the three settlements met in conference to consider this unexpected address, and on the 21st, the latter delivered the following answer to the Half King:

"Uncle! and ye captains of the Delawares and Muncies, our friends and countrymen! Ye Shawanese, our nephews, and all ye other people here assembled! We have heard your words; but have not seen the danger so great, that we might not stay here. We keep peace with all men and have nothing to do with the war, nor do we wish or desire anything but to be premitted to enjoy rest and peace. You see yourselves, that we cannot rise immediately and go with you, for we are heavy, and time is required to prepare for it. But we will keep and consider your words, and let you, uncle! know our answer next winter, after the harvest; upon this you may rely."

The Half King certainly, and perhaps Captain Pipe, were not disposed to press the matter further, and in the Indian camp the current was so strongly in favor of the Christian Indians, that some were disposed to make a shooting target of the British flag, as a retaliation upon the agency of Captain Elliot. That officer, whose zeal for the English cause was stimulated by the prospect of pecuniary advantage in the sacrifice of the stock and other valuable property of the mission, labored zealously to remove the reluctance of Half King and Pipe. He represented to them that the English Governor at Detroit would be greatly dissatisfied, if they returned without the missionaries. It unfortunately happened that two Moravian Indians, whom the missionaries had dispatched to Pittsburgh with information of the existing state of things, were intercepted by the savages, and this circumstance was exaggerated by Elliot into a proof, not only that the missionaries were leagued with their enemies, but that they were instigating a hostile expedition against the party of Half King and Pipe. This turn of affairs greatly exasperated those chiefs. At a second council, held on the 25th, Half King had seemed to waver—at least he listened to the remonstrances of Glikhikan and his associates in silence—but in his altered humor he no longer hesitated. A third council was convened on the second of September, before which Zeisberger, Senseman and Heckewelder, with some of their assistants, were summoned, and Half King insisted upon their giving an immediate answer, whether they would go with him or not, without retiring to consult upon it. The missionaries appealed to their former answer—the assembly broke up without debate and in some confusion, and soon afterwards Zeisberger, Senseman and Heckewelder, were violently seized and imprisoned. They were voluntarily joined by their associates, William Edwards, who was determined to accept no exemption from their fate : and during that night and the subsequent day their residences were pillaged. The other missionaries, Young and Youngman, were also imprisoned, although the latter was released the next day. The wives and children of the five missionaries were brought to Gnadenhutten as captives, but were soon released, as were the missionaries themselves, after five days of close confinement and distressing anxiety.

The life of Isaac Glikhikan was endangered by the heroic act of a young Indian relative, who rode Captain Pipe's best horse to Pittsburgh with the news of the recent violence. As soon as her departure was discovered, she was instantly pursued, but as she could not be overtaken, the savages were enraged in the highest degree, and a party of warriors immediately started to Salem and brought Isaac Glikhikan bound to Gnadenhutten, singing a death song. Loskiel relates that while the savages were binding him, perceiving that they seemed much terrified, he encouraged them, saying, "Formerly, when I was ignorant of God, I should not have suffered any one of you to touch me. But now, having been converted unto him, through mercy, I am willing to suffer all things for his sake. He no sooner arrived in the camp but a general uproar ensued, the savages demanding that he should be cut in pieces. The Delawares, who hated him more particularly for his conversion, thirsted for his blood, but the Half King interfering, would not suffer him to be killed. However, they examined him very severely, and though his innocence was clearly proved, they attacked him with opprobious language. After some hours' confinement, he was set at liberty. Although the young woman reached Pittsburgh, the commandant there deemed it too late, or otherwise unadvisable, to attempt a forcible rescue. It was a prudent decision, and probably prevented a massacre of the missionaries and their families.

On the 10th, the Indians resumed their outrages to such a degree, that emigration seemed the desirable alternative. It was accordingly proposed to the congregations, who sorrowfully assented. "But they never," says Loskiel, "forsook any country with more reluctance. They were now obliged to forsake three beautiful settlements, Gnadenhutten, Salem and Schoenbrun, and the greatest part of their possessions in them. They had already lost above two hundred head of horned cattle, and four hundred hogs. Besides this, they left a great quantity of Indian corn in store, above three hundred acres of corn land, where the harvest was just ripening, besides potatoes, cabbage, and other roots and garden fruits in the ground. According to a moderate calculation, their loss was computed at twelve thousand dollars or two thousand pounds. But what gave them most pain, was the total loss of all books and writings, for the instruction of their youth. These were all burnt by the savages."

On the third day after their departure, they arrived at Goschocking, where a short halt was made to hunt a tamed buffalo cow, which was shot as it came to the river to drink. Here Elliott left for the Scioto to meet McKee, greatly to the relief of the Moravian teachers. They then ascended the Walhonding, partly by water and partly along the banks of that stream. On the 19th, two of their best canoes, heavily laden with provisions were sunk in a violent storm of wind and rain, and the women and children suffered severely from exposure. Half King halted to give the encampment an opportunity to dry their clothes and baggage, and hence dispatched a war-party to the Ohio. "While they were marching so proudly through our camp," adds Heckewelder, "they were not aware of what would befall them: they were defeated with the loss of some of the party, among whom were the Half King's two sons."

At Gockhosink, or the "habitation of owls," (probably Owl Creek, now Vernon River) they left the river, traveling altogether by land, and on the 11th of October, (a calendar month in making a journey of one hundred and twenty-five miles) they arrived at the Sandusky River. Here the Half King left them, and after roving to and fro for some time, they "pitched upon the best spot they could find in the dreary waste, and built small huts of logs and bark, to screen themselves from the cold, having neither beds nor blankets, and being reduced to the greatest poverty and want. The savages had by degrees stolen every thing both from the missionaries and the Indians on the journey, only leaving them the needful utensils for making maple sugar." Loskiel mentions as an extraordinary proof of the general distress, that "even the missionaries, who had hitherto always lived upon their own produce, were now obliged to receive alms, they and their families being supported by contributions gathered in the congregation." A party was sent back to the Muskingum to gather a portion of the corn yet standing in the fields; and returned with about four hundred bushels. Six of their number including the missionary Shebosch, were taken prisoners at Schoenbrun, and carried to Pittsburgh, but were released soon after their arrival there.

The month of October had not passed, before a message was received from the British commmandant at Detroit, requiring the missionaries to appear before him. On the 25th, Zeisberger, Heckewelder, Senseman and Edwards, with four Indian assistants, started upon the journey, and after enduring the hardships and dangers of the land route to the mouth of the Maumee River, (called Tawa or Ottawa by Heckewelder,) and thence along the western shore of Lake Erie, they reached Detroit at the expiration of nine days. In their first interview with the Governor, Arend Schuyler Depeyster, he informed them that the reason of calling them from their settlements on the Muskingum, was because he had heard that they carried on a correspondence with the Americans to the prejudice of the English interest. The missionaries justified themselves from such an imputa tion, and a further investigation was postponed until the arrival of Captain Pipe. Fortunately, that chief was not accompanied by Elliott or Girty, and when he was confronted with the missionaries on the 9th of November, he bore a frank and honorable testimony to their impartiality and worth, and in answer to a direct appeal by the Governor, advised that they should be allowed to return to their congregations. "I never witnessed," Heckewelder piously observes, "a more manifest instance of the powerful workings of conscience than during the whole of this transaction. Of course, all who were present, immediately acquitted us of all the charges brought against us; expressing their sincere regret that we had innocently suffered so much."

The missionaries were thenceforth treated with much kindness by the commandant, his officers, and the inhabitants of Detroit, and soon returned to Upper Sandusky. Here, as the winter advanced, the unfortunate Indians were often on the verge of starvation; while Half King and Pipe, instigated by Elliott and Girty, resumed their persecutions, and demanded that the Governor of Detroit should remove the teachers from Sandusky. Their threats were too significant to be disregarded, and an order was received on the 1st of March, 1782, directing Girty and Half King to remove the missionaries and their families to Detroit: but as they had just arranged an expedition to the Ohio, one Francis Levallie, a Canadian Frenchman, living at Lower Sandusky, was appointed to accompany them. This was a fortunate exchange, for their conductor proved himself courteous and humane, even surrendering his own horse to the missionary Zeisberger, who was sixty years old, and insisting that respect for his age and station alike prompted the act. Levallie, instead of urging the party, among whom were the wives and children of the missionaries, through the dreary wilderness beyond Lower Sandusky, tarried at the latter place and sent a messenger to Detroit for further iustructions, while, until his return, two English traders, Messrs. Arundel and Robbins, hospitably received the fugitives into their houses. In due course, two vessels arrived from Detroit, under directions from the Governor to transport the missionaries and their families by Sandusky Bay and Lake Erie. They embarked on the 14th of April, greatly to the chagrin of Girty, who had complained in the most brutal manner of their indulgent treatment, and made the voyage safely to Detroit, where they were generously received, and allowed their choice, either to remain under the protection of Col. Depeyster, or be returned to Bethlehem. They chose to remain in the vicinity of their beloved Indian congregation, although restrained from living among them.

Simultaneously with the removal of Zeisberger and his fellow-teachers to Detroit, a tragedy was enacted on the Muskingum, which fills the darkest page in the border history of the American Revolution. We refer to the cruel and cowardly massacre of a party of Moravian Indians, who had again repaired to their deserted cornfields to glean the scattered ears for the relief of their suffering brethren on the Sandusky plains. Unhappily, while this peaceable party were thus engaged on the Muskingum, a band of Indians from Sandusky had made a descent upon the Pennsylvania frontier, and murdered the family of Mr. William Wallace, consisting of his wife and five or six children. A man named John Carpenter was taken prisoner at the same time. Enraged at these outrages, a band of one hundred and sixty men, from the settlements on the Monongahela, turned out in quest of the marauders, under the command of Col. David Williamson. Each man provided himself with arms, ammunition and provisions, and the greater number were mounted. They struck immediately for the settlements of Salem and Gnadenhutten, arriving within a mile of the latter place at the close of the second day's march. Colonel Gibson, commanding at Pittsburgh, having heard of Williamson's expedition, dispatched messengers to apprise the Indians of the circumstance, but they arrived too late.

Still, the Christian Indians were aware of the approach of Williamson's band, but having recently been accustomed to regard the savage allies of the English as the source of their injuries, they made no effort to escape, although their labors were accomplished and they were about to retrace their steps to Sandusky. The bloody sequel we prefer to give in the words of Loskiel:

"Meanwhile, the murderers marched first to Gnadenhutten,

where they arrived on the 6th of March. About a mile from the settlement they met young Shebosch in the wood, fired at him, and wounded him so much that he could not escape. He then, according to the account of the murderers themselves, begged for his life, representing that he was Shebosch, the son of a white Christian man. But they paid no attention to his entreaties, and cut him in pieces with their hatchets. They then approached the Indians, most of whom were in their plantations, and surrounded them almost imperceptibly, but feigning a friendly behavior, told them to go home, promising to do them no injury. They even pretended to pity them on account of the mischief done to them by the English and the savages, assuring them of the protection and friendship of the Americans. The poor believing Indians, knowing nothing of the death of young Shebosch, believed every word they said, went home with them and treated them in the most hospitable manner. They likewise spoke freely concerning their sentiments as Christian Indians, who had never taken the least share in the war. A small barrel of wine being found among their goods, they told their persecutors, on inquiry, that it was intended for the Lord's Supper, and that they were going to carry it to Sandusky. Upon this, they were informed that they should not return thither, but go to Pittsburgh, where they would be out of the way of any assault made by the English or savages. This they heard with resignation, concluding that God would perhaps choose this method to put an end to their present sufferings. Prepossessed with this idea, they cheerfully delivered their guns, hatchets and other weapons to the murderers, who promised to take good care of them, and in Pittsburgh to return every article to its rightful owner. The Indians even showed them those things, which they had secreted in the woods, assisted in packing them up, and emptied all their bee-hives for their pretended friends.

"In the meantime, the assistant, John Martin, went to Salem, and brought the news of the arrival of the white people to the believing Indians, assuring them that they need not be afraid to go with them, for they were come to carry them to a place of safety, and to afford them protection and support. The Salem Indians did not hesitate to accept of this proposal, believing unanimously that God had sent the Americans to release them from their disagreeable situation at Sandusky, and imagining that when they had arrived at Pittsburgh, they might soon find a safe place to build a settlement and easily procure advice and assistance from Bethlehem. Thus, John Martin, with two Salem brethren, returned to Gnadenhutten, to acquaint both their Indian brethren and the white people with their resolution. The latter expressed a desire to see Salem, and a party of them was conducted thither and received with much friendship. Here they pretended to have the same good will and affection towards the Indians as at Gnadenhutten, and easily persuaded them to return with them. By the way they entered into much spiritual conversation with the Indians, some of whom spoke English well, giving these people, who feigned great piety, proper and scriptural answers to many questions concerning religious subjects. The assistants, Isaac Glikhikan and Israel, were no less sincere and unreserved in their answers to some political questions started by the white people, and thus the murderers obtained a full and satisfactory account of the present situation and sentiments of the Indian congregation. In the meantime, the defenceless Indians at Gnadenhutten were suddenly attacked and driven together by the white people, and, without resistance, seized and bound.

The Salem Indians now met the same fate. Before they entered Gnadenhutten, they were at once surprised by their conductors, robbed of their guns, and even of their pocket knives, and brought bound into the settlement."

The officers, unwilling to take on themselves the whole responsibility of a massacre, agreed to refer the question to a vote of the detachment. The men were drawn up in a line, and Williamson put the question, "whether the Moravian Indians should be taken prisoners to Pittsburgh or put to death?" requesting all in favor of saving their lives to advance in front of the line. On this, sixteen, some say eighteen, stepped out of the rank, and formed themselves into the second line. In this manner was their fate decided.[10]

"Those who were of a different opinion," continues Loskiel, "wrung their hands, calling God to witness that they were innocent of the blood of these harmless Christian Indians. But the majority remained unmoved, and only differed concerning the mode of execution. Some were for burning them alive, others for taking their scalps, and the latter was at last agreed upon; upon which one of the murderers was sent to the prisoners to tell them that as they were Christian Indians, they might prepare themselves in a Christian manner, for they must all die to-morrow.

"It may easily be conceived how great their terror was at hearing a sentence so unexpected. However, they soon recollected themselves, and patiently suffered the murderers to lead them into two houses, in one of which the brethren, and in the other the sisters and children were confined like sheep ready for slaughter. They declared to the murderers, that though they could call God to witness that they were perfectly innocent, yet they were prepared and willing to suffer

10) Doddridge's Notes, 251.

death. But as they had at their conversion and baptism made a solemn promise to the Lord Jesus Christ, that they would live unto him and endeavor to please him alone in this world, they knew that they had been deficient in many respects, and therefore wished to have some time granted to pour out their hearts before him in prayer, and in exhorting each other to remain faithful unto the end. One brother, called Abraham, who for some time past had been in a lukewarm state of heart, seeing his end approaching, made the following public confession before his brethren :

"'Dear brethren! it seems as if we should all soon depart unto our Saviour, for our sentence is fixed. You know that I have been an untoward child, and have grieved the Lord and my brethren by my disobedience, not walking as I ought to have done. But yet I will now cleave to my Saviour with my last breath, and hold him fast, though I am so great a sinner. I know assuredly, that He will forgive me all my sins and not cast me out.' The brethren assured him of their love and forgiveness, and both they and the sisters spent the latter part of the night in singing praises to God their Saviour, in the joyful hope that they should soon be able to praise him without sin.

"When the day of their execution arrived, namely, the 8th of March, two houses were fixed upon, one for the brethren and another for the sisters and children, to which the wanton murderers gave the name of slaughter-houses. Some of them went to the brethren and showed great impatience that the execution had not yet begun, to which the brethren replied that they were all ready to die, having commended their immortal souls to God, who had given them that divine assurance in their hearts that they should come unto him and be with him forever.

"Immediately after this declaration the carnage commenced. The poor, innocent people, men, women and children, were led, bound two and two together with ropes, into the above mentioned slaughter-houses, and there scalped and murdered.[11]

"According to the testimony of the murderers themselves, they behaved with uncommon patience, and went to meet death with cheerful resignation. The above mentioned brother Abraham was the first victim. A sister called Christina, who had formerly lived with the sisters in Bethlehem, and spoke English and German well, fell on her knees before the captain of the gang, and begged her life, but was told that he could not help her.

"Thus ninety-six persons magnified the name of the Lord by patiently meeting a cruel death. Sixty-two were grown persons, among whom were five of the most valuable assistants, and thirty-four children.

"Only two youths, each between sixteen and seventeen years old, escaped almost miraculously from the hands of the murderers. One of them, seeing that they were in earnest,

11) As to the precise manner of this tragedy, Heckewelder differs from Loskiel, whose narrative is preserved above. Heckewelder does not speak of their removal from the place of their confinement. His language is (Narrative, 319): "The murderers, impatient to make a beginning, came again to them, while they were singing, and inquiring whether they were now ready for dying, they were answered in the affirmative; adding, 'that they had commended their immortal souls to God, who had given them the assurance in their hearts that he would receive their souls.' One of the party now taking up a cooper's mallet, which lay in the house (the owner being a cooper), saying, 'How exactly this will answer for the business,' he began with Abraham, and continued knocking down one after the other, until he had counted fourteen, that he had killed with his own hands. He now handed the instrument to one of his fellow-murderers, saying, 'My arm now fails me; go on in the same way! I think I have done pretty well.' In another house, where the women and children were confined, Judith, a remarkably pious, aged widow, was the first victim," &c., &c.

was so fortunate as to disengage himself from his bonds, then slipping unobserved from the crowd, crept through a narrow window into the cellar of that house in which the sisters were executed. Their blood soon penetrated through the flooring, and according to his account, ran in streams into the cellar, by which it appears probable that most, if not all of them, were not merely scalped, but killed with hatchets or swords. The lad remained concealed until night, providentially no one coming down to search the cellar, when having, with much difficulty, climbed up the wall to the window, he crept through and escaped into a neighboring thicket. The other youth's name was Thomas. The murderers struck him only one blow on the head, took his scalp, and left him. But after some time he recovered his senses, and saw himself surrounded by bleeding corpses. Among these, he observed one brother, called Abel, moving and endeavoring to raise himself up. But he remained lying as still as though he had been dead, and this caution proved the means of his deliverance; for soon after, one of the murderers coming in and observing Abel's motions, killed him outright with two or three blows. Thomas lay quiet until dark, though suffering the most exquisite torment. He then ventured to creep towards the door, and observing nobody in the neighborhood, got out and escaped into the wood, where he concealed himself during the night. These two youths met afterwards in the wood, and God preserved them from harm on their journey to Sandusky, though they purposely took a long circuit and suffered great hardships and danger. But before they left the neighborhood of Gnadenhutten, they observed the murderers from behind the thicket making merry after their successful enterprise, and at last setting fire to the two slaughter-houses filled with corpses.

"Providentially, the believing Indians who were at that time in Schoenbrun escaped. The missionaries had, immediately on receiving orders to repair to Fort Detroit, sent a messenger to the Muskingum to call the Indians home, with a view to see them once more, and to get horses from them for their journey. This messenger happened to arrive at Schoenbrun the day before the murderers came to Gnadenhutten, and having delivered his message, the Indians of Schoenbrun sent another messenger to Gnadenhutten to inform their brethren there, and at Salem, of the message received. But before he reached Gnadenhutten, he found young Shebosch lying dead and scalped by the way-side, and looking forward, saw many white people in and about Gnadenhutten. He instantly fled back with great precipitation, and told the Indians in Schoenbrun what he had seen, who all took flight and ran into the woods. They now hesitated a long while, not knowing whither to turn or how to proceed. Thus, when the murderers arrived at Schoenbrun, the Indians were still near the premises, observing every thing that happened there, and might easily have been discovered. But here the murderers seemed, as it were, struck with blindness. Finding nobody at home, they destroyed and set fire to the settlement, and having done the same at Gnadenhutten and Salem, they set off with the scalps of their innocent victims, about fifty horses, a number of blankets and other things, and marched to Pittsburgh, with a view to murder the few Indians lately settled on the north side of the Ohio, opposite to the fort. Some of them fell a sacrifice to the rage of this blood-thirsty crew, and a few escaped. Among the latter was Anthony, a member of the [Moravian] congregation, who happened then to be at Pittsburgh, and both he and the Indians of Schoenbrun arrived, after many dangers and difficulties, safe at Sandusky.

"The foregoing account of this dreadful event was collected partly from what the murderers themselves related to their friends at Pittsburgh, partly from the account given by the two youths, who escaped in the manner above described, and also from the report made by the Indian assistant Samuel of Schoenbrun, and by Anthony from Pittsburgh, all of whom agreed exactly as to the principal parts of their respective evidences."

The Rev. Joseph Doddridge, in his Notes upon the Settlement and Indian Wars of Western Virginia and Pennsylvania, published at Wheeling, in 1824, closes his narrative of this transaction with some observations, which, in justice to Colonel Williamson and his detachment, should accompany the indignant sketch of the Moravian historian:

"The pressure of the Indian war along the whole of the western frontier," Doddridge remarks, "for several years preceding the event under consideration, had been dreadfully severe. From early in the spring, until the commencement of winter, from day to day, murders were committed in every direction by the Indians. The people lived in forts which were in the highest degree uncomfortable. The men were harrassed continually with the duties of going on scouts and campaigns. There was scarcely a family of the first settlers, who did not, at some time or other, lose more or less of their number by the merciless Indians. Their cattle were killed, their cabins burned, and their horses carried off. These losses were severely felt by a people so poor as we were, at that time. Thus circumstanced, our people were exasperated to madness, by the extent and severity of the war. The unavailing endeavors of the American Congress to prevent the Indians from taking up the hatchet against either side in the revolutionary contest, contributed much to increase the general indignation against them; at the same time that those pacific endeavors of our government divided the Indians amongst themselves, on the question of war or peace with the whites. The Moravians, part of the Delawares, and some others, faithfully endeavored to preserve peace; but in vain. The Indian maxim was: "He that is not for us, is against us.' Hence the Moravian missionaries and their followers were several times on the point of being murdered by the warriors. This would have been done, had it not been for the prudent conduct of some of the war-chiefs.

"On the other hand, the local situation of the Moravian villages excited the jealousy of the white people. If they took no direct agency in the war, yet they were, as they were then called, 'Half way houses,' between us and the warriors, at which the latter could stop, rest, refresh themselves and traffic off their plunder. Whether these aids, thus given to our enemies, were contrary to the laws of neutrality between belligerents, is a question which I willingly leave to the decision of civilians. On the part of the Moravians, they were unavoidable. If they did not give or sell provisions to the warriors, they would take them by force. The fault was in their situation, not in themselves.

"The longer the war continued, the more our people complained of the situation of these Moravian villages. It was said that it was owing to their being so near us, that the warriors commenced their depredations so early in the spring, and continued them until late in the fall.

"In the latter end of the year 1781, the militia of the frontier came to a determination to break up the Moravian villages on the Muskingum. For this purpose a detachment of our men went out under the command of Col. David Williamson, for the purpose of inducing the Indians with their teachers to move further off, or bring them prisoners to Fort Pitt. When they arrived at the villages they found but few Indians, the greater number of them having removed to Sandusky. These few were well treated, taken to Fort Pitt and delivered to the commandant at that station, who, after a short detention, sent them home again.

"This procedure gave great offence to the people of the country, who thought that the Moravians ought to have been killed. Col. Williamson, who, before this little campaign, had been a very popular man, on account of his activity and bravery in war, now became the subject of severe animadversions on account of his lenity to the Moravian Indians. In justice to the memory of Col. Williamson I have to say, that although at that time very young, I was personally acquainted with him, and from my recollection of his conversation, I say with confidence that he was a brave man, but not cruel. He would meet an enemy in battle, and fight like a soldier; but not murder a prisoner. Had he possessed the authority of a superior officer in a regular army, I do not believe that a single Moravian Indian would have lost his life; but he possessed no such authority. He was only a militia officer, who could advise, but not command. His only fault was that of too easy a compliance with popular opinion and popular prejudice. On this account his memory has been loaded with unmerited reproach.

"Several reports unfavorable to the Moravians had been in circulation for some time before the campaign against them. One was, that the night after they were liberated at Fort Pitt, they crossed the river and killed or made prisoners of a family of the name of Montour. A family on Buffalo creek had been mostly killed in the summer or fall of 1781, and it was said by one of them, who, after being made prisoner, made his escape, that the leader of the party of Indians who did the mischief was a Moravian. These, with other reports, of similar import, served as a pretext for their destruction, although no doubt they were utterly false.

"Should it be asked, what sort of people composed the band of murderers of these unfortunate people?—I answer, they were not miscreants or vagabonds: many of them were men of the first standing in the country. Many of them were men who had recently lost relatives by the hand of the savages: several of the latter class found articles which had been plundered from their own houses, or those of their relatives, in the houses of the Moravians. One man, it is said, found the clothes of his wife and children, who had been murdered by the Indians but a few days before. They were still bloody: yet there was no unequivocal evidence, that these people had any direct agency in the war. Whatever of our property was found with them, had been left by the warriors in exchange for the provisions which they took from them. When attacked by our people, although they might have defended themselves, they did not. They never fired a single shot. They were prisoners, and had been promised protection. Every dictate of justice and humanity required that their lives should be spared. The complaint of their villages being 'half-way houses for the warriors,' was at an end, as they had been removed to Sandusky the fall before. It was, therefore, an atrocious and unqualified murder. But by whom committed? By a majority of the campaign? For the honor of my country, I hope I may safely answer this question in the negative. It was one of those convulsions of the moral state of society, in which the voice of the justice and humanity of a majority is silenced by the clamor and violence of a lawless minority. Very few of our men imbrued their hands in the blood of the Moravians. Even those who had not voted for saving their lives, retired from the scene of slaughter with horror and disgust. Why then did they not give their votes in their favor? The fear of public indignation restrained them from doing so. They thought well: but had not heroism enough to express their opinions. Those who did so, deserve honorable mention for their intrepidity. So far as it may hereafter be in my power, this honor shall be done them: while the name of the murderers shall not stain the pages of history from my pen at least."

Thus much for the amiable Doddridge. We leave his plea for the friends and neighbors of his childhood undiminished, committing it freely to the discrimination of the reader. But there was still another construction placed upon this bloody deed—that of the savage fatalists of the woods. As the sad tale passed from village to village of the Ohio tribes, the Indians, particularly the scattered Delawares, recognized with simple reverence a providential design. They said they had envied the condition of their relations, the believing Indians, and could not bear to look upon their peaceful and happy lives in contrast with their own lives of privation and war. Hence they had endeavored to take them from their own tranquil homes, and draw them back into heathenism, that they might be reduced again to a level with themselves. But the Great Spirit would not suffer it to be so, and had taken them to himself.

Soon after the massacre on the Muskingum, the congregation at Sandusky, reduced in numbers and deprived of their teachers, yielded to the solicitations of their Delaware and

Shawanese friends, and abandoned their settlement at Sandusky. They were ordered to do so by Half King, who persisted in holding them in some degree responsible for the fate of his two sons; but in their present situations, it was doubtless a prudent resolution. Loskiel informs us, that on their dispersion, "one part went into the country of the Shawanese: the rest stayed some time in the neighborhood of Pipestown, and then resolved to proceed farther—to the Miami River." Heckewelder is more explicit, and mentions the Scioto and Miami of the Lake, now Maumee, as their respective destinations.

We have previously considered the probability, that Cornstalk and the Shawanese tribe on the Scioto, were disposed to peace, and perhaps to accept Christianity, through the influence of the missionaries. Indeed, after the death of Cornstalk, a tribe of Shawanese removed to the Muskingum and concurred in the pacific policy of the Delaware chiefs, only retiring to the Scioto when that policy was reversed. These Indians doubtless tendered an asylum to the Moravians. Their friends on the Maumee were the band of Delawares, who were the immediate followers of the magnanimous Pachgantschihilas, whose friendly solicitude and timely warning to the missionaries had been so fully justified by recent events as to seem almost prophetic. There is ample evidence that in 1791, nine years afterwards, Delawares inhabited the banks of the Auglaize River near its junction with the Maumee; and here, while the heathen, aboriginal and European, raged around them, the simple-hearted proselytes of a religion of peace, found a refuge from the persecutions of those professing the same benignant faith.

CHAPTER XXII.

PENNSYLVANIA CAMPAIGNS AGAINST THE OHIO INDIANS.

THE border war of the Revolution upon the Ohio, consisted of two series of expeditions in retaliation for Indian outrage —those already considered, which issued from the region of Kentucky traversed by the Kenhawa, the Licking and the Kentucky Rivers, usually led by George Rogers Clark, and designed to restrain the inveterate Shawanese, and those which had Wheeling and the vicinity of Pittsburgh for their base of operations, and aimed to chastise the bands of Wyandots, Ottawas, Mingoes, and finally the Delawares, whose villages were scattered upon the sources of the Muskingum and Sandusky Rivers and along the Lake shore. The latter may be called the Pennsylvania Campaigns, from the fact that the western counties of Pennsylvania furnished the volunteer militia, which composed the main force of these expeditions.

To the Coshocton campaign of Col. Daniel Brodhead, incidental allusion has already been made. In the correspondence of that officer recently published,[1] he says, under date of March 27, 1781, that he had called upon the County Lieutenants for a few of the militia, and intended to surprise the Indian towns about Coochocking—written Goschocking by Heckewelder, and now familiar as Coshocton. Soon afterwards, probably before the close of April, these levies

1) Craig's Olden Time, vol. ii, p. 392.

assembled at Wheeling, and their number, including a few continental troops from Pittsburgh, are estimated by Doddridge[2] at eight hundred men. In justice to those upon whom was imposed the responsibility of command, it should be borne in mind that the army was mostly composed of the tumultuous and intractable population of the frontiers.

When in the vicinity of the Moravian towns, it has been mentioned, that Col. Brodhead and Col. Shepherd of Wheeling could with difficulty restrain a foray of the militia upon the peaceful inhabitants. The remaining details of the expedition rest upon the authority of Doddridge.

At White Eyes Plain, a few miles from Coshocton, an Indian prisoner was taken. Soon afterwards two more Indians were discovered, one of whom was wounded, but he as well as the other made his escape.

The commander knowing that these two Indians would make the utmost despatch in going to the town, to give notice of the approach of the army, ordered a rapid march, in the midst of a heavy rain, to reach the town before them and take it by surprise. The plan succeeded. The army reached the place in three divisions. The right and left wings approached the river a little above and below the town, while the center marched directly upon it. The whole number of the Indians in the village, on the east side of the river, together with ten or twelve from a little village

2) Rev. Joseph Doddridge, M. D. Frequent allusion has already been made to this narrator of frontier manners and incidents. In the infancy of the Protestant Episcopal Church of Ohio, his services as a minister of the Gospel were cheerfully given to the settlements opposite Wheeling; but in 1820, he announces an intention of resuming the medical profession, as the means of acquiring a competency for his approaching age. See a Republication of the Journals of Episcopal Conventions in Ohio, from 1818 to 1827, edited by Rev. W. C. French, 1853. The citations of the text are from Doddridge's Notes of Western Virginia.

some distance above, were made prisoners, without firing a single shot. The river having risen to a great height, owing to the recent fall of rain, the army could not cross it, and the villages with their inhabitants on the west side of the river escaped destruction.

Among the prisoners, sixteen warriors were pointed out by Pekillon, a friendly Delaware chief, as engaged in a recent excursion upon the frontiers of Virginia, during which all the male captives had been put to death by torture in the presence of their weeping families. A council of war was held in the evening to determine the fate of the warriors in custody. They were doomed to death, and by the order of the commander, they were bound, taken a little distance below the town, despatched with tomahawks and spears, and scalped.

Early the next morning, an Indian presented himself on the opposite bank of the river and asked for the "Big Captain." Brodhead came forward and inquired what he wanted? to which he replied, "I want peace." "Send over some of your chiefs," said the Colonel. "May be you kill," said the Indian. "They shall not be killed," was the answer. A fine looking sachem thereupon crossed the river, and entered into conversation with the commander in the street, but while thus engaged, a man of the name of Wetzel[3] came up behind him, with a tomahawk concealed in the bosom of his hunting shirt, and struck him on the back of his head. He fell and instantly expired.

On the retreat from Coshocton, Col. Brodhead committed the care of the prisoners, about twenty in number, to the militia. After marching half a mile, the men commenced

3) Lewis Wetzel, a noted borderer. See Appendix No. IX, for a biographical notice of this type of a numerous class.

killing them, and soon, all except a few women and children were despatched in cold blood.

The reduction of Detroit, for which Congress had collected troops and munitions in 1778, with no other result than the useless fortifications of Laurens and McIntosh, was again proposed in 1780–1. Thomas Jefferson, then Governor of Virginia, authorized Gen. George Rogers Clark to raise a force adequate to march from the Falls of the Ohio through the valleys of the Wabash and the Maumee to Detroit. The expedition was approved by Washington, who wrote to Col. Brodhead, the commandant at Pittsburgh, to send a detachment with four field pieces and one eight inch howitzer, besides other stores. Accordingly, Captain Isaac Craig descended the Ohio with two companies of artillery to the place of rendezvous, but Gen. Clark was obliged to relinquish the expedition—his whole force, although nearly a year had passed in exertions to recruit it, not exceeding seven hundred and fifty men. Captain Craig returned to Pittsburgh on the 26th of December, 1781, having been forty days on the voyage from the falls. He was obliged to throw away his gun-carriages, but brought back the pieces themselves, and the best of the stores.

The most melancholy incident in connection with Clark's projected expedition against Detroit, was the massacre of a party of Pennsylvania volunteers. In a letter from General William Irvine, who assumed the command at Pittsburgh, in the fall of 1781, addressed to General Washington, and dated in December of that year, the affair is thus noticed: "A Col. Lochry, of Westmoreland county, Pennsylvania, with about one hundred men in all, composed of volunteers and a company raised by Pennsylvania, for the defence of that county, started to join General Clark, who, it is said, ordered him to unite with him (Clark) at the mouth of the Miami, up which river it was previously designed to proceed; but the General having changed his plan, left a small party at the Miami, with directions to Lochry to follow him to the mouth of the falls. Sundry accounts agree that this party, and all of Lochry's troops, to a man, were waylaid by the Indians and British, (for it is said they had artillery) and all killed or taken, not a man escaping, either to join General Clark or to return home." In a journal kept by General Richard Butler, while attending a conference with the Ohio Indians at the mouth of the Great Miami, in the winter of 1785–6, he designates Lochry's creek, about seven miles south of the Great Miami, on the north side of the Ohio, as the scene of this tragedy. "Col. Lochry," he says, "and his party were defeated and cut to pieces by Brant and his people, who perfectly surprised Lochry." It is singular that our historical compilations contain so slight a reference to a battle which resulted in the destruction of more than a hundred whites, especially as, in the language of Gen. Irvine, "Lochry's party were the best men of the frontier." In the disastrous battle of Blue Licks, the Kentucky loss was but seventy-six, although on that occasion there were many survivors, to report as well as to revenge the horrors of the day. But at Lochry's creek a hecatomb of brave spirits died and gave no sign.[4]

In the spring of 1782, occurred the Moravian campaign, already noticed in the narrative of the mission on the Muskingum.

It was immediately followed by active preparations for a

4) Craig's Olden Time, vol. ii., 541. Gen. Butler was doubtless mistaken, if he supposed that the leader of the Indians engaged in the slaughter of Lochry's party, was the Mohawk chieftain, Joseph Brant.

volunteer expedition against the new settlement of the Christian Indians and the Wyandot and Delaware towns, on the head waters of the Sandusky. The enterprise was conducted with secrecy and dispatch; the men were all mounted, and furnished themselves with all their outfits, except some ammunition which was supplied by the Lieutenant Colonel of Washington county.

On the 20th of May, 1782, the volunteers assembled at the deserted Mingo village, on the west bank of the Ohio, seventy-five miles below Pittsburgh. No estimate of their number is less than four hundred and fifty. Here, Colonel William Crawford, the agent and friend of Washington, was elected to the command. Col. David Williamson was an unsuccessful candidate for the post, and accompanied the expedition.

On Saturday, the 25th of May, the army commenced its march, and on the fourth day reached Shoenbrun, on the Muskingum, finding sufficient corn in the adjacent fields for a night's forage of their horses. On the morning of the 30th, Major Brunton and Capt. Bean, being a few hundred yards in advance of the troops, observed two Indians skulking through the woods, apparently observing the movements of the detachment. Although fired upon, they escaped. From the excitement and confusion of his troops on this slight occasion, Crawford was held to apprehend the worst consequences from their want of discipline.

It had been supposed that the expedition would surprise the Indians, but the spies of the latter had hovered near the army during the whole route, visiting each encampment the day after it was abandoned, and transcribing from the trees where some loungers had carved the words, that "No quarter was to be given to any Indian, whether man, woman or child."

The savages were alert and ready to repel the invaders, who now pressed rapidly forward.

"Nothing material happened," says Doddridge, "until the sixth day, when their guides conducted them to the site of the Moravian village, on one of the upper branches of the Sandusky river, but here, instead of meeting with Indians and plunder, they found nothing but vestiges of desolation. The place was covered with high grass, and the remains of a few huts alone announced that the place had been the residence of the people whom they intended to destroy." The removal of the missionaries to Detroit, and the dispersion of the congregation a few weeks before, thus proved a providential interposition in their behalf.

The accounts of what followed are very conflicting. The men here insisted upon returning, as their horses were jaded and the stock of provisions nearly exhausted. The officers held a council and determined to march one day longer, and if they should not meet the enemy in the course of the day, to retreat. Doddridge states that the army commenced their march next morning, which was continued until two o'clock in the afternoon, when the advance guard was attacked and driven in by the Indians, who were discovered in large numbers in the high grass with which the plain was covered. Another version is,[5] that on the eleventh day of the march, "the army reached the spot where the town of Sandusky had formerly stood, but from which the Indians had lately removed to a spot about eighteen miles below"—that here a council was held with the result already mentioned; and that "just as the council broke up," one of the advance guards arrived with the intelligence that the Indians had appeared in force "a few miles in advance." If the army, all of whom were

5) McClung's Western Adventure, 120.

mounted, had advanced beyond the Moravian town from sunrise on a June day, until two hours after noon, the distance to the place where the Indians were discovered would have been more than a "few miles."

The traditions of Wyandot county represent the scene of the engagement which ensued as three miles north of the Upper Sandusky of a modern map, and one mile west of the Sandusky River. A spot near Leesville or Leesburg in Crawford county, is called "the battle ground," from a tradition that there, Crawford, on his way to Upper Sandusky, had a skirmish with the Indians. If the route of his march was so far north as Leesville, and we admit the statement of a six hours' progress between the Moravian towns and the battle field, it becomes probable that the temporary settlement of the Christian Indians was in the vicinity of Bucyrus, whence a westward march of six hours before meeting the enemy, might have occurred.

The discrepancy is not merely whether the alarm of an enemy in advance, was communicated to the army "just as the council broke up" or after a six hours' further march; but it includes a contradiction as to the locality of the Moravian settlement on the Sandusky. McClung makes it within a short distance of the Indian ambuscade—Doddridge, a full half day's journey by a mounted body of men. McClung's Narrative is consistent with the opinion that the council was held at the old Indian town of Upper Sandusky, which would also be the site of the Moravian settlement, and stood on the bank of the Sandusky River, four miles north-east of the present town of Upper Sandusky. Heckewelder's Narrative describes the destination of the captive congregation in a manner favorable to this view of the case. "On the 11th of October" (1781,) he says "they arrived at the old Up per Sandusky town, which is on the east branch of the river of that name, where the Half King and his party left them and proceeded nine or ten miles further to their homes." Heckewelder also mentions that Pipestown was ten miles distant.[6]

All the accounts unite that there were two Wyandot villages (of which one, Upper Sandusky Old Town, was probably deserted at this time) and one Delaware village, the residence of Captain Pipe. The latter was situated on the Tymochtee, about eight miles above its junction with the Sandusky, and we assume that New Wyandot Town, probably the residence of Half King, was at Big Spring, now Springville in Seneca county. These localities are ascertained with a fair degree of certainty, and rest upon the authority of Col. John Johnston, and Joseph McCutchen Esq., of Wyandot county. The only doubt is raised by Doddridge's Narrative, whether Old Town of Upper Sandusky was the Moravian village. We incline to the affirmative belief, and that the council of war was held within a short distance of the battle field.

With these explanations, we resume the narrative of the battle of Sandusky Plains.

The main body of the Indians had stationed themselves in a grove of trees. Crawford immediately ordered his men to dismount, tie their horses, and force the enemy from this position, which was done. The Indians continued their fire from the high grass of the prairie. Doddridge relates that the savages attempted to gain a small skirt of wood on Crawford's right flank, but were prevented by the vigilance and bravery of Major Leet, who commanded the right wing; while McClung's statement is, that Crawford was outflanked and exposed, except as the wood was a partial shelter, to a severe fire on every side. From four o'clock until dark, the

6) Heckewelder's Narrative of Indian Missions, 281, 285.

contest was very animated. Doddridge admits only "three killed and several wounded" on the American side, which was certainly an inconsiderable loss in so close an engagement. At night, the enemy drew off, and Crawford's party slept on their arms upon the field of battle.

On the next day, the Indians did not resume the attack, as they were awaiting reïnforcements, but were seen in large bodies traversing the plains in every direction. Some of them appeared to be employed in carrying off their dead and wounded.

As soon as it was dark, the field officers assembled in council; and, as the numbers of the enemy were evidently increasing every moment, it was unanimously determined to retreat by night, as rapidly as was consistent with order and the preservation of the wounded. The resolution was quickly announced to the troops, and the necessary dispositions made for carrying it into effect. The outposts were silently withdrawn from the vicinity of the enemy, and as fast as they came in the troops were formed in three parallel lines, with the wounded borne upon biers in the centre. By nine o'clock at night, all necessary arrangements had been made, and the retreat began in good order.

Unfortunately, they had scarcely moved a hundred paces, when the report of several rifles was heard in the rear, in the direction of the Indian encampment. The troops soon became unsteady. At length a solitary voice, in the front rank, called out, that their design was discovered, and that the Indians would soon be upon them. A panic, accompanied by an immense uproar, ensued—the wounded were abandoned to the mercy of the enemy—straggling parties wandered away from the main body, under the delusive expectation of more safety by so doing: and of the whole number, scarcely three hundred reached the settlements. The Indians soon ceased their attacks upon the main body, but pursued the small parties with such activity that few of them escaped.

Dr. Knight, the surgeon of the detachment, was in the rear when the flight commenced, and hurried forward. He had not advanced more than three hundred yards, when he heard the voice of Colonel Crawford, a short distance in front, calling aloud for his son, John Crawford, his son-in-law, Major Harrison, and his two nephews, Major Rose and William Crawford. Dr. Knight joined him, and they tarried until the last straggler had passed, without meeting or hearing of the young men. Presently a heavy fire was heard at the distance of a mile in front, accompanied by yells, screams, and other indications of a fierce attack. Crawford had lost all confidence in his men, and not choosing to unite his fortune with them, he changed his course to the northward in such a manner as to leave the combatants on the right. Dr. Knight, and two others, accompanied him. They continued in this direction for nearly an hour, until they supposed themselves out of the line of the enemy's operations, when their course was turned eastward. They were guided by the north star, soon crossed the Sandusky, and pressed forward until daybreak, when their horses failed, and were abandoned.

Continuing their journey on foot, they soon fell in with Captain Biggs, who had generously surrendered his horse to a wounded officer, Lieutenant Ashley, and was composedly walking by his side, with a rifle in his hand and a knapsack on his shoulders. This casual meeting was grateful to both parties, and they continued their journey with renewed spirits. At three o'clock in the afternoon a heavy rain fell and compelled them to encamp. A temporary shelter was formed by barking several trees, after the manner of the Indians, and spreading the bark over poles. Here they passed the night.

Resuming their route next morning, they were so fortunate as to find the carcass of a deer, neatly sliced and bundled in the skin, and a mile farther fell in with a white man, who had kindled a fire. They breakfasted heartily after the fatigues and abstinence of thirty-six hours, and continued their march. By noon, they had reached the path by which the army had marched a few days before, in their advance upon the Indian towns, and some discussion took place as to the propriety of taking that road homeward. Biggs and Knight strenuously insisted upon continuing their course through the woods, and avoiding all paths, but Crawford overruled them, representing that the Indians would not urge the pursuit beyond the plains, which were already far behind. Unfortunately the colonel prevailed, and abandoning their due eastern course, the party pursued the beaten path. They had not advanced a mile, when a party of Delaware Indians sprang up within twenty yards of Crawford and Knight, who were one hundred and fifty yards in front of their comrades, presented their guns, and ordered the fugitives in good English to stop. Crawford and Knight surrendered themselves prisoners, but the rest of the party made their escape, although Captain Biggs and Lieutenant Ashley were overtaken and killed the next day.

Col. Crawford and Doctor Knight were immediately taken to an Indian encampment, at a short distance from the place where they were captured. Here they found nine other prisoners, and passed the following day. The next morning, Monday, June 10, they were paraded (and our quotations in this connection are from Dr. Knight's own narrative) "to march to Sandusky, about thirty-three miles distant;" but "Col. Crawford was very desirous to see Simon Girty, who lived with the Indians, and was on this account permitted to go to town the same night, with two warriors to guard him." The other prisoners "were taken as far as the old town, which was within eight miles of the new."

Crawford had known Girty, before the latter's adherence to the British, and hoped to make some arrangements for his ransom from captivity and torture. Girty promised to do every thing in his power to save Crawford, and it is probable that the former made a proposition to Captain Pipe, offering three hundred and fifty dollars for the release of the American commandant, intending, unquestionably, to exact a much larger amount from Crawford. The Delaware chief treated the proposition as a gross insult, and threatened Girty himself with torture at the stake, if it was renewed. This threat had such an effect, that Girty appeared subsequently at the execution of Crawford, an acquiescent, perhaps an exultant spectator.

On the morning of June 11th, Crawford returned to his companions in misfortune at the Old Town, but Captain Pipe had preceded him and painted the faces of Dr. Knight and the other nine prisoners black. Upon Crawford's arrival, Pipe painted him also, but without any ferocity of language or manner. On the contrary, he dissembled so far as to assure Crawford that he would be adopted at the Wyandot village. When the Indians marched, Col. Crawford and Dr. Knight were kept back between Pipe and Wingemand, the two Delaware chiefs, while the other nine persons were sent forward. As they proceeded towards the Tymochtee, Crawford and his friend were shocked to see the bodies of four of the pris oners scattered along the path, and were themselves witnesses of the slaughter of the remaining five by a crowd of squaws and boys. Among them was one John McKinley, formerly an officer in a Virginia regiment, whose head was severed from his body by an old hag, and kicked about among the savages. Half a mile further, they reached the spot selected for Crawford's execution, which was attended with all the horrors of savage cruelty. Three hours of torture, during which he entreated Girty in vain for the mercy of a bullet through his heart, elapsed before the unfortunate victim was released from his unutterable anguish.

His companion and friend, Dr. Knight, was compelled to witness the horrible spectacle, and was taunted by Girty with the certainty of a similar fate when he should reach the Shawanese villages on the Mad River, whither, on the next morning, (after passing the night at the house of Captain Pipe, three quarters of a mile north of the scene of Crawford's fate,) he started under charge of a Delaware Indian. The first day they traveled about twenty-five miles and encamped for the night. In the morning the gnats becoming very troublesome, the Doctor requested the Indian to untie him that he might help him make a fire to keep them off. With this request the Indian complied. While the latter was on his knees and elbows, blowing the fire, the Doctor caught up a dogwood stick, about eighteen inches long, with which he struck the Indian on his head, knocking him forward into the fire. He sprang to his feet, but Knight had seized the Indian's gun, and the latter fled. After twenty-one days of wandering, Knight reached the frontier of Virginia, nearly famished to death.

Another captive, John Slover, who was doomed to the stake at the Shawanese villages, but who made a wonderful escape from his savage persecutors, saw the dead bodies of William Crawford, a nephew of Col. Crawford and of Major Harrison, his son-in-law, at Wakatomika. The unfortunate Crawford had been assured by Pipe, that these relatives would be admitted to mercy, but they, as well as Colonel McLelland, the second in command, were beaten to death soon after reaching the valley of Mad River.

Thus, life for life were the atrocities on the Muskingum avenged at the sources of the Sandusky. It was the cry of vengeance for the Christian Delawares slaughtered at Gnadenhutten, which was raised by Pipe on the banks of the Tymochtee, drowning every appeal or suggestion of mercy for one so estimable as all contemporary accounts represent Col. William Crawford to have been. Although the Muskingum proselytes were the objects of persecution by their heathen brethren, yet it was far from being a persecution unto death. It had for its object their restoration to the customs and associations of their former lives, and was entirely consistent with warm personal attachments. Loskiel narrates that the wife of Captain Pipe had been strongly moved by the persuasions of the missionaries; and the chief himself, when not instigated by Elliott, Girty or McKee, was disposed to be just and tolerant even to the teachers. He was a magnanimous savage, and his indignant repulse of all compromise with his rude sense of justice—when Girty sought to invoke his influence to save Crawford by an offer of money—gives a heroic air to the dreadful tragedy which followed. "Sir, do you think I am a squaw?" replied the indignant Delaware. "If you say one word more on the subject, I will make a stake for you and burn you along with the white chief."

With Crawford's defeat, and the carnage at Blue Licks in

August following, closed the drama of the American Revolution upon the wilderness of Ohio. Soon the motive power of British intrigue and gratuities was withdrawn, as the termination and result of the struggle became apparent, and the ravages of their Indian allies also abated. The latter were glutted with vengeance and plunder, and while their villages rang with their savage festivals, there was comparative indisposition to assume the risks of fresh forays upon the frontiers of Pennsylvania.

On the 30th of November, 1782, provisional articles of peace had been arranged at Paris: on the 20th of January following, hostilities ceased: on the 19th of April, 1783, peace was proclaimed to the army of the United States, and on the 3d of September a definite treaty was concluded.

CHAPTER XXIII.

SUBSEQUENT MOVEMENTS OF THE MORAVIAN CONGREGATION.

THE removal of the Moravian missionaries to Detroit, and the dispersion of their Indian congregation, did not terminate the labors of Zeisberger, Heckewelder, and their associates in the Western wilderness. There is no doubt that the interposition of Col. Depeyster was prompted by a disinterested regard for their safety; and the departure of the Christian Indians from Upper Sandusky, which soon followed, is commemorated by Loskiel and Heckewelder as a manifest token of the Divine protection, specially vouchsafed to arrest a repetition of the massacre at Gnadenhutten.

On the arrival of the missionaries at Detroit, Governor Depeyster offered to provide means for the removal of themselves and their families to Bethlehem in Pennsylvania, but they "resolved, from motives of duty and affection, to use their utmost exertions to gather their scattered flock." In this design, they received the countenance and aid of the English officer. A site was selected in Michigan, thirty miles distant from Detroit, and on the Huron River. The Chippewas were induced, by the influence of Col. Depeyster, to assent to such an occupation of a portion of their hunting grounds: the settlement was affectionately called New Gnadenhutten; and thither the Christian Indians, by messages directed to them on the Scioto and the Miami of the Lake, were invited to come. The Governor accompanied the invitation by an assurance, that they should enjoy perfect liberty of conscience, and be supplied with provisions and other necessaries of life.

On the second of July, 1782, two families arrived from the Miami, who were soon joined by Abraham, a venerable assistant, and two other families: a seasonable remittance of one hundred pounds sterling by their brethren in London, reached the missionaries about the same time; and on the 20th of July, the new settlement was commenced. On the 5th of November, the missionaries (namely, Zeisberger, Heckewelder, Youngman and Senseman, with their families, and the "single brethren," Edwards and Young) had the gratification of meeting fifty-three of their converts at the consecration of a chapel. Loskiel says that the fugitives to the Shawanese had been in great danger of their lives, and had only escaped by a precipitate flight. The larger portion had sought the protection of their Delaware kindred on the Miami—the personal adherents of Pachgantschihilas, or Bockengehelas, the great war chief of the Delawares, whose magnanimous conduct at the Muskingum villages, in 1781, has already been detailed. When Bockengehelas was urged by Captain Pipe "not to suffer the believing Indians to leave his territory," his reply is thus reported by Loskiel: "I shall never hinder any one of my friends from going to their teachers. Why did you expel them? I have told you beforehand, that if you drive the teachers away, the believing Indians would not stay. But yet you would do it, and now you have lost the believing Indians, together with their teachers. Who murdered the believing Indians on the Muskingum? Did the white people murder them? I say, no! You have committed the horrid deed! Why could you not let them live in peace where they were? If you had let them alone, they would all have been living at this day, and we should now see the faces of our friends: but you determined otherwise."

The other Delaware chiefs made extraordinary exertions to dissuade their converted kindred from joining the missionaries; and although forty-three of their number returned in the summer of 1783, yet many relapsed into savage life.

The manner in which the Indian congregation sustained the severe winter of 1784, with other incidents of that period, are thus narrated by the European historian of the Mission: "In the beginning of the year 1784, a most extraordinary frost set in, extending over the whole country about New Gnadenhutten. All the rivers and lakes were frozen, and the oldest inhabitants of Detroit did not remember ever to have seen such a deep fall of snow. In some places it lay five or six feet deep. The long continuance of this severe weather was the cause of great distress. March 6th, the snow was still four feet deep; about the end of the month it began to melt, but the ice on the River Huron did not break till the 4th of April, and Lake St. Clair was not free from ice in the beginning of May.

"As no one expected so long and severe a winter, there was no provision made either for man or beast. The extraordinary and early night frosts of the autumn before, had destroyed a great part of the promising harvest of Indian corn, and thus the Indians soon began to feel want; for what was bought at Detroit was very dear, and the bakers there refused to sell bread at a Spanish dollar per pound. The deep snow prevented all hunting. The Indians were therefore obliged to seek a livelihood wherever they could get it, and some lived upon nothing but wild herbs. At length a general famine prevailed, and the hollow eyes and emaciated countenances of the poor people were a sad token of their distress. Yet they appeared always resigned and cheerful, and God in due season relieved them. A large herd of deer strayed unexpectedly into the neighborhood of New Gnadenhutten, of which the Indians shot above an hundred, though the cold was then so intense, that several returned with frozen feet, owing chiefly to their wearing snow-shoes."[1]

Heckewelder mentions that the cattle were saved from starvation, by the discovery that the deer fed upon a species of rushes, or scrub grass, which grew along the river banks, or the borders of the ponds. "Strange as it may appear," he says in his narrative, "even our hogs lived chiefly upon those rushes, or the sap or juice thereof, for after chewing the stalks, until they had drawn the juicy substance out, they would drop the cud and take a fresh bite. Both these and the horned cattle, were not only saved from starving during the winter, but were in fine order in the spring. Even the fowls would eat it greedily after being cut up in small pieces of the size of a grain of Indian corn: and the Indians say, that they lay more eggs when fed with rushes, than when fed with corn: but to the horses (who are equally fond of it) it proved fatal. A lean horse would get fat on them in four or five weeks, but if left to feed a few weeks longer, they would surely die. On examining into the cause of this, it was discovered, that their stomachs were cut up, or worn quite thin, and full of small holes like a sieve: whereas, with horn cattle and deer who chewed the cud, the roughness or sharpness of the grass had not this effect."[2]

We resume Loskiel. "They now began again to barter venison for Indian corn at Detroit, and thus were delivered from the danger of suffering the same extremity of distress

1) Loskiel, part iii., p. 199.
2) Heckewelder's Narrative, p. 355.

as in Sandusky. As soon as the snow melted, they went in search of wild potatoes and came home loaded with them. When the ice was gone, they went out and caught an extraordinary number of fishes. Bilberries were their next resource, and they gathered great quantities, soon after which they reaped their crops of Indian corn, and God blessed them with a very rich harvest, so that there was not one who lacked any thing.

"Towards the end of May, the Governor of Detroit, Colonel Depeyster, removed to Niagara, and both the missionaries and the believing Indians sincerely regretted the loss of this humane man, their kind friend and benefactor. He recommended them to the favor of his worthy successor, Major Ancrom, in whom they found the same benevolent disposition towards them.

"The more the good fame of New Gnadenhutten spread, the more frequent were the visits of the white people, who could not sufficiently admire the expedition with which the believing Indians had raised this pleasant settlement. They also heard here the Gospel of Jesus Christ, which doubtless had a good effect on some. As it happened that no ordained Protestant divine resided in Detroit at that time, the missionaries, at the request of the parents, baptised several children, when they visited the fort. Some parents brought their children to New Gnadenhutten, to be baptised there, and a trader, who had two unbaptised children, went thither with his wife and whole family, and publicly presented his children to the Lord in holy baptism. But as to the ceremony of marriage, which several persons desired the missionaries to perform, they wished on many accounts to be excused as much as possible.

"The industry of the Christian Indians had now rendered

New Gnadenhutten a very pleasant and regular town. The houses were as well built as if they intended to live and die in them. The country, formerly a dreadful wilderness, was now cultivated to that extent that it afforded a sufficient maintenance for them. The rest they now enjoyed was particularly sweet, after such terrible scenes of trouble and distress. But towards the end of the year 1784, it appeared that they would likewise be obliged to quit this place. Some of the Chippewas had, the year before, expressed their dissatisfaction that the believing Indians should form a settlement in a country which had been their chief hunting place; but the governor of Detroit pacified them at that time with good words. Now they renewed their complaints, pretending that they had only allowed the Christian Indians to live there till peace should be established, and even threatened to murder some of them in order to compel the rest to quit the country. After many consultations, it evidently appeared that the complaints and vexatious demands of this nation would not cease. Added to this, the governor of Detroit sent word to the believing Indians that they should not continue to clear land and build, nothing being yet fixed, either as to the territory or government. The missionaries therefore thought it most prudent to take steps to return with their congregation to the south side of Lake Erie, and to settle near the river Walhonding. This proposal being approved by the congregation, the governor of Detroit was informed of it, and preparations were made to emigrate in the spring of 1785."

But these preparations were suspended by the unsettled condition of affairs on the Ohio frontier, and another year passed on the Huron River. In May, 1785, the missionaries Youngman and Senseman returned with their families to

Bethlehem, and the mission remained under the care of Zeisberger, Heckewelder and Edwards. "The latter" (to continue the selections from Loskiel) "went in July, with three Indian brethren, to Pittsburgh, with a view to gain certain information concerning the state of affairs in the Indian country, and to search out a proper situation on the river Walhonding for a new settlement. In Pittsburgh he was told that strictly speaking, not an inch of land to the east of Lake Erie could be called Indian country, the United States having claimed every part of it; and though they did not intend to drive the Indians away by force, yet they would not permit them to live in the neighborhood of the white people. He also received letters from Bishop John de Waterville, who had arrived from Europe to hold a visitation in the congregations of the brethren in North America, by which he was informed that Congress had expressly reserved the district belonging to the three settlements of the Christian Indians on the Muskingum, to be measured out and given to them with as much land as the surveyor should think proper. The same intelligence he likewise received from the Philadelphia papers, and hastened home to acquaint the Indian congregation with this unexpected decision in their favor, which occasioned universal joy. An Indian is naturally very averse to dwelling in any place where one of his relations has been killed, but the believing Indians had even parted with this kind of superstition, and longed to be there as soon as possible."[3]

3) The Moravian society at Bethlehem had memorialized Congress on the 28th of October, 1783, to reserve to the remnants of the Muskingum mission their three towns and the surrounding lands. A favorable report was made in March, 1784, and on the 20th of May, 1785, Congress ordered that "the said towns and so much of the adjoining lands as, in the judgment of the geographer of the United States, (might) be sufficient for them,

Immediately after Easter, 1786, New Gnadenhutten was abandoned, and its inhabitants proceeded to Detroit in twenty-two canoes, with the purpose of thence returning to Ohio. They were hospitably received by the governor, and after a parting interview with the Chippewa chiefs, to whom a bundle of some thousands of wampum was presented in token of gratitude, the congregation embarked on the 28th of April, in two trading sloops, the Beaver and the Mackinaw, which had been generously placed at their service by the agent of the Northwest company. Their destination was the mouth of the Cuyahoga, and in twenty-four hours the vessels had reached the Bars Islands of Lake Erie, adjacent to the Sandusky peninsula. Here the winds became adverse, and a detention of four weeks ensued. The sea-sick voyagers pitched their camp upon Cunningham's, or Kelley's Island, going on board at every prospect of release from their bondage to the northeast wind. Once they set forward with a brisk and favorable breeze, and were in sight of the coast of Cuyahoga, when the wind shifted and drove them back to their station on the Island. They lived by hunting and fishing, and found wild potatoes, onions, and "several kinds of wholesome herbs in abundance." At length this Island was

together with the buildings, &c., (should) be reserved for the sole use of the Christian Indians formerly settled there." Congress passed another ordinance, dated 27th of July, 1787, "that the property of ten thousand acres, adjoining to the former settlements of the Christian Indians, should be vested in the Moravian Brethren at Pennsylvania, or a society of the said Brethren for civilizing the Indians and promoting Christianity, in trust and for the uses expressed in the ordinance of May 20, 1785, including Killbuck and his descendants, and the nephew and descendants of the late Captain White Eyes, Delaware chiefs who have distinguished themselves as friends of the cause of America." The three town plats were six hundred and sixty-six and two-thirds acres each, making, with the ten thousand above mentioned, twelve thousand acres, which were surveyed in 1797, and patented on the 4th of February, 1798.

cleared of game, and they went to another, ("Hope's Love, or Put-in Bay," according to Heckewelder) where they found "a better haven and good hunting, but a remarkable number of rattlesnakes."

On the 28th of May, a vessel arrived from Detroit to recall the Beaver, and it was determined that the Mackinaw should transport the baggage and a few of the company to Cuyahoga, while most of them should make the journey along the coast. They were landed at Rocky Point, about eight miles from Sandusky Bay (probably the promontory now known as Scott's Point, or Ottawa City, in Ottawa county). "Here," says Loskiel, "they had to ascend very high and steep rocks, and to cut a way through the thicket to their summit. Heckewelder records the capture and cure of "five hundred white fish that had retired, during the high blowing wind, between Rocky Island and the shore, where the water was about two feet deep."

The travelers organized themselves into two divisions. One, led by Zeisberger, proposed to make the journey by land, while the second division of the congregation, led by Heckewelder, constructed canoes of elm bark for a coasting voyage to Cuyahoga. Zeisberger's party "had hardly pitched their camp (proceeds Loskiel) before a party of Ottawas, who were hunting in that neighborhood, rode towards them and expressed great astonishment to find such a large number of people encamped in the pathless desert. The Christian Indians treated them as hospitably as their circumstances would permit, and were in return presented by the Ottawas with some deer's flesh, and informed of the manner in which they might best make a way through the forests through which they had to pass. The day following, they all set out on foot, and every one, the missionary and his wife not excepted, was loaded with a proportionable part of the provisions. Those who formed the van had the greatest difficulties to encounter, being obliged to cut and break their way through the thicket. They soon arrived at a large brook running through a swamp, through which all the Indians, both men and women, waded, some being up to their armpits in the water. Some of the children were carried, others swam, and brother Zeisberger and his wife were brought over upon a barrow, carried by four Indian brethren. When they arrived at Sandusky Bay, they hired boats of the Ottawas, from whom also they received frequent visits during their stay. One evening the savages had a dance,[4] and none of the Christian Indians appearing at it, as they expected, some came and endeavored to persuade the young people to join them; but meeting with a refusal, they addressed brother Zeisberger, begging him to encourage them. He replied that the Christian Indians lived no more after the manner of the heathen, having found something better. June 3d, they crossed the Sandusky Bay, and the day after, the river Petquotting, in a vessel belonging to a French trader.[5] During this journey they celebrated the Whitsuntide holydays, and rejoiced to see many attentive hearers among the heathen.

"June 4th, the second division, led by John Heckewelder, overtook them in slight canoes, the sloop Mackinaw having sailed with the heavy baggage straight for Cuyahoga. The whole congregation now traveled together, one half on foot along the coast of the lake, and the others in canoes, keeping as close to the shore as possible. June 7th, they arrived at

4) Johnson's Island, near the mouth of Sandusky Bay, and separated from the Peninsula by a narrow strait, was a favorite resort of the Ottawas, for festivals and dances. It is probable that the transaction narrated above occurred on that island.

5) Now Huron River.

the celebrated rocks on the south coast of Lake Erie. They rise forty or fifty feet perpendicular out of the water, and are in many places so much undermined by the waves, that they seem considerably to project over the lake. Some parts of them consist of several strata of different colors, lying in a horizontal direction, and so exactly parallel that they resemble the work of art." In Heckewelder's narratives, the ceremonies of a party of Chippewas, who sought, by supplications and gifts of tobacco to propitiate the spirits of the winds and waves, are fully described. They preceded the Moravian party, and had scarcely passed the rocky range when a terrific storm arose. When it subsided, Heckewelder's little fleet also achieved the voyage without accident. Zeisberger's land party reached the Cuyahoga simultaneously. "The sloop also arrived safely, and drifted so near the shore in a calm, that the baggage could be taken out and carried to land in canoes, upon which the sloop returned to Detroit."

Both the Moravian annalists concur in mentioning "a large store-house filled with flour, at the mouth of Cuyahoga," which, Heckewelder adds, was owned by "Messrs. Duncan & Wilson, of Pittsburgh, who carried on a trade in articles of provisions to Detroit."

As soon as additional canoes could be provided, the party ascended the Cuyahoga to "an old town about one hundred and forty miles distant from Pittsburgh, which had been forsaken by the Ottawas." Here the forest, which had been unbroken from the mouth of the river, was cleared, and the recent growth was easily removed, allowing them to plant corn. Their encampment was on an elevated plain east of the river, about twelve miles from its mouth, and received the name of Pilgerruh, or Pilgrim's Rest.[6] "Here," as Loskiel narrates, "they regulated their daily worship in the usual manner, reëstablished the statutes of the congregation, and God blessed their labors. August the 13th, they partook of the Lord's Supper for the first time on this spot, which to them was the most important and blessed of all festivals.

"In externals, God granted them his gracious assistance. Brother Zeisberger, having given information of the arrival of the Indian congregation at the Cuyahoga creek to the governor of Pittsburgh, and brother Shebosch having been at that place to endeavor to procure provisions, Messrs. Duncan & Wilson were so kind as to provide a sufficient supply, trusting them for a great part of the payment. Congress likewise ordered a quantity of Indian corn and blankets to be given them.[7] They also found means to purchase several necessary articles from traders passing through on their way from Pittsburgh to Detroit, and as they had an opportunity of going by water to Sandusky and Petquotting, they easily procured Indian corn from those places. The two hundred dollars which they received for their houses and fields on the river Huron, enabled them to make their payments good. In hunting deer, bears, and moose-deer, they were remarkably successful. The congregation at Bethlehem had charitably collected a considerable quantity of different articles to supply the necessities of the Christian Indians; but these having been detained on the road, did not arrive at Pilgerruh till August, 1786, when they were equally divided

6) "Within the present limits of Independence, Cuyahoga county."—*Howe's Hist. Coll.*, 120.

7) Lieut. Col. Harmar, then in command at Fort McIntosh, was directed to furnish the Christian Indians with five hundred bushels of Indian corn, one hundred blankets and other necessaries. The supplies were not delivered, however.—*American State Papers, Indian Affairs*, vol. ii., p. 373.

among all; the children even received their share, and the whole congregation expressed, in the most lively terms, their sincere acknowledgments to their kind benefactors. Salt was not so easily procured here as on the river Huron, the salt springs being a great way off."

The summer and winter passed without material change in the situation and prospects of the little community. In October, 1786, John Heckewelder returned to Bethlehem, leaving David Zeisberger and William Edwards in charge of the congregation; and on the 10th of November, "a new and spacious chapel was consecrated: but the Indians only furnished themselves with frail huts, hoping soon to reach the Muskingum. In this they were destined to disappointment. Every day added to the exposure and danger which would attend a removal thither; and towards the close of the year 1786, Captain Pipe sent a message, urging them to remove westward to the Petquotting or Huron River. Another message from the Delawares, was a pressing invitation to Sandusky. Thus a dilemma was presented to the leaders of the congregation. While their own inclination was decidedly in favor of a speedy occupation of their former seats on the Muskingum, they were advised by Gen. Richard Butler, the Indian Agent of the United States, to remain for the present on the Cuyahoga, and the Indians insisted on their removal to localities still more remote. The dispositions and final action of the missionaries, with the attending circumstances, are thus stated by Loskiel:

"Accustomed to venture their lives in the service of the Lord, they were unconcerned as to their own safety, and if that alone had been the point in question, they would not have hesitated a moment to return to the Muskingum: but they durst not bring the congregation committed to their care, into so dreadful and dangerous a situation. They rather thought it their duty to sacrifice every other consideration to the welfare and safety of their flock, and therefore, after mature deliberation, resolved to propose to them, that they should give up all thoughts of returning to the Muskingum for the present, but at the same time not remain on the Cuyahoga, but rather seek to find some spot between that river and Petquotting, where they might procure a peaceable and safe retreat. This proposal was solemnly accepted, first by the Indian assistants, and then by the whole congregation. Soon after this, the following message arrived from a Delaware chief to Brother Zeisberger: 'Grandfather! having heard that you propose to live on the Muskingum, I would advise you not to go thither this spring. I cannot yet tell you my reason; nor can I say whether we shall have war or peace, but so much I can say, that it is not yet time. Do not think that I wish to oppose your preaching the word of God to the Indians. I am glad that you do this; but I advise you for your good. Go not to the Muskingum.'[8] This message tended to confirm the people in the above mentioned resolution, which was undoubtedly the most prudent at the time; and in the beginning of April, some Indian brethren set out, with a view to seek a place for a new settlement, and found one much to their mind.

"Meanwhile the Indian congregation of Pilgerruh, celebrated Lent and Easter in a blessed manner. The public reading of the history of our Lord's passion, was attended with a remarkable impression on the hearts of all present. The congregation could not sufficiently express their desire to hear more of it, and it appeared as if they now heard this great and glorious word for the first time.

8) No one was more likely to send such a message than the noble-hearted Bockengehelas.

"April 19th, 1787, the Christian Indians closed their residence at Pilgerruh, by offering up solemn prayer and praise in their chapels, which they had used but a short time. They thanked the Lord for all the internal and external blessings he had conferred upon them in this place, and then set out in two parties, one by land, led by Brother Zeisberger, and the other by water, with Brother Edwards. The latter were obliged to cross over a considerable part of Lake Erie. But before they had left the Cayahaga creek, a dreadful storm arose, the wind blowing from the lake. The waves beat with such violence against the rocks described above, that the earth seemed to tremble with the sound. The travelers thanked God that they were yet in safety in the creek, and being in want of provisions, spent the time in fishing. One night they fished with torches, and pierced above three hundred large fish of a good flavor, resembling pikes, and weighing from three to five pounds, part of which they roasted and ate, and dried the rest for provisions on the voyage. April 24th, the travelers by land, and the day following those who went by water, arrived at the place fixed upon for their future abode. It appeared like a fruitful orchard, several wild apple and plum trees growing here and there. They had never settled upon so good and fertile a spot of ground. The camp was formed about a league from the lake, which in these parts abounded with fish. Wild potatoes, an article of food much esteemed by the Indians, grew here plentifully. The brethren rejoiced at the thoughts of establishing a regular settlement in so pleasant a country, especially as it was not frequented by any of those savages who had hitherto proved such troublesome neighbors.[9]

"But their joy was of short duration. April 27th, a

9) This was the fertile valley of the Black River in Lorain county.

Delaware Captain arrived in the camp, and informed them that they should not remain in this place but live with them at Sandusky, adding, that they should consider it a matter positively determined, and not first deliberate upon it. He added, as usual, the most solemn declarations of protection and safety. The Captain assured them likewise, that the place appointed for their habitation was not in the vicinity of any heathen towns, but ten miles distant from the nearest. To the missionary, David Zeisberger, he had brought the following particular message. 'Hear, my friend, you are my grandfather. I am not ignorant of your having been formally adopted by our chiefs as a member of our nation. No one shall hurt you, and you need not have any scruples about coming to live at Sandusky.' He then delivered a string of wampum. Disagreeable as this message was to the Christian Indians, and though they represented to the Captain the malice, deceit and treachery of the Delaware Chiefs, which they had painfully experienced for these six or seven years past: yet after many serious consultations, they and the missionaries could not but resolve to submit to the will of the chiefs, lest they should bring new troubles and persecutions upon the mission. Their answer was therefore in the affirmative. Brother Zeisberger answered likewise the particular message sent to him to the same effect, yet, with this express condition, that all the other white brethren should have the same privileges granted them, and his successor in office enjoy the same rights.

"Nothing appeared in this affair so dreadful to the missionaries as the prospect of being again subject to heathen rule and government. Yet they could not deny that it was more agreeable to their peculiar calling to live in the midst of those heathen, to whom they were to preach the gospel, and therefore write: 'We must be satisfied to live in the very nest of Satan, for it appears indeed, as if every savage Indian was possessed by a number of evil spirits, with whom we must be at war.'"

"In the beginning of May, they with great joy welcomed two assistants in the work of the mission, sent by the congregation at Bethlehem, Michael Young and John Weygand, and soon after left a country so pleasing in every respect, with great regret, proceeding partly by water on Lake Erie, partly by land along its banks to Petquotting, where they encamped about a mile from the lake. Here they found that the greatest part of the message brought by the above mentioned Captain from the Delaware chiefs was fallacious; for the place fixed upon for their residence was not above two miles from the villages of the savages. Our Indians therefore, and the missionaries, resolved not to go any farther for the present, lest they should be entangled in some snare, but to settle near Petquotting, and even to maintain their situation in opposition to the will of the Delaware chiefs. They then sought and found an uninhabited place situated on a river called also Huron, which empties itself into the lake at Petquotting, whither they all went in canoes on the 11th of May, and before night a small village of bark huts was erected. Hence they sent deputies to the chiefs to inform them of their resolution and their reasons for it, and obtained leave to stay at least one year in that place without molestation. They hoped also that during that period, circumstances might alter in their favor, and that they might perhaps be permitted to continue there longer.

"They therefore made plantations on the west bank of the river, and chose the east, which was high land, for their dwellings. This place was called New Salem.[10] Here they celebrated Ascension Day and Whitsuntide in the usual manner, meeting in the open air, and on the sixth of June, finished and consecrated their new chapel, which was larger and better built than that at Pilgerruh. They indeed wanted more room, for a larger number of heathen Indians attended their public worship here, than at the Cayahaga, and hardly a day passed without visits from strangers. June 9th, the whole congregation held a love-feast, for which flour had been sent from Bethlehem. A letter to the believing Indians from Bishop Johannes Von Wateville, was read to them on this occasion, and heard with much emotion. He had held a visitation in all the settlements of the Brethren in North America, but to his sorrow found it impossible to go to the Indian congregation, and was then on his return to Europe. On the same day the congregation at New Salem partook of the Lord's Supper, rejoicing in God their Saviour, whose gracious presence comforted their hearts in an inexpresible degree."

And here, with an enthusiastic narrative of the reclamation of "many of the poor lost sheep," and "the increase of the Indian assistants in grace and knowledge of the truth," the truthful chronicle of Loskiel draws to its close. "According," he says, "to the accounts transmitted to the middle of the year 1787, the missionaries were full of courage and confidence, and diligent in the work of God committed to them."

Although the limitation of Loskiel's narrative is contemporaneous with the period to which this volume relates, yet we cannot resist the inclination to follow the subsequent fortunes

10) Near the north line of the township of Milan, Erie county.

of the missions. For this purpose, Heckewelder will be our principal authority.

Three years after the settlement of New Salem, in the winter of 1789–90, the Ohio Indians joined a league of the Western savages against the United States, and it was determined at a general council to remove the Christian Indians and their teachers from Petquotting to Kegeyunk, now Fort Wayne, and that the former should then be required to take part in the impending hostilities. Information of this plot was secretly communicated to Zeisberger by some friendly Indians, and the missionary Edwards was instantly despatched to Detroit, with a request that the British commandant would grant them an asylum. He readily consented, and in April, 1790, a vessel arrived at the Huron River, and the whole Indian congregation abandoned their settlement of New Salem. They were at length removed to the river Thames, seventy miles northeast of Detroit, where a town was built and called Fairfield.

In 1797, three separate tracts of four thousand acres each, including the sites of Gnadehutten, Schoenbrun and Salem were surveyed and laid off to the mission. In the spring of 1798, John Heckewelder and the Rev. Benjamin Mortimer repaired to Fairfield "by way of the Genessee county, Black Rock, Niagara, Grand River, and the Pinery in Upper Canada, to inform the congregation that the Congressional grant was perfected:" and thence, after a week's stay, Heckewelder and Edwards, with two young Indians, started for the Muskingum, to make the necessary preparations for a permanent settlement. Their route was by Detroit, Brownstown, River Raisen, rapids of the Maumee, Upper Sandusky, Owl Creek (now Vernon River) and the Forks of the Muskingum. In October, Zeisberger and Mortimer, with "a large number of the Christian Indians from Fairfield," arrived on the Muskingum and founded Goshen. In 1804, a part of the Fairfield congregation removed to Petquotting, and renewed their missionary settlement, which the late Rev. E. Judson of Milan supposed to have been situated on the spot where Milan now stands. It was under the charge of Rev. Christian Frederic Dencke, but was relinquished in 1809, when the lands had been surveyed, and began to be appropriated by the whites. The Moravians returned to Fairfield.

David Zeisberger passed the remnant of his useful life at Goshen, Tuscarawas county, where he died November 7, 1808, aged 87 years, 7 months and 6 days. At the same place, in 1801, William Edwards had rested from his labors, aged about seventy. John Heckewelder, after remaining in the scenes of his early missionary life from 1801 to 1810, returned to Bethlehem, and became widely known as the author of the "Narrative of the Missions of the United Brethren among the Delaware and Mohegan Indians," and of an "Account of the History, Manners and Customs of the Indian Nations, who once inhabited Pennsylvania and the neighboring States," besides many other publications. He died at Bethlehem on the 31st of January, 1823, aged seventy-nine years, and nearly eleven months.

The influence of the white settlements upon the Indian colony of the Muskingum was so unfavorable,[11] that their

11) At the session of the Territorial Legislature for 1799–1800, an act was passed to protect the Moravian Indians from the traffic in intoxicating liquors. The missionaries were authorized to seize the same whenever brought within the Schoenbrun tract, and "do with it as they should think proper;" and Heckewelder mentions that on one occasion "the missionary, Zeisberger, although then in his eightieth year, in his zeal for the cause in which he was engaged, took up an axe and stove the kegs so that the liquor ran into the river." The Moravian annalist adds, that "although this act

spiritual guardians at length induced Congress to adopt such measures as would tend to the removal of the Indians, and enable the society to divest itself of the trusteeship in the land. On the 4th of August, 1823, an agreement or treaty was entered into at Gnadenhutten between Lewis Cass, then Governor of Michigan, on the part of the United States, and Lewis de Schweinitz, on the part of the Moravian Missionary Society, as a preliminary step towards the retrocession of the land to the government. By this agreement, the members of the society relinquished their right as trustees, conditioned that the United States would pay six thousand six hundred and fifty-four dollars, being but a moiety of the money they had expended. The agreement could not be legal without the written consent of the Indians, for whose benefit the land had been donated. These embraced the remainder of the Christian Indians formerly settled on the land, "including Killbuck and his descendants, and the nephews and descendants of the late Captain White Eyes, Delaware chiefs." The Goshen Indians, as they were then called, repaired to Detroit for the purpose of completing the contract. On the 8th of November, they signed a treaty with Governor Cass, by which they relinquished their right to the lands, on condition that Government would pay them an annuity of four hundred dollars as long as they remained on the River Thames in Canada, or in lieu thereof, should they choose to return to the United States, secure to them a reservation of twenty-four thousand acres.

The trustees could not, however, divest themselves of all

of the missionary served as a check on some other disorderly people from their making similar attempts of bringing liquor to the town, yet, upon the whole, this act of the Assembly became highly offensive, and was termed an infringement on the rights and liberties of a free and independent people; and, consequently, soon repealed."

the associations of the Muskingum Mission. It is interesting to observe, that the fourth article of the treaty secures in perpetuity to the Society of United Brethren, free from any condition or limitation whatever, "ten acres of ground, including the church called Beersheba, and the grave yard on the Gnadenhutten tract; also the church lot, parsonage house and grave yard in the town of Gnadenhutten, * * * and also the missionary house and grave yard at Goshen." These still constitute links between the period, when the message of the cross was announced in the depth of a wilderness and amid the horrors of border warfare, and the passing era of material development and spiritual privileges.[12]

12) See Appendix No. X, for this final negotiation with the remnant of the Moravian congregation.

CHAPTER XXIV.

EMBASSIES AND NEGOTIATIONS BETWEEN THE UNITED STATES AND THE OHIO TRIBES

THE student of diplomacy, either as an art or in its relation to the events of history, will find no more suggestive field of inquiry, than is presented by the negotiations of the Indian tribes of North America. At the council fire, the loftiest qualities of their character have been conspicuous—self-control, courtesy, dignity, eloquence, and that instinctive sagacity, which is the first requisite of statesmanship. Of this, Jefferson seemed conscious, when he triumphantly rested his defence of the native race of the American continent, against Buffon's imputation of inferiority, upon the terse and touching speech of the desolate Cayuga warrior, Logan.

The present chapter will relate to the negotiations with the Ohio Indians, between 1768 and the Territorial epoch.

The American Revolution interrupted the dreams of power and wealth, in which the leading spirits of the Middle Colonies had indulged at the consummation of the Treaty of Fort Stanwix, on the 24th of October, 1768. Sir William Johnson, who conducted that negotiation, hoped to found a colony south of the Ohio; the envoys of Pennsylvania exulted at the extinction of the Indian title between the Alleghanies and the Ohio River, as far north as Kittaning;[1] while Virginia was no less gratified by a still more westward extension of

1) The northwest corner of Cambria county, Pennsylvania.

her territorial occupation. Land speculation was the mania of that age, and the disbanded soldiery of the long wars with France, desired the widest possible range of selection in the location of their bounties.

The conference of Fort Stanwix only transferred the claim of the Six Nations of New York. The Delawares, who were seated upon the Upper Ohio, and the Shawanese, who had formerly occupied Kentucky, and now shared its range as a hunting ground with the Cherokees and other Southern Indians, were no parties to the treaty. As has been shown, a prominent cause of the hostilities, which were terminated by Dunmore's expedition of 1774, was the dissatisfaction of the Shawanese with the settlement of Kentucky. The Delawares were more willing to transfer their villages to the west bank of the Ohio, for their name implies former removals westward, and experience had convinced them of the futility of any other than a passive policy.

There is but little doubt, that a condition of the treaty between the Shawanese of the Scioto and Lord Dunmore, besides the surrender of prisoners and plunder, made the Ohio River the boundary between themselves and the whites. But this agreement to abandon the lands south of the Ohio, did not probably include the Shawanese warriors and hunters of the Miami villages; and it was only after many bloody campaigns, that the whole tribe acquiesced in a partition, which was more a trophy of conquest by the bold Kentuckians, than a treaty stipulation on the part of the Indians.

When Lord Dunmore concluded the treaty of Camp Charlotte, he required the delivery of four hostages by the Shawanese, and also detained twelve Mingo prisoners. The latter were still imprisoned on the 9th of February, 1775, as, on that date, Dr. John Connolly wrote to Col. George Washington, asking what should be done with them.[2] The Shawanese hostages seem to have been released in the summer, and would have been previously, if their tribe had more promptly surrendered the white captives which they held. A Williamsburg publication of Feb. 10, 1775, mentions that a few days before, Cornstalk, the chief of the Scioto Shawanese, arrived at the mouth of the Great Kenawha, where a Capt. Russell was then in command, and delivered to him "several of the old white prisoners, and a number of horses."

On the 12th of July, 1775, Congress organized an administration of Indian Affairs. Almost simultaneously, an envoy of Virginia, Capt. James Wood, afterwards Governor of that State, was traversing Ohio, having been deputized by the General Assembly of Virginia to invite the Indian tribes to a council at Fort Pitt, on the 10th of September. While thus employed, he ascertained that the British commandant at Detroit, and one Mons. Baubee, a Canadian Frenchman, had distributed belts and wampum among seventeen Western tribes, with a message, that the Virginians were about to invade their country and attack them from two directions—by the Ohio and by the Lakes. Hamilton's only object in making such a statement, was to provoke a border war.

Capt. Wood, on the 22d and 23d of July, had a satisfactory interview with Newcomer,[3] and other Delaware chiefs, at Coshocton; and on the 25th, arrived at a "Seneca Town," where he found Logan, with some of the Mingoes who had been prisoners at Fort Pitt. They appeared very desirous to know his errand. He called them together, and made the

2) American Archives, fourth series, vol. i., p. 1222.

3) Netawatwes. The details of Wood's journey are compiled from American Archives, fourth series, vol. iii., p. 76—an account dated August 15, 1775—without change in the names of persons and places.

same speech to them as to the Delawares; but their only answer was, that they would acquaint the rest of the tribe with what he had said. These Indians, Wood remarks, appeared very angry, and behaved with great insolence.

On the 27th of July, Capt. Wood had a hearing at the Wyandot Town. A chief, War Post, postponed a reply until the next day, when they would meet him in the Council House. Meanwhile, War Post and six others came privately to the Virginian, "to talk with him as friends," they said. They had always understood the English had but one king, who lived over the Great River; they were much surprised lately to hear that there was a war, and several engagements at Boston, where a great many men were killed on both sides; and as they had heard many different stories, they would be glad to know the truth. Capt. Wood then explained to them the nature of the dispute, and the general union of the colonies; removing an error into which the Wyandots had been led, that the Virginians were a distinct people from the other colonies. On the following day, War Post replied publicly, that they had fully considered the message, and thought it good, but they would be ruled in the matter by their chiefs beyond Lake Erie.

Wood reached the Shawanese towns on the 31st. Here he found much excitement from the alarming reports brought by one Chennsan, or the Judge, who had just escaped from Williamsburg, where he had been detained as a hostage. He said that all the people of Virginia, except the Governor, were determined on war with the Indians; that he had barely escaped with his life, but there was no doubt that his fellow-hostages, Cuttenwa and Newa, were killed. Capt. Wood was soon confronted with the fugitive, denied his whole story, and assured the Shawanese present that Cuttenwa and Newa were on the way, riding leisurely back to their towns, and that Chennsan, by his flight, had lost a horse, saddled and bridled, besides other presents. This explanation quieted the crowd, and on the 2d of August, the Shawanese were likewise invited to the council at Fort Pitt, and responded with pacific assurances.[4]

On the return of Wood to Virginia, it was known that Messrs. Franklin, Henry and Wilson had been appointed by Congress Commissioners of Indian Affairs for the Middle Department (including the Ohio tribes), and we presume that it was under their direction that the conference at Fort Pitt, of September, 1775, was held. Perhaps Mr. John Gibson, who then represented the Virginia commissioners at that place, may have held a separate interview with the chiefs; but Heckewelder is an authority, that the Delawares then heard from the representatives of Congress the celebrated allegory of the oppressive father and his pack-laden son. This address was forwarded to all the Indian tribes of the country, and its purport is apparent from a brief extract:—"We desire you will hear and receive what we have now told you, and that you will open a good ear and listen to what we are going to say. This is a family quarrel between us and Old England. You Indians are not concerned in it. We do not wish you to take up the hatchet against the king's troops. We desire you to remain at home, and not join on either side, but keep the hatchet buried deep. In the name and behalf of all our people, we ask and desire you to love peace and maintain it, and to love and sympathize with us in

4) The reader will readily identify the localities visited by Wood—first at Coshocton; two days afterwards, either near the mouth of Vernon River, or at the village on the Lake fork of the Muskingum; then two days after at Upper Sandusky, and finally at the Shawanese villages within what is now Logan county

our troubles: that the path may be kept open with all our people and yours, to pass and repass without molestation."

It is probable that in the spring of 1776, some confusion resulted from the fact that Richard Butler was acting as United States agent, and John Gibson as agent of Virginia, to the Western Indians: while Alexander McKee, formerly a deputy of the British superintendent, was still at Pittsburgh, although under parol "not to transact any business with the Indians on behalf of the crown or ministry." On the 8th of April, Mr. Butler wrote to Col. James Wilson, that Guyasotha (he calls him Kiosola, but it can be no other than the noted Seneca chief who lived on the head waters of the Ohio,) had failed, in the fall of 1775, to carry a big belt from the United States to the Western tribes, as he had agreed to do. When asked by Butler the reason for this failure, Guyasotha said that Captain Pipe did not meet him at the Moravian town, nor had two Delawares joined him at Wyandot town, according to the promises of Gibson. Butler also mentions, that Logan had threatened Gibson, and that the latter arrived on the 9th of April, with some Shawanese white prisoners and slaves, probably in further redemption of Cornstalk's stipulations with Lord Dunmore, in October, 1774. Perhaps Congress proposed, by the appointment of Col. George Morgan on the 10th of April, as Indian agent for the Middle Department, to adjust any local jealousy or conflict of jurisdiction, which might have existed between Butler and Gibson.

On the date of Morgan's appointment, Congress resolved —partly on the petition of *Coquataginta* or Captain White Eyes, then on a visit to Philadelphia—to employ a preacher, a schoolmaster, and a blacksmith, to live among the Delaware Indians in Ohio; to provide for the entertainment of their chiefs whenever they should visit Fort Pitt, and that a treaty should be effected with the Indians to the westward by the Commissioners of the Middle Department!

The first letters of Col. Morgan, after reaching Pittsburgh, indicated a critical state of affairs on the Ohio frontier. Under date of May 16, he alludes to a council of the Six Nations, then being held at Niagara by Col. John Butler, a British agent, from which he apprehended unpleasant consequences. The proceedings at that conference were well calculated to excite alarm. Nearly one hundred Indians, representing the Six Nations and "a number of the back nations," were induced to visit Col. Guy Johnson at Quebec, after pledging themselves to Butler to "support the King's peace or government." Gen. Schuyler wrote, on the 17th of July, that "one Cajughsoda, from some town toward the Ohio, inveighed bitterly against Butler, on this occasion, for attempting to make the Indians parties to the war." This was undoubtedly the Guyasotha, who is so prominent in the contemporary annals of the Alleghany region.

One William Wilson seems to have been a trusted agent of the United States among the Ohio Indians at this time. Col. Morgan hearing that the Niagara conference was soon to be followed by another at Detroit, which Governor Hamilton would be sure to manage with even less scruple than Butler had exhibited, sent this Wilson in June to prevent the attendance of the Shawanese, until Morgan should visit them. When the latter arrived, he was referred to the Wyandots (by no means a favorable indication,) and in July, Wilson, accompanied by Cornstalk, a chief called Hardman, and several others, started for the Wyandot towns, with a message from Morgan inviting the Indians to a treaty at Pittsburgh.

This party first proceeded to a small Shawanese town, about ten miles from the principal towns, where they remained ten days. Hardman remained at this village, to meet the "Shade" (another Shawnee chief, who was expected soon to return from Niagara,) while the rest continued their journey to Pluggy's town.[5] Here they heard a rumor that the Kentuckians had killed two Shawanese, and it was afterwards ascertained that a party of Shawanese and Cherokees had killed two men, and captured a woman on the Kentucky River. Immediate pursuit was made by the whites: the savages overtaken: two Shawanese killed, and the woman rescued.

While at Pluggy's Town, a French blacksmith residing there overheard the Mingoes plotting to make Wilson and one Joseph Nicholson prisoners and carry them to Detroit; whereupon Cornstalk advised that they should escape by night to Coochocking. They did so, and remained with the friendly Delawares eleven days, King Newcomer (Netawatwes) dissuading Wilson from going to the Wyandot Towns. Captain Killbuck was sent thither with Col. Morgan's invitation, and returned with a message that the Wyandots of Sandusky must first consult their chiefs on the other side of the lake, but desired that Wilson should come on, assuring him of safety. Accordingly, Wilson, the Delaware Killbuck, and two young men started, but were turned back, after going ten miles, by the sickness of Killbuck. Captain White Eyes took his place, and at *Winganons* Town, six miles from Coochocking, the party was joined by the half-breed, John Montour. Arrived at Detroit, whither Montour piloted them

5) We incline to the opinion that Pluggy's Town was on the west branch of the Muskingum, near the junction with the Vernon River, or Owl creek. See the narrative of Smith's captivity, ante pp. 82, 86.

"by a nearer way than Sandusky," Col. Morgan's message to the Wyandots, "the purport of which was to ask their assistance in brightening the chain of friendship with all the western tribes of Indians, and inviting them to a treaty to be held at Pittsburgh in twenty-five days from that time, or the 2d of December," was delivered with a belt by Wilson, and was at first favorably received by the chiefs assembled at the Wyandot village opposite Detroit. As soon, however, as governor Hamilton heard of the arrival and message of the American deputies, he induced the Indians to return the belt, and at a subsequent council held in Detroit, addressed the Wyandots as follows:

"CHILDREN, I am your father, and you are my children. I have always your good at heart. I am sent here to represent the great king over the waters and to take care of you. Those people from whom you received this message are enemies and traitors to my king, and before I would take one of them by the hand, I would suffer my right hand to be cut off. When the great king is pleased to make peace with his rebellious children in this big island, I will then give my assistance in making peace between them and the Indians."

"With that," says Wilson, "he tore the speech and cut the belt to pieces, and contemptuously strewed it about the council-house." The governor then made a speech on a tomahawk belt in French to the Wyandots. Their chief delivered the belt to the Cornstalk, who was asked by the governor if he knew what it meant. Cornstalk answered that he did not, and Hamilton then informed him that the belt was put into the hands of the Wyandots in March, desiring them to request the nations who lived next the river from Presque Isle downwards, to be watchful, and inform him if any army attempted to cross the Ohio, but now the belt had a greater meaning, and referred Cornstalk to the Wyandots for an explanation. He added that the Cherokees had joined the general cause.

The Mingoes present then produced a black belt, which they said was received from Guy Johnson, in the spring of 1775, and intimated very clearly their hostility to the colonies.

Hamilton had previously ordered Wilson to return immediately, and he now ordered White Eyes "to leave Detroit before the sun set, as he regarded his hea d." He told him "that he knew his character well, and so did all the nations present"—adding "that he would lose the last drop of his blood before he would suffer any one nation to come there and destroy the union which was brought about by so many nations."

The Half King of the Wyandots—Pomacan of Sandusky—was at Detroit, and while drinking with John Montour, expressed himself hostile to the Big Knives; he had accepted a tomahawk belt from Hamilton, but believed that one half of the Wyandots would not join the British. The Cornstalk and Hardman avowed their concurrence in the sentiments of White Eyes, and, upon the whole, Wilson returned to Coochocking and thence to Pittsburgh, with a report not so unfavorable as was apprehended.

Still, it was not until the last of October, that the council was convened at Fort Pitt. The commissioners—Messrs. Thomas Walker, John Harvey, John Montgomery and J. Yeats—were in attendance early in September, and on the 25th, wrote to a committee of Congress that the frontier had been alarmed by a rumor that fifteen hundred Chippewas and Ottawas were about to rendezvous at Tuscarawas, but which proved unfounded. A letter from Col. Morgan to the president of Congress, dated November 8, announces that the Six Nations, Delawares, Muncies, Mohicans and Shawanese had assembled to the number of six hundred and forty-four, with their principal chiefs and warriors, and gave the strongest assurances of peace and neutrality. The most troublesome band in Ohio was an assemblage of "Mingo, Wyandot and Cockanawaga warriors at the Kispapoo town, (as they are described by the commissioners in their letter of September 25) the chief part of whom consist of a banditti, headed by one Pluggy." Col. Morgan thus describes them: "About sixty or seventy families, composed of most of the different tribes of the Six Nations, and a few of the lake Indians, but principally of the Senecas, who removed from near the mouths of Cross creeks, on the Ohio, a few years ago, and are now seated on the heads of the Scioto,[6] have been the perpetrators of all the mischief and murders committed on the frontiers of Virginia since the last treaty." Notwithstanding their hostility, he writes that the cloud which threatened to break over the frontiers of Pennsylvania and Virginia, had nearly dispersed, and the winter of 1776–7, passed in comparative quiet.

We have elsewhere sketched the Indian administration of Col. George Morgan, and shall hasten to the consideration of the more prominent negotiations with the Ohio tribes.

In 1778, an expedition against Detroit was contemplated, and on the 17th of September, Andrew Lewis and Thomas Lewis, commissioners of the United States, obtained from Captain White Eyes, The Pipe and John Killbuck, Jr., a formal stipulation that the United States might have a free passage through the Delaware country for any expedition against British posts. The treaty also contained an agree-

6) Pluggy's town was probably on the Muskingum.

ment by the United States to construct a fort in the Delaware country, and the tribe are guaranteed all territorial rights as bounded by former treaties.

There are provisions for the mutual forgiveness of offences; of perpetual peace and defensive alliance—that neither party shall inflict punishments on the citizens of the other, without a fair and impartial trial by judges or juries of both parties, as Congress and Delaware deputies shall prescribe—for the delivery of criminal fugitives—that the United States will appoint an agent to trade with the Delawares on the principles of mutual interest—and, finally, "it is further agreed on between the contracting parties, should it for the future be found conducive for the mutual interest of both parties, to invite any other tribes who have been friends to the interest of the United States, to join the present confederation, and to form a State, whereof the Delaware nation shall be the head, and have a representative in Congress. Provided, nothing contained in this article to be considered as conclusive until it meets with the approbation of Congress."[7]

The treaty is signed by the commissioners and chiefs, as named above, in presence of Lachn. McIntosh, Brigadier General, commandant of the western department; Daniel Brodhead, Colonel of the 8th Pennsylvania regiment; William Crawford, Colonel; John Gibson, Colonel 13th Virginia regiment; A. Graham, Brigade Major; Lach. McIntosh, Jr., Brigade Major; Joseph L. Finley, Captain 8th Pennsylvania regiment; John Finley, Captain 8th Pennsylvania regiment.

It is a sad commentary upon the beneficent professions of these "Articles of Agreement and Confederation," that Col. Morgan, who was absent in Philadelphia, should write in the following January, that "there never was a conference with

7) United States Statutes at Large, vol. vii, p. 14.

the Indians so improperly or so villainously managed," and that he is "only surprised it had not worse effects."

The friendly Delaware chiefs were occasionally the guests of Congress at Philadelphia, and their territorial claims, on these visits, were very fluctuating. In March, 1776, Captain White Eyes thus defines the grant to the Delawares by their uncles, the Wyandots: "The Ohio River on the south, the west branch of the Muskingum and the Sandusky on the west, Lake Erie on the north, and Presque Isle on the east;" while on the 10th of May, 1779, the Delaware chiefs communicate the boundaries of their country, "From the mouth of the Alleghany River at Fort Pitt, to Venango, and from thence up French creek, and by LeBoeuf, along the old road to Presque Isle, *on the east;* the Ohio River, including all the islands in it from Fort Pitt to the Onabache, on the south; thence up the river Onabache to the branch Opecomeecah, and up the same to the head thereof, and from thence to the head waters and springs of the most northwestern branches of the Scioto River, thence to the head westernmost springs of Sandusky River, thence down the said river, including the islands in it, and the Little Lake, to Lake Erie, on the west and northwest; and Lake Erie on the north."

Allusion has already been made, with sufficient particularity,[8] to the submission of *Doonyontat*, a Wyandot chief, and *Keeshmatsee*, a chief of the Maginchee, or Machacheek tribe of Shawanese, to Col. Brodhead, which occurred September 14th, 1779, at Fort Pitt, on the return of that officer from his expedition against the Seneca towns. The mediator on that occasion was *Kelleleman*, or Killbuck.

Very soon, there was no room for negotiation with the

8) See Chapter xix., p. 308.

Western savages. Except a few Delawares—who were become a minority of the tribe—the whole wilderness of Ohio succumbed to British influence; and it was not until after the peace of 1783 with Great Britain, that the humbled tribes, abandoned by their ally, rekindled the council fires.

TREATY OF FORT STANWIX IN 1784.[9]

The site of Rome, in New York, was the scene of a highly important negotiation between Oliver Wolcott, Richard Butler and Arthur Lee, commissioners on the part of the United States, and the representatives of the Six Nations, which continued from the 3d to the 22d of October, when the treaty was signed.

The attitude assumed on this occasion by the commissioners was closely connected with the history of the West during the next twenty years. A full abstract of their transactions will therefore be presented.

On the first day, the commissioners met several of the Indians from the different nations at the council place, and announced their official character and purpose. The usual formula was varied so far as to add, that they proposed to "give peace and good counsel to those who have been unfortunately led astray by evil advisers." It was stated that the head men and warriors of the Western nations would attend in a few days, when they would speak more fully. Meanwhile, the Indians were desired to "hearken to the voice of Kayenlaa, the Marquis de Lafayette, a great man among the French, one of the head warriors of the great Onondio," &c.

9) The following particulars of this important negotiation are gathered from the Journal of Gen. Richard Butler, preserved in that valuable historical compilation, Craig's Olden Time, vol. ii., p. 404.

The reply of Kayenthogle, an Alleghany chief of the Senecas, was dignified and courteous, responding appropriately to every topic of the commissioners' address, except the suggestion, that the Indians had been "unfortunately led away by evil advisers."

Most of the time until the 11th of October, was occupied by efforts to prevent the sale of intoxicating liquors to the Indians. The commissioners directed Lieut. John Mercer, who attended them with a detachment of New Jersey troops by resolution of Congress, to seize and store all spirituous liquors until the conclusion of the treaty. For the execution of this order, a writ from a court of Montgomery county was issued for his arrest, but the commissioners would not suffer any compliance with its mandate.

Another collision, which might have been more serious, took place before the Indians were fully assembled. The Legislature of New York had already manifested a disposition to expel the Six Nations from all the country within the bounds of the State, which had not been ceded by them previous to the war. This state of feeling had excited much concern in Congress and elsewhere, and the commissioners were probably prepared for some annoyance, if not palpable interference, in the discharge of their duties. In a letter to the President of Congress, dated Fort Stanwix, Oct. 5, they state, that notwithstanding due notice to the Governor of New York, that he might transact any business with the Indians under the patronage of the United States, the governor chose to hold a separate treaty with the Six Nations. This procedure is contrasted with the course of Pennsylvania, whose commissioners were in attendance, with credentials and instructions entirely satisfactory to the Continental commissioners.

It happened that a Mr. Peter Schuyler was present at Fort Stanwix, and soon attracted the attention of the commissioners. He also assumed an official character, and was notified on the 6th of October to desist from all interference with the Indians. Schuyler produced a paper to the Secretary of the Commission, of which no particulars are given, except that it was without seal or signature, and "directed the said Peter Schuyler, together with one Peter Rightman, as an interpreter, to attend at Fort Stanwix during the time of the Commissioners of the United States holding their treaty with the Indians, to observe the conduct of the said commissioners, and to oppose and frustrate any of their proceedings which might eventually affect the interests of the State of New York." After this discovery, particular care was taken to include Messrs. Schuyler and Rightman in the execution of the liquor ordinance, and to exclude them from the councils.

On the 12th of October, the commissioners made an address to the sachems and warriors, in which they asserted their authority from the Congress of the United States to treat with the Indian Nations, and that the latter should not listen to any overtures made by any person or body of men, or by any particular State not authorized by Congress—exhibited the definitive treaty between the United States and the King of Great Britain, expressing the readiness of Congress to "give peace to the Indian nations upon just and reasonable terms, and to receive them into the friendship, favor and protection of the United States"—called particular attention to the sixth article, whereby the King of Great Britain "renounces and yields to the United States all pretensions and claims whatsoever of all the country south and west of the great Northern Rivers and Lakes, as far as the

Mississippi," making no reservation in favor of any Indian nation, but leaving those tribes to seek for peace with the United States, upon such terms as the United States shall think just and reasonable; and, after impressing upon them, that the delivery of all prisoners, white and black, was essential to any peace, the commissioners closed by asking the tribes present at the council, to propose such a boundary line between the United States and themselves, as would be just for them to offer and the United States to accept. It was intimated to the American allies—Oneidas, Tuscaroras, and Caughnewaghas—that the foregoing address was not intended for them.

At the opening of the session, Capt. Aaron Hill, a Mohawk, who had just arrived, explained that his tribe had received frequent messages from the Governor of New York to meet him in council, but they were unwilling to partake in any but a continental treaty, and that the message of the Commissioners of the United States had been received so recently, that it was difficult for many to attend, and impossible to deliver the prisoners at this time, but Capt. Brant would instantly collect and send down the latter. He added, that numbers of their brothers to the Westward, the Wyandots in particular, had returned home, by reason of the advanced season of the year, after coming as far as Niagara, so that themselves and their brothers, the Shawanese, were only present.

Capt. O'Bail, or Cornplanter, was then recognized by the commissioners as authorized to transact all business with the United States on behalf of six towns.

It was not until the 17th of October, that the assembled Indians were ready to reply. Capt. Aaron Hill first spoke. After intimating that they could not answer so fully and satisfactorily as they might do, if a copy of the commissioners' speech had been furnished to them, allusion was made to the statement, that the council fire was kindled for the purpose of settling all differences and disputes between the United States and the Indian nations, the speaker begged attention to the words of the warriors, and thus proceeded: "The words of the warriors are strong: they are persons who have so traveled through the world, and borne all the difficulties of the war, that it is in their power to make a lasting peace. You told us that it was solely on us to make peace, but we apprehend that it is mutually dependent upon both parties. I speak in the name of the Six Nations, and not only in their name, but also in the name of all the other tribes—my voice, therefore, is strong—our minds are deep, and persevering, and our wish to make peace is great. We are neither haughty, nor proud, nor is it our disposition ever, of ourselves, to commence hostilities. Our adherence to our covenant with the Great King, drew us into the late war, which is a great proof to the commissioners of our strict observance of our ancient covenant with the white people; and you will find the same attachment to the covenant now to be made, as that which signalized our conduct during the late war. We are free and independent, and at present under no influence. We have hitherto been bound by the Great King, but he having broken the chain, and left us to ourselves, we are again free and independent."

Recapitulating, without dissent, the points of the commissioners' speech in respect to their exclusive authority to conclude a treaty, and the terms of peace between the United States and Great Britain, the orator feelingly remarked: "You also assured us that the Great King in settling this peace with the United States, made no mention of us, but left us to treat for ourselves. Certainly the Great King did not look up to that Great Spirit, which he had called as a witness to that treaty, otherwise common justice would not have suffered him to be so inattentive, as to neglect those who had been so just and faithful to him; and we think that our brothers, the United States, did not think of the Great Spirit, otherwise they would have mentioned to the Great King those persons who had been so faithful to him, when they found that he had entirely neglected them."

The speaker claimed that the Indians present were adequate to treat of, and conclude a peace, not only on the part of the Six Nations, but also on that of the Ottawas, Chippewas, Hurons, Potowatames, Messasagas, Miamis, Delawares, Shawanese, Cherokees, Chicasaws, Choctaws, and Creeks.

The sarcasm of the following paragraphs—at least that in respect to the cession by France—is very apparent:

"You acquainted us that the King of France had ceded to the United States all claim and title to any lands within their boundary. We have only to thank the Great Spirit for putting it into the mind of the King of France to make this cession, as it is well known that he is extremely saving of his lands, and that the United States are in great want of them.

"You informed us that it was indispensably essential to the making of peace, that all the prisoners should be delivered up, and that nothing could be finally done therein, until that should be the case. We would propose to the commissioners that for this purpose they should depute persons of their own nation to go and collect them, lest if it should rest with us, the commissioners might apprehend that they were not all brought, and for this purpose we will give them all the assistance in our power."

On the following day, the 18th, Cornplanter or Capt. O'Bail, resumed and closed the speech on behalf of the Six Nations.

After an unsatisfactory attempt to explain the conduct of his own tribe, the Senecas, in joining the British, after their repeated pledges to observe a neutrality, Cornplanter approached the boundary question, which he treated with consummate tact. That entire portion is here given:

"Brothers, Representatives of the Thirteen United States:

"You have allotted to me the task of drawing a line between us to your satisfaction. I feel the weight of it: I feel for many of my brothers, who will be left destitute of any lands, and have therefore taken care in my deliberations to mark out that line which will give peace to both our minds.

"I hope that in our present negotiations, nothing but friendship will prevail, and I am fully sensible that you will never conduct yourselves towards us, as the King of Great Britain has in throwing us away.

"Brothers, Commissioners of the Thirteen United States, now hearken:

"When we shall have drawn the line between us, whatever shall remain within the boundary allotted to us, shall be our own—it shall continue forever, as the sun which rolls over from day to day.

"Brothers, Commissioners of the Thirteen United States:

"Let us go on with this business of peace with tenderness and caution, as it is of the utmost importance, and should what I now say not meet with a kind reception into your breasts, it will greatly distress me, for I who stand before you am a warrior, and should it not meet your approbation, inform me whilst I am here:

"Brothers, I have several times repeated the words to

proceed tenderly in this business, for I regard future generations, and to them I attend while engaged in making peace with you.

"Our fires will be a considerable distance from each other, when I come to describe the boundary between us. This will tend to our mutual peace.

"I think, brothers, that we warriors must have a large country to range in, as indeed our subsistence must depend on our having much hunting ground, and as it will also bring in money to you, will tend to our mutual advantage.

"Now, brothers, I am about to draw the line—this we Senecas do of ourselves, as the land belongs solely to us. Let it begin at Tioga, and run thence by a straight line inclining a little to the North to Ohigee, and when it strikes the River Ohio, let it go down its stream to the old boundary on the Cherokee River. As to the territory westward of that, you must talk respecting it with the Western Nations, towards the setting of the sun—they must consult of what part they will cede to the United States.

"Brothers, should you approve of this boundary, you will direct your people not to trespass upon our territory, or pass over the line, and should any of our nation attempt to pass over, or intrude upon your lands—let us know it—we will take care to reprimand them, and prevent it.

"Brothers, by this belt you now see my mind. If what I have mentioned be approved of by you, lay it along the Tioga, as I have said—if not, I again request you to inform me."

On the 20th of October, the commissioners replied to Hill and Cornplanter. No part of this speech is omitted:

"Sachems and Warriors:—We are now going to reply to the answer you made to our speech—therefore open your ears and hear.

"You informed us that your words were not the words of the Six Nations only, but that you were empowered to speak for all the western nations of Indians. This surprises us. We summoned the Six Nations only to this treaty—that nations not called should send their voices hither, is extraordinary. But you have not shown us any authority, either in writing or by belts, for your speaking in their names. Without such authority, your words will pass away like the winds of yesterday that are heard no more.

"You have complained that we refused you a copy of our speech, which might lead you into errors. When we refused it we gave our reason, which was this, that having explained our minds publicly and clearly to you all, and given belts and strings to remind you of every proposition, we did not choose you to be deceived, and our meaning to be misrepresented by the few persons among you who understand English, and might have explained our speech, if we had given a copy of it, as they pleased. We knew there were such persons among you who wished to deceive you, and under the direction of those who led you into the war against us, were planning to mislead you again for their own purposes. We did not wish to put you into the power of such persons, but to clear your eyes and understandings. We explained, at your desire, over and over again, our speech to you, and the strings and belts which accompanied every part of it.

"You next excused your having taken up arms against us, by alleging you were drawn into it by your ancient covenant with the king of England.

"Where was your sense of covenants, when, after solemnly covenanting with us in 1775, and again as solemnly in 1776, receiving our presents to cover you, to comfort and to strengthen you—immediately you took up the hatchet against us and struck us with all your might? Could you have so soon forgotten your recent engagements with us, and yet be influenced by those long past with the king of England?

"We asked you—we exhorted you for your own sakes, to remain neuter, though as living on the same ground with us, we had a right to expect your assistance against all invaders. You twice solemnly covenanted not to join in the war against us—and without the smallest provocation on our part, you violated your covenants and spilt our blood.

"We should not have called to mind this conduct, had you not attempted to justify it. You must not deceive yourselves, nor hope to deceive us. To justify errors may lead to a recommission of them, and it will be more safe and honorable to repent of, than to palliate, a conduct which, though mischievous to us, has been fatal to you, and has left you at our mercy.

"Again, you are mistaken in supposing that having been excluded from the treaty between the United States and the king of Great Britain, you are become a free and independent nation, and may make what terms you please. It is not so. You are a subdued people; you have been overcome in a war which you entered into with us, not only without provocation, but in violation of most sacred obligations. The Great Spirit, who is at the same time the judge and avenger of perfidy, has given us victory over all our enemies. We are at peace with all but *you; you* now stand out *alone* against our *whole force*.

"When we offer you peace on moderate terms, we do it in magnanimity and mercy. If you do not accept it now, you are not to expect a repetition of such offers. Consider well, therefore, your situation and *ours*. Do not suffer yourselves to be again deceived so as to raise our arm against you. You feel the sad effects of having refused this counsel before—beware how you do it again.

"Compassionating your situation, we endeavored to make the terms on which you were to be admitted into the peace and protection of the United States, appear to spring from your own contrition for what you had done, rather than from a necessity imposed by us. We therefore proposed to you to deliver up the prisoners, and to propose a boundary line, such as it became the United States to agree to.

"On neither of these points have you given us the smallest satisfaction. You propose we should deputise people of our nation to go and collect the prisoners. This you know from experience is impracticable; that it would only provoke insults, and perhaps the murder of such deputation, by the persons who hold our fellow citizens in bondage. You only can collect them; you only ought to collect them; you must collect and deliver them up. Our words are strong, and we mean you should feel them. With regard to the boundary line you have proposed, the lands to the northwest of it have almost all been sold already to Onas, and all the land south-east of it, to the Cherokee River, was sold by you in the year 1768, at this place, and is all granted and settled by the white people.

"We shall now, therefore, declare to you the condition on which alone you can be received into the peace and protection of the United States. The conditions are these:

"The United States of America will give peace to the Senecas, Mohawks, Onondagas and Cayugas, and receive them into their protection upon the following conditions:

"ARTICLE 1. Six hostages shall be immediately delivered to the commissioners by the said nations, to remain in the possession of the United States till all the prisoners, white and black, which were taken by the said Senecas, Mohawks, Onondagas and Cayugas, or by any of them, in the late war, from among the citizens of the United States, shall be delivered up.

"Article 2. The Oneida and Tuscarora nations shall be secured in the possession of the lands on which they are settled.

"Article 3. A line shall be drawn, beginning at the mouth of a creek about four miles east of Niagara, called Oyonwayea, or Johnston's Landing Place, upon the lake named by the Indians Oswego, and by us Ontario; from thence southerly, in a direction always four miles east of the carrying path, between lakes Erie and Ontario, to the mouth of the Tehoseroron, or Buffalo creek, on Lake Erie, thence south to the north boundary of the State of Pennsylvania; thence west to the end of the said north boundary; thence south along the west boundary of the said State to the river Ohio; the said line from the mouth of the Oyonwayea to the Ohio shall be the western boundary of the lands of the Six Nations, so that the Six Nations shall and do yield to the United States, all claims to the country west of the said boundary, and then they shall be secured in the peaceful possession of the lands they inhabit east and north of the same, reserving only six miles square round the fort of Oswego, to the United States, for the support of the same.

"Article 4. The commissioners of the United States, in consideration of the present circumstances of the Six Nations, and in execution of the humane and liberal views of the United States, upon the signing of the above articles, will order goods to be delivered to the said Six Nations for their use and comfort.

"We shall make a few remarks on these articles, though the moderation and equity of them are manifest:

"1st. It is more than six months since you were informed by General Schuyler, in the name of Congress, that you must deliver up all the prisoners before peace could be granted to you. Our message gave you the same information, yet you have not delivered them up.

"As the delivery of them is indispensable, so you have rendered hostages necessary by your delay.

"2d. It does not become the United States to forget those nations who preserved their faith to them, and adhered to their cause—those, therefore, must be secured in the full and free enjoyment of those possessions.

"3d. The line proposed leaves as extensive a country to the remaining four nations as they can in reason desire, and more than, from their conduct in the war, they could expect.

"The king of Great Britain ceded to the United States *the whole;* by the right of conquest they might *claim the whole.* Yet they have taken but a small part compared with their numbers and their wants. Their warriors must be provided for. Compensations must be made for the blood and treasures which they have expended in the war. The great increase of their people renders more lands essential to their subsistence. It is therefore necessary that such a boundary line should be settled as will make effectual provisions for these demands and prevent any future cause of difference and dispute.

"4th. It ought to be felt by you as a signal proof of the magnanimity of the United States, that though the present distresses of most of the Six Nations have been incurred by their own fault in fighting against them, yet they have determined to minister such relief to them as is at present in their power.

"These are the terms on which you may obtain perpetual peace with the United States, and enjoy their protection.

"You must be sensible that these are blessings which cannot be purchased at too high a price. Be wise, and answer us accordingly."

The speech of Captain Aaron Hill, on the 21st, presents no new points, and is tame and unimpressive. The written proofs or belts of their right to speak in the name of the western tribes, he said, had been left at the council fire which was burning among the Shawanese, on the river Miami. There is a tradition that young Red Jacket boldly opposed the burial of the hatchet, and spoke with vehement eloquence against the treaty. When the Marquis De Lafayette revisited the United States, in 1824–5, he met Red Jacket at Buffalo, and the General was reminded, by the venerable chief, of the circumstance of their former meeting at Fort Stanwix. This is the earliest allusion to the Seneca orator, afterwards so widely renowned.

But the experienced and sagacious Cornplanter saw that total banishment, perhaps a bloody extirpation, was the only alternative, and his influence in favor of the treaty prevailed. The motto of the commissioners was *Voe Victis*—woe to the vanquished!

The official publication of the treaty at Fort Stanwix is identical with the proposition dictated by the commissioners. The sword of victory was in the American scale, and it was signed without the addition or diminution of a syllable. Its future consequences will appear in the sequel.

TREATY AT FORT McINTOSH IN 1785.

The treaty with the New York Indians having extinguished their western claims, measures were promptly taken to prescribe terms and boundaries to the Ohio tribes. On the 21st of January, George Rogers Clark, Richard Butler and Arthur

Lee met a body of Indians at Fort McIntosh, who asserted themselves to be representatives of the Wyandots, Delawares, Chippewas and Ottawas. We present this document with its signatures and attestation:

"The Commissioners Plenipotentiary of the United States in Congress assembled, give peace to the Wyandot, Delaware, Chippewa, and Ottowa nations of Indians, on the following conditions:

ARTICLE 1. Three chiefs, one from among the Wyandot, and two from among the Delaware nations, shall be delivered up to the Commissioners of the United States, to be by them retained till all the prisoners, white and black, taken by the said nations, or any of them, shall be restored.

ARTICLE 2. The said Indian nations do acknowledge themselves and all their tribes to be under the protection of the United States, and of no other sovereign whatever.

ARTICLE 3. The boundary line between the United States and Wyandot and Delaware nations, shall begin at the mouth of the River Cayahoga, and run thence up the said river to the portage between that and the Tuscarawas branch of Meskingum; then down the said branch to the forks at the crossing place above Fort Lawrence [Laurens]; then westerly to the portage of the Big Miami, which runs into the Ohio, at the mouth of which branch the fort stood which was taken by the French in one thousand seven hundred and fifty-two; then along the said portage to the Great Miami or Ome River, and down the southeast side of the same to its mouth; thence along the south shore of Lake Erie, to the mouth of Cayahoga, where it began.

ARTICLE 4. The United States allot all the lands contained within the said lines, to the Wyandot and Delaware nations, to live and to hunt on, and to such of the Ottowa nation as now live thereon: saving and reserving for the establishment of trading posts, six miles square at the mouth of Miami or Ome River, and the same at the portage on that branch of the Big Miami which runs into the Ohio, and the same on the Lake of Sanduske where the fort formerly stood, and also two miles square on each side of the lower rapids of Sanduske River, which posts, and the lands annexed to them, shall be to the use, and under the Government of the United States.

Article 5. If any citizen of the United States, or other person not being an Indian, shall attempt to settle on any of the lands allotted to the Wyandot and Delaware nations in this treaty, except on the lands reserved to the United States in the preceding article, such person shall forfeit the protection of the United States, and the Indians may punish him as they please.

Article 6. The Indians who sign this treaty, as well in behalf of all their tribes as of themselves, do acknowledge the lands east, south and west of the lines described in the third article, so far as the said Indians formerly claimed the same, to belong to the United States; and none of their tribes shall presume to settle upon the same or any part of it.

Article 7. The post of Detroit, with a district beginning at the mouth of the River Rosine, on the west end of Lake Erie, and running west six miles up the southern bank of the said river, thence northerly and always six miles west of the strait, till it strikes the Lake St. Clair, shall be also reserved to the sole use of the United States.

Article 8. In the same manner, the post of Michillimachinac with its dependencies and twelve miles square about the same, shall be reserved to the use of the United States.

ARTICLE 9. If any Indian or Indians shall commit a robbery or murder on any citizen of the United States, the tribe to which such offenders may belong, shall be bound to deliver them up at the nearest post, to be punished according to the ordinances of the United States.

ARTICLE 10. The commissioners of the United States, in pursuance of the humane and liberal views of Congress, upon this treaty's being signed, will direct goods to be distributed among the different tribes for their use and comfort.

SEPARATE ARTICLE.—It is agreed that the Delaware chiefs, Kelelarrand, or lieutenant-colonel Henry [alias Killbuck,] Hengue Pushees or the Big Cat, Wicocalind or Captain White Eyes, who took up the hatchet for the United States and their families, shall be received into the Delaware Nation, in the same situation and rank as before the war, and enjoy their due portion of the lands given to the Wyandot and Delaware Nations in this treaty, as fully as if they had not taken part with America, or as any other person or persons in the said nations:

GEO. CLARK,	TALAPOXIE,
RICHARD BUTLER,	WINGENUM,
ARTHUR LEE,	PACKELANT,
DAUNGHQUAT,	GINGEWANNO,
ABRAHAM KUHN,	WAANOOS,
OTTAWERRERI,	KONALÁWASSEE,
HOBOCAN,	SHAWNAQUM,
WALENDIGHTUN,	QUECOOKIA.

WITNESS.—Samuel J. Atlee, Francis Johnston, Commis sioners of Pennsylvania; Alexander Campbell; Joseph Har mar, Colonel Commandant; Alexander Lowrey; Joseph Nicholas, interpreter: J. Bradford; George Slaughter; Van Swearingen; John Boggs; G. Evans; D. Luckett."[10]

10) U. S. Statutes at Large, vol. vii., p. 16.

Of the Indian names signed to this treaty, Daunnghquat was the Wyandot chief who negotiated with Col. Brodhead at Fort Pitt in 1779; Abraham Kuhn was a Wyandot from Lower Sandusky, mentioned by Heckewelder as engaged in the removal of the Moravians in 1781, from the Muskingum to the Sandusky: "Hobocan" was the Indian name of Captain Pipe: Talapoxie we suppose to be the friendly Delaware chief called Tetepachksi by Heckewelder; Wingenum was also a Delaware; and Packelant may have been the same as the Packgantschihilas of Heckewelder's Narrative, or our favorite Bockengehelas. The other names are not recognizable—probably Chippewas and Ottawas.

TREATY OF FORT FINNEY IN 1786.

In pursuance of a resolution of Congress, March 18th, 1785, preparations had been made to hold a treaty with the Wabash Indians at Fort Vincent, (now Vincennes) on the 20th of June, 1785, but these tribes were impracticable, and by a resolution of the 29th of June, the place was changed to the mouth of the Great Miami, and the time postponed until January, 1786. The conference was finally held at Fort Finney—a post established for the occasion on the left bank of the Great Miami at its junction with the Ohio—by George Rogers Clark, Richard Butler and Samuel H. Parsons, Commissioners of the United States, and the Shawanese Indians.

The journal of General Butler, while engaged upon the mission, has recently been published,[11] and a summary of its contents will best reflect the posture of affairs, and the aspect of the frontier, as well as the dispositions of the savages, at that period. Its author, originally a trader of Pittsburgh,

11) Craig's Olden Time, vol. ii, p. 431.

distinguished himself in the war of the Revolution, enjoyed in a high degree the confidence of Washington, and sealed his devotion to the country, by the sacrifice of his life on the bloody field of St. Clair's defeat. Having borne a part in the negotiations which resulted in the treaties of Forts Stanwix and McIntosh, he left his residence in Carlisle, Pennsylvania, on the 9th of September, 1785, on a service in all respects more arduous and uncertain. General Butler was accompanied until the 11th of October, and as far as Limestone, now Maysville, on the Ohio River, by Colonel James Monroe, then a member of Congress from Virginia, and afterwards President of the United States.

On the 27th of September, Butler caused three boats to be loaded with goods for the treaty, and one large scow with provisions for the troops that were to join him at Fort McIntosh, and started for the mouth of Beaver—the site of that post—where he arrived next day. Here he found the detachment in readiness (its strength is not mentioned), and before again embarking, prepared and left a paper with Col. Harmar, the commandant, in which the opinion was expressed that the "mouth of the Muskingum would be a proper place for a post to cover the frontier inhabitants, prevent intruding settlers on the lands of the United States, and secure the surveyors." At the west line of Pennsylvania, then being run by David Rittenhouse and his assistants, the party met Thomas Hutchins, the geographer of the United States, and a corps of surveyors. "They had made a beginning," says Butler, "at right angles on the Pennsylvania line at the post set up by Mr. Rittenhouse, and had gone on westward six miles, the breadth of one range of townships, on which Capt. Martain begins to-morrow (October 1,) having won it by lots: the other gentlemen will follow in rotation, and some are very anxious to get to business. The gentlemen were very polite and seemed happy to see us. Capt. Hutchins had a very good dinner ready, which we partook of with great pleasure, as it was with a set of gentlemen who are the first at work on a fund which will eventually, and I think in a short time, extinguish the debt of the United States, and fix a permanent prosperity on legal right, for millions of people."

There was some discord among the gentlemen of this surveying party, as afterwards transpired in their private interviews with Butler, which the latter labored to assuage. He also found Captain Hutchins apprehensive of the safety of his company, unless the Indian chiefs should personally assure him of their good will.

From Yellow Creek to Cross Creeks—the present front of Jefferson county on the Ohio River—Butler was often ashore to warn off settlers upon the right bank of the Ohio. He notified them that "Congress was determined to put all the people off the lands, and that none would be allowed to settle but the legal purchasers, and that these, and these only, would be protected: that troops would be down next week, who had orders to destroy every house and improvement on the north side of the river, and that garrisons would be placed at Muskingum and other places, and that if any person or persons attempted to oppose Government, they might depend on being treated with the greatest rigor." Certainly a short method with squatters.

Wheeling, in 1785, is thus noticed: "This is a fine settlement, and belongs to one Zane; an Island which is opposite the mouth of Wheeling Creek, containing about 400 acres of most excellent land, and is a situation not only of great profit, but real beauty. He says he sells to amount of £300 per annum of the produce of his farm for cash, exclusive of the other advantages by traffic. He is an intelligent man, but seems either timid through real doubt or affects it through design."

General Butler visited and describes the antiquities at Grave Creek. "The Grave is an extraordinary pile of human bones covered with earth. It is about sixty feet perpendicular high, and about one hundred eighty feet in diameter at the base; a conical figure, with large trees on its sides and top, where is one of three feet in diameter. Supposing the annual growth one-tenth of an inch, it is one hundred and eighty years old; how long its sides were naked may be supposed fifty years, as these kinds of mounds do not produce trees so soon as the land which is on a level with the country round. There are two small forts, which, with the Grave, form a triangle. Near one of these forts are three large holes, which appear to have been places of deposit for provisions. About one-fourth of a mile from these, forming an angle of about twenty-five degrees, is a large fort which the owner of the land has begun to plow up, where they find pieces of earthen kettles, arrow points and stone tomahawks, all marks of savage antiquity."

From Muskingum (where a letter, recommending the site of the fort at a point on the Ohio side, was "left fixed to a locust tree") to the mouth of the Great Kenawha, the journal, beyond the ordinary incidents of a voyage, dwells upon the beauty and fertility of the bottoms, and the abundance of wild game, pouncing occasionally upon a luckless squatter. On reaching the Great Kenawha, Gen. Butler digresses into a town-lot speculation. It was a common impression then, that by the James River or Potomac, and the Kenawha, the Muskingum or the Cuyahoga, the great commercial avenue between the lakes and tidewater would be established, and the confluence of the Kenawha and Ohio, seemed clearly indicated as the site of a flourishing city. Here Butler met "young Col. Lewis, a most sensible young gentleman, very interesting and communicative." They dined together—Col. Lewis being "treated with attention, who received it very politely. I inquired," Butler continues, "if they did not intend to lay out a town at the point [Point Pleasant, probably]: he told me it was laid out and the lots generally sold, but if I wanted a lot, or more, I might still be supplied, as many of the lots were forfeited. I told him I would purchase, on which we went to look over the ground; and he took me up the Ohio bank to a fine dry lot which fronts the street on the river Ohio, a street that runs at right angles from the river and the main street, or first parallel street with the Ohio, which gives it three fronts, being west, north, and east. This I agreed for." Butler also purchased a lot fronting on the Kenawha. The prices were "ten pounds for front lots on each river, five pounds the first back lots, and four pounds the further back."

As the voyage continued, the enthusiasm of the journalist becomes irrepressible. "This delightful country," he writes on the 13th of October, "involuntarily draws from my pen praises: it is fine, it is rich, and only wants the cultivating hand of man to render it the joyous seat of happy thousands. Here are the wild animals provided for the assistance of the first settlers. Here are the finest and most excellent sites for farms, cities and towns. This seems provided as a reward for the adventurous and industrious, by the Divine hand, whose good providence appears in all his works. Here we have nothing to do but spring from our boats among flocks of turkeys, kill as we please, for sport or gust; the bear growls in your hearing, and the deer, timid by nature, bounds along before your eye; in short, there is no end to the beauty and plenty. I have just stepped from my boat and killed, at one shot, two fine turkeys; and our whole party feasts on fine venison, bear meat, turkeys and cat-fish, procured by themselves, at pleasure."

Passing a river below Guyandot, which is the most southerly point between Fort Pitt and sixty miles below the Great Miami, Butler called it South River, and then adds: "Near the mouth of Big Sandy, Mr. Zane (Isaac Zane, who had accompanied the party from Wheeling) killed a fine buffalo."

The following description evidently refers to the vicinity of Ironton, Lawrence county: "About ten miles below Big Sandy Creek, is a hill on the north side with fine trees on it: there also a body of rocks appears with a southeast front, below which, about five miles, opposite to a large sand bar on the south side of the river, is an old Indian town and grave, where we encamped. It is a body of as fine land as I have seen, and well worthy attention; indeed, there are on both sides of the river fine lands: here Mr. Zane killed three buffalo, one of which seems to be a real curiosity for size. Several of the gentlemen went to see it, viz: Lieut. Smith, Lieut. Doyle and Mr. Peebles; they brought with them the head and one of the shoulders, with the whole leg to it. The head weighed one hundred and twenty-nine pounds, and the tongue six—total, one hundred and thirty-five pounds. The head was cut off as close as possible, or at the large joint, so that the neck was but a small addition to the weight. The leg and shoulder, when set upright, was as high as my head, which is five feet eight and a half inches: this, when on the body, including that extraordinary protuberance called the hump, Mr. Zane assured me, is higher than his head, which is six feet (eighteen hands): and it was agreed by all who saw this amazing wild animal, that it weighed at least fifteen hundred pounds. Part of the beef of these fine animals was delivered to the troops, and part salted for future use.

"I cannot help here describing the amazing plenty and variety of this night's supper. We had fine roast buffalo beef, soup of buffalo beef and turkeys, fried turkeys, fried cat-fish, fresh caught, roast ducks, good punch, madeira, claret, grog and toddy, and the troops supplied in the most abundant manner. They are all cheerful, and generally in perfect health, and enjoying the bounties of heaven, the land and the water. The industry and judgment of one man could certainly supply many families. Mr. Zane killed this day, on the lowest computation, three thousand weight of as fine beef as need be used, all in about four hours' hunting."

There is special mention of "that sweet and delightful little river Sciota, whose charming banks are not only beautiful to a wonder, but the richest and most luxuriant soil." Here he was "alarmed by a prodigious gust of wind, which caused a great and extraordinary fog, that smelt of sulphur."

Next morning, Oct. 17, they passed the mouth of Scioto, and twenty-four miles below, reached Buffalo Lick Creek, where the indefatigable Zane was soon in successful pursuit of a drove of buffaloes, killing a fine one.

Limestone, or Maysville, is described as containing "about fifteen good cabins for families, kitchens, &c., included, and about twenty-five houses, with a good wagon road to Lexington and other places." Here information was received that Gen. Clark, one of the commissioners, was at the Miami with a number of troops, and that some of the messengers had arrived, accompanied by a few Indians.

The allusions to the vicinity of Cincinnati, are dimly prophetic: "About three o'clock (Oct. 21), passed the mouth of the Little Miamis. About two miles below is a piece of high ground, which, I think, will be the site of a town. * * Pushed on to the mouth of Licking Creek, which is a pretty stream: at the mouth, both above and below, are very fine bottoms. The bottom below the mouth seems highest and most fit to build a town on; it is extensive, and whoever owns the bottoms should own the hill also. Passed this at five o'clock, and encamped two miles below on the north side."

General Butler arrived at the Great Miami on the 22d of October, and found General Clark at a station, (defined as "a few families collected for mutual safety to one place, and a little fort erected,") a short distance below, on the Kentucky side; but it was not until the 13th of November that their colleague, General Parsons, arrived. Fully two months elapsed before the Shawanese could be induced to attend the council. Meanwhile, "four block houses and quadrangular work" were constructed under the superintendence of Major W. Finney, (by whose name they were designated,) on the Ohio, above the mouth of Miami. Excursions were made by the leaders of the party to Big Bone Lick and the falls of the Ohio; and at Louisville, Butler found the people engaged "in selling and buying lots in the back streets, but not liking the situation, bought none."

There was no considerable arrival of Indians until the 18th of November, when fifty Wyandots, ten Delawares and ten Shawanese approached the fort. The Wyandot camp was on the banks of the Miami, about three miles north of Fort Finney. Thenceforth, private interviews, accompanied by presents, frequently occurred with the Half King and Crane of the Wyandots; with Wingenum, Pipe, White Eyes, (a son of the celebrated Indian so called,) old Abraham, (probably

Kuhn,) who were Delawares, and John Harris and Micanimsica, Shawanese. It transpired that Simon Girty and one Robert Suphlet, (cousin to the well-known British agent, Alexander McKee,) were then in the Shawanese towns, using every persuasion to prevent an attendance at the conference. Their labors proved so far successful, that another month elapsed without any further arrival of Shawanese, except "the Grenadier Squaw's daughter, Fanny, (Cornstalk's niece) and her brother Morgan, with one other Shawnee man and woman." At length, on the 27th of December, Captain Wingenum, (chronicled by Butler as "old, experienced and sensible") was sent to the nations with a final message of invitation. This embassy seems to have been effective, for, on the 14th of January, one hundred and fifty Shawanese men, and eighty women, were received with due ceremony by the commissioners and the garrison. The formal reception of this "proud little nation" is thus described. "The oldest chief leads, and carries a small drum, on which he beats time and sings; two young warriors, who dance well, carry each the stem of a pipe painted and decorated with feathers of the bald eagle and wampum; these are joined in the dance by several other young men, who dance and keep time to the drum—the whole of the party painted and dressed in the most elegant manner, in their way, which is truly fantastic, but elegant though savage. The chief who headed this party is called Melonthe. These were followed by the chief warrior, Aweecauny, and last, the warriors armed; then came the headwoman, called Ca-we-chile, in front of all the women and children. When they came near the council house, Aweecauny got on a stump and ordered the whole to halt. They then sung for some time, when he gave a signal and the song ceased. He then ordered the armed men to make ready, which they did; then to fire, which was performed in the Indian style of a running fire. This was repeated three times, on which our troops returned the salute with three vollies from a platoon, well performed, the drum beating an American march. We then entered the council house and took our seats; they then arrived, and after dancing a short time at the door, by way of salute, they entered at the west door, the chiefs on our left, the warriors on our right and round on the east end till they joined the chiefs—the old chief beating the drum, and the young men dancing and waving the feathers over us, whilst the others were seated. This done, the women entered at the east door, and took their seats on the east end with great form. This over, the chief inquired who were the commissioners, which the young warrior, John Harris, told them, and pointed us out. After a short song, the chiefs called on Ke-kewepellethe, a Wagatommochie man, who immediately rose to address us. His speech was short, but pathetic and sensible. He said, that in consequence of our invitation they had come to our council fire—that they had also brought their women and children—that they had shut their ears against all that advised them not to come, and now stood before us. They hoped, on our part, we would also shut our ears against evil stories, and banish from our memory every evil impression; that they cleared our ears, wiped our eyes, and with the strings of wampum removed all sorrow from our hearts. They hoped, therefore, we would be strong, pity their women and children, and go on with the good work of peace, and suffer no evil reports to prevent our carrying it into effect."

The commissioners replied complaisantly, and the affair ended with a dinner and an allowance of "grog and tobacco."

It was noticed that the Sachems only shook the hands of the commissioners, but the warriors and women ("the strength of the nation") postponed that ceremony "until peace was certain." Another usage of the Shawanese, was subsequently found to be, to transact business relating to peace before noon, the day afterwards being the time for the business of war.

An interview, on the 20th of January, between Bockengehelas and George Rogers Clark, has been the subject of much literary embellishment. Butler's simple narrative is as follows: "This morning early, (Friday, January 20,) the Pipe, a chief of the Delawares, came in and informed us that the strange chief Pacanchichiles, or Iskittapiecica, in Shawanese, with others, were at hand, and would salute us, on which we ordered the usual salute of three platoons to return it. When they advanced, this piece of ceremony was performed, and our messengers showed them into the council house, on which the flag of the United States is kept displayed. When they were all seated, the commissioners were notified, and went to the council house with the officers. After being seated, Packanchichiles rose and spoke. His first address was to the Great Spirit, returning thanks for the preservation of his own and General Clark's life through the war, and for putting it once more in their power to see each other, adding that he felt very happy at the prospect which now opened to his view, and thanked God for giving us this great day to meet and declare the pleasure he felt. That now he felt the advantages his nation may experience by the good work his kings have been transacting with the commissioners of the United States; that he is determined to support it with all his endeavor, and recommended to General Clark, as a warrior, to assist on our part, with much more to the same purport.

General Clark told him he was glad to see him, and advised him to be strong and sincere in his determination."[12]

On this occasion, "the old chief called Tetapaxicca," spoke to the same purport, and the Big Cat, who had been employed as a messenger to the western tribes, reported that a deputation of the Twightwees, and other Wabash and Miami Indians, had reached the Shawanese towns, "where they received such advice and accounts from Detroit as put them back." He also charged the Shawanese with giving the tomahawk to a town of Mohicans on the White River. The statements of Big Cat were afterwards denied very stoutly by the Shawanese.

On the 30th of January, the main business of the conference proceeded. The commissioners addressed the Indians so nearly in the spirit and terms employed at the treaty of Fort Stanwix, as to render a transcript unnecessary. They closed with a recital of the terms of a treaty which they should impose upon the Shawanese. Immediately ensued a scene of great excitement. The younger warriors of the nation, as Butler admits under date of January 17th, "who had grown up through the course of the war," had been "trained like young hounds to blood, and were greatly under British influence. When the latter were informed of the stringent terms dictated to them—especially the surrender of hostages for the delivery of prisoners—intense dissatisfaction prevailed. The chief from Wakatomaka, Kekewepellethy, became the organ of this indignant feeling, and addressed the commissioners as follows:

"Brothers, by what you said to us yesterday, we expected everything past would be forgotten; that our proposals for

12) For a more detailed sketch of Bockengehelas, the distinguished Delaware chief, see Appendix No. XI.

collecting the prisoners were satisfactory, and that we would have been placed on the same footing as before the war. To-day you demand hostages till your prisoners are returned. You next say you will divide the lands. I now tell you it is not the custom of the Shawnese to give hostages; our words are to be believed; when we say a thing, we stand to it; *we are Shawnese!* As to the lands, God gave us this country; we do not understand measuring out the lands; it is all ours. You say you have goods for our women and children; you may keep your goods, and give them to the other nations; we will have none of them. Brothers, you seem to grow proud because you have thrown down the king of England; and as we feel sorry for our past faults, you rise in your demands on us. This we think hard. You need not doubt our words—what we have promised we will perform. We told you we had appointed three good men of our nation to go to the towns and collect your flesh and blood; they shall be brought in. We have never given hostages, and we will not comply with this demand." A string of black wampum was likewise delivered.

After a short consultation, the commissioners determined not to recede from any of the articles, and General Butler thus addressed the turbulent assemblage:

"SHAWNEES: You have addressed us with great warmth. We think the answer unwise and ungrateful; and, in return for just and generous proposals, you have not only given us improper language, but asserted the greatest falsehoods. You say you cannot give hostages for the performance of your promises, as it is contrary to your usages, and that you never break your word. Have you forgotten your breach of treaties in the beginning of the late war with Britain, between the United States and your chiefs, in '75 and '76? Do you think us ignorant of those treaties? Do you think we have forgotten the burning of our towns, the murder and captivity of our people in consequence of your perfidy, or have you forgotten them? Don't you remember when Col. Bouquet came up to Tuscarawas, that you there gave hostages? Do you forget that you gave hostages to Lord Dunmore? Do you forget that when he had agreed to send people to collect the prisoners, that they had like to have been murdered in your towns? Recollect, and you might know that these are truths. You gave to both of these great men hostages for the performance of your promises; and, even under that engagement, you paid so little regard to your faith, which you had pledged, that it was with difficulty our people got from amongst you; and although you had promised to do the business yourselves, you did not even attempt to protect these men who went to assist you. We know these things to be truths, with much more we could relate equally aggravating. You cannot, therefore, expect we will believe you; I tell you we cannot believe you, or rely on your words; are the burning the houses of our people, and barbarously ravaging our frontier, besides the repeated violations of treaties of the most sacred nature—are your barbarous murders, and the cruelty shown our prisoners, marks of your fidelity, or proofs of your pacific disposition, or a desire of enjoying the blessings of peace in common with us? I say, they are not. These are the gifts of heaven, and they cannot be enjoyed under such circumstances. You joined the British king against us, and followed his fortunes; we have overcome him, he has cast you off, and given us your country; and Congress, in bounty and mercy, offers you country and peace. We have told you the terms on which you shall have it. These terms we will not alter; they are liberal, they are just, and we will not depart from them. We now tell you, if you have been so unfortunate and unwise as to determine and adhere to what you have said, and to refuse the terms we have offered to give to your nation peace, friendship and protection, you may depart in peace; you shall have provisions to take you to your towns, and no man shall touch you for eight days after this day; but after that time is expired, be assured that we shall consider ourselves freed from all the ties of protection to you, and you may depend the United States will take the most effectual measures to protect their citizens and to distress your obstinate nation. It rests now with you. The destruction of your women and children, or their future happiness, depends on your present choice. Peace or war is in your power; make your choice like men, and judge for yourselves. We shall only add this: had you judged as it is your interest to do, you would have considered us as your friends, and followed our counsel; but if you choose to follow the opinion which you have expressed, you are guided either by evil counsel or rashness, or are blinded. We plainly tell you that this country belongs to the United States—their blood hath defended it and will forever protect it. Their proposals are liberal and just; and you, instead of acting as you have done, and instead of persisting in your folly, should be thankful for the forgiveness and offers of kindness of the United States, instead of the sentiments which this string imports, and the manner in which you have delivered it. [I then took it up and dashed it on the table.] We therefore leave you to consider of what hath been said, and to determine as you please."

The commissioners then threw down a black and a white string, to signify that they might choose either war or peace, and retired. "It was worthy of observation," Butler continues, "to see the different degrees of agitation which appeared in the young Indians at the delivery of Kekewapellathe's speech." They were "ready for war," but the outside pressure was too strong for that sentiment to prevail: and at a subsequent interview on the same day, the chief, who had spoken so boldly, succumbed to the demands of the American officers. Although the treaty is dated January 31, it was actually signed on the 1st of February. It is here transcribed from the United States Statutes at Large, Vol. vii., p. 26:

ARTICLE 1. Three hostages shall be immediately delivered to the commissioners, to remain in the possession of the United States until all the prisoners, white and black, taken in the late war from among the citizens of the United States, by the Shawanoe nation, or by any other Indian or Indians residing in their towns, shall be restored.

ARTICLE 2. The Shawanoe nation do acknowledge the United States to be the sole and absolute sovereigns of all the territory ceded to them by a treaty of peace made between them and the King of Great Britain, the fourteenth day of January, one thousand seven hundred and eighty-four.

ARTICLE 3. If any Indian or Indians of the Shawanoe nation, or any other Indian or Indians residing in their towns, shall commit robbery or murder on, or do any injury to the citizens of the United States or any of them, that nation shall deliver such offender or offenders to the officer commanding the nearest post of the United States, to be punished according to the ordinances of Congress; and in like manner, any citizen of the United States, who shall do an injury to any Indian of the Shawanoe nation, or to any other Indian or Indians residing in their towns, and under their protection, shall be punished according to the laws of the United States.

ARTICLE 4. The Shawanoe nation having knowledge of the intention of any nation or body of Indians to make war on the citizens of the United States, or of their counselling together for that purpose, and neglecting to give information thereof to the commanding officer of the nearest post of the United States, shall be considered as parties in such war, and be punished accordingly: and the United States shall in like manner inform the Shawanoes of any injury designed against them.

ARTICLE 5. The United States do grant peace to the Shawanoe nation, and do receive them into their friendship and protection.

ARTICLE 6. The United States do allot to the Shawanoe nation, lands within their territory to live and hunt upon, beginning at the south line of the lands allotted to the Wyandots and Delaware nations, at the place where the main branch of the Great Miami, which falls into the Ohio, intersects the said line; then down the River Miami to the fork of that river, next below the old fort which was taken by the French in one thousand seven hundred and fifty-two; thence due west to the River de la Panse; then down that river to the River Wabash, beyond which lines none of the citizens of the United States shall settle, nor disturb the Shawanoes in their settlement and possessions; and the Shawanoes do relinquish to the United States, all title or pretence of title, they ever had to the lands east, west and south of the east, west and south lines before described.

ARTICLE 7. If any citizen or citizens of the United States shall presume to settle upon the lands allotted to the Shawanoes by this treaty, he or they shall be put out of the protection of the United States.

In testimony whereof, the parties hereunto have affixed their hands and seals the day and year first above mentioned:

G. CLARK,	MUSQUAUCONOCAH,
RICHD. BUTLER,	MEANYMSECAH,
SAML. H. PARSONS,	WAUPAUCOWELA,
AWEECONY,	NIHIPEEWA,
KAKAWIPILATHY,	NIHINESSICOE,
MALUNTHY.	

Attest: ALEXANDER CAMPBELL, Sec'y Commissioners.

WITNESSES.—W. Finney, Maj. B. B.; Thos. Doyle, Capt. B. B.; Nathan McDowell, Ensign; John Saffenger; Henry Govy; Kagy Calloway; John Boggs; Sam. Montgomery; Daniel Elliot; James Rinker; Nathl. Smith: Joseph Suffrein, or Kemepemo Shawno; Isaac Zane (Wyandot); The Half King of the Wyandots; The Crane of the Wyandots; Capt. Pipe of the Delawares; Capt. Bohongehelas; Tetebockshieha; The Big Cat of the Delawares; Pierre Droullar.

The orthography of the names of the Shawanese chiefs varies considerably in Butler's journal. "The treaty was signed," he says, "by Aweecanny, Kewepelathy, Captains Melontha, Musquackhoonaka, Mianimsicca, Wapachcawela, Nihipeewa, kings, and Nehinessica, a young chief. The last named, Mianimsicca and four others were delivered as hostages—six instead of three. The witnesses were military officers, and inhabitants of the vicinity: Joseph Suffrein, mentioned as the White Shawnee, and probably an adopted son of the tribe and the Wyandot and Delaware chiefs, whose names are already familiar by their connection with the treaty of Fort McIntosh.[13]

During the period of these negotiations, the vigilance of

13) See Appendix No. XII.

the commissioners was unable to prevent depredations upon the Indians by white borderers,[14] and it required an extraordinary exertion to check the organization of an expedition to proceed from Lexington to the Falls of the Ohio, and thence strike across the country to a point on the Great Miami, forty miles north of its mouth, for the purpose of intercepting and plundering the returning party of Shawanese. Such a condition of the frontier (for the savages, either in provocation or refusal, were constantly making depredations), in connection with the ill-suppressed dissatisfaction of the Shawanese with the treaty itself, augured most unfavorably for the future. Indeed, the treaty of Fort Finney, or the Great Miami, was not worth the paper on which it was engrossed. The savage inroads continued through the summer of 1786, and in the autumn of that year Col. Logan led his expedition against their towns, on the Mad River and Great Miami, as already narrated.

It will be observed that the terms of this treaty were peculiarly calculated to excite the jealousy of the Indians. The Shawanese were made to "acknowledge the United States to be the sole and absolute sovereign of all the territory ceded by Great Britain"—a claim unintelligible to the savages, except in a sense fatal to their independence and territorial rights. Nor was this an erroneous construction. In a communication to President Washington, by H. Knox, Secretary of War, dated June 15th, 1789, the following admission occurs: "By having recourse to the several Indian

14) An old Wyandot chief, called Runtandy, who came to camp as early as Oct. 23, with three young lads and a white interpreter, lost several horses, and on account of his absence in pursuit of the thieves, his name does not appear in the attestation. *Quere.*—Is the "Doonyontat" of Brodhead's Conference, in 1779, the "Daungquat," of Fort McIntosh, and "Runtandy," the same name?

treaties, made by the authority of Congress, since the conclusion of the war with Great Britain, excepting those made January, 1789, at Fort Harmar, it would appear, that Congress were of opinion, that the treaty of peace of 1783, absolutely invested them with the fee of all the Indian lands within the limits of the United States; that they had the right to assign or retain such portions as they should judge proper."[15]

So general was the sensation of alarm, that the active and intelligent Brant succeeded in reviving his favorite project of the New York and Northwestern tribes; although there is reason to doubt whether the former were ever represented therein, except by himself and his Mohawks, already refugees in Canada. There had been some indications of such a combination at the Treaty of Fort Stanwix, but the commissioners on that occasion had sternly and peremptorily refused to recognize any other Indian parties to the negotiation than the Six Nations. When, however, the transactions at the Ohio conferences had penetrated the recesses of the Western wilderness, it was not difficult, near the close of 1786, to assemble a formidable body of savage protestants at the Huron village opposite Detroit. The Indian archives of the United States contain a document, addressed to Congress, and purporting to proceed from the Five Nations, Hurons, Delawares, Shawanese, Ottowas, Chippewas, Powtewattimies, Twichtwees, Cherokees, and the Wabash confederates, assembled in confederate council near the mouth of the Detroit River, from the 28th of November to the 18th of December, 1786. Their speech is of the latter date, and expressed a desire for peace, while temperately yet firmly insisting, that the first step towards a lasting reconciliation should be, "that all treaties

15) American State Papers, vol. v., p. 13.

carried on with the United States, should be with the general voice of the whole confederacy, and in the most open manner, without any restraint on either side, holding all partial treaties as void and of no effect." They attributed recent "mischief and confusion" to the fact that the United States had "managed every thing their own way," and concluded treaties separately. Congress was also urged to order surveyors and others to cease from crossing the Ohio River. Notwithstanding the mischief that had happened, the council professed a sincere wish for peace and tranquillity. "This," they said, "is the determination of all the chiefs of the confederacy now assembled, notwithstanding that several Indian chiefs were killed in our villages, even when in council, and when absolutely engaged in promoting peace with you, the thirteen United States." For this purpose, they proposed a treaty at some half-way house early in the spring of 1787. This important address closed with these words: "Brothers! It shall not be our faults, if the plans which we have suggested to you should not be carried into execution. In that case, the event will be very precarious; and if fresh ruptures ensue, we hope to be able to exculpate ourselves, and shall most assuredly, with our united force, be obliged to defend those rights and privileges which have been transmitted to us by our ancestors; and if we should be thereby reduced to misfortunes, the world will pity us when they think of the amicable proposals we now make to prevent the unnecessary effusion of blood. These are our thoughts and firm resolves, and we earnestly desire that you would transmit to us, as soon as possible, your answer, be it what it may." The address was not signed by the individual chiefs, but opposite the name of each nation was drawn the figure of the bird or animal, which had been adopted as a national emblem.

In a letter to Col. Joseph Brant, dated "War Office, July 23, 1787," Gen. Knox explains that the Shawanese neglected to forward the original speech; and it appears by a letter from Captain Pipe of the Delawares, and the Half King of the Wyandots, dated June 3, 1787, that they finally forwarded the despatches to Fort Pitt, whence they reached the War Office on the 17th of July.

Such a communication could not fail to produce a profound sensation in Congress. That body was almost powerless by the weakness of the old system of confederation. The fighting population of the tribes apparently represented at the council near Detroit, was estimated at five thousand warriors; while the British still held the frontiers, and their agents ranged the valleys of the St. Lawrence, the Ohio and the Mississippi. Under these circumstances, Congress wisely modified their policy; recognized the Indians as the rightful proprietors of the soil; and, on the 2d of July, appropriated twenty-six thousand dollars "solely to the purpose of extinguishing Indian claims to lands already ceded to the United States, by obtaining regular conveyances for the same, and for extending a purchase beyond the limits hitherto fixed by treaty." The clause in relation to limits, was a mere salvo to pride, as the treaties of Fort Harmar, negotiated on the 9th of January, 1788, by Governor St. Clair, with the Six Nations and the Ohio Indians, respectively, were only a reiteration of the boundary stipulations at Fort Stanwix and Fort McIntosh.

The jealousies between the New York and the Western tribes, soon interrupted the Indian confederacy, which Brant and Sir John Johnson had hoped to make an efficient agency of embarrassment to the United States, but long and bitter was the struggle, before the Western Indians acquiesced in the surrender of the valley of the Ohio. It was not until the treaty of Greenville, August 3, 1795, that the terrors of savage warfare passed from the annals into the traditions of the frontiers: but the campaigns of Wilkinson, Harmar, St. Clair, and Wayne, are beyond our present design, and we pause at a period when, with the territorial organization, the idea of conquest had ceased to guide our Indian administration, and the more generous policy, of the recognition and purchase of an aboriginal right to the soil, which Washington was the first to urge, became the usage of his own and subsequent administrations of the General Government.

CHAPTER XXV.

COLONIAL CLAIMS TO WESTERN LANDS, AND THEIR CESSION TO THE UNITED STATES.

On the 5th of March, 1496, King Henry VII. of England granted to the Venitian adventurer, John Cabot and his three sons, Sebastian, Lewis, and Sanctius, a commission by which they had authority and leave to sail to all parts, countries and seas of the east, of the west, and of the north, and upon their own proper cost and charges, to seek out and discover countries of the heathen and infidels, unknown to all Christians; there to set up the king's banner; to occupy and possess, as his vassals and lieutenants, the countries they should find, on condition of paying him one-fifth of all the gains obtained by them. Under this commission, John Cabot and his son Sebastian, sailed from England in May, 1497, and in June came in sight of land, supposed to be a part of Newfoundland. Thence they sailed along the coast north and south, and returned without attempting a settlement, although they took possession of the country in behalf of the crown of England.

In 1534 the celebrated Jaques Cartier made several voyages along the northern coast of North America, sailed up the River St. Lawrence as far as Montreal, and took possession of the country in the name of the King of France. On the 17th of June, 1673, Father Marquette and M. Joliet reached the Mississippi by the channels of the Fox and Wisconsin Rivers, and descended as far as the Arkansas; while on the 9th of April, 1683, M. de la Salle, the commandant of Fort Frontenac on Lake Ontario, discovered the mouth of the Mississippi, and took formal possession of the country in the name of Louis XIV. of France.

Colonization gave significance to discovery. England chiefly occupied the Atlantic sea-board: Canada and Louisiana became colonies of France, and, before the treaty of 1763, France had so successfully asserted her dominion to the valley of the Ohio, that England proposed to limit her American colonies on the west by a line drawn from Lake Erie through French creek to its mouth, and thence direct to the nearest mountains of Virginia.

When, in 1763, after a struggle of various fortune, the title to the vast region of the Ohio, the Mississippi and St. Lawrence was yielded by France, the government of England proclaimed that all the land west and northwest of the sources of the Atlantic rivers was reserved under the sovereignty, protection and dominion of the King of Great Britain, for the use of the Indians, and the governors of the colonies were forbidden to make any grants of the lands thus reserved.

Such a disposition of the conquest from France was inconsistent with the pretensions of some of the colonies, whose early charters included in their limits the whole breadth of the continent—"from sea to sea." The adjustment of these claims greatly embarrassed the country at the most critical period of our national history, and is so closely related to individual rights in the soil of Ohio, as to justify a detailed statement of their nature and extent.

In the year 1606, on the 10th of April, James I., King of England, on the application of a number of gentlemen, for a license to settle a colony in that part of America called

Virginia, not possessed by any Christian prince or people, between the thirty-fourth and forty-fifth degrees of north latitude, granted them a charter. In order to facilitate the settlement of the country, and at the request of the adventurers, he divided it into two colonies. To the first colony, consisting of Sir Thomas Gates, Sir George Somers, Richard Hackluyt, Edward Maria Wingfield and their associates, called the London Company, he granted, "That they might begin their first plantation and habitation at any place on the said coast of Virginia or America, where they shall think fit and convenient, between the said four-and-thirty and one-and-forty degrees of the said latitude; and they shall have all lands, &c., from the said first seat of their plantation and habitation, by the space of fifty miles of English statute measure, all along the said coast of Virginia and America, towards the west and southwest, as the coast lieth, with all the islands within one hundred miles directly over and against the same sea-coast; and also all the lands, &c., from said place of their first plantation and habitation, for the space of fifty like English miles, all along the said coast of Virginia and America, towards the east and northeast, or towards the north as the coast lieth, with all the islands, within one hundred miles, directly over and against the said sea coast; and also all the lands, &c., from the same fifty miles every way on the sea coast, directly into the main land, by the space of one hundred like English miles, and that no other subjects should be allowed to settle on the back of them, towards the main land, without written license from the council of the colony."

To the second colony, consisting of Thomas Hanman, Raleigh Gilbert, William Parker, George Popham, and others, principally inhabitants of Plymouth, Bristol, and the eastern parts of England, King James granted the tract between the thirty-eight and forty-fifth degrees of north latitude, under the same description, as the grant of the first colony. To these grants a consideration was annexed, that a plantation should not be made within one hundred miles of a prior plantation.

By the same charter, the king agreed that he would give and grant, by letters patent, to such persons, their heirs and assigns, as the council of each colony, or the most part of them, should nominate or assign, all the lands, tenements and hereditaments, which should be within the precincts limited for each colony, to be holden of him, his heirs and successors as for the manor of East Greenwich, in the county of Kent, in free and common socage only, and not in capite. And that such letters patent should be sufficient assurance from the patentees, so distributed and divided amongst the undertakers of the plantations of the several colonies, and such as should make their plantations in either of the said several colonies in such manner and form, and for such estates, as shall be ordered and set down by the council of said colony, or the most part of them respectively, within which the same lands, tenements or hereditaments shall lie, or be; although express mention of the true yearly value or certainty of the premises, or any of them, or of any other gifts or grants by the king, or any of his progenitors or predecessors, to the guarantees, was not made, or any statute, &c., to the contrary notwithstanding.

On the 23d of May, 1609, King James, on the application of the first colony for a further enlargement and explanation of the first grant, gave them a second charter, in which they were incorporated by the name of "The Treasurer and Company of Adventurers and Planters of the city of London, for the first colony of Virginia."

In this charter, the king grants to them all the lands, &c., in that part of America called Virginia, from the point of land called Cape or Point Comfort, all along the sea-coast to the northward, two hundred miles; and from the said Point or Cape Comfort, all along the sea-coast, to the southward, two hundred miles; and all the space and circuit of land, lying from the sea-coast of the precinct aforesaid *up into the main land throughout, from sea to sea, west and northwest;* and also all the islands within one hundred miles along the coast of both seas of the precinct aforesaid.

On the 12th of March, 1611–12, on the representation that there were several islands without the foregoing grant, and contiguous to the coast of Virginia, and on the request of the said first colony, for an enlargement of the former letters patent, as well for a more ample extent of their limits and territories into the seas adjoining to, and upon the coast of Virginia, as for the better government of the said colony, King James granted them another charter. After reciting the description of the second grant, he then proceeds to give, grant and confirm, to the Treasurer and Company of Adventurers and Planters of the city of London for the first colony of Virginia, and their heirs, &c., "all and singular those islands, whatsoever, situate and being in any part of the ocean, seas, bordering on the coast of our said first colony in Virginia, and being within three hundred leagues of any of the parts heretofore granted to the said treasurer and company in said former letters patent as aforesaid, and being within the one and-fortieth and thirty degrees of northerly latitude, with all the lands, &c., both within the said tract of land on the main, and also within the said islands and seas adjoining, &c. *Provided, always*, that the said islands, or any premises herein mentioned, or by these presents intended or meant to be conveyed, be not actually possessed or inhabited by any other Christian prince or state; nor be within the bounds, limits, or territories of the northern colony heretofore by us granted, to be planted by our loving subjects in the north part of Virginia."

On the 15th day of July, 1624, James I. granted a commission for the government of Virginia, in which it is alleged that the charters to the Treasurer and Company of Adventurers and Planters of the city of London, for the first colony of Virginia, had been avoided upon a quo warranto brought, and a legal and judicial proceeding therein by due course of law.

On the 20th day of August, 1624, James granted another commission for the government of Virginia, in which it is alleged: "Whereupon we, entering into mature and deliberate consideration of the premises, did, by the advice of our Lords of the Privy Council, resolve, by altering the charters of the said company, as to the point of government, wherein the same might be found defective, to settle such a course as might best secure the safety of the people there, and cause the said plantation to flourish; and yet, with the preservation of the interests of every planter and adventurer, so far forth as their present interests shall not prejudice the public plantations; but because the said treasurer and company did not submit their charters to be reformed, our proceedings therein were stayed for a time, until, upon quo warranto brought, and a legal and a judicial proceeding therein, by due course of law, the said charters were, and now are, and stand avoided."

On the 13th of May, 1625, Charles I., by his proclamation, after alleging that the letters patent to the colony of Virginia had been questioned in a legal course, and thereupon judicially repealed and judged to be void, declares that the government of the colony of Virginia, shall immediately depend on himself, and not be committed to a company or corporation.

From this time, Virginia was considered to be a royal government, and it appears that the kings of England, from time to time, granted commissions for the government of the same.

The right of making grants of lands was vested in and solely exercised by the crown.

The colonies of Maryland, North and South Carolina, Georgia, and part of Pennsylvania, were erected by the crown, within the chartered limits of the first colony of Virginia.

In the year 1620, on the 3d of November, King James gave a charter to the second colony of Virginia. After citing the grants made to the first colony of Virginia, and stating an application from the second colony for a further enlargement of privileges, he proceeded to declare, "that the tract of land, in America, between the fortieth and forty-eighth degrees of north latitude, from sea to sea, should be called New England; and for the planting and governing the same, he incorporated a council at Plymouth, in the county of Devon, and granted to them and their successors all that part of America lying and being in breadth, from forty degrees of northerly latitude from the equinoctial line, to forty-eight degrees of the said northerly latitude inclusively, and in length of and within all the said breadth aforesaid, throughout all the main lands from sea to sea, together with all the firm lands, &c., upon the main, and within the said islands and seas adjoining. Provided, the said islands, or any of the premises before mentioned, and intended by said charter to be granted, be not actually possessed or inhabited by any Christian prince or state, nor be within the bounds, limits or territories of the southern colony, granted to be planted in the south part." King James, by said charter, commanded and authorized said council at Plymouth, or their successors, or the major part of them, to distribute and assign such portions of land to adventurers, &c., as they shall think proper.

In 1628, 4th March, the council of Plymouth, pursuant to the authority vested in them by their charter, granted to Sir Henry Roswell, Sir John Young, Thomas Southcoat, John Humphrey, John Endicott and Simon Whetcomb, their heirs and associates, a tract of land called Massachusetts; and King Charles I., on the 4th of March, 1629, confirmed the sale and granted them a charter. After reciting the description of the grant to the council of Plymouth, and their grant to Sir Henry Roswell and others, he grants and confirms to them "all that part of New England in America, which lies and extends between a great river there commonly called Morromack River, alias, Merrimack River, and a certain other river there called Charles River, being in the bottom of a certain bay, there called Massachusetts, alias, Mattachusetts, alias, Massactusetts Bay; and also all and singular those lands and hereditaments whatsoever, lying within the space of three English miles, on the south part of the said river, called Charles River, or of any or every part thereof; and also all and singular, the lands and hereditaments whatsoever, lying and being within the space of three English miles to the southward of the southernmost parts of the said bay, called Massachusetts, alias, Mattachusetts, alias, Massactusetts Bay; and also all those lands and hereditaments whatsoever, which lie and be within the space of three English miles to the northward of the said river, called Morromack, alias, Merrimack; or to the northward of any and every part thereof; and all lands and hereditaments whatsoever, lying within the limits aforesaid, north and south, in latitude and in breadth, and in length and longitude of and within all the breadth aforesaid, throughout the main lands there from the Atlantic and Western sea and ocean on the east part *to the South Sea on the west part*, with a proviso not to extend to lands possessed by a Christian prince, or within the limits of the southern colony.

In the year 1631, on the 19th of March, the Earl of Warwick (to whom the territory had been granted the year before by the council of Plymouth) granted to Lord Say and Seal, Lord Brooke, Lord Rich, Charles Fiennes, Sir Richard Saltonstall, Sir Nathaniel Rich, Richard Kingsly, John Pym, John Humphrey, John Hampden and Herbert Pelham, "all that part of New England in America which lies and extends itself from a river there called Narragansett River, the space of forty leagues, upon a straight line near the sea shore, towards the southwest, west and by south or west as the coast lieth towards Virginia, accounting three English miles to the league, and also all and singular the lands and hereditaments whatsoever, lying and being within the lands aforesaid, north and south, in latitude and in breadth, and in length and longitude of, and within all the breadth aforesaid, throughout the main lands there from the Western ocean to the South sea, &c., and also all the islands lying in America aforesaid, in said seas, or either of them, on the western or eastern coasts." In 1644, the patentees, in consequence of the new state of things in England, relinquished their plan of removal and sold their grant to the people of Connecticut. On the 23d of April, 1662, King Charles II. granted a charter in which he constituted and declared John Winthrop and others, his associates, "a body corporate and politic, by the name of the governor and company of the English colony of Connec-

20*

ticut, in New England, in America, with privileges and powers of government, and granted and confirmed to the said governor and company and their successors, all that part of his dominions in New England, in America, bounded on the east by Narraganset River, commonly called Narragansat Bay, where the said river falls into the sea; and on the north by the line of Massachusetts plantation, and on the south by the sea, and in longitude as the line of Massachusetts colony, running from east to west, that is to say, from the said Narraganset Bay on the east, to the South sea on the west, with the islands thereto adjoining." On the 23d of April, 1664, King Charles addressed a letter to the governor and company of Connecticut, in which, among other things, he speaks of having renewed their charter.

On the 12th of March, 1664, Charles II. granted to James, Duke of York, the region extending from the western bank of the Connecticut to the eastern shore of the Delaware, together with Long Island and Hudson River. This grant was inconsistent with the western limits of Massachusetts and Connecticut, and soon after, commissioners on the part of the crown met those appointed by the General Assembly of Connecticut for the settlement of this conflict of boundaries. On the 30th of November, 1664, the royal commissioners ordered "that the creek or river which is called Monoromock, which is reputed to be about twelve miles to the east of Westchester, and a line to be drawn from the east point or side where the fresh water falls into the salt, at high water mark, north-northwest to the line of Massachusetts, be the western bound of said colony of Connecticut, and all plantations lying westward of that creek and line so drawn shall be under his Royal Highness' government; and all plantations lying eastward of that creek and line to be under the government of Connecticut." To this the commissioners of Connecticut subscribed in the following manner: "We, the underwritten, on behalf of the colony of Connecticut, have assented unto the determination of His Majesty's commissioners in relation to the bounds and limits of his Royal Highness the Duke's patent and the patent of Connecticut." A re-settlement of this line was finally effected in 1730, when Borain River, the present line, was established.

On the 4th of March, 1681, Charles II. granted to William Penn, the first proprietary and governor of Pennsylvania, "all that tract or part of land in America, with the islands therein contained, as the same is bounded on the east by Delaware River, from twelve miles distance northward of Newcastle town, unto the three and fortieth degree of northern latitude, if said river doth extend so far northward; but if the said river shall not extend so far northward, then by the said river so far as it doth extend, and from the head of the said river the eastern bounds are to be determined by a meridian line to be drawn from the head of said river unto the said forty-third degree; the said land to extend westward five degrees in longitude to be computed from the said eastern bounds; and the said lands to be bounded on the north by the beginning of the three and fortieth degree of northern latitude; and on the south by a circle drawn at twelve miles distance from Newcastle, northward and westward, unto the beginning of the fortieth degree of northern latitude, and then by a straight line, westward, to the limits of longitude above mentioned."

In 1754, some settlements were made from Connecticut, on lands on the Susquehannah, about Wyoming, within the chartered limits of Pennsylvania, and also within the chartered limits claimed by Connecticut. Pennsylvania resisted these occupants as intruders; and the organization by Connecticut, of a county of Westmoreland, in the valley of Wyoming, led to many scenes of civil strife. The controversy was finally determined in 1782, by the intervention of Congress. The articles of confederation of 1779, provided for the settlement of territorial disputes between the States by a federal court, to be composed of judges selected by the parties litigant and commissioned by Congress. Such a tribunal of five judges, having been in session six weeks at Trenton, unanimously determined that the State of Connecticut had no right to the lands included in the charter of Pennsylvania. Congress confirmed this decision and Connecticut submitted.

In 1774, the Parliament of Great Britain passed an act by which the whole country north of the forty-fifth parallel of latitude, and northwest of the west boundary of Pennsylvania and the Ohio River, was annexed and made parcel of the province of Quebec, as created and established by the royal proclamation of October 7, 1763, with a proviso, however, that the act should not affect the boundaries of other colonies.

Thus it is obvious that, before the American Revolution, the claims of any of the colonies to extend their limits to the "South Sea," were of little importance or value—entirely disregarded by the crown, and constantly yielded by the colonies. It remains to be seen, that a sentiment of hostility to Great Britain tended to revive these claims until they became a serious obstacle to the harmony of Congress and the national defence.

The first demonstration proceeded from Virginia. In 1776 that colony adopted a State Constitution, in which the following provision occurred: "The territories contained within the charters, erecting the colonies of Maryland, Pennsylvania, North and South Carolina, are hereby ceded, released, and forever confirmed to the people of these colonies respectively, with all the rights of property, jurisdiction and government, and all other rights whatsoever, which might, at any time heretofore, have been claimed by Virginia, except the free navigation and use of the rivers Potomaque and Pokomoke, with the property of the Virginia shores and strands, bordering on either of the said rivers, and all improvements which have been, or shall be made thereon. The western and northern extent of Virginia shall, in all other respects, stand as fixed by the charters of King James I., in the year one thousand six hundred and nine, and by the public treaty of peace, between the courts of Britain and France, in the year one thousand seven hundred and sixty-three: unless, by act of this Legislature, one or more governments be established westward of the Allegheny Mountains. And no purchases of lands shall be made of the Indian natives, but on behalf of the public, by authority of the General Assembly." North Carolina inserted a similar assertion of western boundary in her Constitution. Massachusetts, Connecticut and New York did not refer to the subject in that connection.

Maryland led the resistance to these pretensions. When the Articles of Confederation were under consideration, her delegates contended, unsuccessfully, that Congress should have the power to limit and ascertain the boundaries of those colonies which claimed to the South Sea, and to dispose of all lands beyond such boundaries for the benefit of the Union. In June, 1778, it appeared that Maryland, New Jersey and Delaware were the only colonies that had declined to ratify the Articles, and the instructions to their delegates concurred on the subject of the public lands. Maryland now proposed an amendment, vesting Congress with power "to appoint commissioners, who should be fully authorized and empowered to ascertain and restrict the boundaries of such of the confederated States which claim to extend to the river Mississippi or South Sea." It was negatived by the following vote: *Aye*, Rhode Island, New Jersey, Pennsylvania, Delaware, Maryland; *No*, New Hampshire, Massachusetts, Connecticut, Virginia, South Carolina, Georgia—New York divided, and North Carolina absent. The whole subject was postponed, and the compact only contained a provision for the arbitration, under the direction of Congress, of disputes and differences between the States concerning boundary jurisdiction or other causes—with the condition carefully added, that "no State [should] be deprived of territory for the *benefit* of the United States."

Virginia, in 1779, opened an office for the sale of unappropriated lands. Congress earnestly recommended the reconsideration of the act, and directed Col. Brodhead, who was then stationed with a detachment of continental troops at Fort Pitt, to prevent any occupation of the west bank of the Ohio by settlers. In the execution of these orders, that officer, in October, 1779, being informed that certain inhabitants of Virginia had crossed the Ohio and made improvements on the Indian lands, from the river Muskingum to Fort McIntosh, ordered them to be apprehended as trespassers, and destroyed their huts. Information of this was immediately given to the Governor of Virginia, but Congress resolved, April 18th, 1780, that Colonel Brodhead should be supported in any act or order which the nature of his service had made, or should make necessary.

The example of Virginia was contagious, and other States revived their dormant claims to the valley of the Mississippi.

Some of them did so, it must be admitted, with better reason than the former State could adduce. "The charter of Virginia had been vacated by a judicial proceeding; the company to which it was granted had been dissolved; the grant itself had been resumed by the crown, and large tracts of the country included by its original limits, had been patented to various individuals and associations, without remonstrance on the part of Virginia."[1] We have already described the charters of Massachusetts: the Carolinas had received similar grants; under the proclamation of 1763, annexing to Georgia the country west of the Altamaha and north of Florida, that State also claimed to extend to the Mississippi: and so did New York, under color of certain alleged acknowledgments of her jurisdiction over the Six Nations, whom it had long been colonial usage to regard as the conquerors of the whole western territory on both shores of Lakes Ontario and Huron, and both banks of the Ohio, as far south as the Cumberland Mountains.

The Articles of Confederation, dated, in the preamble, November 15, 1777, were signed by the representatives of ten colonies, on the 9th of July, 1778. New Jersey deferred her signature to the 25th of November, 1778, and Delaware ratified the Articles on the 22d of February, 1779. Maryland, however, still persisted in a refusal. In December, 1778, the Legislature of Maryland made a communication to their delegates in Congress, in which they insisted, "that a country unsettled at the commencement of the war, claimed by the British crown, and ceded to it by the treaty of Paris, if wrested from the common enemy by the blood and treasure of the thirteen States, should be considered as a common property, subject to be parceled out by Congress into free,

1) Historical Sketch of Ohio, by S. P. Chase. Statutes, vol. i., p. 13.

convenient and independent governments, in such manner and at such times as the wisdom of that assembly shall hereafter direct. Thus convinced," they proceed to say, "we should betray the trust reposed in us by our constituents, were we to authorize you to ratify on their behalf the confederation, unless it be further explained. We have coolly and dispassionately considered the subject; we have weighed probable inconveniences and hardships against the sacrifice of just and essential rights: and do instruct you not to agree to the confederation, unless an article or articles be added thereto in conformity with our declaration. Should we succeed in obtaining such article or articles, then you are hereby fully empowered to accede to the confederation."

The above are but the closing paragraphs of an able document, to which the State of New York was the first to respond by a contribution of individual interest to the general welfare. In February, 1780, the legislature of that State passed an act "to facilitate the completion of the Articles of Confederation and perpetual union among the United States of America;" whereas, nothing under Divine Providence, can more effectually contribute to the tranquillity and safety of the United States of America, than a federal alliance, on such liberal principles as will give satisfaction to its respective members; and, whereas, the Articles of Confederation and perpetual union recommended by the honorable the Congress of the United States of America have not proved acceptable to all the States, it having been conceived that a portion of the waste and uncultivated territory, within the limits or claims of certain States, ought to be appropriated as a common fund for the expenses of the war: and the people of the State of New York, being on all occasions disposed to manifest their regard for their sister States, and their earnest desire to promote the general interest and security; and more especially to accelerate the federal alliance, by removing, so far as it depends upon them, the before mentioned impediment to its final conclusion," &c. By this act the delegates of the People of New York in Congress, were empowered "to limit and restrict the western boundaries of that State, by such line or lines, and in such manner and form, as they shall judge to be expedient, either with respect to the jurisdiction as well as the preëmption of soil, or reserving the jurisdiction in part, or in the whole, over the lands which may be ceded or relinquished, with respect only to the right and preëmption of the soil." This act, also, declared that the territory thus ceded, "should be and enure for the use and benefit of such of the United States, as should become members of the federal alliance of the said States, and for no other use or purpose whatever."

A remonstrance of Virginia in behalf of her title, and the act of New York just cited, were referred to a committee of Congress, who declined to examine into the merits or policy of the instructions by Maryland and the remonstrance of Virginia, but reported a resolution, which Congress adopted, September 6th, 1780, earnestly recommending to those States who had claims to the western country, to pass such laws and give their delegates in Congress such powers, as would effectually remove the only obstacle to a final ratification of the Articles of Confederation; and that the legislature of Maryland be earnestly requested to authorize their delegates in Congress to subscribe the said articles.

A resolution of still more importance, since the terms of it subsequently became conditions of the cessions by the States, was adopted in Congress on the 10th of October, to wit:

"*Resolved*, That the unappropriated lands that may be

ceded or relinquished to the United States, by any particular State, pursuant to the recommendation of Congress of the 6th day of September last, shall be disposed of for the common benefit of the United States, and be settled and formed into distinct Republican States, which shall become members of the federal union, and have the same rights of sovereignty, freedom and independence as the other States: that each State which shall be so formed shall contain a suitable extent of territory, not less than one hundred, nor more than one hundred and fifty miles square, or as near thereto as circumstances will admit; that the necessary and reasonable expenses which any particular State shall have incurred since the commencement of the present war, in subduing any British posts or in maintaining forts or garrisons within and for the defence, or in acquiring any part of the territory that may be ceded or relinquished to the United States, shall be reimbursed: that the said lands shall be granted or settled at such times, and under such regulations as shall hereafter be agreed on by the United States in Congress assembled, or any nine or more of them."

The immediate results were a cession by Connecticut in October, 1780, and by Virginia in January, 1781. Neither of these cessions were accepted by Congress, but Maryland was encouraged by their terms, and stimulated by her own patriotism to accede to the articles of the confederation, which thus became, on the 1st of March, 1781, the law of the whole union. On the same day, James Duane, William Floyd and Alexander M'Dougall, the delegates of New York, executed a deed of cession, by which the western bounds of that state were limited by "a line from the northeast corner of the State of Pennsylvania, along the north bounds thereof, to its northwest corner, continued due west until it shall be intersected by a meridian line, to be drawn from the forty-fifth degree of north latitude, through a point twenty miles due west from the most westerly bent or inclination of the river or strait of Niagara; thence by the said meridian line to the forty-fifth degree of north latitude, thence by the said forty-fifth degree of north latitude." The delegates reserved a right of retraction, unless the same guaranty was given to New York as to any other State making cessions.

The New York delegates alluded, in the qualification of their cession last mentioned, to a proposition of Virginia, which retarded the consummation of her cession for several years, and was finally relinquished by that State: namely, that Congress should guaranty to Virginia all the territory southeast of the Ohio and included between the boundaries of Pennsylvania, Maryland and North Carolina to the Atlantic.

Connecticut offered at this time, to cede all her claim to the soil of the territory west of Pennsylvania, excepting the tract south of Lake Erie and immediately adjoining Pennsylvania, since known as the Connecticut Reserve, but Congress was then averse to making so material a concession. On the other hand, Connecticut never receded from her demand. Even after the Council of Trenton, on the 30th of December, 1782, had excluded the Connecticut claim from the chartered limits of Pennsylvania, the former state reässerted her title to the lands beyond the western boundary of Pennsylvania. At a General Assembly, held at New Haven on the second Thursday of October, 1783, the following act was passed, viz:

"Whereas this State has the undoubted and exclusive right of jurisdiction and preëmption to all the lands lying west of the western limits of the State of Pennsylvania, and east of the River Mississippi, and extending throughout from the latitude forty-one degrees, to latitude forty-two degrees and two minutes north, by virtue of the charter granted by King Charles the Second to the late colony, now State of Connecticut, bearing date the 23d day of April, A. D. 1662, which claim and title to make known, for the information of all, to the end that they may conform themselves thereto,

"*Resolved*, That his excellency the Governor, be desired to issue his proclamation, declaring and asserting the right of this State to all the lands within the limits aforesaid; and strictly forbidding all persons to enter or settle thereon, without special license and authority first obtained by the General Assembly of this State."

Pursuant to this resolution, Governor Trumbull issued a proclamation, bearing date the 15th of November, 1783, making known the determination of the State to maintain their claim to said territory, and forbidding all persons to enter thereon, or settle within the limits of the same.

It is interesting to observe the importance which Congress attributed to the claim of New York, after the cession of March, 1781. A committee, to whom the whole subject of the public lands had been referred, reported on the 3d of November in the same year, that "it clearly appeared to them, that the crown of England had always considered and treated the country of the Six Nations, and their tributaries, inhabiting as far as the 45th degree of north latitude, as appendant to the government of New York; that the neighboring colonies of Massachusetts, Connecticut, Pennsylvania, Maryland and Virginia, had also, from time to time, by their public acts, recognized and admitted the said Six Nations, and their tributaries, to be appendant to the government of

New York; and that the acceptance by Congress of the New York cession, would vest the whole western territory belonging to the Six Nations and their tributaries, in the United States, greatly to the advantage of the nation." The committee also reported against a federal guaranty to Virginia of the territory southeast of the Ohio, and maintained that large tracts west of the mountains had been sold by Great Britain before the Revolution; "that in the year 1763, a very large part thereof was separated and appointed for a distinct government and colony by the King of Great Britain, with the knowledge and approbation of the government of Virginia," and that the west boundary line of Virginia had been otherwise declared by the King of Great Britain, in council, previous to the Revolution. This report elicited much and warm debate, postponing the formal acceptance of the deed of New York to October 31, 1782—"an acceptance intended," says Hildreth, "as a means to compel the other States to make satisfactory cessions."[2] Massachusetts and Virginia voted against it; the Carolinas were divided; all the other States in the affirmative.

The subject of the Virginia cession was again referred, on the 4th of June, 1783, to a select committee consisting of Messrs. Rutledge, Ellsworth, Bedford, Gorham and Madison. They recommended that Congress should accept all the conditions proposed by Virginia, except the territorial guaranty already mentioned, and a condition "that all Indian purchases, which had been or should be made for the use of private persons, and all royal grants inconsistent with 'the chartered rights, laws and customs of Virginia,' should be declared void." This report was agreed to by all the States except New Hampshire, New Jersey and Maryland; and the

2) History of the United States, by Richard Hildreth, vol. iii., p. 427.

General Assembly of Virginia, at their session commencing on the 20th of October, 1783, passed an act accepting the proposition of Congress, and authorized their delegates in Congress to make the cession.

Accordingly, on the 1st day of March, 1784, Thomas Jefferson, Samuel Hardy, Arthur Lee and James Monroe, delegates of Virginia, executed a deed of cession to the United States in Congress assembled, of all right, title and claim, as well of soil as jurisdiction, which that commonwealth had to the "territory or tract of country within the limits of the Virginia charter, situate, lying and being to the northwest of the river Ohio," upon six enumerated conditions, namely: *Firstly*, distinct Republican States, not less than one hundred, nor more than one hundred and fifty miles square, were to be formed and admitted members of the Federal Union, having the same rights of sovereignty, freedom and independence as the other States—a recital of the resolution of Oct. 10, 1780. *Secondly*, Virginia to be reimbursed the expenses of subduing British posts, and acquiring or defending the territory conveyed, as the same should be adjusted by commissioners, according to the intent and meaning of the aforesaid resolution of Congress. *Thirdly*, the French and Canadian inhabitants, who had professed themselves citizens of Virginia, to be confirmed in their possessions and titles, and protected in their rights and liberties. *Fourthly*, one hundred and fifty thousand acres of land to be selected by the officers and soldiers of Clark's regiment, who were engaged in the reduction of Kaskaskia and St. Vincents, which should be laid off in one tract not more than twice its breadth in length. *Fifthly*, "that in case the quantity of good land on the southeast side of the Ohio, upon the waters of the Cumberland River, and between the Green River and Tennessee

River, which had been reserved by law for the Virginia troops upon continental establishment, should, from the North Carolina line, bearing in further upon the Cumberland lands than was expected, prove insufficient for their legal bounties, the deficiency should be made up to the said troops in good land, to be laid off between the rivers Sciota and Little Miami, on the northwest side of the river Ohio, in such proportions as have been engaged to them, by the laws of Virginia." *Sixthly*, "that all the lands within the territory so ceded to the United States, and not reserved for, or appropriated to, any of the before mentioned purposes, or disposed of in bounties to the officers and soldiers of the American army, shall be considered a common fund, for the use and benefit of such of the United States as have become, or shall become members of the confederation, or federal alliance of the said States, Virginia included, according to their usual respective proportions in the general charge or expenditure, and shall be faithfully and *bona fide* disposed of for that purpose, and for no other use or purpose whatsoever."

Congress declared, by resolution, that the United States were ready to receive the foregoing deed. The delegates of Virginia then proceeded and signed, sealed and delivered the same; whereupon Congress came to the following resotion: "The delegates of the Commonwealth of Virginia having executed the deed; *Resolved*, That the same be recorded and enrolled among the acts of the United States in Congress assembled."

On the 29th of April, 1784, Congress adopted the following resolution:

"Congress, by their resolution of September 6th, 1780, having thought it advisable to press upon the States, having claims to the western country, a liberal surrender of a portion of their territorial claims; by that of the 10th of October, in the same year, having fixed conditions to which the Union should be bound on receiving such cessions; and having again proposed the same subject to those States, in their address of April 18th, 1783, wherein, stating the national debt, and expressing their reliance for its discharge on the prospect of vacant territory in aid of other resources, they, for that purpose, as well as to obviate disagreeable controversies and confusions, included in the same recommendations a renewal of those of September 6th and October 10th, 1780, which several recommendations have not yet been fully complied with:

"*Resolved*, That the same subject be again presented to the said States; that they be urged to consider, that the war being now brought to a happy termination, by the personal services of our soldiers, the supplies of property of our citizens, and loans of money from them as well as foreigners; these several creditors have a right to expect that funds will be provided, on which they may rely for indemnification; that Congress still consider vacant territory as an important resource; and that, therefore, said States be earnestly pressed, by immediate and liberal cessions, to forward these necessary ends, and to promote the harmony of the Union."

Massachusetts, on the 13th of November, 1784, having authorized her delegates in Congress to cede to the United States so much of her claims to western territory as they might see fit, it was proposed by Rufus King, one of her delegates, on the 16th of March, 1785, to modify a report on the western territory, which had been accepted by the late Congress, by inserting a total and immediate prohibition of slavery. This resolution, substantially adopted by the vote of seven States, including Maryland; Delaware unrepresented; Virginia, the two Carolinas and Georgia in the negative. This was a test vote, and having thus secured the welfare of future generations, rather than any temporary advantage to the ceding States, the delegates of Massachusetts, Rufus King and Samuel Holten, on the 19th of April, 1785, executed a deed of cession as to all the territory west of the present western boundary of New York; whereupon Congress resolved "to accept said deed of cession, and that the same be recorded and enrolled among the acts of the United States in Congress assembled."

Another year elapsed, when Connecticut resumed the consideration of a cession of western territory, and at a general assembly of the State, on the second Thursday of May, 1786, passed the following act:

"*Be it enacted by the Governor, Council and Representatives, in General Court assembled, and by the authority of the same,* That the delegates of this State, or any two of them, who shall be attending the Congress of the United States, be, and they are hereby directed, authorized, and fully empowered, in the name and behalf of this State, to make, execute and deliver, under their hands and seals, an ample deed of release and cession of all the right, title, interest, jurisdiction and claim of the State of Connecticut, to certain western lands, beginning at the completion of the forty-first degree of north latitude, one hundred and twenty miles west of the western boundary line of the commonwealth of Pennsylvania, as now claimed by said commonwealth, and from thence by a line to be drawn north, parallel to, and one hundred and twenty miles west of the said west line of Pennsylvania, and to continue north until it comes to forty-two degrees and two minutes north latitude; whereby all the right, title, interest, jurisdiction and claim of the State of Connecticut to the lands lying west of the said line, to be drawn, as aforementioned, one hundred and twenty miles west of the western boundary line of the commonwealth of Pennsylvania, as now claimed by said commonwealth, shall be included, released, and ceded to the United States in Congress assembled, for the common use and benefit of said States, Connecticut inclusive."

This pertinacity succeeded, and on the 26th of May, 1786, it was resolved, "that Congress, in behalf of the United States, are ready to accept all the right, title, interest, jurisdiction and claim of the State of Connecticut to certain western lands, beginning at the completion of the forty-first degree of north latitude, one hundred and twenty miles west of the western boundary line of the commonwealth of Pennsylvania, as now claimed by said commonwealth; and from thence, by a line to be drawn north, parallel to, and one hundred and twenty miles west of the said west line of Pennsylvania, and to continue north until it comes to forty-two degrees two minutes north latitude, whenever the delegates of Connecticut shall be furnished with full powers and shall execute a deed for that purpose."

On the 14th of September, 1786, William Samuel Johnson and Jonathan Sturges, delegates from Connecticut, executed a deed of cession agreeably to the above resolution, and it was resolved "that Congress accept the said deed of cession, and that the same be recorded and enrolled among the acts of the United States in Congress assembled."

The western boundary of Pennsylvania, so frequently mentioned in these transactions, had been in dispute between the colonies of Virginia and Pennsylvania, but on the 31st of August, 1779, an agreement was concluded between commissioners appointed by those States respectively, that the line run in 1767, by Jeremiah Mason and Charles Dixon, and which had been established as the boundary between Maryland and Pennsylvania, should be extended due west five degrees of longitude, to be computed from the river Delaware for the southern boundary of Pennsylvania; and that a meridian drawn from the western extremity thereof to the northern limit of the said States respectively, should be the western boundary of Pennsylvania forever. Both States concurred in the action of the commissioners.

One of the conditions of the cessions just enumerated—originally contained in the resolution of Congress of October 10th, 1780, and recognized in the deed of Virginia—pledged the government of the Union to the formation of States, each with an extent not less than one hundred nor more than one hundred and fifty miles square. By a resolution of Congress, dated July 7, 1786, to which Virginia responded by an act dated December 30, 1788, this condition was changed so as to empower Congress to make a division of the territory northwest of the Ohio, into not less than three nor more than five States.

Some further particulars upon the subject considered in this chapter should here be added:

Connecticut, in 1786, provided for the survey of that portion of the Reserve east of the Cuyahoga River, and opened a land office—in 1792, granted five hundred thousand acres, the west part thereof, to certain citizens of the State as a compensation for property burned and destroyed in the towns of New London, New Haven, Fairfield and Norwalk, by the British troops during the Revolution—in 1795, sold the balance of the Reserve, and in 1800, ceded her jurisdiction over the tract to the United States, in consideration of an act of Congress, passed April 28th, authorizing the President to issue letters patent to the Governor of Connecticut in trust for the grantees of the soil. The proceeds of the Western Reserve were applied to the school fund of Connecticut.

On the 9th of August, 1787, South Carolina, by John Kean and Daniel Huger, her delegates in Congress, ceded to the United States the territory west of the mountains which divide the western from the eastern streams. A similar cession, but by no means so liberal in its terms, was made by North Carolina on the 25th of February, 1790, while the Western limits of Georgia were not adjusted until 1802.

CHAPTER XXVI.

THE SETTLEMENT OF THE NORTH WESTERN TERRITORY.—ORDINANCE OF 1787.

To dispose of the soil and to determine the political institutions of the valley between the Alleghanies and the Mississippi, was recognized by the Congress of the Confederation, as a grave and urgent duty. The members exaggerated the value of the lands, as a resource of revenue and credit to the government; but there was no error, either of purpose or policy, in their political regulations for the undeveloped empire of the west.

Still, the necessity of the case was substituted for any direct constitutional authority. The Articles of Confederation conferred upon Congress the power of "regulating the trade and managing all affairs with the Indians, not members of any of the States, provided that the legislative right of any State within its own limits be not infringed or violated," and of admitting other colonies into the confederacy with the assent of nine States by their delegates; but we look in vain for any other warrant of the legislation by Congress for the disposition and government of the western territory. The power to raise a revenue, from which the requisite implication might have been derived, consisted only of a right to make requisitions upon the respective States without the authority to enforce their compliance. But, in the course of events, Congress had acquired a public domain, and the proposition that checked or answered cavil, was, that the right to acquire, necessarily implied the right to dispose of the soil and protect the settlers by territorial governments.

The intrusions of settlers forced a public system of survey and sale upon the attention of Congress. On the 20th of May, 1785, "an ordinance for ascertaining the mode of disposing of lands in the Western Territory" was perfected by Congress, and became the foundation of the existing system. A corps of surveyors—one from each State, and appointed by Congress—were placed under the direction of Thomas Hutchins, Geographer of the United States, and instructed to divide the territory into townships of six miles square, by lines running due north and south, and others crossing these at right angles, as far as practicable. The first line running north and south was to begin on the Ohio River, at a point due north from the western termination of the southern boundary of Pennsylvania, and the first line running east and west was to begin at the same point and extend through the territory. The townships, whole or fractional, were to be numbered from south to north—the ranges of townships progressively westward. The townships were to be subdivided into thirty-six sections, each containing a mile square, or six hundred and forty acres. The survey has since been carried to half sections, quarter sections and eighths, and in some cases to sixteenths.

When the survey of seven ranges of townships was completed, plats were to be returned to the Board of Treasury, and the Secretary of War was to reserve, by lot, one-seventh part for the use of the late continental army, and so of every subsequent seven ranges, when surveyed and returned. Lots eight, eleven, twenty-six and twenty-nine in each township were reserved by the United States for future sale: lot sixteen for the maintenance of public schools within the township, and "also one-third part of all gold, silver, lead and copper mines to be sold or otherwise disposed of as Congress should direct."

With these exceptions, the townships were to be drawn in the name of the different States, in the proportion of the latest requisitions by Congress upon them, and sold at public vendue, after a prescribed notice, by the commissioners of the loan office of the several States, in the following manner: The township or fractional part of a township number one, in the first range, to be sold entire; and number two in the same range, by lots: and thus in alternate order through the whole of the first range. In the second range, the first township to be sold in lots, the second entire: and so alternately through the subsequent ranges. "*Provided*, That none of the lands within the said territory be sold under the price of one dollar the acre, to be paid in specie, or loan office certificates reduced to specie value by the scale of depreciation, or certificates of liquidated debts of the United States, including interest, besides the expense of the survey and other charges thereon, which are rated at thirty-six dollars, the township in specie or certificates as aforesaid, and so in the same proportion for a fractional part of a township, or of a lot, to be paid at the time of sales; on failure of which repayment, the lands shall again be offered for sale."

If lands remained unsold by a State after eighteen months, they were to be returned to the Board of Treasury, and sold as Congress might direct.

This ordinance also gave the mode for dividing among the continental soldiers the lands set apart for them: reserved three townships adjacent to Lake Erie for refugees from Canada and Nova Scotia, on account of their devotion to the

American cause:[1] secured to the Moravian Indians the towns of Gnadenhutten, Schoenbrun and Salem on the Muskingum, and such adjacent lands as would, in the judgment of the geographer, be sufficient for them to cultivate: and excluded from sale the territory between the Little Miami and Scioto, in accordance with the provisions made by Virginia in her deed of cession in favor of her own troops.[2]

On the 15th of June, 1785, Congress instructed the commissioners empowered to conclude a treaty with the western Indians, to warn off "several disorderly persons who had crossed the Ohio River and settled upon unappropriated lands," which was industriously, however ineffectually, done by General Richard Butler, on his journey to the conference with the Shawanese at the mouth of the Great Miami.

Congress instructed Hutchins and his body of surveyors, by a resolution of May 9th, 1786, not to proceed with their survey further north than the east and west line (the extension of the southern boundary of Pennsylvania) mentioned in the ordinance of May 20th, 1785. A year afterwards, Congress directed that the sale of lands, after the deduction of one-seventh for army bounties, should be held at the place where Congress was in session.

The bounties to the officers and soldiers of the Revolution, who had continued in service until the close of the war, or until discharged, and the representatives of those who were slain by the enemy, had been granted by resolutions of Congress, dated September 16th and 18th, 1776, and August

1) This tract was afterwards located eastwardly from the Scioto River, near and including the city of Columbus. It is a narrow strip of country, 4½ miles broad from north to south, and 48 miles in length—having the United States twenty ranges of military or army lands north, and twenty-two ranges of Congress lands south, and consisting of 100,000 acres.

2) Land Laws of the United States, edition of 1828, p. 349.

12th and September 22d, 1780, and were as follows: a Major General, eleven hundred acres; Brigadier General, eight hundred and fifty; Colonel, five hundred; Lieutenant Colonel, four hundred and fifty; Major, four hundred; Captain, three hundred; Lieutenant, two hundred; Ensign, one hundred and fifty; each non-commissioned officer and soldier, one hundred.[3] The possession of these and other claims upon the government of the Union, by the disbanded and often impoverished soldiery of the Revolution, became a prominent agency in the settlement of Ohio. In June, 1783, peace having been proclaimed, General Rufus Putnam, of Massachusetts, forwarded to Washington a memorial from a number of persons holding these claims for an appropriation of western lands, which Washington transmitted to Congress, but the States had not made their cessions, and Congress was obliged to postpone the consideration of the subject. In July, 1785, Benjamin Tupper, a Revolutionary officer of Massachusetts, was appointed a surveyor of western lands, and during the year visited Pittsburgh. The survey was interrupted by Indian troubles, and he went no further, but returned with such impressions of the Ohio country that Putnam and himself united in a publication, dated January 10, 1786, which proposed an association for the purchase and settlement of Ohio lands. Whoever desired to promote the scheme were invited to meet in their respective counties of Massachusetts, (enumerating the places) on the 15th of February, and choose a delegate or delegates to meet at "the Bunch of Grapes tavern, in Boston, Essex."

This convention assembled on the 1st of March, and consisted of the following persons: Winthrop Sargent and John Mills, of Suffolk county; Manassah Cutler, of Essex; John

3) Land Laws of the United States, p. 336.

Brooks and Thomas Cushing, of Middlesex; Benjamin Tupper, of Hampshire; Crocker Sampson, of Plymouth; Rufus Putnam, of Worcester; John Patterson and Jahlaliel Woodbridge, of Berkshire; and Abraham Williams, of Barnstable. General Rufus Putnam was elected chairman, and Major Winthrop Sargent clerk.

On the 3d of March, a committee consisting of Messrs. Putnam, Cutler, Brooks, Sargent and Cushing, reported a plan of association, which was adopted. The leading features of the organization were these: a fund of a million dollars, mainly in continental specie certificates, was to be raised for the purchase of lands in the western territory; there were to be a thousand shares of one thousand dollars each, and upon each share ten dollars in specie were to be paid for contingent expenses. One year's interest on the certificates was to be appropriated to the charges of making a settlement and assisting those who were unable to remove without aid. The owners of every twenty shares were to choose an agent to represent them, and attend to their interests, and these agents were to choose five directors, a treasurer and secretary.

The next meeting of the associates was held at Bracket's tavern, in Boston, on the 8th of March, 1787, called by special advertisement. At this meeting it appeared that two hundred and fifty shares had been subscribed in this "company's funds," and "that many in the commonwealth of Massachusetts, Connecticut, Rhode Island and New Hampshire, were inclined to become adventurers, and restrained only by the uncertainty of obtaining a sufficient tract of country, collectively, for a great settlement." It was resolved that three directors be appointed for the company, who were to make immediate application to Congress for a private grant of lands. General Samuel H. Parsons, General Rufus Putnam, and the

Rev. Manassah Cutler were chosen. Major Winthrop Sargent was elected secretary. The appointment of the other two directors and treasurer was postponed until another meeting.

The directors employed Dr. Cutler to make a contract with Congress, and for that purpose he passed the month of July in New York, with the exception of a week's attendance upon the federal convention, then engaged in Philadelphia in framing the constitution of the United States. An interview with Thomas Hutching, shortly after Cutler's arrival in New York, confirmed the previous impressions of the New England adventurers in favor of a location inclusive and westward of the Muskingum valley. General Parsons, as a commissioner to the Shawanese, in 1786, had shared the enthusiasm of all the early voyagers along the river coast of that region of Ohio, and Hutchins doubtless spoke from his prepossessions while the companion of Colonel Bouquet twenty years before. In a published journal of Dr. Cutler, under date of July 9, he says that Hutchins advised him "by all means to make the location on the Muskingum, which was decidedly, in his opinion, the best part of the whole western country." Another circumstance in favor of the Muskingum, was the security to the colonists from the establishment, since the autumn of 1785, of a post—Fort Harmar—at the confluence of the Muskingum and the Ohio.

The journal of Cutler indicates very distinctly, that his embassy to New York would have been unsuccessful if he and Sargent (whom he associated with himself in the negotiation) had not consented to extend their contract for the benefit of another company. He was also obliged to surrender General Samuel H. Parsons, as a candidate for governor of the territory, in favor of the appointment of General

Arthur St. Clair, who was a delegate from Pennsylvania, and also president of Congress. On the 20th of July, Colonel William Duer, and "a number of the principal characters of the city," induced Cutler to extend his purchase so as to include their own speculations, although this part of the transaction was to be kept "a profound secret;" and Cutler admits that "matters went on much better" after St. Clair and his friends had been informed that Parsons was given up for the governorship.

On the 23d, Congress authorized the Board of Treasury to contract with any person or persons for a grant of a tract of land which should be bounded by the Ohio from the mouth of the Scioto to the intersection of the western boundary of the seventh range of townships then in course of survey; thence by the said boundary to the northern boundary of the tenth township from the Ohio; thence by a due west line to Scioto; thence by the Scioto to the beginning."

Cutler, Sargent and Duer, as the former admits in his diary, "now entered into the true spirit of negotiation with great bodies. Every machine in the city that it was possible to work was now put in motion," &c. They succeeded, and it appears from the resolution of July 23, authorizing the Board of Treasury to contract on certain terms therein enumerated, from a communication by Cutler and Sargent, as "agents of the Ohio Company of Associates," dated July 26, and from the final resolution of Congress on the 27th, that the following were the terms of sale for the tract above described.

A survey of the tract, ascertaining its contents and plainly marking the northern boundary, was to be made by the United States, but the company should lay off the tract into townships and lots, pursuant to the ordinance of May 20th, 1785.

The reservations in each township were: lot sixteen, for schools; twenty-nine, for the purposes of religion; and eight, eleven and twenty-six, for future disposition by Congress. The price to be one dollar per acre, "payable in specie, loan office certificates reduced to specie value, or certificates of liquidated debts of the United States," liable to a reduction of one-third for bad lands and all contingencies. The principal of the certificates was only to be received, but military bounties were admitted, acre for acre, in payment of one-seventh of the lands. Of the whole amount, five hundred thousand dollars were to be paid down; another five hundred thousand when the tract above described should be surveyed by the proper officer of the United States, and the remainder in six equal semi-annual instalments, with interest on the sums due from the completion of the United States survey.

Congress, by their resolution of July 23, had stipulated for a reservation of two townships to be given perpetually for the uses of an university, and laid off by the purchasers in good land as near the centre (of the whole tract) as might be—that good and sufficient security be given for the completion of the contract—and that the grant should be made upon the full payment of the consideration money, and a right of entry and occupancy be acquired immediately for so much of the tract as should be agreed upon between the Board of Treasury and the purchasers.

On these points the agents of the Ohio company submitted the following conditions, and induced Congress to acquiecse in them as modifications of the original proposition:

"The lands assigned for the establishment of an university to be nearly as possible in the centre of the first million and a half of acres we shall pay for; for to fix it in the centre of the proposed purchase, might too long defer the establishment.

"When the second payment is made, the purchasers shall receive a deed for as great a quantity of land as a million of dollars will pay for, at the price agreed on; after which we will agree not to receive any further deeds for any of the lands purchased, only at such periods and on such conditions as may be agreed on betwixt the board and the purchasers.

"As to the security, which the act says shall be good and sufficient, we are unable to determine what those terms may mean, in the contemplation of Congress, or of your honorable board; we shall, therefore, only observe that our private fortunes and those of our associates being embarked in the support of the purchase, it is not possible for us to offer any adequate security but that of the land itself, as is usual in great land purchases.

"We will agree so to regulate the contract that we shall never be entitled to a right of entry and occupancy but on lands actually paid for, nor receive any deeds till our payments amount to a million of dollars, and then only in proportion to said payment. The advance we shall always be under, without any formal deed, together with the improvements made on the lands, will, we presume, be ample security, even if it was not the interest as well as the disposition of the company to lay the foundation of their establishment on a sacred regard to the rights of property."

This communication was dated July 26; "Friday, July 27," as recorded in Dr. Cutler's diary, was occupied very effectively in obtaining the consent of Congress. "I rose very early this morning," writes Cutler, "and after adjusting my baggage for my return, (for I was determined to leave New York this day) I set out on a general morning visit, and paid my respects to all the members of Congress in the city, and informed them of my intention to leave the city that day. My expectations of obtaining a contract, I told them, were nearly at an end. I should, however, wait the decision of Congress, and if the terms I had stated—and which I conceived to be very advantageous to Congress, considering the circumstances of that country—were not acceded to, we must turn our attention to some other part of the country. New York, Connecticut and Massachusetts, would sell us lands at half a dollar, and give us exclusive privileges beyond what we have asked of Congress. The speculating plan concerted between the British of Canada was now well known. The uneasiness of the Kentucky people, with respect to the Mississippi, was notorious. A revolt of that country from the Union, if a war with Spain should occur, was universally acknowledged to be highly probable; and most certainly a systematic settlement in that country, conducted by men thoroughly attached to the federal government, and composed of young, robust and hardy laborers, who had no idea of any other than the federal government, I conceived to be an object worthy of some attention."

Such tactics could hardly fail of success. Before the day closed, the order of July 27th was obtained, of which Dr. Cutler remarks: "By this ordinance we obtained the grant of near five million of acres, amounting to three million and a half of acres for the Ohio Company, and the remainder for a private speculation, in which many of the principal characters of America are concerned. Without connecting this speculation, similar terms and advantages could not have been obtained for the Ohio Company."

On the 27th of October, 1787, the verbal arrangement of July was consummated by two contracts of purchase—the first being the actual transaction of the Massachusetts association, and the other in secret trust for William Duer and the "principal characters of America." In both instruments, Cutler and Sargent appear as agents of the Ohio Company. Their first purchase began where the Ohio is intersected by the western boundary of the seventh range of townships, and ran due north on that boundary one thousand three hundred and six chains and twenty-five links; thence due west, to the western boundary of the seventeenth range of townships (as afterwards surveyed by the government); thence due south to the Ohio and up the river to the beginning; the whole area containing one million seven hundred and eighty-nine thousand seven hundred and sixty acres of land, of which two hundred and eighty-one thousand seven hundred and sixty acres constituted the reservations of the United States.

The second purchase of Cutler and Sargent began at the northeastern angle of the tract just described, and ran due north to the northern boundary of the tenth township from the Ohio; thence, due west to the Scioto; thence down the same and up the Ohio to the southwestern angle of the first purchase, and along the western and northern boundaries thereof, to the beginning, the whole area estimated by Jefferson, in a communication from the Department of State in 1791, to contain 4,901,480 acres, including the reservations of the United States. Although Cutler and Sargent, on the 29th of October, (two days after their contracts with the Board of Treasury,) executed an assignment to William Duer and his associates of a moiety of the tract last described, and the latter proceeded to organize a Scioto Land Company, yet they made no payments either to the Ohio Company or the government in execution of their agreement, and the lands finally reverted to the United States.

The Ohio Company did not even retain the whole of their

purchase proper—the subject of their first contract with the Board of Treasury. By an act of Congress, dated April 21st, 1792, it was confirmed so far as to include a tract bounded by the Ohio on the south, the seventh range of townships on the east, the western bounds of the fifteenth range of townships on the west, and a line on the north so drawn as to make seven hundred and fifty thousand acres, besides the reservations enumerated in the contract of October 27th, 1787. The President of the United States was authorized to issue letters patent for the tract above described, to Rufus Putnam, Manassah Cutler, Robert Oliver and Griffin Green, in trust for the persons composing the Ohio Company of Associates, besides a tract of two hundred and fourteen thousand acres for the liquidation of army bounties under the resolutions of 1776 and 1780, and a third tract of one hundred thousand acres, which the company received on condition that they would, within five years, convey the same in tracts of one hundred acres to actual settlers. The whole were to be located with the original purchase of a million and a half acres. The company finally became possessed of nine hundred and sixty-four thousand two hundred and eighty-five acres.[4]

Simultaneously with the cessions of the Atlantic States, the negotiations for the Indian title, and the preliminaries of settlement, Congress was engaged upon a scheme of republican government for "the transmontane half of the American Republic." Before the cession by Virginia, the subject had been considered by a committee, consisting of Jefferson of Virginia, Howell of Rhode Island, and Chase of Maryland; and on the 1st of March, 1784—the date of the Virginia

4) A full abstract of Dr. Cutler's Journal is given in the North American Review, for October, 1841 (vol. liii., 334 to 343). See also Perkins' Western Annals, 287 to 292; U. S. Land Laws, p. 362.

cession—Thomas Jefferson, as chairman of the committee, reported a plan for the government of the Western Territory—not lying north of the Ohio merely, but the whole territory, ceded or to be ceded, from the north line of Florida to the north line of the United States.

This plan proposed to divide the territory into seventeen States; eight between the Mississippi and a north and south line through the Falls of the Ohio, each to contain two parallels of latitude, except the northernmost, which was to extend from the forty-fifth parallel to the northern boundary; eight more between this line and another parallel to it, drawn through the mouth of the Great Kanawha, to be laid out in plots corresponding to the first eight; the remaining tract east of this last line, and between the Ohio, the Pennsylvania boundary and Lake Erie, to constitute the seventeenth State.

"The settlers," to repeat the language of the report, "shall, either on their own petition or on the order of Congress, receive authority, with appointments of time and place, for their free males, of full age, to meet together for the purpose of establishing a temporary government. * * * * * * Such temporary government shall only continue in force, in any State, until it shall have acquired twenty thousand inhabitants; when, giving due proof thereof to Congress, they shall receive from them authority, with appointments of time and place, to call a convention of representatives, to establish a permanent constitution and government for themselves: *Provided*, that both the temporary and permanent governments, be established upon these principles as their basis—

"*First:* That they shall forever remain a part of this confederacy of the United States of America.

"*Second:* That they shall be subject to the Articles of Confederation in all those cases in which tho original States shall be so subject, and to all the acts and ordinances of the United States in Congress assembled, conformable thereto.

"*Third:* That they in no case shall interfere with the primary disposal of the soil by the United States in Congress assembled, nor with the ordinances and regulations which Congress may find necessary, for securing the title of such soil to the *bona fide* purchasers.

"*Fourth:* That they shall be subject to pay a part of the Federal debts, contracted or to be contracted, to be apportioned on them by Congress, according to the same common rule and measure by which apportionments thereof shall be made on the other States.

"*Fifth:* That no tax shall be imposed on lands, the property of the United States.

"*Sixth:* That their respective governments shall be republican.

"*Seventh:* That the lands of non-resident proprietors shall, in no cases, be taxed higher than those of residents within any new State, before the admission thereof to a vote by its delegates in Congress.

"*Eighth:* That after the year 1800 of the Christian era, there shall be neither slavery nor involuntary servitude in any of the said States, otherwise than in the punishment of crimes, whereof the party shall have been duly convicted to have been personally guilty."

The States thus authorized, were to be admitted by their delegates into Congress, when any of them should have, of free inhabitants, as many as the least numerous of the thirteen original States, provided the consent of nine States to such admission was given. An amendment of the Articles of

Confederation, substituting the vote of two-thirds of the States, wherever nine had been previously requisite, was also proposed. During the temporary government, Congress might take measures for the preservation of peace and good order among the settlers in any of the said new States; and the latter were allowed, before their temporary organization, to "keep a member in Congress, with a right of debating but not voting." The plan under consideration closed with the following provision:

"That the preceding articles shall be formed into a charter of compact; shall be duly executed by the President of the United States in Congress assembled, under his hand, and the seal of the United States; shall be promulgated, and shall stand as fundamental constitutions between the thirteen original States, and each of the several States now newly described, unalterable from and after the sale of any part of the territory of such State, pursuant to this resolve, but by the joint consent of the United States in Congress assembled, and of the particular State within which such alteration is proposed to be made."

On the 19th of April, Mr. Spaight of North Carolina moved that the anti-slavery proviso be stricken out. Under the Articles of Confederation, which governed the proceed ings of Congress, a majority of the thirteen States was ne cessary to an affirmative decision of any question; and the vote of no State could be counted, unless represented by at least two delegates.

The question upon Mr. Spaight's motion was put in this form:

"Shall the words moved to be struck out stand?"

The vote stood—

For the Proviso, six States, viz: New Hampshire, Massachusetts, Rhode Island, Connecticut, New York and Pennsylvania.

Against the Proviso, three States, viz: Virginia, Maryland and South Carolina.

Delaware and Georgia were not represented. New Jersey, by Mr. Dick, voted *aye*, but her vote, only one delegate being present, could not be counted. The vote of North Carolina was divided—Mr. Williamson voting *aye*, Mr. Spaight, *no*. The vote of Virginia stood—Mr. Jefferson, *aye*, Messrs. Hardy and Mercer, *no*. Of the twenty-three delegates present and voting, sixteen voted for, and seven against the proviso, which was thus defeated by a minority vote. It so happened that Mr. Beatty of New Jersey, the colleague of Mr. Dick, had left Congress a day or two before, and returned a day or two after. Had he been present, or had one of Mr. Jefferson's colleagues voted with him, the result would have been changed.[5]

The ordinance of 1784, with this material omission, was passed on the 23d of April following. In 1785, Mr. Jefferson went as minister to France, and on the 16th of

5) Journals Cong. Confed., vol. iv. p. 374: See also Congressional Globe, 1848-9, Appendix, 294, Speech of John A. Dix; also Speech of S. P. Chase, on Mr. Clay's Compromise Resolutions, in U. S. Senate, March 26, 1850. Besides the general provisions for the division of the Western Territory, Jefferson's original draft designated the States north of the Ohio—ten in number—by specific boundaries and names. This paragraph, which the committee suppressed on a recommitment, was as follows:

"That the territory northward of the forty-fifth degree, that is to say, of the completion of forty-five degrees from the equator, and extending to the Lake of the Woods, shall be called *Sylvania;* that of the territory under the forty-fifth and forty-fourth degrees, that which lies westward of Michigan, shall be called *Michigania;* and that which is eastward thereof, within the peninsula formed by the lakes and waters of Michigan, Huron, St. Clair, and Erie, shall be called *Cheronesus*, and shall include any part of the peninsula which may extend above the forty-fifth degree. Of the territory under the forty-third and forty-second degrees, that to the westward

March, Rufus King of Massachusetts, preceded the assent of his colleague and himself to a cession of western lands in behalf and by the authority of the State of Massachusetts, with a motion that the following proposition be committed to a committee of the whole House:

"That there shall be neither slavery nor involuntary servitude in any of the States described in the resolves of Congress of the 23d of April, 1784, otherwise than in the punishment of crimes, whereof the party shall have been personally guilty; and that this regulation shall be an article of compact, and remain a fundamental principle of the constitutions between the thirteen original States, and each of the States described in the said resolve of the 23d of April, 1784."

The motion was seconded by Mr. Ellery of Rhode Island, and prevailed by the votes of New Hampshire, Massachusetts, Connecticut, Rhode Island, New York, New Jersey, Pennsylvania and Maryland—eight; against the votes of Virginia, North Carolina, South Carolina and Georgia—four. Delaware was not represented. The vote of Maryland was determined by two ayes against one no, while that

through which the Assenisipi or Rock River runs, shall be called *Assenisipia;* and that to the eastward, in which are the fountains of the Muskingum, the two Miamies of Ohio, the Wabash, the Illinois, the Miami of the Lake, and the Sandusky Rivers, shall be called *Metropotamia.* Of the territory which lies under the forty-first and fortieth degrees, the western, through which the river Illinois runs, shall be called *Illinoia;* that next adjoining, to the eastward, *Saratoga;* and that between this last and Pennsylvania, and extending from the Ohio to Lake Erie, shall be called *Washington.* Of the territory which lies under the thirty-ninth and thirty-eighth degrees, to which shall be added so much of the point of land within the fork of the Ohio and Mississippi as lies under the thirty-seventh degree, that to the westward, within and adjacent to which are the confluences of the rivers Wabash, Shawnee, Tanisee, Ohio, Illinois, Mississippi and Missouri, shall be called *Polypotamia;* and that to the eastward, farther up the Ohio, otherwise called the Pelisipi, shall be called *Pelisipia.*"

of Virginia was determined by two noes against one aye—the single affirmative from Virginia being the vote of Mr. Grayson, the successor of Mr. Jefferson.[6]

The resolution of Mr. King differed from the proposition of Mr. Jefferson, inasmuch as the prohibition of slavery was total and immediate, and not deferred to the year 1800: but was identical with it in the extension of the prohibition over the whole western territory, from the thirty-first parallel of north latitude to the northern boundary of the United States. No expression could be more conclusive of a determination by the statesmen and patriots of the revolutionary epoch, to confine slavery to the Atlantic States.

The division of States contemplated by the ordinance or resolution of 1784, was found inexpedient, and an act exclusively applicable to the recent cessions by New York, Massachusetts, Virginia and Connecticut—the entire territory then belonging to the United States—was proposed in Congress, and resulted in the celebrated ordinance of July 13, 1787. It was reported in September, 1786, by a committee composed of Messrs. Johnson of Connecticut, Pinckney of South Carolina, Smith of New York, Dane of Massachusetts, and Henry of Maryland. Subsequently it was submitted to another committee, consisting of Messrs. Carrington of Virginia, Dane of Massachusetts, R. H. Lee of Virginia, Keen of South Carolina, and Smith of New York. On its final passage, the Ordinance received the unanimous vote of the States, and with a single exception from New York, of all the delegates.

This well-known enactment organized a single territory northwest of the Ohio and eastward of the Mississippi, but

6) Journals Cong. Confed., vol. iv. p. 481.

subject to a future division, if deemed expedient by Congress, into two districts.

The important principles of the equal inheritance of intestate estates, and the freedom of alienation by deed or will, were established and defined, with a reservation in favor of the laws and customs in the French and Canadian settlements.

A governor, for the term of three years, a secretary for four years, and three judges during good behavior, were to be appointed by Congress. The governor was invested with the appointment of civil and military officers, and authorized to establish the territorial divisions of counties and townships. The legislative power was to be exercised by the governor and judges, by the adoption of such laws of the original States, criminal and civil, as were suitable to the circumstances of the country, but which remained in force, only on condition that Congress and the territorial legislature, when created, should approve thereof. The other powers of the officers above mentioned, were not unusual.

This was only a temporary system, however. A more popular form would displace it, when there should be five thousand free male inhabitants of full age in the district. That fact ascertained, the people would be authorized to elect representatives to a Territorial Legislature, and from their nomination of ten persons, Congress (or the President of the United States, after the adoption of the Federal Constitution) would select five names, to constitute a legislative council. The representatives were to serve two, and councilmen five years—the two bodies constituting a Territorial Legislature, with power to make any laws, not repugnant to the National Constitution or the Ordinance of 1787. The judges were thenceforth to be confined to purely judicial functions. The governor was to retain his appointing power, his general executive authority, and to have an absolute negative upon all legislative acts. By a joint ballot of the council and house of representatives, a delegate to Congress might be chosen, with the right of debate but no vote.

The Ordinance concludes with six articles of compact, between the original States and the people and States in the Territory, which should forever remain unalterable, unless by common consent. The first declared that no person, demeaning himself in a peaceable and orderly manner, should ever be molested on account of his mode of worship or religious sentiments. The second prohibited legislative interference with private contracts, and secured to the inhabitants trial by jury, the writ of *habeas corpus*, a proportionate representation of the people in the legislature, judicial proceedings according to the course of the common law, and those guaranties of personal freedom and property, which are enumerated in the Bills of Rights of most of the States. The third provided for the encouragement of schools, and for good faith, justice and humanity towards the Indians. The fourth secured to the new States, to be erected out of the territory, the same privileges with the old ones; imposed upon them the same burdens, including responsibility for the federal debt; prohibited them from interfering with the primary disposal of the soil by the United States, or taxing the public lands, or taxing the lands of non-residents higher than those of residents; and established the navigable waters, leading into the Mississippi and St. Lawrence, and the portages between them, as common highways for the use of all the citizens of the United States.

The fifth article related to the formation of new States within the territory, and to their admission into the Union. There were to be not less than three nor more than five States.

The western State was to include all the country between a line from the mouth of the Wabash along that river to Vincennes, and thence due north to the territorial line, and by that line to the Lake of the Woods and Mississippi. The middle State was to comprehend all within a line drawn due north from the mouth of the Great Miami, to the territorial line and the eastern boundary of the western State. The residue was to constitute the eastern State, but Congress reserved the power of forming one or two States north of an east and west line, drawn through the southern bend or extreme of Lake Michigan. These States, having a population of sixty thousand, or at an earlier period, if consistent with the general interest of the confederacy, were to have the right of admission into the Union, agreeably to the terms of the Virginia cession and the resolution of October 10th, 1780, and were to remain forever members of the confederacy.

The sixth and last article was in these words: "There shall be neither slavery nor involuntary servitude in the said territory, otherwise than in the punishment of crimes, whereof the party shall have been duly convicted. *Provided, always*, That any person escaping into the same, from whom labor or service is lawfully claimed in any one of the original States, such fugitive may be lawfully reclaimed and conveyed to the person claiming his or her labor or service as aforesaid."

The resolutions of the 23d of April, 1784, on the subject of the Ordinance, were repealed.[7]

In October following, Congress ordered seven hundred troops for the defence of the western frontiers and to aid in the organization of civil authority under their Ordinance of July, and on the 5th of the month, appointed General Arthur

7) The Ordinance will be found in Appendix, No. xiii. See Western Law Journal, vol. v. p. 529.

St. Clair, Governor of the Northwestern Territory, associating with him, Winthrop Sargent of Massachusetts as Secretary, and Samuel Holden Parsons of Massachusetts, James Mitchel Barnum of Pennsylvania and John Cleves Symmes of New Jersey, as Judges of the territory.

On the SEVENTH OF APRIL, 1788, a party of forty-eight men, with General Rufus Putman at their head, disembarked at the mouth of the Muskingum River. They were the pioneers of the Ohio Company, and they had made their voyage from Pittsburgh in a vessel constructed for the purpose—the "Adventure Galley" afterwards called the "Mayflower." The aniversary of this interesting occasion will always be cherished, as it is often celebrated by the people of Ohio.

On the FIFTEENTH OF JULY, Governor St. Clair, who had arrived at Fort Harmar six days before, was formally received upon the site of Marietta—the "Seat of Government"—by the veteran Parsons, the Secretary and Judges of the territory, and an assemblage of inhabitants. Under a bower of foliage, contributed by the surrounding forest, the Ordinance of 1787 was audibly read—congratulations exchanged—and three cheers, startling the solitude of the streams, and the denizens of the wilderness around them, closed the simple, but impressive inauguration of Territorial Government beyond the Ohio.

APPENDIX.

I.

(Page 21.)

FURTHER PARTICULARS OF THE ERIES, NEUTRALS, AND ANDASTES.

THE testimony of the Jesuit missionaries confirms the opinion expressed in the text, that the Neutrals were one of several tribes, that suffered from Iroquois hostility. In 1654, Father Simon Le Moine visited the country of the Onondaga Indians, near the mouth of Lake Ontario. His party were received by some Iroquois fishermen; and among them was "a Huron prisoner, and a good Christian," and some Huron squaws, for the most part Christian women, formerly rich and at their ease, whom captivity had reduced to servitude. "They requested me," the missionary continues in his Journal, "to pray to God; and I had the consolation to confess there at my leisure Hostagehtax, our ancient host of the Petun nation. His sentiments and devotion drew tears from my eyes: he is the fruit of the labors of Father Charles Garnier, that holy missionary whose death has been so precious before God."

At the principal Onondaga village, the missionary met other Huron captives, and names Terese, a good Christian woman, who had with her a young captive of the Neutral Nation—*de la Nation Neutre*—who became "the first adult baptism at Onondago."

In a conference with the Indians, Le Moine, who bore a message and various presents from M. de Lauson, then Governor of New France, delivered "a hatchet to each of the four Iroquois Nations, for the new war they were waging against the Cat Nation," with many other references to existing hostilities. "Finally," he adds, "by the nineteenth present, I wiped away the tears of all the young warriors for the death of their great chief Anneneraos, a short time prisoner with the Cat Nation." In reply, a captain of the Oneida Nation "produced four large belts, to thank Onnontio (the French Governor) for having encouraged them to fight bravely against their new enemies of the Cat Nation."

Another Missionary Journal, in 1658, alludes to the subjugation of the dreaded Cat Nation, as having been then accomplished. See Documentary History of New York, vol. i., pp. 30, 31, 32, 37.

A map published in Amsterdam in 1720, founded on a great variety of memoirs of Louisiana, and attached to a work called *Receuil de Voyages*, represents within the present limits of Erie county, and directly east of "*Lac San dou ske*," some villages of the "*Eries—Nation du chat*," adding, that they were then destroyed (*detruite*). See French's Historical Collections of Louisiana, Part II.

There are many traditions among the Senecas of a tribe, by them called Kahkwahs, whose villages were west of the Genesee, and thence south to the sources of the Alleghany. We suppose them to have been the Andastes, who were vanquished by the New York confederates in 1672. H. R. School craft (Notes on the Iroquois, p. 318) has preserved the following Seneca tradition of the Kahkwahs. It will be seen that the writer identifies the Eries with the Kahkwahs. The terms may be synonymous, but if so, the seats of the Eries were certainly extended to the western extremity of Lake Erie.

"My inquiries," Schoolcraft proceeds to say, "were answered one evening at the mission house in Buffalo, by the Alleghany chief, *Ha-yek-dyoh-kunh*, or the Wood-cutter, better known by his English name of Jacob Blacksnake. He stated that the Kahkwahs had their chief residence, at the time of their final defeat, on the Eighteen Mile Creek. The name by which he referred to them, in this last place of their residence, might be written perhaps with more exactitude to the native tongue, *Gah-Gwah-ge-o-nuh*—but as this compound word embraces the ideas of locality and existence along with their peculiar name, there is a species of tautology in retaining the two inflections. They are not necessary in the English, and besides, in common use, I found them to be generally dropped, while the sound of *g* naturally changed in common pronunciation into that of *k*.

"Blacksnake commenced by saying, that while the Senecas lived east of the Genesee, they received a challenge from the Kahkwahs to try their skill in ball-playing and athletic sports. It was accepted, and after due preliminaries, the challengers came accompanied by their prime young men, who were held in great repute as wrestlers and ball players. The old men merely came as witnesses, while this trial was made.

"The first trial consisted of ball playing, in which, after a sharp contest, the young Senecas came off victorious. The next trial consisted of a foot race between two, which terminated also in favor of the Senecas. The spirit of the Kahkwas was galled by these defeats. They immediately got up another race on the instant, which was hotly contested by new runners, but it ended in their losing the race. Fired by these defeats, and still confident of their superior strength, they proposed wrestling, with the sanguinary condition, that each of the seconds should hold a drawn knife, and if his principal was thrown, he should instantly plunge it into his throat and cut off his head. Under this terrible penalty, the struggle commenced. The wrestlers were to catch their holds as best they could, but to observe fair principles of wrestling. At length the Kahkwah was thrown, and his head immediately severed and tossed into the air. It fell with a rebound, and loud shouts proclaimed the Senecas victorious in four trials. This terminated the sports, and the tribes returned to their respective villages.

"Some time after this event, two Seneca hunters went out to hunt west of the Genesee River, and as the custom is, built a hunting lodge of boughs, where they rested at night. One day, one of them went alone, and having walked a long distance, was belated on his return. He saw, as he cast his eye to a distant lodge, a body of the Kahkwahs marching in the direction of the Seneca towns. He ran to his companion, and they instantly fled and alarmed the Senecas. They sent off a messenger post-haste to inform their confederates towards the east, who immediately prepared to meet their enemies. After about a day's march, they met them. It was near sunset when they descried their camp, and they went and encamped in the vicinity. A conference ensued in which they settled the terms of the battle.

"The next morning the Senecas advanced. Their order of battle was this. They concealed their young men, who were called by the narrator *burnt knives*,* telling them to lie flat, and not rise and join in the battle until they received the war cry, and were ordered forward. With these were left rolls of peeled bark to tie their prisoners. Having made this arrangement, the old warriors advanced and began the battle. The contest was fierce and long, and it varied much. Sometimes they were driven back, or faltered in their line—again they advanced, and again faltered. This waving of the lines to and fro, formed a most striking feature in the battle for a long time. At length the Senecas were driven back near to the point where the young men were concealed. The latter were alarmed, and cried out, 'Now we are killed!' At this moment the Seneca leader gave the concerted war-whoop, and they arose and joined in battle. The effects of this reinforcement, at the time that the enemy were fatigued with the day's fight, were instantaneously felt. The young Senecas pressed on their enemies with resistless energy, and after receiving a shower of arrows, beat down their opponents with their war-clubs, and took a great many prisoners. The prisoners were immediately bound with their arms behind, and tied to trees. Nothing could resist their impetuosity. The Kahkwah chiefs determined to fly, and leave the Senecas masters of the field.

"In this hard and disastrous battle, which was fought by the Senecas alone, and without aid from their confederates, the Kahkwahs lost a very great number of their men, in slain and prisoners. But those who fled

* A term to denote their being quite young, and used here as a cant phrase for prime young warriors.

were not permitted to escape unpursued, and having been reinforced from the east, they followed them and attacked them in their residence on the Droseona (Buffalo Creek), and Eighteen Mile Creek, which they were obliged to abandon, and fly to the *Oheeo*, the Seneca name for the Alleghany. The Senecas pursued them, in their canoes, in the descent of this stream. They discovered their encampment on an island in numbers superior to their own. To deceive them the Senecas, on putting ashore, carried their canoes across a narrow peninsula, by means of which they again entered the river above. New parties appeared, to the enemy, to be thus continually arriving, and led them greatly to overestimate their numbers. This was at the close of the day. In the morning not an enemy was to be seen. The Eries had fled down the river and have never since appeared. It is supposed they yet exist west of the Mississippi.

"Two characteristic traits of boasting happened in the first great battle above described. The Kahkwah women carried along, in the rear of the warriors, packs of moccasins for the women and children, whom they expected to be made captive in the Seneca villages. The Senecas, on the other hand, said as they went out to battle, 'Let us not fight them too near for fear of the stench,' alluding to the anticipated heaps of slain.

"It may here be inquired, perhaps, whether the Kahkwahs were not a remnant, or at least allies of the ancient Alleghans. The French idea, that the Eries were exterminated, is exploded by this tradition of Blacksnake, at least if we concede that Erie and Kahkwah were synonyms. A people who were called Erierions by the Wyandots, and Kahkwahs by the Iroquois, may have had many other names from other tribes. It would contradict all Indian history, if they had not as many names as there were diverse nations to whom they were known."

II.

(Page 57.)

FRENCH OCCUPATION BY A PROCESS VERBAL.

The French government still retain this rather theatrical method of asserting their sovereignty. When La Salle reached the mouth of the Mississippi, it was with similar tokens that he proclaimed the dominion of his royal master; and recently, when a French squadron occupied New Caledonia, in the Pacific, it was observable that the lapse of centuries had not materially changed the traditional ceremonies of such an occasion.

III.

(Page 64.)

THE DELAWARE VILLAGES ON THE SCIOTO.

Gist by no means found the bulk of the Delawares upon the "east bank of the Scioto," although "several villages" might have been scattered along its course. His route was doubtless by the "Standing Stone," now Lancaster, and thence to the fertile Pickaway Plains, where the Shawanese were afterwards assembled in considerable force. When the Delaware chiefs, who were in the American interest, visited Philadelphia during the Revolution, they spoke of "placing the Shawanese in their laps"—a figurative expression for the surrender of the Scioto valley to them, as they ascended from the mouth of the river. But the Delawares continued their occupation of the region now bearing their name in Ohio; and George Sanderson, Esq., in his "History of the Early Settlement of Fairfield county," mentions them as joint occupants of that vicinity with the Wyandots. On a further examination of Gen. Sanderson's interesting treatise, we have noticed that he thus obviates the difficulties suggested in the text (chap. xi. p. 160.) While the Wyandots occupied the present site of Lancaster, a Delaware chief, called Tobey, ruled over a village, called Tobeytown, near Royalton. The reader is requested to note the error, on page 160.

IV.

(Page 88,)

THE LOCALITY OF THE CANESADOOHARIE.

There are some circumstances mentioned by Smith, which might induce the opinion, that the Canesadooharie was the Huron, and not the Black River. He says that it "interlocks with the west branch of the Muskingum, runs nearly a north course and empties into the south side of Lake Erie, *about eight miles east from Sandusky*, or betwixt Sandusky and Cuyahoga." A Wyandot camp would also be more likely to be found at the mouth of Huron River. On the other hand, the Falls of Canesadooharie, are a marked feature of analogy to Black River; and a party ascending the west branch of Muskingum, with Lake Erie for their destination, would hardly extend their route to the westward sources of the Mohican or west branch of Muskingum, when the Lake Fork led them northwardly and directly to their destination. The mouth of Huron is certainly "about eight miles east from

Sandusky," while the distance to Black River is at least twenty-five miles, but this is probably an inaccuracy of Smith's memory—his Journal having been published after an interval of more than forty years.

V.

(Page 247.)

CONTEMPORARY ACCOUNTS OF THE INDIAN HOSTILITIES OF 1774.

In the first volume of the fourth series of the American Archives, occurs the following contemporary allusions to the border war, commenced or precipitated by the massacre of Logan's family:

A communication to Lord Dunmore, dated March 24, 1774, speaks of the unhappy murder near the Ohio, not long before, of "young Russell," by a Cherokee chief, and anticipates further hostilities. (Page 278.)

Extracts are given from a "Journal of the United Brethren's Mission on the Muskingum." These mention a rumor, May 6, 1774, from *Mochwesung*, a Munsie village, that a Shawanese chief was killed on the Ohio, by white people, and another wounded. May 8, the journal states that "an express arrived from Gekelemuckepuck with the disagreeable news, that the white people on the Ohio had killed nine Mingoes and wounded two." (p. 283.)

May 24, David Zeisberger writes (p. 284) that twenty Shawanese warriors from *Woakatameka* had gone to make an incursion where the Mingoes were killed, but that the lower Shawanese were peaceable and had protected the traders. The missionary adds, "we are more than 200 souls in Schoenbrun, besides the congregation at Gnadenhutten."

John Heckewelder was an Englishman by birth, and it is barely possible that he is "the Cosh, alias John Bull," who thus writes from the Muskingum Mission on the 24th of May:

"About three weeks ago, John Jungman and myself were at Fort Pitt. On the way thither, we heard that three Cherokee Indians, going down the river, had killed one trader and wounded another, and plundered the canoe: the traders had imprudently shewn their silver things they had for trading. In the Fort, we heard that the Mingoes had stolen that night fifteen horses, and that they were all gone off from below Logtown. The white people began to be much afraid of an Indian war. We hastened to get home again, and after our return, received the news that a company of Virginians, under one Cresap, enticed some of the Mingoes, living at the mouth of Yellow Creek, to the other side of the river, and gave them rum to make them drunk, and then they killed five; two others, crossing the river to look after their friends, were shot down as soon as they came ashore. Five more were going over the river, whom they also waylaid, but the Indians perceiving them, turned their canoe to make their escape, but being immediately fired at, two were killed and two wounded. The day following they killed one Shawanese and one Delaware Indian, in a canoe down the river with two traders. The same party killed John Gibson's wife, a Shawanese woman; they further pursued a canoe, killed a Shawanese chief, and wounded another man. They said they would kill and plunder all that were going up and down the river. But they soon fled and left the poor settlers as victims to the Indians; many are fled and left all their effects behind. The Mingoes took their way up Yellow Creek, and struck our road just where it turns off from the road to *Gekelemuckepuck*, where they hunted for ten days to catch some traders, but as the Delawares had found them out, they stopped the traders from going that road. The Mingoes having sent word to the Shawanese, they fetched them to their town, *Woakatameka*, where they had a council of war. * * * We are in great distress, and don't know what to do; our Indians keep watch about us every night, and will not let us go out of town, even not into our corn fields. If there should be more bad news, we will be forced to move from here, for we are in danger from both sides. I heard from some, that if the white brethren should be forced to leave them, the greatest part would return to the Susquehanna. But if only the Delawares continue in their peaceful mind, it may go better than we now think. At the council at Woakatameka, were several head men of the Delawares present, who live at Schoenbrun and Gnadenhütten, being particularly sent for by *Netawatenees*, to assist them in the good work of preserving peace. The chief addressed the Shawanese and Mingoes present in a fatherly manner, shewing unto them the blessing of peace and folly of war; and pressed it very much upon their reason, what misery they would bring upon themselves and others by their madness, and told them positively that they had not to expect any help or assistance from the Delawares, and enjoined them very earnestly not to stop the road to Philadelphia, but to let it be free and open. The Shawanese gave him in answer, they did believe his words to be good, and they would take notice of them, and desired him to give also a fatherly admonition to their wives to plant corn for them; which he did, but they seemed more inclined to move off than to plant." (p. 285.)

May 29, Arthur St. Clair writes to Gov. Penn from Ligonier. He had lately been to Pittsburgh. Capt. White Eyes protected Duncan, a trader, from the hostile Shawanese, keeping him at Newcomerstown. Cresap and Greathouse killed thirteen Indians. Cresap declares publicly that he acted by Connolly's orders. (p. 286.)

From a speech of the Shawanese, it appears that Cornstalk sent his brother to accompany and protect the traders to Pittsburgh. (p. 288.)

A newspaper publication at Philadelphia, dated May 23, 1774, gives the following version of the affair at Yellow Creek, on the authority of "Capt. Crawford and Mr. Neville, of Virginia:"

"That a number of Indians encamped at the mouth of Yellow Creek, opposite to which two men named Greathouse and Baker, with some others, had assembled themselves, at a house belonging to the said Baker, and invited two men and two women of the Indians over the creek to drink with them, when, after making them drunk, they killed and scalped them; and two more Indian men then came over, who met with the like fate. After which six of their men came over to seek their friends, and on approaching the bank, where the white men lay concealed, perceived them, and endeavored to retreat back, but received a fire from the shore, which killed two Indians, who fell in the river; two fell dead in the canoe, and a fifth was so badly wounded that he could hardly crawl up the bank." Among the unfortunate sufferers was an Indian woman, wife to a white man, one of the traders; and she had an infant at her breast, which these inhuman butchers providentially spared and took with them. Mr. Neville asked the man who had the infant, if he was not near enough to have taken its mother prisoner without killing her. He replied that he was about six feet from her, when he shot her exactly in the forehead, and cut the hoppase with which the child's cradle hung at her back; and he thought to have knocked out its brains, but remorse prevented him, on seeing the child fall with its mother. This party further informed them, that after they had killed these Indians, they ran off with their families, and that they thought the whole country was fled, as Cresap, who was the perpetrator of the first offence, was then also on his way to Red Stone. (p. 345.)

A letter from Fort Pitt, June 19, 1774, says: "We have an account of Logan's being returned to the Shawanese towns, and that he took with him thirteen scalps." (p. 429.)

A letter from Pittsburgh, June 24, states that one of the Shawanese escort of the traders was shot near the mouth of Beaver Creek, by a party of twelve whites sent out by Connolly. (p. 449.)

"Newcomerstown" also mentioned—also Snakestown, on the Muskingum. (p. 464.)

A letter from Devereux Smith (Pittsburgh, June 10), mentions a complaint by the Shawanese "down the Ohio," that Connolly's militia had fired on their camps at the mouth of Sawmill Run, on the 25th of January—that Butler's canoe was attacked by the Cherokees on the 16th of April—that the attack on the second canoe by the whites under Cresap, was on the 27th of April; and about the same time a party headed by one Greathouse, had barbarously murdered and scalped nine Indians at the house of one Baker, near Yellow Creek, about fifty-five miles down the river." The letter reports White Eyes as stating that "a Mingo man named Logan (whose family had been murdered in the number), had raised a party to cut down the Shawanese town traders at Canoe Bottom, on the Hockhocking Creek, where they were pressing their peltry. On the 6th of June, an account was received of a family of eight killed on Monongahela by Logan's party." (p. 407)

The following persons, described as "chiefs of the Delawares," concur in pacific assurances, dated "Newcomerstown, June 21st, 1774:" King Newcomer, White Eyes, Thomas McKee, Epaloined, Neolige, Killbuck, William Anderson, and Simon Girty. (p. 545.)

Carlisle, June 30, 1774. "Logan's party has returned, and had thirteen scalps and one prisoner. Logan says he is now satisfied for the loss of his relations, and will sit still until he hears what the Long Knife (the Virginians) will say."—(John Montgomery to Gov. Penn, p. 546.)

Speech of friendly Delawares refers to towns on Muskingum, as *Kakelellamapeking*, *Gnadenhütten* and *Tripiakeng*, and mentions a Shawanese chief, *Keesmatela*, as hostile. (p. 680.)

In a letter of Col. Wm. Preston, dated Fincastle, August 13, 1774, the name of Jacob Sodousky is mentioned, as one of a surveying party on the Kentucky River, that had been in danger from an Indian attack. (p. 707.) It has been supposed that the word Sandusky was derived from the father of this person, who was a native of Poland, and had traded in Northwestern Ohio about 1740, losing his life while returning from an excursion thither; but there is evidence (see Appendix No. I) that as early as 1720, *Lac San dou ske* is found on European maps.

At Lord Dunmore's conference with the Ohio Indians (probably) at Fort Pitt, in October, King Custaloga, and Captains White Eyes and Pipe, Delawares, and Captains Pluggy and Big Apple Tree, Mohawks, were present. There is an allusion, by Pipe, to the "Standing Stone, near the Lower Shawanese towns"—now Lancaster, Fairfield county.

During Dunmore's campaign, Capt. William Crawford was sent with a detachment to destroy a Mingo town. He did so, making the prisoners afterwards taken to Pittsburgh.

VI.

(Page 263.)

FURTHER PARTICULARS OF CONNOLLY'S SCHEME.

It is mentioned in Sabine's American Loyalists, p. 225, that this noted character was born in Lancaster county, Pennsylvania, and was bred a physician. His Revolutionary movements are thus detailed in American Archives, Fourth Series:

In a letter to John Gibson, dated Portsmouth, August 19, 1775, Connolly urged the former to "avoid an over-zealous exertion of what is now ridiculously called patriotic spirit;" including a speech from Lord Dunmore to Captain White Eyes, which was immediately handed by Gibson to the Committee of West Augusta. (Vol. iii. p. 72.)

On the 5th November, 1775, Lord Dunmore commissioned John Connolly, Lieut. Col. of the Queen's Rangers. Afterwards Connolly was arrested and confined at Fredericktown, Md. On the 16th of December, he wrote to Captain Lernoult, at Detroit, and Captain Lord, on the Illinois, intimating that his intention had been to penetrate to Detroit, and thence conduct an expedition through Virginia, thus dividing the Southern from the Northern governments. These letters were sent by one Dr. Smyth.

This J. F. D. Smyth, in his "Tour," says: "It was proposed that I should pass through Pittsburgh, with despatches to Mr. McKee, the Indian Superintendent, and to some other friends of Government, then proceed down the river Ohio to the mouth of the Sciota, and from thence up that river, through the Shawanese, Delawares and Wyandots, and down Sandusky River to Sandusky Old Fort; from thence I was to cross Lake Erie, by the Rattlesnake Islands, to Detroit: while Lieut. Col. Connolly and a Mr. Cameron were to cross the Alleghany River, at the Kittaning, and proceed by the nearest and most direct route to Detroit. Here a very considerable force was to be collected from all the nearest posts in Canada, and transported, early in the spring, across the Lake Erie to Presque Isle, where I was to be employed during the winter, with a detachment of 200 men, in covering and conducting the building batteaus, and collecting provisions, in order to proceed by the French Creek, Venango, and the Alleghany River, to Pittsburgh." Here were to be Head Quarters, and thence the design was to strike through Virginia to the Potomac, or that scheme failing, to fall down the Ohio, and, reinforced by the garrison, artillery and stores from Fort Gage, at Kaskaskia on the Illinois, to proceed to the Gulf, and thence join Lord Dunmore at Norfolk. (Vol. iv. p. 615.)

Prior to the Revolution, Connolly, in connection with one John Campbell, claimed lands at the Falls of the Ohio (now Louisville), by grant of Lord Dunmore, laid out a town there, and invited settlers. The interests of Campbell in this locality were not forfeited.

Sabine states that Connolly was at Detroit in 1788, and that he and other disaffected persons held conferences with some of the prominent citizens of the West as to the seizure of New Orleans, and the control of the navigation of the Mississippi by force; but were baffled by the vigilance of Washington.

VII.

(Pages 267, 310.)

INCIDENTS IN THE LIFE OF JAMES DEAN.

James Dean, the founder of Westmoreland, New York, was no less active and influential than Samuel Kirkland, in preserving the Oneida tribe as the friends and allies of the Americans. His descendants are still living in Oneida county, upon a portion of the tract allotted to their ancestor by his Indian brethren.

In the Fourth Series of the American Archives (vol. ii. p. 152), a letter is preserved from Rev. Eleazer Wheelock to Gov. Trumbull of Connecticut, dated Dartmouth College, March 16, 1775, in which, after stating the high importance of conciliating the Indians, the following passage occurs:

"I have this spring sent Mr. James Dean (who, among other excellent qualifications, is a great master of the language of the Indians at *Caghnawaga*), as a missionary, to itinerate for a short time among the tribes in Canada. Ten of their sons at Durtmouth—eight descendants of English captives, one a son of the chief Sachem at St. Francis, and another, a brother to the youth who was lately elected and crowned Sachem at Caghnawaga.

"Mr. Dean was brought up and naturalized among the Six Nations; is a great master of their language, and much esteemed as an orator among them; and his influence among them I apprehend to be greater than any other man's, unless it be their present Superintendent, and is esteemed by the best judges to be a man of genius, learning, piety, and great prudence, —might induce the Six Nations to join the colonies—will return as soon as the Lake shall be clear of ice," &c.

Another letter (March 22) repeats the above, adding that Mr. Dean could also speak the Huron language—was early naturalized among the Indians, had great interest in their affections, and was the fittest man to be employed on behalf of the colonies among the Western and Northern Indians.

Gov. Trumbull, on the 17th of April, responded to these letters, that "the ability and influence of Mr. Dean to attach the Six Nations to the interest of the colonies, is considered an instance of Divine favor."

In a letter of Volkert P. Douw, to the President of Congress, dated Albany, Nov. 6, 1775, it is mentioned that Mr. Dean, who was sent by the Commissioners of Indian Affairs for the Northern Department, to the Six Nations, had returned with information that the Cayugas, Mohawks and Senecas had taken up the hatchet against the colonies. (Vol. iii. p. 1372.)

On the 21st of March, 1776, James Dean, in company with the Oneidas and a deputation from the seven tribes in Canada, set out from *Kanonwaro-*

haro to attend a meeting of the Six Nations, at their Central Council-House at Onondaga. They stopped at *Kanaghsorage*, a small village inhabited by the Onondagas and Tuscaroras, about sixteen miles west of Oneida. Here, where they remained four days, they heard that the Mohawks were determined to kill Dean. Little Abraham, a friendly Mohawk sachem, preceded the party of Oneidas, and dissuaded his countrymen from their purpose, sending back a message to that effect. When it was received, a council of Oneidas, Caughnawagas and Tuscaroras was held, and it was concluded best that Dean should go on with them.

The female governesses of the town, and those who were present from Oneida, hearing of this purpose, took the matter into their consideration, and about eight in the evening presented the following speech:

"*Brother:* We, the female governesses, take this opportunity to speak a word, and let you know our minds. In truth, our hearts have trembled and our eyes have not known sleep since you have been here, while we consider the danger that appears to us to threaten you at Onondaga, and the dreadful consequences that must ensue, should some fatal blow be given you. We desire you to consider well of these things, and to return back from this place."

To which the following answer was made:

"*Sisters, Female Governesses:* I sincerely thank you for what you have said, and the concern you appear to have for my safety; but, sisters, possess your minds in peace, and let it not offend you if I do not comply with your request. I am sent by the great men upon important business, and must proceed as far as directed."

Next morning, they started for Onondaga, but found, on approaching the village, that it was proposed to lodge the party, not altogether, but by two or three in a place. This looked suspicious, and they chose to encamp in a hemlock grove near by.

On the 28th, the council commenced and continued until the 3d of April. Various speeches were made, and a general disposition exhibited to observe neutrality between the English and the Americans. (Vol. v. p. 1079.)

Though not appurtenant to the foregoing note, still the reference on page 310, requires the insertion of the following communication, descriptive of the Shawanese towns on the Mad River and Upper Miami, now Logan county:

"House of Representatives,
"*Columbus*, April 20, 1854.

"Dear Sir: In respect to the Indian localities of Logan county, the most prominent was Wappatomica, two miles south of Zanesfield. My impression is, that it was a Wyandot town, or a common rendezvous for Wyandots, Shawanese and Mingoes—Wappatomica signifying the *capital* or *head* town. Perhaps the name, like that of Wakatomaka Creek, in Muskingum county, is of Shawanese origin. The village of Zanesfield, and the township of Zane, in the southeast corner of Logan county, are thus called from Isaac Zane, who was an adopted member of tne Wyandot tribe.

"About nine miles southeast from Wappatomica, and not far from King's Creek, near the line of Champaign county, was a Mingo village: and such probably was Solomon's Town, which was on the waters of Cherokee Man's Run, near the line between McArthur and Richland townships, and about nine miles northwest from Bellefontaine. It was named from a chief called Mohawk Solomon—a New York or Mingo Indian.

"The Shawanese towns were more numerous--the Wyandots and Mingoes being sojourners among the Shawanese. Lewistown, named from a Capt. Lewis, who was living as late as 1820, was as prominent as any other Shawanese village. Lewistown was situated four miles south of Solomon's Town, and about eight miles northwest from Bellefontaine. The Mackacheek towns were two in number—one on the west bank of Mad River, and not over three-quarters of a mile northeast from the present site of West Liberty, and the other about a mile east from the former village, including the farm of R. E. Runkle, and traversed by Mackacheek Creek, which runs southwestwardly into the Mad River. A mile and a half south of the village last described, was a mound—still visible on the farm of John Enoch—from the summit of which Simon Kenton was compelled, in 1778, to run the gauntlet to the Council House, at or near the village. The whole vicinity was an Indian settlement, but denser at the above points than elsewhere.

"Simon Kenton is buried about five miles northeast of Bellefontaine, in Jefferson township, on the east side of the road leading from Zanesfield to Big Spring, near the line of Hardin county—the old Indian trace to the Wyandot towns of the Sandusky. His grave is situated on a knoll, about a quarter of a mile from the spot where the closing years of his life—at least fifteen years—were passed. He died in 1836, and the impression produced by his appearance and conversation is among the most cherished recollections of my early life—so much so, that I have deemed it my duty, as a Representative of Logan county in the current Legislature, to submit a bill for the erection of a monument to his memory, as one of the most marked and noble characters in our annals.

"There is a tradition, that there was a Shawanese settlement on the creek, which rises within the limits of Bellefontaine, and flows westwardly until it falls into the Bokongahelas, the latter being a tributary of the Miami. This village was called Blue Jacket Town, probably from the chief of that name, but I cannot exactly identify its locality. It was doubtless in Lake township.

"The above are the impressions derived from my personal recollections, and the traditions of the first settlers. Perhaps prior to 1787, which I understand to be the period included in your volume, the localities and the inhabitants of these towns might have been different; and it is quite likely that the population, about this time of the Revolution, was more exclusively Shawanese. Yours, &c.,

"JOSEPH NEWELL.

"JAMES W. TAYLOR, Esq."

VIII.

(Page 332.)

NETAWATWES, AND OTHER DELAWARE CHIEFS.

Heckewelder says (Transactions of American Philosophical Society, vol. iv. p. 388) that Netawatwes had been a signer of a treaty held at Conestogo, near Lancaster, Pennsylvania, in 1718, and was then a young man, between twenty or thirty years of age. As an hereditary chief of the Turtle Tribe, he was intrusted with "all verbal speeches, with wampum, bead vouchers," &c., from the time of William Penn. He died at a great age—upwards of ninety. He was settled on the Cuyahoga, on his first arrival in Ohio, but in 1773 was on the Muskingum, at a point still called from him, Newcomerstown.

WHITE EYES or Coquethagechton (as Heckewelder writes his name) succeeded Netawatwes in 1776, or "at least accepted the appointment for a limited time, and until the young chief by lineal descent should be of proper age." (See Biography in Am. Phil. Trans., p. 391.) His character and career are sufficiently apparent from the text.

GELELEMEND or Killbuck, after the death of White Eyes in 1778, was installed as temporary chief during the minority of the heir of Netawatwes. He became a devoted adherent of the Americans, receiving the rank of colonel.

MACHENGIVE PUSHIS or Big Cat afterwards removed to the Auglaise, as appears from the interesting narrative of John Brickell, late of Franklin county, who was a captive, from 1791 to 1795, among the Delawares. During that time, he was adopted as a son by "Whingwy Pooshies or Big Cat." (See Brickell's Narrative in American Pioneer, vol. i. p. 46.) His description of the parting with his Indian protector, when the tribe was compelled to deliver their prisoners, is extremely touching—sufficiently so to warrant its quotation.

"On the breaking up of spring [in 1795] we all went up to Fort Defiance, and on arriving on the shore opposite we saluted the fort with a round of rifles, and they shot a cannon thirteen times. We then encamped on the spot. On the same day Whingwy Pooshies told me I must go over to the fort. The children hung around me crying, and asked me if I was going to leave them? I told them I did not know. When we got over to the fort, and were seated with the officers, Whingwy Pooshies told me to stand up, which I did; he then rose and addressed me in about these words: 'My son, there are men the same color with yourself. There may be some of your kin there, or your kin may be a great way off from you. You have lived a long time with us. I call on you to say if I have not been a father to you? if I have not used you as a father would use a son?' I said, 'You have used me as well as a father could use a son.' He said, 'I am glad you say so. You have lived long with me; you have hunted for me; but our treaty says you must be free. If you choose to go with the people of your own color, I have no right to say a word, but if you choose to stay with me your people have no right to speak. Now reflect on it and take your choice, and tell us as soon as you make up your mind.'

"I was silent a few minutes, in which time it seemed as if I thought of almost every thing. I thought of the children I had just left crying; I thought of the Indians I was attached to, and I thought of my people which I remembered; and this latter thought predominated, and I said, 'I will go with my kin.' The old man then said, 'I have raised you—I have learned you to hunt. You are a good hunter—you have been better to me than my own sons. I am now getting old and I cannot hunt. I thought you would be a support to my age. I leaned on you as on a staff. Now it is broken —you are going to leave me and I have no right to say a word, but I am ruined.' He then sank back in tears to his seat. I heartily joined him in his tears—parted with him, and have never seen nor heard of him since."

Heckewelder mentions another prominent Delaware, Tetepachksi, whose name will be readily identified at the subsequent treaties. In the Philosophical Transactions (vol. iv. p. 391), the Moravian biographer thus speaks of him: "Tetepachksi, also called by the whites the Glaze King, was for a number of years a counsellor of the Great Council of the Turtle Tribe at Goshacking (forks of the Muskingum); afterwards he became a chief of the Delawares, who resided on White River in Indiana. He was rather timorous, and easily prompted to become jealous or mistrustful, though he meant no harm to any body, and rather than make a mistake, would leave others to act in his stead. Yet harmless and innocent as he was, he was by the prophet brother of Tecumseh declared a *witch*, and condemned to die; in consequence of which sentence, his executioners took him to the distance of eight or ten miles from their village, and there tomahawked him, and then burnt his body on the piles.—See Heckewelder's Narrative, page 410." At a treaty with the United States, August 18, 1804, his name is written Tetabuxika.

Hopocan or Pipe appears seldom, except as narrated above. He signed the treaty of Jan. 9, 1789, at Fort Harmar, and is frequently mentioned in the journals of the Marietta settlers. He probably died before the Treaty of Greenville in 1795, as his signature does not appear.

Heckewelder speaks of Newalike and Nihmha, as chiefs of the Munsie tribe (of Delawares), at Minisink in Pennsylvania, afterwards on the Susquehanna, and finally at Sandusky.

IX.

(Page 376.)

LEWIS WETZEL, THE BORDERER.

We have been favored with the following communication from Hon. E. R. Eckley, of Carroll county; which presents some facts of the later history of this noted borderer, that are not generally known, besides vindicating his memory in respect to his Indian hostilities:

"J. W. Taylor, Esq.:

"Sir,—In compliance with your request, I send you such facts, in connection with the history and services of Lewis Wetzel, as are in my possession, or within my power to furnish. I do it with the more pleasure, because it may tend to wrest from oblivion the history of one who, in that stirring time in our frontier history, filled so conspicuous a place. The date of events, in the life of that distinguished man, are now perhaps beyond the reach of certainty. The date of facts contained in this letter, I cannot even approximate. They were given me by my venerable father, who, though cognizant to many of them, kept no record, and would not undertake to fix even the year. He, at the time Wetzel was in Louisiana, was engaged in the river trade, and was personally acquainted with him; visited him while in prison at New Orleans, also after he was released from prison, while he lived with a relative near Natchez.

"Lewis Wetzel was supposed to have been born in the vicinity of what is now the city of Wheeling; at all events, his father occupied a small farm at that place when he was a small boy. Of his family I am unable to learn much, except that they were comparatively poor, which circumstance may account for the dangers and privations of a frontier life, to which he and his family were exposed. Wetzel had a sister and brother (John or Jack) who, with him, performed many daring adventures and exploits in the spy department, at that day so important to the defence of the frontier. In those days, every frontiersman man was, more or less, a hero; every frontiersman was compelled to defend himself and family against marauding savages, who were constantly committing depredations upon the property and persons of themselves and families. Such circumstances, and the services they were compelled to perform, inured them to dangers and deeds of daring, that make up that record of thrilling events of which our past history is so fruitful. In the midst of these stormy scenes, Wetzel's early impressions were formed; and doubtless from the fireside, on hearing tales of daring adventure and personal courage, he conceived the idea of arresting the savage on his war-path, and shivering from his hand the deadly weapon, while aimed at the head of helpless females and unsuspecting children.

"The first feat in the life of Wetzel, worthy of notice, that has been preserved, happened when he was about sixteen years of age. A party of Indians had crossed the river and stolen off several horses, and were making their way back to their towns on the Muskingum, and further west. A party of the hardy pioneers were soon assembled and enroute to recapture the property and bring the aggressors to justice. In the pursuit the party passed the farm of the elder Wetzel. Lewis was engaged in cultivating a crop of growing corn. They solicited him to join their party. He had been forbidden by his father to leave his home, but the adventure was too great a temptation for the spirit of young Wetzel, and he was easily persuaded to join them. He accordingly took from the plow a favorite mare of his father's and started in pursuit of the fugitive Indians. They had not proceeded far until they came upon the enemy, who were carelessly loitering about their camp, apparently off their guard, and probably thinking they had safety on their side, as the Ohio River was between them and the neighborhoods upon which they lately committed depredations. The stolen horses were spanceled and grazing at a short distance. They were easily surprised and fled, leaving the horses, which were recovered. The party of settlers having accomplished their purpose, prepared to return, but their horses were jaded and hungry, and they agreed that the horses they had rode should be turned out to grass, three of their number left to bring them after they had refreshed a short time, and the balance of the company, with the recaptured horses, should commence their retreat back to the settlements. They had not proceeded many miles until they were overtaken by the three of their number they had left behind to bring their horses, who informed them that soon after their departure they were surprised by the savages, who made their appearance between them and their horses, leaving them no alternative in saving their lives but to abandon everything and escape by flight, which they succeeded in doing, overtook their companions, but left their horses in the hands of the enemy. A parley was called, and the hasty determination was soon formed to continue their way homeward and leave the Indians in possession of the horses. To this determination Wetzel earnestly remonstrated. The loss of a favorite animal improperly taken from home, the disappointment of his first adventure, and the wrath of a father whom he both feared and loved, drove him almost to desperation. He protested he would never return alive to his father without the mare—swore he preferred the mare without his scalp, to his scalp without the mare, and urged the company to return and retake the horses. In this he was overruled in council, against which decision he uttered bitter anathemas. He next proposed that if only one man would join him he would return and contest the right to the horses, but no *one* would volunteer. He then *swore* that he would go alone, that the mare he must and would have, and was actually upon the point of starting, when two others, who had been active in inducing him to go, reluctantly agreed to accompany him. The three left their companions on their way to their homes, and started back in search of their horses. They soon reached the camp and found the Indians engaged at their meals with the horses safely secured at a short distance. The Indians were three in number, equal only to themselves, but the companions of Wetzel hesitated and desired to return, but Wetzel counted chances and insisted upon success. The plan of attack was soon agreed upon. They were to advance in single file, Wetzel in front, until they passed two trees, behind which his companions were to ambush. When he reached the third it was the signal for an attack. Wetzel reached his tree, and discovered that the Indians had also treed; but in looking around for his companions he found they had retreated and were nearly out of sight, at the top of their speed. His condition was really critical; to come out in an open field was almost certain death. His only hope was in stratagem. He therefore placed his hat on the end of his ramrod and gently pushed it partly from behind the tree. This was no sooner done than all the Indians fired at it. The hat was literally riddled, and Wetzel, still secure behind the tree, quick but cautiously dropped it to the ground. At this, the Indians believing they had killed their adversary, all sprung from their ambush and rushed towards him. Wetzel now held the trump, and taking advantage of the enemy, whose guns were empty, he left his tree, and firing on the foremost brought him to the ground, and then, with the fleetness of the wind, ran from the scene, and was followed by the survivors. Wetzel loaded as he ran, and wheeling quickly, fired into the breast of the foremost savage; again ran, loaded and fired on the last of the Indians, just as he was in the act of hurling his tomahawk at the head of Wetzel. His fire was successful, and the whole three were thus dead on the plain. Wetzel secured the evidence of his victory, obtained the horses and overtook his companions before they had stopped for the night. The exhibition of the bloody trophies of victory, and the lost horses safely recaptured, all in the hands of their captor, a boy but sixteen years of age, of course from that time made him a hero, one whose counsel was sought by men of riper years and more experience.

"The news of this daring adventure very soon made him the man of the frontier, eminently qualified as a leader in the spy department, in which position he and his brother John rendered such important services to the then western country, until Lewis, feeling himself deeply wounded by the treatment of that country for which he had so often risked his life, and for which he had rendered such great services, left the northern frontier for the Spanish province of Louisiana. The many hazards and adventures of which Lewis Wetzel was the hero, during his service in the spy department, would fill a volume, and could not be abridged, had I the material arranged into an ordinary letter. And as most, if not all of his western adventures, have been collected and given to the public by others better able to perform the task, and as my object is only to embody the outlines of the life of one of the daring spirits of the early pioneers of our own land, I pass over all that interesting, and to the frontiers valuable, part of his service.

"About the year 1790, Wetzel being on what was then called a scout, in what is now the State of Ohio, killed and scalped an Indian warrior on the Tuscarawas River, who, it was claimed by recent negotiations at Fort Harmar, was protected from harm from our spies and others employed in our defence. The Indians made bitter complaints to the commandants of our forts and garrisons, and insisted that unless Wetzel was punished they would again turn loose their horde of warriors. Col. Harmar could not do otherwise than offer a reward for the arrest of Wetzel. He accordingly offered, with great reluctance, a reward of two hundred dollars for the arrest of a man who had spent his life in the woods, standing as a bulwark between the deadly weapon of the barbarian and the struggling settlements of the Christian frontier; a name that was dear to every man, woman and child on the whole line of western settlements; one whose deeds of daring and adventure were taught to the children in their earliest lispings, and whose achievements were to fill the brightest page in the history of their early and desperate struggles. To place a price on a man as a criminal, who had made such sacrifices, of course met with bitter denunciation from all who could appreciate his eminent services: particularly so when they considered Wetzel guilty of nothing criminal whatever. True, he had captured a warrior in the woods, at a time and under circumstances when he (Wetzel) had good reason to believe the warrior was attempting his life; he was out-generaled by this hero of the forest and himself made a victim to his unconquered adversary,—an Indian that belonged to a warlike tribe; a tribe that had committed numerous murders and other depredations upon the very settlement in which lived the aged father and mother of the daring Wetzel. Besides all this, there was good reason to believe this identical warrior had been concerned in the very outrages alluded to. That any white man would attempt to arrest him, no one believed, and that any red man could, the friends of Wetzel did not fear. To avoid the constant clamor of the Indians for the arrest of Wetzel, he was advised by his friends to leave for a time, until the feeling on the part of the Indians should subside. Wetzel accordingly, for the last time, left the humble frontier abode of his venerable parents, and the place where he had played many a tragic scene where life was the stake; not, however, to arrest the merciless savage on his mission of blood, but to avoid the action of his own country which he had so faithfully served. He proceeded to the vicinity of Cincinnati, where he engaged in the service of the country as a spy, going where commanded, and returning when his mission was performed. He was often heard to say that no one would ever attempt his arrest because he had killed an Indian, but that the love of the reward might find some one heartless enough to, Judas like, sacrifice him for the money. Against the danger of arrest he doubtless felt secure. In his security, however, he was not safe. While he was enjoying the confidence and receiving the admiration of all the people of the west, Col. Parks was ordered to remove with two hundred men from Louisville to Fort Pitt. He stopped at Fort Washington (Cincinnati) with his keel-boats, in which he was transporting his troops. Wetzel was there, and from a regard for his duty, or some other cause, he ordered a file of his men to arrest Wetzel, which, after a violent opposition, they succeeded in doing, and he was placed in irons and dragged on board the boats. The people of Cincinnati made every exertion to procure his release. But to the efforts and appeals of the people in behalf of Wetzel, Col. Parks was immovable, and with a stoic coldness, informed them that Wetzel must be delivered to the officers of justice. Finding that nothing but force could procure his release, they, during the night, rallied the entire force on both sides of the river, and at the dawn of day next morning, five hundred strong men, under arms, marched to the boats and peremptorily demanded the release of Wetzel. Parks at first refused, but he was informed by their leader that if he did not deliver Wetzel in ten minutes he would sink his boats and take Wetzel by force. The ferocious spirit of the people, and the determination of their leader, compelled Parks to knock the irons off of Wetzel and surrender him to his friends.

"At this conduct of his countrymen, Wetzel was deeply mortified, and to avoid what he called the persecution of his own people, he declared his determination of immediately leaving the country for ever. Accordingly he left, the first opportunity, for the Spanish province of Louisiana. He stopped at Natchez, and at once engaged in his favorite business of frontier service, and soon became a general favorite with the settlers. In his new home, Wetzel appeared to have every thing to make it comfortable, and the change from his native to his adopted country appeared a happy one. But the smooth current of his life was doomed soon again to be ruffled, and his meridian sun again obscured by the clouds of trouble.

Wetzel was an unlettered man, and his whole life proved his character of unbending integrity. Placing no value upon money, none believed that he would do a dishonest act for mere gain. But notwithstanding his character and the circumstances of his life, he was arrested for counterfeiting the coin of the king.

"A man by the name of Piatt, from near Pittsburgh, who had for some cause sought refuge in Louisiana, was the accuser of poor Wetzel. Whether he was actuated by motives of malice, self-protection, or other cause, is, and perhaps ever will be, locked up in the secrets of the past. That an unlettered man, like Wetzel, could counterfeit, was he ever so willing, was preposterous. Besides, all who knew him were confident he would not do it if he could. But, upon the testimony of Piatt, he was convicted and sentenced to the calaboose at New Orleans.

"The news of Wetzel's misfortunes soon reached the upper country, and the first office of the western boatman, on reaching New Orleans, was to visit the prison of poor Wetzel and offer whatever was in his power for his comfort and relief. Petition after petition was sent to the Spanish Governor, praying for his release, but without effect. Col. Richard Brown, and the Hon. F. McGuire, both distinguished men at that day in Western Virginia, upon their own personal responsibility, at different times, offered the Governor two thousand dollars for his release. The Governor, placing it on the grounds of having no discretion in the matter, declined a compliance with their request; expressing, at the same time, a desire for Wetzel's relief, but refusing a pardon, on the grounds that his sovereign required the judgments of his majesty's courts executed to the letter.

"In that dark and loathsome prison, denied of all the comforts of life, even the light of heaven, did the poor sufferer drag out four years and a half of his mortal existence, with no other inmates than the meanest malefactors that were ever incarcerated for crime. Hope of obtaining his liberty had fled. His friends that had previously made such disinterested and noble efforts for his relief, had long since given over in despair, or regarded him as having fell a victim to his confinement, and by that unwelcome monster been released from his chains. Wetzel regarded himself, for the balance of his days, as a permanent fixture to the damp floor of his prison, and almost ceased to pray for liberty.

"While Wetzel was counting with fevered anxiety every day as it passed, as bringing him nearer the day of his deliverance from his miserable and loathsome dungeon 'to that house not made with hands,' the light of hope suddenly broke upon the solitude of his cell. Previous to this time, there existed in Western Pennsylvania, what was familiarly known as the Whisky Insurrection. One of the leaders of the insurgents was General Bradford of Pennsylvania, who was prosecuted for resisting the execution of the laws, and to avoid which he fled to Louisiana. Bradford was a man of education, talents, and fine address. He claimed the protection of the Spanish Governor, and soon became a favorite at his court. He soon learned the condition of Wetzel. He knew his former character and great services, and deeply sympathized with him in his misfortunes. Bradford immediately set himself about procuring the release of his old friend and countryman from that loathsome prison house in which he was dying by the inch. He approached the Governor in person, in behalf of Wetzel. He represented his services, his sufferings, and former good character, and soon found that the kind nature of the Governor, too, sympathized with the unfortunate prisoner in his sufferings. Bradford's hopes of success soon ripened into reality, and through him Wetzel once more enjoyed his liberty.

"In those days a story was current, concerning the manner in which Bradford effected the release of Wetzel, that savored strongly of the marvelous. The Governor, it was said, through fear of his sovereign, refused to exercise the pardoning power, although he very much desired that Wetzel should be discharged from imprisonment; and to supply the want of unbiassed power, resort was had to stratagem. The plan was briefly this: Wetzel was to feign himself sick; a report was to be put in circulation that he had died; a coffin-maker and undertaker was to be called on. His body was coffined and carried out of the prison and delivered to his friends, amongst whom was Bradford, and by them carried out of the city, where the *dead man* was taken alive out of the coffin and it sunk in the Mississippi. Wetzel was conveyed to Natchez, and was taken into the family of a relative of his, who was a wealthy planter near that place. Whether this story was true or not, could make but little difference to the unfortunate victim of circumstances; but the facts, about which there is no dispute, give it the color of probability. Certain it was that Wetzel was taken from prison to Natchez, where he lived for a number of years in the family of a Mr. Sicks, a cousin of Wetzel's. His long confinement in the damp and unhealthy prison had undermined his constitution and rendered him unfit for his former vocation of frontier service. From long inactivity, his limbs had grown stiff and clumsy; his stalwart arms had lost their strength, and his whole system lacked the physical power to qualify him for the woods. He was kindly treated and cared for by his friends, working when it suited him and playing when he pleased.

"After the purchase of Louisiana by the United States, Sicks removed on to the Brasos, in Texas, taking Wetzel with him. He remained a member of the family of his friend for a number of years, gradually yielding to the encroachments of disease, until his powerful form could resist no longer, when he died. On the banks of the Brasos, in the yet far distant wilderness, sleeps, without mark or monument, the ashes of the intrepid scout, the fearless and gallant spy. Who can listen to the winds as they moan among the branches that overhang his grave, and reflect upon the services, persecutions and sufferings of the fearless spirit that once animated the entombed remains, without shedding a tear of sympathy for the name of LEWIS WETZEL?

"Wetzel never could forget the wrongs he had suffered from his own country and countrymen. Piatt, in particular, he denounced as a villain. Inasmuch as he (Piatt) is one of the prominent characters mentioned in this letter, a brief notice of his career and end might, by the curious, be desirable.

"After the conviction of Wetzel, Piatt was arrested for killing an Indian on Red River, was tried, convicted, and placed in the calaboose at New Orleans, where he remained nine years, and was then taken out and hung.

"I have thus given you all the facts within my knowledge, not already before the public. I regret my inability to fix dates, but I have given certain historical events, about the date of which there is no dispute, from which to infer the date of the events mentioned in the letter.

"Yours, truly, &c.,

"E. R. ECKLEY."

X

(Page 411.)

SURRENDER OF THE MORAVIAN TRACT TO THE UNITED STATES.

Articles of agreement made and concluded at Gnadenhütten, in the county of Tuscarawas, and State of Ohio, between Lewis Cass, on the one part, of the United States, being thereto specially authorized by the President of the United States, and Lewis D. Schweinitz, on the part of the Society of the United Brethren for propagating the Gospel among the Heathen, being thereto specially authorized by the said Society.

I. The said Society agree to retrocede to the United States the three tracts of land, lying on the Muskingum River, in the county of Tuscarawas, and State of Ohio, containing each four thousand acres; which said tracts of land were granted to the said Society by patent from the United States, on the 24th day of February, 1798, for certain purposes therein expressed, which will more fully appear by reference to the said patent, and to the act of Congress of June 1st, 1796, entitled "An act regulating the grants of land appropriated for military services, and for the Society of the United Brethren for propagating the Gospel among the Heathen," by authority of which act, said patent was issued.

The conveyance required by this article shall be made by a good and sufficient deed, at the expense of the said Society, as soon after the ratification of this agreement as possible; which deed shall convey to the United States all the right and title vested in the said Society by the patent and act of Congress aforesaid.

II. The schedule hereunto annexed, contains a descriptive list of all the leases which have been granted by said Society, together with the number of the lots, and the quantity of acres granted to each person, the commencement and expiration of the lease, and the rent which each tenant is bound to pay. These leases, as soon as this agreement is ratified, shall, by a sufficient conveyance in law, be assigned by the said Society to the United States, after which the rights and duties created by the said leases shall be vested in, and performed by the United States.

III. Whereas, by the documents which accompanied the President's message to the Senate, of December 9th, 1822, it appears that the sum of $43,356 was actually expended by the said Society upon the objects connected with the trust created by the acceptance of the said patent, to the 21st of August, 1822, and that the whole receipts from the said land were $9,998.58¼ cents, leaving a balance due to the said Society of $32,587.50¾ cents, of which sum $15,840.10¼ cents were actually expended in procuring the title of the said land, and in surveying the same (the repayment of which, amounting now, with the interest, to $2,596.13 cents, was guarantied by the ordinance of Congress, of September 3d, 1788), and in the settlement at an early period of these remote tracts, being more than seventy miles distant from the nearest white settlement, in cutting roads, building temporary mills, and making other improvements, which have greatly added to the value of the said lands, all which will more fully appear by a reference to the said documents; and, whereas, the committee of the Senate, to whom the said documents were referred, state that "it appears satisfactorily to the committee, that the Society, ever since they assumed the trust, have, under circumstances of great difficulty and embarrassment, exerted their best endeavors to effect the great and benevolent purposes of civilizing, improving, and protecting the Indians thus placed under their charge, and have, with persevering industry, care, and fidelity, performed the duty and trust reposed in them by Congress;" and, whereas, by an account this day exhibited by the treasurer of said Society, it appears that the said three tracts of land are actually holden for the payment of a debt of $6,654.25 cents, being part of the said sum of $15,840.10¼ cents, expended as aforesaid: Now, therefore, it is reasonable, and it is hereby agreed, that the sum of six thousand six hundred and fifty-four dollars and twenty-five cents, shall be paid by the United States to the said Society, out of the first proceeds of the sales of the said land, in full consideration of the retrocession hereby made, and of all the expenses which the said Society have incurred in the execution of the trust aforesaid, in relation to the said land.

IV. It is also agreed that ten acres of ground, including the church, called Beersheba, and the grave yard, on the Gnadenhütten tract; and, also, the church lot, parsonage houses, and grave yard in the town of Gnadenhütten; the house and lot occupied by John G. Demuth; the house and lot occupied by David Peter, both which lots are about five rods in front by sixteen rods in depth; and the house and lot occupied by Frederick Dell, which lot does not exceed two acres; and, also, the Missionary house and grave yard at Goshen; shall be conveyed, by the United States, in perpetuity to the said Society, free from any condition or limitation whatever.

V. Whereas, John Andreas, Neigaman, Jacob Winsch, and Catharine Tschudy, have erected houses in the town of Gnadenhütten upon lots of five by fifteen rods, under leases from the said Society, conditioned for the payment, the two former of the annual rent of $1.65 cents each; and the two latter of $3.60 cents each, with an understanding that the said lessees should hold the said lots, as long as they complied with the conditions of the lease, and should also be allowed the privilege of selling the same at their option; it is therefore agreed, that the said John Andreas, John Neigaman, Jacob Winsch, and Catharine Tschudy, shall be allowed a preëmption right to the said lots, to be exercised in such manner as may be determined by the United States.

VI. Five of the leases, yet unexpired, to wit: those to Isaac Simmers, Jesse Walton, Barzillai Walton, and Boaz Walton, on the Gnadenhütten tract, and to Jesse Hill, on the Salem tract, contain clauses for the payment of such sums, as may be awarded to them in the mode pointed out by the said leases, for certain improvements upon the tracts leased to them. It is therefore agreed, that a sum not exceeding one thousand eight hundred dollars shall be paid, by the United States, out of the proceeds of the said land, should that amount be awarded to the said persons. But should the amount awarded to them fall short of them, then the United States shall be held to pay only the amount actually awarded. Joseph Rhoads having leased a lot for the term of thirty-three years, from the 1st of April, 1821, and having advanced to the said Society the consideration therefor, amounting to $215.25 cents, under an agreement that the same, at the expiration of the lease, shall be refunded to the said Rhoads, without interest, the said Society agree to procure a surrender to the United States of the said lease within the term of four years, and to save the United States harmless from the effect of any stipulation in the said lease.

VII. It is expressly understood and declared, that this agreement, and every part thereof, is to be null and void, unless the assent of those persons can be obtained, for whose benefit the trust specified in the said act of

Congress, was created, and who are in the said patent declared to be the "Christian Indians who were formerly settled there, or the remains of that Society, including Killbuck and his descendants, and the nephew and descendants of the late Captain White Eyes, Delaware Chiefs," or such persons as are now entitled to the benefits of the trust. It being the intention of the parties hereunto that no responsibility shall be incurred by the said Society in consequence of the retrocession herein provided for. The motives of the Society being to divest themselves of a trust burdensome to them and useless to the Indians, that their funds devoted to charitable purposes may be applied where there is a prospect that they will produce some permanent advantage.

VIII. This agreement, after the same shall be ratified by the United States, and by the said Society, and after the assent aforesaid shall be obtained, shall be obligatory on the parties hereunto.

LEWIS CASS,
LEWIS D. DE SCHWEINITZ.

GNADENHUTTEN, AUGUST 4th, 1823.

I do hereby certify that the above is a true copy of the original.

JACOB KUMMER,
Secretary of the Society.

Whereas, at a stated annual meeting of the Society of United Brethren for promulgating the Gospel among the Heathen, held at Bethlehem, on the twenty-sixth day of September, in the year of our Lord one thousand eight hundred and twenty-three, agreeable to adjournment, duly notified to the members of said Society by the President and Directors thereof, an agreement made and entered into on the fourth day of August last, at Gnadenhütten, Tuscarawas county, State of Ohio, between Lewis D. de Schweinitz, as Agent of said Society, thereunto specially authorized by said Society, and Lewis Cass, as Agent of the United States, thereunto specially authorized by the President of the United States, whereof the foregoing is a certified copy was submitted to the said Society for consideration and ratification, whereupon the same was by a unanimous vote of said Society duly accepted, confirmed, and ratified. Now, therefore, we, the President and Secretary of the said Society, do, by these presents, certify that the said agreement, and each and every article thereof, is hereby, on the part of said Society, duly adopted, confirmed, and ratified.

In testimony whereof, we, the President and Secretary of the Society, have hereunto signed our names, and affixed the Seal of the Society this 26th day of September, in the year of our Lord, 1823.

[L. S.]

C. G. HUEFFEL, EP. U. FRR.
President United Brethren's Society for propagating the Gospel.

JACOB KUMMER,
Secretary of the Society.

Articles of agreement, made this eight day of November, in the year of our Lord one thousand eight hundred and twenty-three, between Lewis Cass, Commissioner on the part of the United States, and Zacharias, or Kootalees, John Henry, or Killbuck, Charles Henry, or Killbuck, Francis Henry or Killbuck, John Peter, Tobias, John Jacob, and Matthias, or Koolotshatshees, being the descendants and representatives of the Christian Indians, who were formerly settled upon three tracts of land, lying on both sides of the Muskingum River, in the State of Ohio, containing four thousand acres each, which were granted by patent from the United States, dated February twenty-fourth, seventeen hundred and ninety-eight, in pursuance of the act of Congress of June first, seventeen hundred and ninety-six, entitled "An act regulating the grants of land appropriated for military services, and for the Society of the United Brethren for propagating the Gospel among the Heathen," to the said Society for the use of the said Christian Indians, or the remains of that society, including Killbuck and his descendants, and the nephew and descendants of the late Captain White Eyes, Delaware Chiefs.

Article I. The descendants and representatives aforesaid, for themselves and for the society of the Christian Indians aforesaid, do hereby declare their full assent to the agreement concluded at Gnadenhütten, in the State of Ohio, on the fourth day of August, one thousand eight hundred and twenty-three, between Lewis Cass, Commissioner on the part of the United States, and Lewis D. de Schweinitz, Agent for the Society of United Brethren aforesaid.

Article II. The said descendants and representatives do for themselves, and for the Christian Society of Indians aforesaid, forever cede to the United States all right and interest in and to the tracts of land before described, the use of which was granted to them by the patent and act of Congress aforesaid.

Article III. The United States agree to pay to the United Christian Society of Indians, an annuity of four hundred dollars, which annuity shall commence as soon as a sum is received from the sale of the said lands sufficient as a principal stock to produce the amount of four hundred dollars, at an interest of six per centum per annum. But the proceeds of the sales of the lands are to be applied to the sums secured to be paid to the Society of United Brethren, and to the lessees described in the sixth article of agreement, executed at Gnadenhütten aforesaid, before the creation of the principal stock provided for in this agreement, and the annuity of four hundred dollars shall continue so long as the said Society of Christian Indians shall occupy their present residence.

Article IV. It is further agreed, that, should the said Society of Christian Indians be desirous of removing from their present residence, the United States will secure to them a reservation, containing not less than twenty-four thousand acres of land, to be held by them upon the usual condition of Indian reservations, so long as they shall live thereon; and when the said Christian Society shall remove to the said reservation, then the annuity herein granted shall cease.

ARTICLE V. This agreement shall be obligatory upon the parties, when the same shall be ratified by the United States.

Done at Detroit, in the Territory of Michigan, the day and year aforesaid.

LEWIS CASS,
ZACHARIAS, or KOOTALEES, his x mark,
JOHN HENRY,
CHARLES HENRY, or KILLBUCK, his x mark,
FRANCIS HENRY, or KILLBUCK, his x mark,
JOHN PETER, his x mark,
TOBIAS, his x mark,
JOHN JACOB, his x mark,
MATTHIAS, or KOOLOTSHASKEES, his x mark.

In presence of

R. S. FORSYTH,
ADAM AAMAN,
HENRY S. COLES.

The contract or articles of agreement entered into on the 8th day of November, 1823, between Governor Cass, and the Representatives of the Christian Indians, for the tracts of land specified in the agreement, and on the conditions therein contained, is approved.

JAMES MONROE.

WASHINGTON, FEBRUARY 10, 1824.

NOTE.—The deed of retrocession, in pursuance of the foregoing articles, was executed 1st April, 1824, and is on file in the General Land Office.

XI.

(Page 453.)

BOCKENGEHELAS, THE WAR-CHIEF OF THE DELAWARES.

The name of this noted chief is written Bukongehelas, by Judge Burnet (Notes p. 68), and is still preserved to designate a small tributary of the Great Miami, in Logan county.

Our opinion that he is the same personage who was prominent in Western Pennsylvania during the French and English war, as Shingess, is sustained by the fact that Heckewelder, in his biographies of the prominent Delawares of Pennsylvania and Ohio, omits altogether to mention Shingess (although intimately acquainted with him at Tuscarora, in 1764), but speaks of "Buckengilla, so called by the white people," or Pachgantschihillas, as the name is written in the Moravian Narrative. This adds probability to the proposition that they were the same individual. (Am. Phil. Trans vol. iv. p. 391.)

We first hear of Shingess in 1753. Washington then crossed the Alleghanies on his well known mission to the western tribes, and in his diary, after describing the forks of the Ohio, near Pittsburgh, he says: "About two miles from this, on the south-east side of the river, at the place where the Ohio company intended to erect a fort, lives Shingess, king of the Delawares." Washington called upon him to invite him to council at the Logstown. Shingess at first attended, but afterwards made his wife's sickness an excuse for absence. He was probably in the French interest.

In 1755, Shingess was so active in the border war, that the Governor of Pennsylvania offered a reward of seven hundred dollars for his head, and that of a Captain Jacobs. In Gordon's Pennsylvania (Appendix, p. 618), several of the expeditions led by Shingess are detailed, and it is incidentally mentioned that a prisoner, one John Craig, was adopted by him as a son.

During the French and English war, when the Governor of Pennsylvania sent C. F. Post to negotiate with the Ohio tribes, mention is often made in his journal of Shingess, and uniformly to his advantage. On the first mission, August 28, 1758, Post writes: "We set out from Sawcunk, in company with twenty, for Kushcushkee. On the road, Shingess addressed himself to me, and asked if I did not think that if he came to the English they would hang him, as they had offered a great reward for his head. I told him that was a great while ago, 'twas all forgotten and wiped away now." Post dined with Shingess on the 29th, when the latter observed, that although the English had offered a great reward for his head, yet he had never thought to revenge himself, but was always very kind to such prisoners as were brought in, and that he would do all in his power to bring about a peace, and wished he could be sure the English were in earnest for peace also. Heckewelder says of Shingess, that he was "the greatest Delaware warrior of his time," and that were his war exploits on record, they would form an interesting document, though a shocking one. Mr. Heckewelder gives him a good character, and adds (Hist. Ind. Nations, p. 264): "Passing one day with him, in the summer of 1762, [this was at Tuscarora, on the Muskingum, during Post and Heckewelder's unsuccessful mission, ante p. 187,] near by where his two prisoner boys (about twelve years of age) were amusing themselves with his own boys, and he observing me looking that way, inquired what I was looking at. On my replying that I was looking at his prisoners, he said, 'When I first took them, they *were* such, but they are now *my* children; eat their victuals out of the *same* bowl!' which was saying as much as that they, in all respects, were on an equal footing with his own children — alike dear to him." Though of small stature, Heckewelder observes, Shingess had a great mind.

In a narrative of Hugh Gibson's captivity among the Delaware Indians (Transactions Mass. Hist. Soc., 3d Series, vol. vi. p. 146,) he mentions the chief as living in 1757, at the mouth of Big Beaver, where Gibson "remained, dwelling in king Shingess' tent, until autumn." Gibson states that "about the middle of October, 1758, he was taken to Kus-ko-ra-vis," (Tuscarawas) the western branch of Muskingum. Custalogo, or King Beaver, who lived at this town of Tuscarora until 1764, was a brother of Shingess, and Heckewelder's Narrative describes the latter as dwelling there in 1762, when the ceremony of mourning for the loss of Shingess' wife occurred, as already described. *Ante*, chap. xiv. p. 193.

When, shortly before Col. Bouquet's expedition to the Muskingum, this Indian town was deserted, Shingess removed westward, and finally was seated on the Miami of the Lake, if our hypothesis that he was Bockengehelas is admitted.

His appearances by the latter designation, until 1787, are already detailed in the preceding pages. His salutation of General Clark, at the conference in 1786, at the mouth of the Great Miami, is usually quoted as follows: "I thank the Great Spirit for having this day brought together two such great warriors as Bokongahelas and General Clark." See Gen. Butler's narrative of the incident. *Ante*, p. 452.

In 1791, the government of the United States sent Hendrick Aupaumet, a friendly Mohican, or Stockbridge chief, as an envoy to the Indian villages on the Maumee. His narrative is published in vol. iii. of Pennsylvania Historical Transactions, page 61. He arrived on the 13th of July, at the "grand council fire, called the Rapids, about eighteen miles from the mouth of this Miamie River," where, he adds, were two Delaware towns, in one of which Captain Pipe resided. Here stood Col. McKee's house and stores for the Indians, at that time under the charge of Captain Elliott. Captain Hendricks delivered his messages, and long talks were interchanged—first with a party of Delawares, living sixty miles up the river, whose Sachem was named Tautquhgtheet—then with a deputation of Shawanese; and again with the Delawares, who were represented by "Hobakon, or Pipe-Sachem," and the "*head Heroe of the Delawares, named* PUCKONCHEHLUH." All parties then adjourned, to "meet at the Glaze or Forks—Naukhunwhnauk — where the Shawanese, Delawares, and part of the Miamis had towns." The journey was by water, commencing on the 24th. On the 27th, they "arrived at the first village of the Shawanese, and next day at the Forks, where were other two villages of Shawanny; also, one of the towns of Delawares, and the town of Wenuhtukowuk, and some outcast

Cherokees, and part of the Miamis, and about eight miles from this place the town of Big Cat—this town the last on the river."

On the 1st of August, while waiting the arrival of deputies from western tribes, Hendricks says: "At this time I went up to Big Cat's town with my brother; arrived there in the evening; went to the house of Pohquonnoppet, the Sachem—the Delawares having left word that we should give them notice of my coming. Early in the morning of the 2d instant, my uncle sent a runner to inform the chiefs that we were arrived, and will meet them in council. My business was to comfort Big Cat for the death of his brother, who died last spring. He was the chief Sachem of the Delawares; *also, Pukonchehluh for the death of his son.*" After an expression of condolence, Hendricks mentions that the "Head Heroe, whose name is Puckonchehluh, got up with the strings and belt," and made a suitable response. He alludes to him afterwards as "the great heroe." On the 28th of August, "Wunummon, or Vermillion, a Heroe" (probably Wingemund), appears on the stage, and although the Delaware chiefs seemed pacific in their dispositions, yet the outside pressure was too great for the Mohican envoy to accomplish any thing. McKee was active—an "alarming voice" from the Shawanese villages near the Ohio, announced new aggressions by the Long Knives—Simon Girty made his ill-omened appearance on the 29th, and finally there arrived some messengers from the wily Brant, to turn the scale against the Americans. The peace party went with the tide, "the head warrior, Puckonchehluh, in response to the message of the Five Nations, admitting that the Indians, who were one color, had one heart and one head, and that if one nation was struck all must feel it." Captain Hendricks was wholly unsuccessful, although, as he says, "endeavoring to do his best in the business of peace."

Drake, in his "Book of the Indians," thus notices an act of magnanimity by Bockengehelas in the following year, 1792: "Col. Hardin, Major Trueman, and several others, were sent, in May of that year, by Washington, with a flag of truce, to the Indian nations of the west, particularly the Maumee towns. They having arrived near the Indian town of Au Glaize, on the south-west branch of the Miami of the Lake, fell in with some Indians, who treated them well at first, and made many professions of friendship, but in the end took advantage of them, while off their guard, and murdered nearly all of them. The interpreter made his escape, after some time, and gave an account of the transaction. His name was William Smalley, and he had been some time before with the Indians, and had learned their manners and customs, which gave him some advantage in being able to save himself. He was at first conducted to Au Glaize, and soon after to 'Bukungahela, king of the Delawares,' by his captors. The chief told those that committed the murder, "he was very sorry they had killed the men; that instead of so doing, they should have brought them to the

Indian towns, and then, if what they had to say had not been liked, it would have been time enough to have killed them then. Nothing, he said, 'could justify them for putting them to death, as there was no chance for them to escape.' The truth was, they killed them to plunder their effects. Buckongahelas took Smally into his cabin and showed him great kindness; told him to stay there while he could go safely to his former Indian friends. (He having been adopted into an Indian family in place of one who had been killed in his former captivity.) While here with Buckongahelas, which was near a month, M. Smally said the chief would not permit him to go abroad alone, for fear, he said, that the young Indians would kill him."

Judge Burnet, in his Notes on the North-west Territory, page 68, gives a spirited description of a visit to "the venerable old Delaware chief, Bukongehelas, who was living at the Ottawa town, on the Auglaize," during which an Indian game of ball was ordered for the amusement of the white guests.

At the celebrated treaty of Greenville, August 3, 1795, "Bukongehelas, a Delaware chief," in his speech immediately before the council closed, remarked, proudly: "All who know me, know me to be a man and a warrior; and I now declare, that I will, for the future, be as strong and steady a friend to the United States as I have heretofore been an active enemy." An incident of the war then closed, with some further particulars of this remarkable character, are copied from Thatcher's Indian Biography, vol. ii. p. 177–9, as follows:

"He (Buckongahelas) was indeed the most distinguished warrior in the Indian confederacy, and as it was the British interest which had induced the Indians to commence, as well as to continue the war, Buckongahelas relied on their support and protection. This support had been given, so far as relates to provisions, arms, and ammunition; and in the celebrated engagement, on the 20th of August, 1794, which resulted in a complete victory by General Wayne over the combined hostile tribes, there were said to be two companies of British militia from Detroit on the side of the Indians. But the gates of Fort Mimms being shut against the retreating and wounded Indians, after the battle, opened the eyes of Buckongahelas, and he determined upon an immediate peace with the United States, and a total abandonment of the British. He assembled his tribe and embarked them in canoes, with the design of proceeding up the river, and sending a flag of truce to Fort Wayne. Upon approaching the British fort, he was requested to land, and he did so: 'What have you to say to me?' said he, addressing the officer of the day. It was replied, that the commanding officer wished to speak with him. 'Then he may come here,' was the reply. 'He will not do that,' said the officer, 'and you will not be suffered to pass the fort if you do not comply.' 'What shall prevent me?' said the intrepid chief. 'These,' said the officer, pointing to the cannon of the fort. 'I fear not your cannon,' replied the chief. 'After suffering the Americans to defile your spring, without daring to fire on them, you cannot expect to frighten Buckongahelas;' and he ordered the canoes to push off, and passed the fort.

"Never after this would he, like the other chiefs, visit the British, or receive presents from them. 'Had the great Buckingehelos lived,' says Mr. Dawson, alluding to these circumstances, 'he would not have suffered the schemes projected by the prophet (brother of Tecumseh) to be matured.' And the same writer states, that on his death-bed he earnestly advised his tribe to rely on the friendship of the United States, and desert the cause of the British. This was in 1804.

"In Dawson's Memoirs of Harrison, Buckongahelas is mentioned as being present at a council of the chiefs of various tribes, called at Fort Wayne in 1803, for the purpose of ratifying a negotiation for land, already proposed in a former one which met at Vincennes. The Governor carried his point, chiefly by the aid of an influential Miami chief, and by being '*boldly seconded in every proposition* by the Pottawatamies, who (as Mr. Dawson states), *were entirely devoted to the Governor.*' It is not our intention here to discuss at length the character of this transaction, which rather belongs to the general history of the period. How the Delaware chief and the Shawanees understood it, and how they expressed their sentiments, may be inferred from the following statement of Dawson:

"'When the transaction at the council of Vincennes was mentioned, it called forth all the wrath of the Delawares and the Shawanese. The respected Buckingehelos so far forgot himself that he interrupted the Governor, and declared with vehemence, that nothing that was done at Vincennes was binding upon the Indians; that the land which was there decided to be the property of the United States, belonged to the Delawares; and that he had then with him a chief who had been present at the transfer made by the Piankishaws to the Delawares of all the country between the Ohio and White rivers, more than thirty years before. The Shawanese went still further, and behaved with so much insolence that the Governor was obliged to tell them that they were undutiful and rebellious children, and that he would withdraw his protection from them until they had learnt to behave themselves with more propriety. These chiefs immediately left the council house in a body.'

"Subsequently the Shawanees submitted, though it does not appear that Buckongahelas set them the example: and thus, says the historian, the Governor overcame all opposition, and carried his point.

"It is said of Buckongahelas, that no Christian knight ever was more scrupulous in performing all his engagements. Indeed he had all the qualifications of a great hero—a perfect Indian independence—the independence of a noble nature, unperceived to itself, and unaffected to others."

XII.

(Page 459.)

SUBSEQUENT INDIAN TREATIES.

The following signatures of Ohio Indians to subsequent treaties are compiled for the sake of comparison by the curious. To the treaty at Greenville, Aug. 3, 1795, the following names, among many others, are attached:

Wyandots.—Tarhe, (or Crane), J. Williams, jr., Tey-yagh-taw, Ha-ro-en-yow, (or Half King's son), Te-haaw-to-rens, Aw-me-yee-ray, Staye-tah, Sha-tey-ya-ron-yah, (or Leather Lips), Daugh-shut-tay-ah, Sha-aw-run-the.

Shawanese.—Mis-qua-coo-na-caw, (or Red Pole), Cut-the-we-ka-saw, (or Black Hoof), Kay-se-wa-e-se-kah, Wey-tha-pa-mat-tha, Nia-wym-se-ka, Way-the-ah, (or Long Shanks), Wey-a-pier-sen-waw, (or Blue Jacket), Ne-que-taugh-aw, Hah-goo-see-kaw, (or Captain Reed.)

Delawares.—Teta-boksh-kee, (or Grand Glaise King), Le-man-tan-quis, (or Black King), Wa-bat-thoe, Magh-pi-way, (or Red Feather,) Kik-tha-we-nund, (or Anderson), Bu-kon-ge-he-las, Peikee-lund, Welle-baw-kee-lunds, Peikee-tele-mund, (or Thomas Adams), Kish-ko-pe-kund, (or Captain Buffalo), Ame-na-he-han, (or Captain Crow), Que-shawk-sey, (or George Washington), Wey-Win-gins, (or Billy Siscomb), Moses.

Ottawas.—Au-goosh-away, Kee-no-sha-meek, La Malice, Ma-chi-we-tah, Tho-wo-na-wa, Se-cah, Che-go-nicks-ka, (an Ottawa from Sandusky).

Delawares of Sandusky.—Haw-kin-pum-is-ka, Pey-a-mawk-sey, Reyn-tue-co, (of the Six Nations living at Sandusky).

Witnesses.—H. De Butts, first A. D. C., and Secretary to M. G. Wayne, Wm. H. Harrison, Aid-de-Camp to M. G. Wayne, T. Lewis, Aid-de-Camp to M. G. Wayne, James O'Hara, Quarter Master General, John Mills, Major of Infantry and Adjutant General, Caleb Swan, P. M. T. U. S., Geo. Demten, Lieut. Artillery, Vigo, P. fris La Fontaine, Ant. Lasselle, H. Laselle, Jn. Bean Bien, David Jones, Chaplain U. S. L., Lewis Beufait, R. Lachambre, Jas. Pepen, Baties Coutien, P. Navarre.

Sworn Interpreters.—Wm. Wells, Jacques Laselle, M. Morins, Bt. Sans Crainte, Christopher Miller, Robert Wilson, Abraham ⋈ Williams, Isaac ⋈ Zane.

June 7, 1803.—Gen. Harrison concluded a treaty defining the extent of the reservation at Vincennes by the treaty of Greenville. Among the Delawares signing it was "Bu-kon-ige-helas" and John Johnston, U. S. Factor, and Hendrick Aupaumet, chief of Muhhecon, were witnesses.

On the 18th of August, 1804, the Delawares ceded a tract of country between the Ohio and Wabash rivers, and below the tract ceded by the treaty of Fort Wayne and the road leading from Vincennes to the Falls of the Ohio. The Delawares signing it were, Teta Buxika, Bokongehelas, Alimee, or George White Eyes, Hocking Pomskann, Tomaquee, or the Bearer.

The United States recognized the right of the Delawares to the country bounded by the White River on the north, the Ohio on the south, the general boundary line running from the mouth of the Kentucky river on the east, and the tract ceded by the treaty of Fort Wayne on the west and south.

At the treaty of Fort Industry, on the Maumee river (July 4, 1805), relinquishing the title to the Western Reserve, the following Indians participated:

Ottawas.—Nekirk, or Little Otter, Kanachewan, or Eddy, Mechimenduck, or Big Bowl, Aubaway, Ogonse, Sawgamaw, Tusquagan, or McCarty, Tondawgame, or the Dog, Ashawet.

Shawanees.—Weyapurscawaw, or Blue Jacket, Cutheawcasaw, or Black Hoof, Anonaseehla, or Civil Man, Isaac Peters.

Wyandots.—Tarhee, or the Crane, Miere, or Walk in Water, Thateyyanayoh, or Leather Lips, Tschanendah, Tahunehawetee, or Adam Brown, Shawrunthie.

Munsee and Delaware.—Puchconsittond, Paahmelot, Pamoxet, or Armstrong, Pappellelond, or Beaver Hat.

XIII.

(Page 513.)

ORDINANCE OF 1787.

The following important document is transferred from Land Laws of the United States (Edition of 1828), page 356:

An Ordinance for the government of the Territory of the United States Northwest of the river Ohio.

Be it ordained by the United States in Congress Assembled, That the said territory, for the purposes of temporary government, be one district, subject, however, to be divided into two districts, as future circumstances may, in the opinion of Congress, make it expedient.

Be it ordained by the authority aforesaid, That the estates, both of resident and non-resident proprietors in the said territory, dying intestate, shall descend to, and be distributed among, their children, and the descendants of a deceased child, in equal parts; the descendants of a deceased child or grandchild to take the share of their deceased parent in equal parts among them:

And where there shall be no children or descendants, then in equal parts to the next of kin in equal degree; and, among collaterals, the children of a deceased brother or sister of the intestate shall have, in equal parts among them, their deceased parents' share; and there shall, in no case, be a distinction between kindred of the whole and half-blood; saving, in all cases, to the widow of the intestate her third part of the real estate for life, and one-third part of the personal estate; and this law, relative to descents and dower, shall remain in full force until altered by the legislature of the district. And, until the governor and judges shall adopt laws as hereinafter mentioned, estates in the said territory may be devised or bequeathed by wills in writing, signed and sealed by him or her, in whom the estate may be (being of full age,) and attested by three witnesses; and real estates may be conveyed by lease and release, or bargain and sale, signed, sealed, and delivered by the person, being of full age, in whom the estate may be, and attested by two witnesses, provided such wills be duly proved, and such conveyances be acknowledged, or the execution thereof duly proved, and be recorded within one year after proper magistrates, courts, and registers shall be appointed for that purpose; and personal property may be transferred by delivery; saving, however to the French and Canadian inhabitants, and other settlers of the Kaskaskias, St. Vincents, and the neighboring villages who have heretofore professed themselves citizens of Virginia, their laws and customs now in force among them, relative to the descent and conveyance of property.

Be it ordained by the authority aforesaid, That there shall be appointed, from time to time, by Congress, a governor, whose commission shall continue in force for the term of three years, unless sooner revoked by Congress; he shall reside in the district, and have a freehold estate therein in 1000 acres of land, while in the exercise of his office.

There shall be appointed, from time to time, by Congress, a secretary, whose commission shall continue in force for four years unless sooner revoked; he shall reside in the district, and have a freehold estate therein in 500 acres of land, while in the exercise of his office; it shall be his duty to keep and preserve the acts and laws passed by the legislature, and the public records of the district, and the proceedings of the governor in his Executive department; and transmit authentic copies of such acts and proceedings, every six months, to the secretary of Congress: There shall also be appointed a court to consist of three judges, any two of whom to form a court, who shall have a common law jurisdiction, and reside in the district, and have each therein a freehold estate in 500 acres of land while in the exercise of their offices; and their commissions shall continue in force during good behavior.

The governor and judges, or a majority of them, shall adopt and publish in the district such laws of the original States, criminal and civil, as may be necessary and best suited to the circumstances of the district, and report them to Congress from time to time; which laws shall be in force in the district until the organization of the General Assembly therein, unless disapproved of by Congress; but, afterwards, the legislature shall have authority to alter them as they shall think fit.

The governor, for the time being, shall be commander-in-chief of the militia, appoint and commission all officers in the same below the rank of general officers; all general officers shall be appointed and commissioned by Congress.

Previous to the organization of the General Assembly, the governor shall appoint such magistrates and other civil officers, in each county or township, as he shall find necessary for the preservation of the peace and good order in the same: After the General Assembly shall be organized, the powers and duties of the magistrates and other civil officers, shall be regulated and defined by the said assembly; but all magistrates and other civil officers, not herein otherwise directed, shall, during the continuance of this temporary government, be appointed by the governor.

For the prevention of crimes and injuries, the laws to be adopted or made shall have force in all parts of the district, and for the execution of process, criminal and civil, the governor shall make proper divisions thereof; and he shall proceed, from time to time, as circumstances may require, to lay out the parts of the district in which the Indian titles shall have been extinguished, into counties and townships, subject, however, to such alterations as may thereafter be made by the legislature.

So soon as there shall be 5000 free male inhabitants of full age in the district, upon giving proof thereof to the governor, they shall receive authority, with time and place, to elect representatives from their counties or townships to represent them in the General Assembly: *Provided*, That, for every 500 free male inhabitants, there shall be one representative, and so on progressively with the number of free male inhabitants, shall the right of representation increase, until the number of representatives shall amount to 25; after which, the number and proportion of representatives shall be regulated by the legislature: *Provided,* That no person be eligible or qualified to act as a representative unless he shall have been a citizen of one of the United States three years, and be a resident in the district, or unless he shall have resided in the district three years; and, in either case, shall likewise hold in his own right, in fee simple, 200 acres of land within the same: *Provided, also*, That a freehold in 50 acres of land in the district, having been a citizen of one of the States, and being resident in the district, or the like freehold and two years residence in the district, shall be necessary to qualify a man as an elector of a representative.

The representatives thus elected, shall serve for the term of two years; and, in case of the death of a representative, or removal from office, the governor shall issue a writ to the county or township for which he was a member, to elect another in his stead, to serve for the residue of the term.

The General Assembly, or Legislature, shall consist of the governor, legislative council, and a house of representatives. The legislative council shall consist of five members, to continue in office five years, unless sooner removed by Congress; any three of whom to be a quorum: and the members of the council shall be nominated and appointed in the following manner, to wit: As soon as representatives shall be elected, the governor shall appoint a time and place for them to meet together; and, when met, they shall nominate ten persons, residents in the district, and each possessed of a freehold in 500 acres of land, and return their names to Congress; five of whom Congress shall appoint and commission to serve as aforesaid; and, whenever a vacancy shall happen in the council, by death or removal from office, the house of representatives shall nominate two persons, qualified as aforesaid, for each vacancy, and return their names to Congress; one of whom Congress shall appoint and commission for the residue of the term. And every five years, four months at least before the expiration of the time of service of the members of council, the said house shall nominate ten persons, qualified as aforesaid, and return their names to Congress; five of whom Congress shall appoint and commission to serve as members of the council five years, unless sooner removed. And the governor, legislative council, and house of representatives, shall have authority to make laws in all cases, for the good government of the district, not repugnant to the principles and articles in this ordinance established and declared. And all bills, having passed by a majority in the house, and by a majority in the council, shall be referred to the governor for his assent; but no bill, or legislative act whatever, shall be of any force without his assent. The governor shall have power to convene, prorogue, and dissolve the General Assembly, when, in his opinion, it shall be expedient.

The governor, judges, legislative council, secretary, and such other officers as Congress shall appoint in the district, shall take an oath or affirmation of fidelity and of office; the governor before the president of Congress, and all other officers before the governor. As soon as a legislature shall be formed in the district, the council and house assembled in one room, shall have authority, by joint ballot, to elect a delegate to Congress, who shall have a seat in Congress, with a right of debating but not of voting during this temporary government.

And, for extending the fundamental principles of civil and religious liberty, which form the basis whereon these republics, their laws and constitutions are erected; to fix and establish those principles as the basis of all laws, constitutions and governments, which forever hereafter shall be formed in the said territory: to provide also for the establishment of States, and permanent government therein, and for their admission to a share in the federal councils on an equal footing with the original States, at as early periods as may be consistent with the general interest:

It is hereby ordained and declared by the authority aforesaid, That the following articles shall be considered as articles of compact between the *original States* and the *people and States* in the *said territory*, and forever remain unalterable, unless by common consent, to wit:

ART. 1st. No person, demeaning himself in a peaceable and orderly manner, shall ever be molested on account of his mode of worship or religious sentiments, in the said territory.

ART. 2d. The inhabitants of the said territory shall always be entitled to the benefits of the writ of *habeas corpus*, and of the trial by jury; of a proportionate representation of the people in the legislature; and of judicial proceedings according to the course of the common law. All persons shall be bailable, unless for capital offences, where the proof shall be evident or the presumption great. All fines shall be moderate; and no cruel or unusual punishments shall be inflicted. No man shall be deprived of his liberty or property, but by the judgment of his peers or the law of the land; and, should the public exigencies make it necessary, for the common preservation, to take any person's property, or to demand his particular services, full compensation shall be made for the same. And, in the just preservation of rights and property, it is understood and declared, that no law ought ever to be made, or have force in the said territory, that shall, in any manner whatever, interfere with or affect private contracts or engagements, *bona fide*, and without fraud, previously formed.

ART. 3d. Religion, morality, and knowledge, being necessary to good government and the happiness of mankind, schools and the means of education shall forever be encouraged. The utmost good faith shall always be observed towards the Indians; their lands and property shall never be taken from them without their consent; and, in their property, rights, and liberty, they shall never be invaded or disturbed, unless in just and lawful wars authorized by Congress; but laws founded in justice and humanity, shall, from time to time, be made for preventing wrongs being done to them, and for preserving peace and friendship with them.

ART. 4th. The said territory, and the States which may be formed therein, shall forever remain a part of this confederacy of the United States of America, subject to the Articles of Confederation, and to such alterations therein as shall be constitutionally made; and to all the acts and ordinances of the United States in Congress assembled, conformable thereto. The inhabitants and settlers in the said territory shall be subject to pay a part of the federal debts contracted or to be contracted, and a proportional part of the expenses of government, to be apportioned on them by Congress according to the same common rule and measure by which apportionments thereof shall be made on the other States; and the taxes, for paying their proportion, shall be laid and levied by the authority and direction of the legislatures of the district or districts, or new States, as in the original States, within the time agreed upon by the United States in Congress assembled. The legislatures of those districts or new States, shall never interfere with the primary disposal of the soil by the United States in Congress assembled, nor with any regulations Congress may find necesary for securing the title in such soil to the *bona fide* purchasers. No tax shall be imposed on lands the property of the United States; and, in no case, shall non-resident proprietors be taxed higher than residents. The navigable waters leading into the Mississippi and St. Lawrence, and the carrying places between the same, shall be common highways, and forever free, as well to the inhabitants of the said territory as to the citizens of the United States, and those of any other States that may be admitted into the Confederacy, without any tax, impost, or duty, therefor.

Art. 5th. There shall be formed in the said territory, not less than three nor more than five States; and the boundaries of the States, as soon as Virginia shall alter her act of cession, and consent to the same, shall become fixed and established as follows, to wit: The Western State in the said territory, shall be bounded by the Mississippi, the Ohio, and Wabash rivers; a direct line drawn from the Wabash and Post St. Vincent's, due North, to the territorial line between the United States and Canada; and, by the said territorial line, to the Lake of the Woods and Mississippi. The middle State shall be bounded by the said direct line, the Wabash from Post Vincent's, to the Ohio; by the Ohio, by a direct line, drawn due North from the mouth of the Great Miami, to the said territorial line, and by the said territorial line. The Eastern State shall be bounded by the last mentioned direct line, the Ohio, Pennsylvania, and the said territorial line: *Provided, however*, and it is further understood and declared, that the boundaries of these three States shall be subject so far to be altered, that, if Congress shall hereafter find it expedient, they shall have authority to form one or two States in that part of the said territory which lies North of an East and West line drawn through the Southerly bend or extreme of lake Michigan. And, whenever any of the said States shall have 60,000 free inhabitants therein, such State shall be admitted, by its delegates, into the Congress of the United States, on an equal footing with the original States in all respects whatever, and shall be at liberty to form a permanent constitution and State government: *Provided*, the constitution and government so to be formed, shall be republican, and in conformity to the principles contained in these articles; and, so far as it can be consistent with the general interest of the confederacy, such admission shall be allowed at an earlier period, and when there may be a less number of free inhabitants in the State than 60,000.

Art. 6th. There shall be neither slavery nor involuntary servitude in the said territory, otherwise than in the punishment of crimes, whereof the party shall have been duly convicted: *Provided, always,* That any person escaping into the same, from whom labor or service is lawfully claimed in any one of the original States, such fugitive may be lawfully reclaimed and conveyed to the person claiming his or her labor or service as aforesaid.

Be it ordained by the authority aforesaid, That the resolutions of the 23d of April, 1784, relative to the subject of this ordinance, be, and the same are hereby repealed and declared null and void. Done, &c.